Ethics, Integrity and Aptitude

Ethics, Integrity and Aptitude

S. S. Baredia
Ajab Lal Lilhare

Sangam Books

All rights reserved. No part of this book may be modified, reproduced or utilised in any form, or by any means, electronic or mechanical, including photocopying, recording or by any information storage and retrieval system, in any form of binding or cover other than in which it is published, without permission in writing from the publisher.

ETHICS, INTEGRITY AND APTITUDE

SANGAM BOOKS
(An imprint of The Agricultural Development Commercial Credit and Industrial Investment Company Private Limited)

Registered Office
3-6-747/1/A & 3-6-754/1 Himayatnagar, Hyderabad 500 029, Telangana, India
Email: info@sangambooks.com

© The Agricultural Development Commercial Credit And Industrial Investment Company Private Limited 2024
First published 2024

ISBN 978-93-95308-47-2

Distributed by
Orient BlackSwan Private Limited
3-6-752 Himayatnagar, Hyderabad 500 029, Telangana, India
Email: centraloffice@orientblackswan.com

Other Offices
Bengaluru, Chennai, Guwahati, Hyderabad, Kolkata, Mumbai,
New Delhi, Noida, Patna

Typeset in Adobe Garamond Pro 11/12.75
by Shine Graphics, Delhi 110 094

Printed at
B.B. Press, Tronica City (U.P.) 201102

Published by
Sangam Books
(An imprint of The Agricultural Development Commercial Credit And Industrial Investment Company Private Limited)
3-6-747/1/A & 3-6-754/1 Himayatnagar, Hyderabad 500 029, Telangana, India
Email: info@sangambooks.com

CONTENTS

Introduction   ix

1. **Ethics and Human Interface**   1
   Ethics: Essence, Determinants and Consequence; Why Ethics?; How are Ethical Frameworks Built?; Ethics and Morality; Ethics as a Guide to Life: The End Goal; Free Will and Determinism; Character in Ethics; The Historical Evolution of Ethics; Religion and Morality

2. **Dimensions of Ethics**   14
   Normative Ethics; Meta-Ethics; Applied Ethics; Evolutionary Ethics; Lying and Ethics

3. **Ethics in Private and Public Relationships**   35
   What, Why, How; Types of Conduct; Evolution and Emergence of Morality; Public and Private Relationships; Legal Intervention in the Realm of the Private

4. **Human Values**   41
   What are Values?; Hierarchy and Classification of Values; Value Theory of Milton Rokeach (1918–88); Value Theory of Clare W. Graves (1914–86); Choosing Personal Core Values; Role of Family in Inculcating Values; Role of Society in Inculcating Values; Role of Educational Institutions in Inculcating Values

5. **Lessons from the Lives and Teachings of Great Leaders, Reformers and Administrators**   52
   Mahatma Gandhi; Sardar Vallabhbhai Patel; Jawaharlal Nehru; Dr Bhimrao Ambedkar; Napoleon Bonaparte; Abraham Lincoln; Swami Vivekananda; Raja Rammohan Roy; Nelson Mandela; Martin Luther King Jr; George Washington; Deendayal Upadhyaya; Rammanohar Lohiya; Swami Dayananda Saraswati; Tulsidas; Kabir; Guru Nanak; Guru Ravidas; Sri Ramakrishna Paramhans; Sri Narayan Guru; Maulana Abul Kalam Azad; Rabindranath Tagore; Mother Teresa; A. P. J. Abdul Kalam

6. **Attitude**   74
   What is Attitude?; Components of Attitude: The Tripartite ABC Model; Implicit and Explicit Attitudes; Measuring Attitude; Behaviour, Intention, Beliefs and Goals; Functions of Attitude; Attitude and Behaviour; Attitude Formation and Attitude Change; Factors Controlling Attitude Change; Methods of Attitude Change;

Goals and Attitude Change; Moral, Political and Bureaucratic Attitudes; Persuasion as a Model of Belief Correction for Attitude Change

7. Aptitude — 104

Introduction; Aptitude for the Civil Services; Intelligence; Role of Personality in Learning; Aptitude versus Attitude

8. Emotional Intelligence — 114

Introduction; Why is Emotional Intelligence Important?; Classifying Emotional Intelligence; How to Achieve Emotional Intelligence; Working with Emotional Intelligence; Models of Emotional Intelligence

9. Foundational Values for Civil Servants — 124

Introduction; Integrity; Objectivity; Impartiality and Non-Partisanship; Empathy; Dedication to Public Service; Tolerance; Compassion towards Weaker Sections; Courage of Conviction; Perseverance

10. Contributions of Moral Philosophers and Thinkers from India and the World — 132

Indian Philosophers; Ethics in Religion; Western Philosophers; Chinese Philosophers; Social Contract Theory; Contemporary Critique of Social Contract Theory

11. Ethics in Public Administration — 164

Status and Problem; The Politics-Administration Dichotomy; The Principles of Administration; Public Administration as Political Science; Public Administration as an Independent Discipline; Ethical Concerns in Government; Low Road Approach; High Road Approach; Public Service Ethos; Ethical Minimum and Ethical Maximum; Ethical Dilemma in Government; Ethical Dilemma in Private Institutions

12. Source of Ethical Guidance — 179

Laws, Rules and Regulations as Sources of Ethical Guidance; Conscience as the Source of Ethical Guidance

13. Accountability — 185

Accountability and Ethical Governance; Types of Accountability; Accountability and New Public Management

14. Strengthening of Ethical and Moral Values in Governance — 191

Introduction; Ethics Training for Public Servants; Steps taken by India in Ethics Training

15. Ethical Dilemma — 197

Introduction; Trolley Problem; How to Handle Ethical Dilemma

16. Ethics in International Relations — 203

Introduction; Ethical Theories of International Relations; Different Ideologies of International Relations; Ethics of International Funding

17. Corporate Governance — 210

Introduction; Ethics of Corporate Governance; Corporate Governance in India; Corporate Social Responsibility

18. Public Service — 216

Introduction; Meaning of 'Public' in Public Service; Public Interest; Conflict of Interest; Public Service Values

19. Probity in Governance — 225

Philosophical Basis of Governance; Good Governance; Key Challenges in Governance; Social Capital: A Shared Destiny; Philosophical Basis of Probity; Code of Ethics and Code of Conduct; Citizen's Charter; Utilisation of Public Funds; Probity in Governance and Challenges of Corruption; Measures for Curbing Corruption and Ensuring Probity in Governance; Fourth Report of the Second Administrative Reforms Commission: Ethics in Governance; Causes of Corruption; Ethical Framework; Recommendations Related to Ethical Framework for Ministers; Ethical Framework for Legislatures; Code of Ethics for Civil Servants; Ethical Framework for the Judiciary; Legal Framework for Fighting Corruption; Protecting the Honest Civil Servants; Seventh Report of the Second Administrative Reforms Commission

20. Work Culture — 264

Power Distance, Uncertainty Avoidance, Individualism, Masculinity/Femininity

21. Quality of Service Delivery — 267

Introduction; Framework for Quality Service Delivery; Six Sigma; Lean Methodology

22. Case Studies — 273

Solved Case Studies (UPSC Civil Services Mains Examinations 2013–19); Unsolved Case Studies (UPSC Civil Services Mains Examinations 2020–23); Sample Case Studies with Solutions

Bibliography — 329

INTRODUCTION

This book aims at providing a one-stop solution for the Civil Services (Main) Examination, General Studies Paper IV (Ethics, Integrity and Aptitude). This book has been crafted keeping in mind the syllabus prescribed by the UPSC and the previous years' questions asked in the GS Paper IV. Meticulously researched, the book contains various references for a better understanding of the theoretical aspects of the subject while also providing practical solutions. This book will be greatly beneficial not only for UPSC aspirants, but also for the aspirants of the various state civil services examinations.

This book is lucidly written and offers a holistic coverage of the syllabus, unlike other books commonly available in the market. The readers will find step-by-step explanation of concepts accompanied by practical suggestions to problems, making this book a perfect study guide that addresses the demands of the examination. Important facts and information are highlighted within boxes for easy revision. The chapters are interconnected and gradually evolves in complexity, ensuring that students with all levels of knowledge on the subject find the book useful.

The syllabus has been rearranged and presented in 21 chapters, with each chapter concluding with related questions asked in the previous years' UPSC examinations. Readers will gain confidence that they are advancing in the right direction when they are able to compare the content of each chapter with the nature of the questions being asked in the examination. Chapter 22 contains case studies that have appeared in the GS Paper IV in the last ten years, along with a few model solutions which aspirants will find useful. Some sample questions and answers have also been included in the book for further practice.

The simple language of the book makes it easy for students to read and understand. It will prove to be useful for both the aspirants as well as teachers and mentors in their journey towards success in civil services examinations.

S. S. BAREDIA
A. LILHARE

1

ETHICS AND HUMAN INTERFACE

> **KEY CONCEPTS**
> Ethics: Essence, Determinants and Consequence; Why Ethics?;
> How are Ethical Frameworks Built?; Ethics and Morality;
> Ethics as a Guide to Life: The End Goal; Free Will and Determinism;
> Character in Ethics; The Historical Evolution of Ethics;
> Religion and Morality

ETHICS: ESSENCE, DETERMINANTS AND CONSEQUENCE

Ethics is a pivotal aspect of philosophy, directly and closely related to everyday human affairs. It involves the study of principles that govern human behaviour and evaluating how individuals and societies make ethical decisions and determine what actions are considered virtuous or justifiable. Ethics provides a practical framework for examining and understanding the moral dimensions of various situations and human interactions, guiding us in making choices that align with principles such as fairness, honesty, integrity and respect for others. It provides practical wisdom to discern between right and wrong, and reconciles opposing, conflicting inclinations through mutually beneficial interactions, thereby fostering social equilibrium, overall prosperity, happiness and the advancement of society as a whole for its lasting existence. Ethics thus plays a crucial role in shaping personal values, societal norms and the wellbeing of individuals and communities.

J. S. Mackenzie defines ethics as the 'science of the ideal' in relation to human life and 'the science of conduct' that studies, guides and determines human behaviour with reference to its 'rightness and wrongness' and the tendency of human actions 'to good or to evil'. Ethics examines all aspects of human conduct and helps address the imperfections inherent in human nature such as the tendency to preserve self-interest, suggests guidelines, and sometimes imposes restrictions and penalties for harmony and wellbeing of society. It tries to bring possible happiness in human life which may further culminate in greater good through individual efforts. According to

> Philosophy, or love of wisdom, derives from the Greek words *philo*: love and *sophos*: wisdom. Philosophy is broadly divided into three branches:
>
> 1. *Epistemology*: The study of the origins, structure and methods of human knowledge.
> 2. *Metaphysics*: The study of the nature of reality, being, knowing, the relationship between mind and matter, the soul, things, ideas, etc.
> 3. *Axiology*: The study of values, which is further divided into *ethics* and *aesthetics*.

William Lillie, 'Ethics is the normative science of the conduct of human beings living in societies'. Ethics studies factual knowledge based on the past lived experiences of a society in order to determine its general social norms, rules and regulations. A long social history thus forms the basis of the construction of ethics.

Today the word ethics is rampant in use but narrowly interpreted and inappropriately conceived. It is also used interchangeably with the word *morality*. We will try to define this term in a broader sense throughout the discussion but its differentiation from other similarly conceived terms is inevitable. Ethics is not exactly the same as morality, but it cannot be understood without adequately discussing morality (which we will do).

Ethics originates from the Greek word *ethos*, broadly the customs, habits, practices or set of rules that govern a particular society. That society may conduct its affairs on the basis of certain beliefs, for e.g., in the Indian democracy, the right to vote has the ethical backing of the Constitution of India; likewise in a traditional monarchy, the divine right of kingship has ethical approval. Ethical norms are thus not set in haste but are conceived, contemplated, deliberated and developed over generations as per a society's needs, and its spatial and temporal contexts.

As seen above, ethics is often described as a set of norms meant to regulate human behaviour and conduct for individual and societal wellbeing. As human behaviour is largely influenced and determined by historical, cultural, social and environmental factors which are all dynamic in nature, ethical norms in relation to a society are also subject to change and refinement rather than being fixed. For John Dewey, ethics is not a set of fixed abstract rules to be followed but a dynamic process that is rooted in the continuous interaction between individuals and their environment. As an inseparable, integral part of being human, Dewey holds that ethics must remain flexible to adapt to changing circumstances and address the complexities and challenges of everyday human life.

WHY ETHICS?

One may well ask: why is ethics so important? Why is it essential for human life? Simply put, because everyone wants to live a happy and hassle-free life. We understand that pain and unhappiness cannot be eradicated, but they can be mitigated to some extent. Ethics serves as a guide to alleviate human suffering and find happiness. We also acknowledge that happiness is not everlasting. All sources of happiness, whether material or spiritual in form, in living or non-living entities are ultimately ephemeral and fleeting. The grandeur and beauty of nature, mountains, rivers, oceans, flora and fauna, and all that is created by humans is impermanent. Depending on how one defines happiness, its sources can be said to lie in external elements which are indispensable but transient. Managing the existence of these elements can lead to temporary happiness. However true and lasting happiness lies in the ability to understand, govern and regulate our own conduct, motivations and desires vis-à-vis others. Ethics emerged in order to enhance the sustainability of happiness in society as a whole by helping us to do that.

Ethics provides a framework and a code of conduct by which to live, establishing norms to deter undesirable/unethical behaviour, and to encourage and applaud desirable/ethical behaviour, all in pursuit of well-contemplated goals for individual and societal wellbeing. Built on ethical principles this framework seeks to find the perfect balance between happiness and pain, a concept also known as *moral philosophy* or *moral science*, since morality plays a key role in determining ethical standards. As mentioned earlier, ethics and morality are not synonymous but often treated as such. So what is the source of morality, and to what extent should it define ethics: these questions form the basis of the study of ethics within the humanities and social sciences.

Human beings are largely driven by self-interest, and equate happiness with the fulfilment of desires. However, since the resources that can bestow happiness are scarce, it implies that greater happiness for some would sacrifice that of others. This compels us to ponder the relationship between happiness and morality. Classical moral philosophy emphasises virtue as a means of attaining happiness, but grapples with the fundamental problem of distinguishing between 'I' and 'other'. Morality serves as a bridge connecting these two to ensure happiness is optimally shared by all.

Philosophical discourses on happiness and morality abound in the thoughts of Confucius, Taoists, Greeks, Christian philosophers and modern thinkers. Sonja Lyubomirsky highlights that happiness-enhancing objectives in life should be feasible, realistic, achievable, aligned with high levels of personal commitment, self-agreeable and in congruence with the objectives and desires of others, without fostering rivalry or conflict. An alternative modern concept of happiness however shifts focus to identifying factors that can bring us happiness free from the dichotomy of 'I' and 'other'. The intricate interplay between happiness and morality gives birth to ethics as a vast, dynamic and enduring subject of study, which we will discuss in detail in subsequent chapters.

HOW ARE ETHICAL FRAMEWORKS BUILT?

Ethical principles are systematically and scientifically formulated, based on empirical as well as rational approaches. *Empirical* study involves the collection of facts derived from direct experience in the form of particulars. General norms are then drawn from these particulars by applying the *inductive* methodology. Conversely, *rational* study relies on reasoning, using the *deductive* methodology to derive specific norms from general *a priori* statements. The construction of ethical frameworks involves multiple factors that influence methodological biases and priorities. We can summarise these determinants as follows:

1. *Moral agency*: The construction of an ethical framework is determined by a responsible moral agency. In a monarchy the king serves as the sole agent, while in a democracy the political structure, state/government and the ideals of the ruling party are key determinants. The value system and general attitude of the moral agency play a pivotal role in shaping ethics.

> A proposition can be **a priori** or **a posteriori**. An *a priori* proposition is knowable and true/valid independent of and prior to any empirical experience or observation, e.g.: all bachelors are unmarried; all boys are male; straight lines are not curved; and 2+2 = 4. An *a posteriori* proposition can be known and validated only by empirical experience, e.g.: this apple is very sweet; person X is unmarried; this line has a slope of 45 degrees.
>
> Further, propositions can also be **analytic** or **synthetic**. A proposition is *analytic* if its predicate is contained within its subject, e.g.: in 'all boys are male', the predicate 'male' is contained within the concept of 'boy'. A proposition is *synthetic* if its predicate is not contained within its subject and adds additional information to the subject, e.g.: in 'person X is unmarried', the predicate 'unmarried' provides additional knowledge about the subject 'person X'.

2. *Space and time*: Spatial, i.e., geographical or regional factors and temporal factors serve as important references in determining what is considered ethical and acceptable in a given society at a given point in time. These include cultural aspects, organisational values, contemporary events, the resourcefulness, progress and history of a society or people.

3. *Religion*: Historically, religion has been highly influential in shaping ethical frameworks the world over. While its role has diminished in the modern scenario, its presence is still seen in many countries. The role of religion in personal and societal

morality remains a matter of debate, and will be discussed later.
4. *Ancient texts*: Knowledge written and preserved in scriptures offers guidance in establishing ethical frameworks and principles. In discussions to follow we will quote from ancient texts from cultures around the world as examples.
5. *Society*: Ethics are established for the sake of societal wellbeing and harmony. A society's value system determines its desires and needs, and is also shaped by them. Thus societal needs can also initiate ethical reform. Civil movements and public demonstrations voicing people's demands compel moral agencies to institute ethical reforms through laws and rules. Here we must remember that laws, rules and regulations are shaped and determined by ethics, and not the reverse.
6. *International compulsions*: Internationalism has played a significant role in consolidating scattered and diverse spatial moralities, giving shape to international ethics in various areas such as human development, child labour, war and pandemic situations, gender, environmental issues, etc.

ETHICS AND MORALITY

Ethics and morality are frequently used synonymously, but there can be subtle distinctions in their meanings depending on the context and philosophical approach. Ethics is a subject of study, whereas morality differentiates between proper and improper human actions from a humanistic point of view. In morality, pleasure and pain are not considerations; rather, the focus is on righteousness, regardless of the resulting ratio of happiness and pain. Morality exhibits at least three important features: it commands universal allegiance, urges impartiality and is self-enforcing.

1. *Universality*: This implies that moral norms apply to all members of communities irrespective of their differences. Immanuel Kant's *categorical imperative* emphasises morality in constructing ethical guidelines or 'maxims' which hold good universally and apply equally to everyone in all societies.
2. *Impartiality*: This emphasises the disinterested and unbiased role of moral principles in overcoming the human propensity for selfishness. John Rawls in *A Theory of Justice* discusses the importance of ensuring the impartiality of social moral norms to make all members of a society stand on an equal footing by using what he calls the 'veil of ignorance', which entails determining and choosing norms without knowing who will benefit from them.
3. *Self-enforceability*: Unlike law, morality does not require any external agency, like the state, to enforce it: morality is self-enforceable. English jurist John Fletcher Moulton defines morality as 'obedience to the unenforceable' and differentiates human actions into three categories: legal, moral and voluntary. In the first category, compliance is certain due to the presence of an enforcement agency, and the third category is left to human free will. Between these two exists morality, where the consciousness of duty, rather than the fear of enforcement by punishment, drives moral actions.

Morality pertains to values and beliefs about the distinctions between right and wrong, good and bad, just and unjust, whereas ethics pertains to the scrutiny, rational analysis and justification of morality. Broadly, if seen from a universal humanistic view, morality is an objective concept. It may however become subjective when considering individuals, a smaller society or particular group of people in a particular space and time. For example, killing is objectively unethical and wrong worldwide, but capital punishment is subjectively ethical and right in India in the 'rarest of the rare cases'. Killing in the name of capital punishment here falls under the purview of ethics although it may not be considered moral, which remains a matter of debate.

Ethical norms are practical rules applicable in everyday life and its challenges, and may become habitual ways of doing something. Morality is our own internal compass by which we judge others' and our own actions and intentions. It follows that an action may be both ethical and moral at the same time, or unethical as well as immoral; or it may be unethical but moral, or ethical but immoral. Table 1.1 provides a comparison between the two terms.

Table 1.1: Difference between ethics and morality

Ethics	Morality
1. Pertains to specific groups or cultures.	1. Pertains to personal/internal compass of right and wrong, transcends cultural norms.
2. In specific/spatio-temporal contexts it is objective, but in the general/universal context it is subjective.	2. In specific/personal contexts it is subjective, but in the general/universal context it is objective.
3. It is dependent on spatial and temporal contexts.	3. It is independent of spatial and temporal contexts.
4. It is a general framework that provides broad guidelines to formulate laws and rules, which may also be in written form.	4. It is the unwritten intuitions of individuals on right and wrong, good and bad, just and unjust.
5. Ethical norms are usually explicit and clear, hence easier to standardise and implement.	5. Implicit, intuitive and vague, varies from person to person, hence difficult to implement.
6. Based on external sources like societal norms, habits and practices, philosophy, religion, ancient scriptures, and developed through rational intellectual discourse and analysis.	6. Based on internal sources like intuitions, gut feelings and conscience, also religious, cultural and familial traditions.
7. Enforceable by external agency like the state.	7. Morality is self-enforceable.
8. Can be flexible and adapt to accommodate different belief systems and cultural norms, and may involve more complex and nuanced reasoning.	8. Varies from person to person, and being deeply rooted in personal convictions, may be less flexible and less open to debate or reasoning.
9. Ethics often involves shared standards within a group, organisation or profession. It can be public and may have external consequences.	9. Morality is often a private matter, reflecting an individual's personal convictions and beliefs, and may not necessarily have external consequences.

Source: Created by authors.

Going forward, we will not take into consideration these differences and we will proceed assuming the same meaning for ethics and morality and use the two interchangeably.

ETHICS AS A GUIDE TO LIFE: THE END GOAL

Every individual has a fundamental question related to the objective of their life which encompasses all aspects of life: *How I ought to live my life?* Every individual expects to lead a certain kind of life according to their ideals, expectations and standards, and ponders: *How my life ought to be?* Moral philosophy aims to provide some meaningful answers to these questions.

Aristotle in his *Nicomachean Ethics* emphasises that every individual endeavour, encompassing different skill sets, is directed towards a specific

> Aristotle wrote two major ethical treatises: **Nicomachean Ethics** and **Eudemian Ethics**, which were named after his son Nicomachus, and his friend Eudemus, respectively. Here, Eudemus, who later edited Aristotle's works, has no relationship with the Greek word *eudaimonia*, an ideal state of happiness, contentment, prosperity and wellbeing. Both works are related to happiness, virtue and character. Another treatise titled *Magna Moralia* (Great Ethics) is also considered to be a work of Aristotle, but with some disputes about its authorship.

good. Every human choice (motivated by self-interest) and every action is motivated by the idea of achieving some good. Each action is the result of a deliberate, contemplated choice and oriented towards a particular end. Aristotelian ethics is sometimes aligned with *teleological* ethics as it commences with an individual's choice to achieve a certain end. According to Aristotle, the ultimate end or *telos* for all human beings is happiness. Stoics and sceptics define the final end goal as the ultimate object of desire, distinct from any other good. For Aristotle, happiness is the final and the highest good: it is the culmination of all the goods that an individual aims at, taken together. It is neither one amongst other goods, nor a separate entity from them. The fulfilment of all goods collectively constitutes the final end—happiness. Thus, the final end and goal is the entirety and wholeness of life, encompassing all goods in an active state.

According to Aristotle, the final end or *telos* has two properties: it is complete, and it is self-sufficient. Completeness is characterised by finality and comprehensiveness, while self-sufficiency signifies a state in which an individual lacks nothing. A self-sufficient end leads to a life worthy of living by choice and free of scarcity.

That which is pursued for its own sake demonstrates its property of being complete. Something is complete if it is chosen for its own sake and not as a means to another end. For instance, if someone desires something for the sake of some other thing, and the desire ends at that other thing, this demonstrates finality. That some other thing is complete, but the means used to achieve it is not. This is a *means–end* relationship. Ends for human beings are hierarchically arranged according to their effectiveness in producing happiness. The final good is not something others can bestow upon us—we must achieve it for ourselves. It is not something others can bring about to someone who desires it.

There is no fixed standard which defines the end goal or life goal for an individual. According to Aristotle, the ultimate and final good is living well and doing well, a concept many thinkers equate with happiness or *eudaimonia*. A Greek term used in *Nicomachean Ethics*, eudaimonia combines *eu* which means good or well, and *daimon* which means spirit. In *Eudemian Ethics*, Aristotle emphasised the ways that lead to 'living well and doing well' or a 'blessed individual'. Being happy (eudaimon), being blessed, and final good are terms which can all be used interchangeably, a perspective strongly advocated by Arius. Reinterpreting Aristotelian ethics, Arius asserts that the final good is not related to physical pleasure and external objects but rather to living in accordance with virtues. In this sense, happiness is the active pursuit of preferred things (self-interest) with virtue. While worldly objects contribute to happiness, they lack the ability to fulfill happiness in life, as life is the fulfilment of action. Worldly objects are not actions in themselves because they are not self-active.

Happiness signifies a positive picture of life. Ancient ethics asked questions like: 'What is the content of happiness?' or 'What does happiness consist of?'. Modern interpretations of eudaimonia have been explored in psychology and psychiatry. Abraham Maslow (1970) argues that humans naturally strive for *self-actualisation*—a state representing something greater and more complete in life. Maslow places self-actualisation at the top of his famous 'need hierarchy' or need pyramid, and contends that more self-actualised individuals possess higher levels of emotional awareness. Other psychological theorists define eudaimonia as the evolution of human potential to its fullest. For Carl Jung (1933), happiness is about being self-aware, socially well-integrated and self-reliant. Gordon Allport (1955) describes wellbeing as a maturity that manifests as self-expression, a realistic outlook, constructive interactions and a well-developed conscience. Sigmund Freud emphasises hedonistic satisfaction, asserting that the final goal of life is leading a pleasurable and tension-free life. Richard M. Ryan and Edward L. Deci (2017) define eudaimonia by assigning it three special characteristics: acting with awareness, acting with objectively valid actions based on psychological need (not momentary impulses), and following an ultimate end. The modern concept of eudaimonia is about realising one's potential, personal growth, purposeful living, facing life's challenges, cordial social relations and freedom (autonomy). A. S. Waterman (2013) defines eudaimonia as personal expression, emphasising activities which make us feel alive and complete. For Martin Seligman (2002) eudaimonia is a meaningful life where actions serve a greater good, distinguishing it from the mere pursuit of pleasure or hedonism.

FREE WILL AND DETERMINISM

Freedom of will or free will is understood as the agency and capacity of human beings to choose one action over others. Aristotle in *Nicomachean Ethics* says human beings have the capacity to do or not to do something, and whatever a person does is voluntary. Further, individuals are aware of the consequences of their action. A rational person chooses a course of action after adequate deliberation about all available means to the desired end. Aristotle says that man is the 'father' of his actions, implying that one's character is shaped by his/her actions.

Thomas Aquinas agrees with Aristotle and extends the discussion of free will into Christian theology. He posits that will is rational desire, and freedom is linked to the consideration of all possible means to achieve a given end. Human will is free in the sense that it is not governed or constrained by the nature of any specific means.

Philosophers of the early modern period consider two assumptions related to free will. The first is that if free will is absent then what would be the basis of the principle 'act according to morality'? Morality can be imposed on human beings only when their free will is taken into consideration. The second assumption concerns the afterlife, in which God will reward and punish humans for their good and bad actions respectively.

Determinism is the philosophical doctrine that all events including human actions, decisions and choices are fully and inevitably determined by preceding events and states of affairs and that all facts and events exemplify natural laws and have sufficient causes. And hence, human freedom of choice and free will are illusory.

Despite various contentions, three widely accepted arguments on free will emerge. The first argument is that free will has two aspects: the freedom to act otherwise, and that all individuals must possess sufficient capacity for self-determination. The second argument is that human beings are morally responsible agents, subject to punishment and reward for their actions. Here, the idea of moral responsibility is used to gauge the limitations of free will. The third argument is about the compatibility of free will with determinism. According to Thomas Reid, the determination of the will is an effect which must have a potential cause. This cause may be the individual whose will it is, in which case their action is considered free. Alternately, the cause may be another person or thing (situation), in which case the responsibility for determining the will is attributed to that external factor.

From the above discussion we may conclude that the concept of free will has been conceived to regulate human choices and actions. When an individual exercises free will over their life choices and actions, those choices and actions are considered to be within their control.

CHARACTER IN ETHICS

Character can be understood as a manifestation of an individual's attitude that distinguishes them from others based on the possession of specific virtues or qualities. In the context of morality, moral character involves embodying virtues relevant to ethical principles. Fundamental components of moral character include motivation, ability/capacity and identity. *Motivation* entails understanding others' aspirations and the manner in which our own actions will affect them. *Ability* is the capacity to regulate attitudes which may harm others or potentially lead to more negative outcomes. *Identity* is about giving recognition and priority to moral values to establish oneself as a moral person.

We have seen that morality and ethics are similar but have varying contextual meanings. Morality revolves around discerning good and bad, which is required in social psychology. Ethics involves discerning right and wrong, which is investigated in organisational behaviour. Ethics comprises 'dos' and 'don'ts' while morality comprises 'ought' and 'ought not'.

Moral motivation involves restraining self-interest and respecting others' aspirations so that a conflict-free social order is sustained. These motivations impact social settings, groups, and individuals' relationships with those groups, with varying levels of moral motivation in different contexts. For instance, group-based motivation includes character traits like commitment and communal harmony, while interpersonal motivation includes traits like quid pro quo and fairness. A moral character exhibits different motivations for group morality and interpersonal morality.

According to David C. Funder and Lisa A. Fast, moral character is an individual's distinctive pattern of attitudes together with the psychological mechanisms generating those patterns. Moral motivation is the willingness to act in a manner that is good and right and the reluctance to engage in harmful acts—a trait of being considerate. This consideration involves treating others fairly and understanding social norms. Here the 'H-factor', Honesty-Humility, is an important personality trait which plays a crucial role in fairness, commitment, generosity and temperance in relationships.

The other component of moral character is an individual's ability to do good and right and the reluctance to do bad and wrong. Conscientiousness, another important personality trait, plays a role in determining an individual's moral capacity. Conscientious individuals can discern unproductive and negative behaviours (like abusing, shirking, resentment), have a greater ability to regulate their self-interest and demonstrate a higher ability to consider others in a given situation.

Individuals who value and embody virtue possess moral character, which brings recognition. The identity component of moral character seeks to establish morality as paramount and central in social behaviour. A moral person aspires to present their assimilated moral values before society, and this recognition manifests in social behaviour. Character in ethics serves crucial functions, enabling morally sound individuals to predict and pre-empt unethical conduct, avoid situational conflicts and make ethical decisions. Individuals with moral character contribute to promoting a positive work culture in organisations, earning recognition as leaders and mentors capable of resolving situational complexities stemming from ethical dilemmas, unfair treatment and self-interest sacrificing others' interests.

THE HISTORICAL EVOLUTION OF ETHICS

The study of ethics as a systematic inquiry into questions of morality and conduct has deep historical roots and has evolved over centuries. The historical origins of ethics can be traced to ancient civilisations where early thinkers contemplated the nature of good and evil, morality, virtue and the principles guiding human conduct. They encompass diverse contributions across cultures, religions and philosophical traditions. The field has continued to expand and diversify, incorporating insights and evolving in response to changing social, cultural and intellectual needs.

In theological and religious interpretations, ethics is believed to have originated with the advent of the first man on earth, and played a similar role in the lives of Adam and Eve as it does in our lives today. While ethics was systematically studied first in the Western world, abundant material on ethics exists in classical Indian and Chinese texts as well. In ancient Greece, the intellectual endeavours of foundational Greek philosophers such as Socrates, Plato and Aristotle, among others, to grapple with profound ethical questions were also in response to the unimaginable devastation caused by the Peloponnesian War, which left the Greek polity and economy paralysed and led to the dismantling of Greece's civilisational glory.

While not explicitly focused on ethics, early pre-Socratic philosophers in ancient Greece such as Thales and Heraclitus laid the groundwork for later ethical inquiry by exploring fundamental questions about the nature of reality and human existence. Later Greek philosophers—such as the Sophists, Stoics and Sceptics, Socrates, Plato, Aristotle, Epicurus—profoundly influenced moral guidelines relevant in the lives of both common individuals and public servants today.

Medieval era theologians also contributed significantly to this field, establishing the basis of morality in God, for example, St. Augustine's monumental work, *City of God*. Thomas Aquinas's *Summa Theologica* integrated Aristotelian ethics with Christian theology. During the Renaissance, humanism encouraged a focus on individual moral growth and the pursuit of virtue. Other important moral philosophers include Machiavelli (*The Prince*), Descartes, Thomas Hobbes (social contract theory), Adam Smith, and twentieth-century philosophers like Karl Marx, Jean-Jaques Rousseau, G. E. Moore, Immanuel Kant, Jeremy Bentham and John Stuart Mill. These thinkers employed diverse criteria to define ethics, significantly influencing the moral behaviour of human beings. Kant's deontological ethics and categorical imperative underlined the importance of duty and universality of moral rules, while Bentham's utilitarianism focused on the greatest happiness/good for the greatest number.

In ancient China, Confucianism emphasised moral values, proper conduct, and the cultivation of virtues for social harmony. In ancient India, Hindu and Buddhist philosophies explored ethical principles, *karma*, and the pursuit of right action. Judaeo-Christian and Islamic traditions contributed ethical guidelines through the Bible and the Quran which contain moral codes and commandments that have influenced Western ethical thought.

Ethics involves shifting the focus from identifying the ultimate goal/end or supreme ethical principle to determining a modus operandi for refining our value judgements. Ethical investigation entails the application of reflective intelligence to amend judgements in light of outcomes. Thus, ethics has evolved continuously, seeking to establish practicable norms for human society for living well and harmoniously (as seen in Table 1.2).

Peloponnesian War (431–404 BCE)

Thucydides (born 460 BC or earlier) provides a detailed account of the war in his seminal eight-volume masterpiece, *History of the Peloponnesian War*. The conflict unfolded between two dominant Greek city-states: Athens and Sparta. Athens allied with small coastal and island states to form the Delian League, while Sparta joined forces with major land powers to form the Spartan League. The two engaged in a long and fierce battle that engulfed the entire Greek world. Ultimately the Spartan League emerged victorious, marking the end of the Golden Age of Greece, and leaving a profound and lasting impact on Greek civilians devastated by the war.

'After the Tao was gone, virtue was resorted to.
When virtue was gone, humanity was resorted to.
When this was also lost, justice was sought.
And since there is no longer any justice, we came to depend on rites.'

—Lao-Tzu

Table 1.2: The evolution of ethics: A timeline

Ancient Egypt and Babylonia	Code of Hammurabi: The principle of an eye for an eye, a tooth for a tooth.
	Ten Commandments of God received by Moses (Hebrew Commandments)
India	Vedas (during 1500–1200 BC)
	Charvaka Philosophy
	Jainism
	Buddha (6th–4th century BC)
China	Daoism of Lao-Tzu or Laozi (6th century BC)
	Confucius (551–479 BC)
	Mencius (372–289 BC)
Greece	Pythagoras (580–500 BC)
	Sophists
	1. Protagoras (490–420 BC): Man is the measure of all things (ethical relativism)
	2. Antiphon (480–411 BC)
	Socrates (470–399 BC)
	Plato (428–427 BC to 348–347 BC)
	Aristotle (384–322 BC)
Later Greek and Roman Ethics	Stoics: Zeno of Citium (335–263 BC), Chrysippus (280–206 BC), Cicero (106–43 BC)
	Epicureans: Epicurus (341–270 BC)
Christian Ethics	St. Augustine (354–430 AD)
	St. Thomas Aquinas (1225–1274 AD): Ethics as natural law
Renaissance	Niccolo Machiavelli (1469–1527): *The Prince*
British Tradition	Thomas Hobbes (1588–1679): Psychological hedonism, *Leviathan* (1651)
	Joseph Butler (1692–1752): Self-interest and conscience
	David Hume (1711–1776): Is/ought distinction, *A Treatise of Human Nature*
Intuitionism	Richard Price (1723–1791)
	Thomas Reid (1710–1796)
Utilitarianism	Jeremy Bentham (1748–1832): Father of modern utilitarianism
	John Stuart Mill (1806–1900)
	Henry Sidgwick (1838–1900): *Methods of Ethics*
Continental European Tradition	Benedict de Spinoza (1632–1677)
	Leibniz (1646–1716)
	Jean-Jaques Rousseau (1712–1778): *A Discourse of Inequality*

(*Contd.*)

Table 1.2: (*Contd.*)

	Immanuel Kant (1724–1804): Deontological ethics, categorical imperative
	Hegel (1770–1831): *The Philosophy of Right* (1821)
	Karl Marx: *The Communist Manifesto* (1848), written with Friedrich Engels
	Nietzsche (1844–1900): His famous statement was 'God is dead'; he called morality of ordinary people 'herd morality'.
Twentieth-century Western Ethics	G. E. Moore (1873–1958): *Principia Ethica* (1903), argument against the 'naturalistic fallacy' in ethics.
	Modern intuitionism: Sir David Ross (1877–1971)
	Emotivism: A. J. Ayer (1910–1989); Charles Stevenson (1908–1979), *Ethics and Language* (1945)
	Existentialism: Jean-Paul Sartre (1905–1980)
	Universal Prescriptivism: R. M. Hare (1919–2002), *The Language of Morals* (1952)
	Moral Realism: Philippa Foot and Elizabeth Anscombe; Edward O. Wilson argued for ethics to be removed from the hands of philosophers and conceded to biologists.
	Natural law ethics: Doctrine of double effect
	Virtue ethics: Alasdair MacIntyre, *After Virtue* (1980)
	Feminist ethics: Carol Gilligan, Nel Noddings
	Ethical egoism
	Animal liberation: Peter Singer
	Environmental ethics

Source: Created by authors.

RELIGION AND MORALITY

Religion and morality were considered intertwined and practically inseparable until recent decades. Their relationship has been hotly debated since the time of Socrates, who famously asked 'whether goodness is loved by the gods because it is good or whether goodness is good because it is loved by the gods'. Socrates was in favour of the former proposition. However, many religious philosophers argue that morality is inconceivable without God. According to Phil Zuckerman, one of the reasons behind plummeting moral standards in the modern world is the increasing trend of secularism.

The etymologies of the terms religion and morality do not show a close link. Religion is said to be derived from Latin *religio* (piety, conscientiousness) and *religare* (to tie fast, to bind); while morality has roots in the Latin *moralitas* (right, good behaviour). Both have different value systems. Morality is based on reasoning and intuition while religion is based on faith. According to Ronald M. Green (1987), 'Morality and religion, however intertwined, are at least conceptually distinct phenomena. Religion involves beliefs, attitudes and practices, and relates human beings to supernatural agencies and sacred realities. In contrast, morality has usually been thought as a way of regulating the conduct of individuals in communities.'

There are several and conflicting opinions on the relationship between morality and religion as well as on the need for morality in religion, and vice versa. These may be broadly categorised under the following three groups.

> **Euthyphro's Dilemma**
>
> Euthyphro (400 BC) was a religious prophet of ancient Greece known for his contributions to Plato's *Dialogues*. Euthyphro's dilemma pertains to the relation between morality and God. The question Socrates put before him was: is a pious being loved by the gods because it is pious, or is it pious because it is loved by the gods?

1. *Religion is harmful to morality*: Religion supports the view that man is fundamentally a sinner. Human beings carry the burden of the sin of their ancestors (Adam and Eve's original sin of being defiant towards God). The Christian doctrine of 'original sin' and 'the fall of Adam' dictate that human beings are fundamentally not moral agents. This notion goes against the dignity of human conscience. Religion emphasises the idea of a transcendental world and a future life, which deteriorates the present state of mankind. Religion spreads passion that causes crusades, jihad and inter-religious conflicts, which have violent and immoral consequences.
2. *Religion is distantly related to morality*: As mentioned above, there is no relation between these two concepts in terms of their definitions and meanings. Morality pertains to ethical reasoning, personal intuitions or gut feelings whereas religion is based on faith, dogmas and divine commandments. Morality is self-enforceable whereas religion presupposes a transcendental entity.
3. *Religion and morality are complementary and need each other's support*: It could be said that as religion is also a tradition or custom followed by a large chunk of society, it becomes similar to ethics or morality. Religion provides a foundation for morality in terms of God's commandments. Religion and morality both promote the good character of human beings and peaceful co-existence of mankind. Morality also requires some kind of enforcing legitimising agency which can compel people to follow it. What about conducts which are not evident and which no one sees and no one is accountable for? In such situations the idea of the existence of a transcendental, omniscient, omnipresent entity like God facilitates the construction of moral grounds. Moreover, if we consider atheism to be valid, and there is no moral accountability for human conduct, then the notion of objective moral values defined under ethical naturalism becomes irrelevant.

Theists believe that God, as the ultimate source of meaning and morality, endows them with strength to lead a moral life. They have a strong belief that their good deeds would never go in vain, that evil will be punished and good will be vindicated. Theists would argue that if God does not exist, then morality becomes a mere human convention which is purely subjective. Unless God exists, objective moral values do not exist and we cannot be good in the true sense. Life would become purposeless and all the devotions and sacrifices of good God-fearing individuals would go unrewarded. If morality is an objective idea and not a purely human construct, then theists would argue for the existence of God.

Does that imply that everyone who does not believe in God is evil or incapable of goodness or virtue or altruism or sacrificing their happiness for others or even just being a considerate and kind human being? No. It is irrational and wrong to claim that theists cannot be good and would not lead a good, moral, virtuous life in the absence of God. Neither is it true that all theists are inherently good and moral beings just because they believe in God. It is philosophically illogical, patently absurd and unfair to see human altruism and virtue only through the lenses of religious faith and the fear or love of God. Human beings—theists and atheists alike—are capable of doing good and do good unto others for their own sake, purely for their own happiness and satisfaction. Every human action cannot be judged by moral standards; or life would become impossibly tedious and unliveable. And morality itself cannot be judged by theological or religious standards alone.

REFERENCES

Allport, Gordon W. (1955). *Becoming: Basic Considerations for a Psychology of Personality*. New Haven: Yale University Press.

Green, Ronald M. (1987). 'Morality and Religion'. Encyclopedia of Religion. Encyclopedia.com. Available at https://www.encyclopedia.com/environment/encyclopedias-almanacs-transcripts-and-maps/morality-and-religion (accessed on 15 May 2024).

Jung, Carl G. (1933). *Modern Man in Search of a Soul*. Trans. Cary F. Baynes. London: Kegan Paul, Trench, Trubner & Co.

Maslow, Abraham H. (1970). *Motivation and Personality*. New York: Harper & Row (2nd ed.).

Ryan, Richard M., and Edward L. Deci. (2017). *Self-Determination Theory: Basic Psychological Needs in Motivation, Development, and Wellness*. London, New York: The Guilford Press.

Seligman, Martin E. P. (2002). *Authentic Happiness: Using the New Positive Psychology to Realize Your Potential for Lasting Fulfillment*. New York: Free Press.

Waterman, A. S. ed. (2013). *The Best within Us: Positive Psychology Perspectives on Eudaimonia*. Washington, D.C.: American Psychological Association.

QUESTIONS

1. Explain ethics with the help of real-life examples.
2. Ethics was the necessity of society. Evaluate this, citing historical instances.
3. What is morality, and how is it different from ethics? Explain with the help of suitable examples.
4. The creators of ethics are human beings rather than God; explain.
5. There is no morality without God; elaborate.
6. Morality and religion are complementary to each other; elaborate.
7. The quest for happiness is the basis of the necessity of ethics; critically evaluate.
8. All human beings aspire for happiness. Do you agree? What does happiness mean to you? Explain with examples. (UPSC 2014)
9. What does the study of ethics seek to promote in human life? Why is it all the more important in public administration? (UPSC 2014)
10. Explain how ethics contributes to social and human wellbeing. (UPSC 2016)

2

DIMENSIONS OF ETHICS

> **KEY CONCEPTS**
> Normative Ethics; Meta-Ethics; Applied Ethics; Evolutionary Ethics;
> Lying and Ethics

We have previously explored the indispensability of ethics in human life, its ancient roots and historical evolution. Philosophical traditions down the ages and philosophers across cultures around the world have advocated different and yet overlapping or even convergent paths to try and provide answers to questions and conundrums big and small to do with the human condition, which are intricately linked to the nature of good and evil, right and wrong, the pursuit of meaning, an ultimate purpose and happiness in life. These include religion and religious texts which preached faith and fear of God. The study of ethics as a formal discipline thus commenced through attempts to address fundamental human concerns.

Depending on what kind of questions are being asked in which contexts, different dimensions, approaches and methodologies are considered in the formulation of ethical frameworks and precepts. These approaches or dimensions are broadly categorised as: *normative* ethics, *meta-*ethics and *applied* ethics.

NORMATIVE ETHICS

As the name suggests, normative ethics is concerned with evaluating and establishing moral social norms and provides frameworks for determining what actions and decisions are right or wrong, good or bad, and just or unjust, aimed at achieving the appropriate and desired ends. It encompasses the formulation of rules, regulations, rituals, laws and customs. Different ethical considerations guide different types of normative theories, of which the more important ones may be classified as follows:

1. Deontological Theory
2. Teleological Theory
3. Virtue Theory
4. Ethics of Care or Relational Ethics

Deontological Theory

The term *deontology* is derived from the Greek word *deon*, meaning duty. Deontological theory states that we are morally obliged to follow a certain set of principles, laws, rules and regulations irrespective of the outcomes of the pertinent actions. Now the question is who will decide the rule, and what will be the criteria to judge the righteousness of a particular human action.

Generally, deontology is based on human reasoning free from any biases, emotions and consideration of ends/consequences. Deontology

Dimensions of Ethics

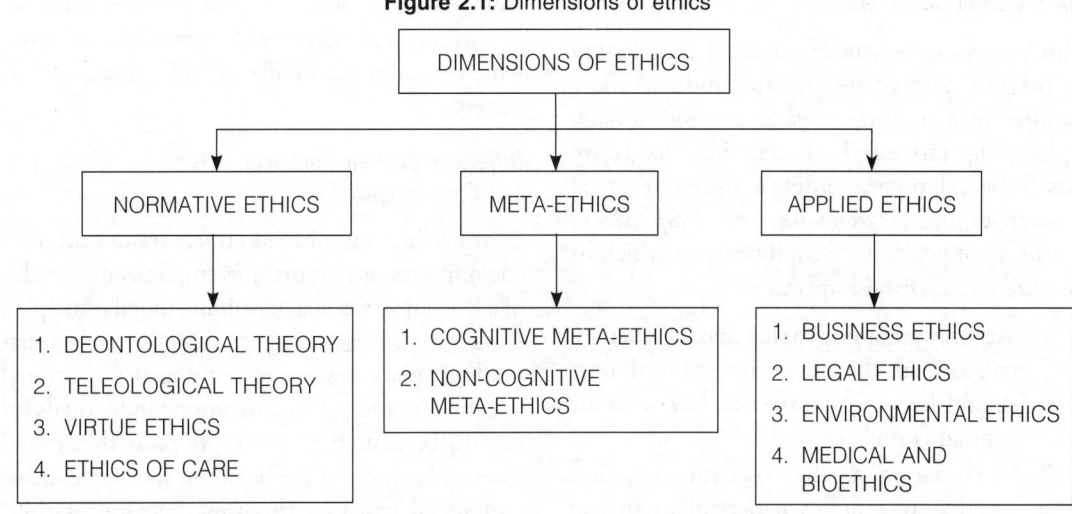

Figure 2.1: Dimensions of ethics

Source: Created by authors.

that seeks to establish the appropriate framework for building moral principles based on reasoning without any involvement of God is known as *secular deontology*, and is grounded in Kantian deontology. Deontology that is derived from divine commandments under religious laws and theology is known as *religious deontology*. In the modern world however, deontology is considered secular and has little to do with divine commandments. Kant is one of the major figures in this field, and it would be no exaggeration to say that deontology exists due to Kantian duty-based ethics and his *categorical imperatives*. John Rawls' theory of contractarianism and Robert Nozick's theory of natural rights also support deontology.

Deontology emphasises means over ends, where means are determined in terms of duties. Kant established a duty-based ethics, famously propounding that 'duty must be done for duty's sake'. Given that individuals find themselves in diverse circumstances at any given moment, determining the right action at the right time based on its consequence can be challenging. It is more practical to establish general principles and rules of conduct based on duties in different contexts. Since the ultimate consequence of any action in the long term is unknown, deciding an action by contemplating its final outcome every time becomes unreasonable. Deontology holds that the motivation behind human action must be based on obligation that is well contemplated before the action takes place. Thus, deontology is an objective theory grounded in the realism of practical morality.

Deontology is categorised into Kantian deontology or Kant's categorical imperatives, and contractualism, which suggests that moral acts are based on collective agreement and social-contract theories.

> **Immanuel Kant (1724–1804)** is one of the foundational and most important moral philosophers whose works remain as influential and relevant today. In his treatise **Groundwork of Metaphysics of Morals**, Kant emphasises moral beliefs based on common sense and proposes moral maxims that are duty-based, universally applicable and universalisable, also known as *categorical imperatives*. In **Metaphysics of Morals**, he focuses on the doctrine of right and the doctrine of virtue.

Kant's Categorical Imperatives

Kant proposes readymade universal moral rules or 'maxims' to regulate human conduct. These maxims must be *categorical* or unconditionally explicit, imperative and commanding, that is, we must be bound to act according to these categorical imperatives. In his *Groundwork of Metaphysics of Morals*, Kant posits three conditions on which to base these categorical imperatives.

1. 'Act only according to that maxim whereby you can at the same time will that it should become a universal law without contradiction.'
2. 'Act in such a way that you treat humanity, whether in your own person or in the person of any other, never merely as a means to an end but always at the same time as an end.'
3. 'Therefore, every rational being must so act as if he were through his maxim always a legislating member in the universal kingdom of ends.'

Contractarianism

The idea of a coercive authority ensuring compliance to the social contract gave rise to the theory of *contractarianism* where morality was constituted by agreed-upon rules that are mutually advantageous and justify morality through self-interest. But these agreed-upon rules do not exist prior to human contracts; we create morality through our agreements within the constraints dictated by self-preservation and self-interest. Antecedent moral truths are not discovered prior to the contract (not a-priori). No action is deemed moral or immoral before the social contract is signed (no retrospective effect). Society forbids some actions, allows others, remains undecided on a few, and continually renegotiates the contract to satisfy rival parties. Thus the moral sphere is one of constant bargaining and power struggles where conflicts are resolved through moral discourse, a political mechanism, and sometimes through violence—a prospect Thomas Hobbes detested. In this way a social contract comes into existence which decides the affairs of individuals in that society.

Difference between Contractarianism and Contractualism

Contractualism is a broad ethical framework that encompasses various theories emphasising the idea of a fair consensus in determining moral principles. *Contractarianism* is a subset of *contractualism* that tends to place a stronger emphasis on rational self-interest and agreement among individuals for mutual benefit. Both concepts posit that moral rules and principles are based on social consensus and social contract theories. Because of their similarities, *contractarianism* is sometimes confused with *contractualism* and used interchangeably. However the two are quite different.

Contractarianism is a moral and political theory that suggests that the legitimacy of moral principles and political authority is based on the hypothetical agreement of rational individuals. It is rooted in Thomas Hobbes' idea of *social contract* where individuals come together and agree upon certain rules for self-preservation and mutual benefit. It emphasises rational self-interest and the idea that individuals would agree to certain rules that maximise their own security and wellbeing. For Hobbes, the *social contract* was a means to escape the chaos and violence of the state of nature and establish a stable social, political order. Morality here thus lies in specific forms of cooperative behaviour that agents engage in for self-preservation. Under contractarianism, we seek to maximise our own interests in a bargain with others.

Contractualism is a broader ethical theory that underlines the importance of the principles or rules that individuals would agree upon under certain conditions. While similar to contractarianism in some respects, contractualism does not necessarily focus only on rational self-interest but also considers the moral principles that people could agree upon when thinking about what is just. The emphasis here is on the fairness of the terms under which individuals come to agree. Contractualism is based on the equal moral status of persons and has its roots in Jean-Jacques Rousseau, who said the general will is what we would collectively will if we were all free and equal citizens. Under contractualism, we seek to pursue our interests in ways that we can also justify to others who have their own interests to pursue.

Social Contract Theory

Social contract theory explains that people coexist in society based on an agreement or contract that establishes moral and political rules of conduct and behaviour. As Stuart Rachels suggests, 'Morality is the set of rules governing behavior that rational people accept, on the condition that others accept them too'. Social contracts contribute to fostering harmony and stability in society, and can take explicit forms like laws, rules and regulations, or implicit forms like raising funds for disaster relief. Each country establishes ideals that describe the social contract among its citizens, and every citizen is bound to follow this contract.

The theory of social contract can be traced back to the earliest philosophical and political thinkers, including Socrates, providing insights into its evolution. While there were several precursors, the modern social contract theory, which has played a central role in moral and political thought throughout the history of the modern West, is associated with the political philosophers Hobbes, Locke and Rousseau, each of whom provided distinct perspectives, contributing to its development.

Thomas Hobbes (1588–1679), in *Leviathan* (1651), presented the first and foundational idea of a social contract, arguing that individuals in their natural state live in a 'state of nature' characterised by chaos and conflict. To escape this condition, they collectively agree to establish a sovereign authority (a commonwealth) to maintain order and protect them. The social contract, according to Hobbes, involves surrendering certain natural rights to the sovereign in exchange for security and stability.

John Locke (1632–1704) believed that individuals in the state of nature have natural rights, including life, liberty and property. Differing from Hobbes, Locke, in his *Second Treatise of Government* (1689), presented the social contract as an agreement among free individuals to establish a government to protect these natural rights. Unlike Hobbes, Locke's view emphasises limited government and the right to resist unjust rule.

Jean-Jacques Rousseau (1712–1778), in *The Social Contract* (1762), proposed that the social contract is not a historical event but a fundamental agreement among citizens to form a collective body politic. He introduced the idea of the 'general will', representing the common interests of the community. Rousseau's social contract theory laid the groundwork for democratic principles and the idea of popular sovereignty.

The theory has continued to be refined and adapted by later thinkers, providing a framework for understanding the relationship between individuals and the political institutions governing them. In the twentieth century, John Rawls brought new perspectives to the study of moral and political theory with his revised version of the social contract. More recently, social contract theories faced criticism from various philosophical schools, notably feminists and race-conscious philosophers who exposed them for their class-dominance perspectives.

Socratic Influence on Social Contract Theory

The concept of a social contract between citizens and the state can be traced back to Socrates, whose contributions to ethical and political philosophy, particularly his ideas on the relationship between individuals and the state, have influenced later thinkers. Socrates' teachings, as documented by his student Plato, involved discussions on justice, morality and the role of the individual in the political community. While Socrates did not explicitly formulate a social contract theory, some themes in the Socratic *Dialogues*, such as the citizens' duty to obey laws of the state and the importance of justice in social life, laid the groundwork for later philosophical explorations in these areas.

> **Crito by Plato** records the historic dialogue between Socrates and his friend Crito during Socrates' imprisonment before his death penalty, on charges of misleading the Athenian youth. Despite Crito's efforts to arrange an escape for Socrates, the 70-year-old philosopher staunchly refuses. Crito endeavours hard to persuade Socrates to flee, but his attempts are in vain. This sparks a profound conversation and debate between them concerning the intricate relationship between citizens and their city, and the nature of justice, as meticulously documented in Plato's work.

In Plato's *Dialogues*, Socrates argues during a conversation with Crito that he must accept the death penalty and not attempt to escape from prison because of the enduring social contract between him and his state, Athens. He lives in accordance with Athenian laws, and his thoughts, words and deeds align with the fundamental laws of the city-state. Importantly, Socrates contends that this relationship, based on a contract between citizens and the rules of the city, is not coercive. Having grown up in Athens and having experienced the city's self-regulation, citizens can choose to leave or stay. By staying, they agree to abide by Athens' laws, rules and traditions and to accept the associated punishments. Having made such an agreement, Socrates asserts that he must also obey the law, in this case, by staying and accepting the death penalty.

In Plato's *Republic* (Book II), in context of a social contract, Plato's brother Glaucon asks: 'What is justice?' He argues that humans would prefer to have the power to commit injustices against others without fear of retaliation and to avoid being unjustly treated without facing the consequences. Glaucon further argues that justice results from the laws, norms and covenants that individuals construct to prevent extreme situations, since, being unable to commit injustice with impunity without victimising themselves, humans decide it is in their self-interest to submit themselves to laws. Socrates, however, rejects this view, asserting that justice is inherently desirable for its own sake, and that the just person is the happiest. From Socrates' perspective, justice holds a value far higher than the prudential value proposed by Glaucon.

Presenting two contrasting views, in *Crito* Socrates employs a social contract-based argument to justify remaining in prison, while in *The Republic* he rejects social contract as the source of justice. Despite this apparent contradiction, these views are reconcilable, revealing the complexity of Socratic thought. According to Socrates, a just person acknowledges their obligation to the state by obeying its laws, considering the state as the highest authority morally and politically. A just person, recognising this, shows the highest allegiance and respect to the state. Justice, for Socrates, involves more than simple reciprocal obedience to the law, as suggested by Glaucon: it includes obedience to the state and the laws sustaining it. Through Socrates, Plato becomes the first philosopher to introduce a representation of this argument in the context of social contract theory, even though Socrates ultimately rejects the idea that the social contract is the original source of justice.

> **The Republic by Plato** is a detailed exploration of the nature of reality, justice, *eudaimonia* (happiness, the highest good), the relationship between justice and *eudaimonia*, virtue, the ideal polity/state and the ideal ruler, in the form of philosophical dialogue between Socrates as the protagonist and various characters, including Adeimantus and Glaucon (half brothers of Plato), Thrasymachus (a sophist), Cephalus (a rich businessman) and Polemarchus (Cephalus' son).

Teleological Theory

Teleology focuses on ends and outcomes rather than means, suggesting that no laws, rules or regulations help in judging consequences. Teleological theory is a subjective and interpretative theory which asserts that there is no objective physical world external to human consciousness, as posited by the deontologists. The emphasis is on desired outcomes, regardless of how they are achieved, prioritising ends over means. Teleology encompasses various branches, including utilitarianism, consequentialism, egoism, situation ethics, intellectualism and welfarism. Notably, this is the only theory of ethics that potentially deems the act of war to be ethical under certain circumstances.

Utilitarianism

Utilitarianism is derived from the concept of utility related to usefulness or instrumentality in achieving a desired end or outcome. Although it emerged fully only in the nineteenth century, it has been one of the most influential moral philosophies and played an integral role in ethical theories throughout history, as evident in the works of ancient Greek philosopher Aristotle (intrinsic utilitarian) and later thinkers like Jeremy Bentham, John Stuart Mill and Henry Sidgwick.

Utilitarianism posits that the moral evaluation of an action is based on its consequences in terms of magnitude and quality. Here, the morally right/good action is one that produces the most good, and the ultimate goal of morality is to enhance human life by maximising the good (pleasure) and minimising the bad (pain). Utilitarianism sharply contrasts with deontological theories by placing greater emphasis on ends rather than means. Rejecting readymade moral codes based on customs, traditions or commands issued by an authority (divine or human), utilitarianism aligns itself with consequentialism and, in some respects, with hedonism.

Classic utilitarian thinkers like Bentham and Mill emphasise the intrinsic value of pleasure and argue for achieving 'the maximum amount of good for the maximum number of people'. Consequently, utilitarian theory adopts an impartial stance regarding the distribution of good among individuals, treating each member of society equally without privileging anyone, and encapsulates the notion that 'My good is same as the good of others.'

Classical Utilitarianism

Jeremy Bentham (1748–1832) believed that humans are governed by two primary masters: pleasure and pain. He argued that all our thoughts, words and actions are dictated by the pursuit of pleasure and the avoidance of pain. Thus an action is deemed morally good, right and virtuous if it enhances pleasure or happiness, and disapproved as bad, wrong and immoral if it causes unhappiness or pain. Influenced by Hobbes' perception of human nature and David Hume's concept of social utility, in Bentham's philosophy the moral evaluation of an action or trait depends on its consequences and the pleasure or utility that it generates, independent of our emotive responses to it. Unlike the deontologists, he argued that laws must not be static and fixed for laws deemed good/right at one point in time may become obsolete or counterproductive at another. Thus lawmakers must remain attuned to changing societal conditions to ensure that laws remain relevant to their context and serve their intended purpose. Bentham was a rationalist who contended that something exists because we perceive it, suggesting that its existence is mind-dependent.

John Stuart Mill (1806–1873) was a disciple of Bentham but diverged from some of Bentham's ideas concerning the nature of happiness. Introducing changes to the utilitarian theory, Mill's approach to hedonism incorporated perfectionist intuitions, acknowledging that certain pleasures are more preferable than others—specifically, intellectual pleasures. He argued that intellectual pleasures, distinct from the more common sensual pleasures found in all animals, are of a higher order, and that our capacity to experience intellectual happiness sets humans apart from other species. Mill asserted that people inherently desire happiness which is the ultimate utilitarian end. Moreover, he regarded general happiness to be a collective good for all individuals.

Henry Sidgwick (1838–1900) proposed a deviation from conventional utilitarianism. According to Sidgwick, the average happiness of human beings constitutes a positive quantity. While utilitarianism commonly advocates for including an increasing number of people to experience happiness, Sidgwick introduced a mathematical consideration often overlooked by traditional utilitarian thinkers. He emphasised that the average happiness increases as the number of individuals decreases, and conversely, it decreases with a larger population. This insight prompts a critical consideration for prescribing utilitarianism to determine overall happiness. To truly evaluate happiness as a whole, one must account for the balance between the happiness gained by additional people and the happiness lost in the process. Sidgwick's approach introduces a nuanced perspective that underscores the complexity of optimising happiness in a utilitarian framework.

Act Utilitarianism and Rule Utilitarianism

In *act utilitarianism*, the principle of utility is decided by weighing the outcomes of all possible actions on a case-by-case basis. The right and chosen action is the one which produces the best overall result in terms of producing maximum utility and, consequently, greater happiness. In this approach, the moral rightness of the means is secondary to the objective of maximising utility. Conversely, *rule utilitarianism* involves collecting all possible moral rules that conform to the ethical codes in a given situation. The outcomes of those rules are weighed, and the rule that generates the most happiness is considered the best as it maximises utility for human beings. While rule utilitarianism may seem close to deontology, it differs in its primary focus on the end result. Deontology is indifferent to the end, while rule utilitarianism focuses primarily on the end goal and evaluates all means that lead to a similar end.

Having explored various interpretations of utilitarianism, it becomes evident that accurately predicting the consequences of an action is challenging. When faced with different choices, it is difficult to predict the diverse possible outcomes associated with each action from a given set of options and precisely identify the best course of action. The long-term consequences of an action are unknown, and the actual outcomes may diverge from the initially foreseeable ones. For example, utilitarianism holds that it is morally right to save someone from drowning. But consider a scenario where the person rescued turns out to be someone like Hitler, ultimately causing the death of many thousands. In this case, the foreseeable consequence significantly differs from the actual consequence in terms of producing a net amount of good. Thus the inherent uncertainty in predicting the consequences of human actions considerably complicates a utilitarian evaluation of actions.

Virtue Ethics

Virtue may be defined as the supreme attribute deeply ingrained in an individual's character, manifesting in various aspects of their life, e.g. courage, generosity, fairness. A virtuous person distinguishes themselves from ordinary individuals through their mindset and habits. Virtue is not practised merely for the sake of following rules and laws or out of fear of the consequences of deviation. Different people possess virtues to different degrees of perfection. *Virtue ethics*, a dimension of normative ethics, establishes the standard for determining good or bad based on the character of the agent/actor. Actions performed by virtuous individuals are considered ethical and good. Virtue ethics stands apart from both deontology, which emphasises rules and laws, and from teleology, which evaluates actions based on their end results. In this theory, virtue is primary while concepts like laws and eudaimonia (highest good) become secondary.

Virtue ethics traces its roots to Greek philosophers like Plato and Aristotle in the West, and figures like Mencius and Confucius in the East. While it remained an important moral theory throughout history, it saw a decline during the nineteenth century. However, it resurfaced in Anglo-American philosophy in the latter half of the twentieth century, particularly with Elizabeth Ancombe's influential article 'Modern Moral Philosophy', which critiqued the shortcomings of deontology and teleology.

Virtue ethics delves into aspects that deontology and teleology might overlook, such as ethical education, ethical wisdom, distinctions between good and bad, the pursuit of happiness and avoidance of pain, and the ideal conduct of human beings. Virtue encompasses all positive attributes or traits in humans, but for virtues to be considered complete, they must possess moral and practical prudence. Practical wisdom introduces a necessary element of flexibility to mitigate rigid virtuousness, which could potentially lead to harmful effects. For example, compassion, if applied indiscriminately, may lead to disastrous consequences. Similarly, telling the truth in certain situations might bring trouble to both the speaker and others. The ability to apply virtue judiciously contributes to the development of full virtue in an individual, achieved through the cultivation of practical wisdom.

Virtue ethics may be classified as Platonistic, eudaimonistic, agent-based and target-centred virtue ethics.

1. ***Platonistic virtue***, the oldest form, is rooted in the teachings of Plato and Socrates, who extensively discussed virtues like wisdom, courage, temperance, justice and fortitude. While some debate Plato's classification as a virtue ethicist due to his focus on intrinsic teleology rather than virtues, there is a plausible argument that links virtue to the pursuit of happiness and goodness in human life. The shift from self-centred thinking to the consideration of others and altruism creates habits aligned with generosity, objectivity and realism—all considered virtues.

2. ***Eudaimonistic virtue*** connects virtues with eudaimonia: the highest good. Eudaimonia in Greek moral philosophy means happiness or wellbeing that is unrelated to worldly pleasures or physical desires. But defining the efficacy of virtue in achieving eudaimonia brings conflicts. Aristotle posits that virtue alone cannot guarantee happiness—the assistance of fortune is necessary. In contrast, Plato and the Stoics contend that virtue alone leads to eudaimonia.

3. ***Agent-based virtue*** acknowledges that virtues are inculcated by individuals, and agents possessing virtue determine eudaimonia based on their motivations and how they unfold. An act is right or wrong depending on the agent's motivation, and if the motive is good, the action is considered good. Virtue in this context cannot be misused with varying motivations. However, virtue alone does not provide a specific course of action in a given situation—agents' dispositions and the results of their actions are crucial. The correlation between the agent's disposition in specific situations defines virtue as conducive to creating eudaimonia.

4. ***Target-centred virtue*** involves an action that duly acknowledges and responds to desired items of good within its field. In other words, target-centred virtue focuses on the objective of a virtue. This emphasis on the target encourages us to pursue

various good things rather than confining our actions to a single virtue. Thus a target-centred act is considered right if it is virtuous in all respects and incorporates the best possible action suitable for a given situation. Conversely, an act is considered right only if it is not overall vicious.

Ancient ethical theories highlight three key characteristics of virtues:

1. Virtues are dispositional in nature.
2. Virtues have an emotional aspect that involves feelings related to pleasure and pain, and inculcating any virtue thus implies transforming those feelings into habitual conduct.
3. Virtues entail practical wisdom or reasoning concerning matters of right and wrong.

There are several drawbacks in the idea of virtue ethics. It lacks specific concrete codified norms that can be universally followed by every member of society, irrespective of their level of virtuousness. Given that everyone possesses varying degrees of virtue, it is unrealistic to expect all individuals to act in a similar fashion. Further, if an individual acts rightly without being virtuous, that action is considered futile. Virtue is thus neither a necessary nor a sufficient condition for doing what is morally right.

Ethics of Care or Relational Ethics

At its core, the ethics of care underscores the fundamental importance and necessity of caring relationships in human survival and consciousness. A caring relationship involves two parties: the 'one caring' and the 'cared for' where both are bound by a reciprocal obligation to care for the other. Here, caring is characterised as an act of 'engrossment' where the 'one caring' is committed to the wellbeing of the 'cared for' for its own sake and on their own terms, devoid of coercion or selfish motives. The ethical dimension of care revolves around the natural sentiments of caring and the recognition of having been cared for, shaping an ideal unselfish self.

Care ethics originated with Carol Gilligan and Nel Noddings, who critiqued male dominance and introduced care as an alternative to the concept of justice in the mid-1980s. While care ethics is occasionally misconstrued to be synonymous with feminist ethics, it encompasses a wide range of issues, delving deep into the moral implications and motivations of relationships, emphasising the fulfilment of needs for both oneself and others, as well as the preservation of humanity. It is an ethical framework that prioritises caring motivations, sentiments and psychological considerations in moral deliberation along with contextual reasoning.

Feminist ethics has contributed significantly to care ethics, covering issues related to femininity, animal and environmental care, international policy, public policy, bioethics, and more. Carol Gilligan describes the ethics of care as 'a different voice'—one that integrates the self with others through relationships, and reason with emotion. By transcending these two extremes, care ethics enables a paradigm shift that redefines both psychological and moral theory. Humans are by nature responsive and interconnected, engaging in responsive actions, listening, answering and transacting affairs, following their inherent interdependence and sense of belonging. Care ethics addresses real-life moral conflicts and choices, demonstrating how we navigate moral disputes and how moral language guides our decisions and behaviour in concrete situations.

META-ETHICS

In epistemology, *meta* is a prefix, meaning 'about'. Meta-ethics focuses on acquiring knowledge about the foundations of ethical statements. It explores and studies the meaning and usage of moral language. Unlike normative ethics, which is concerned with generating ethical courses of action based on rules and regulations, meta-ethics seeks to understand why a particular

Dimensions of Ethics

action is considered ethical. Meta-ethics is not concerned with determining *what* might be a morally appropriate action in a given situation, but rather on understanding *why* a particular moral conduct is considered moral. It concerns itself with deciphering the meaning of terms like good and bad, right and wrong. For instance, 'what does it mean for euthanasia to be wrong?' represents a meta-ethical inquiry, while the question 'is euthanasia right or wrong?' falls under normative ethics. Meta-ethics involves an epistemological investigation, exploring the type of knowledge, its sources, and the methods by which knowledge about ethical statements is acquired.

There are two broadly kinds of meta-ethics: *cognitive* and *non-cognitive* meta-ethics.

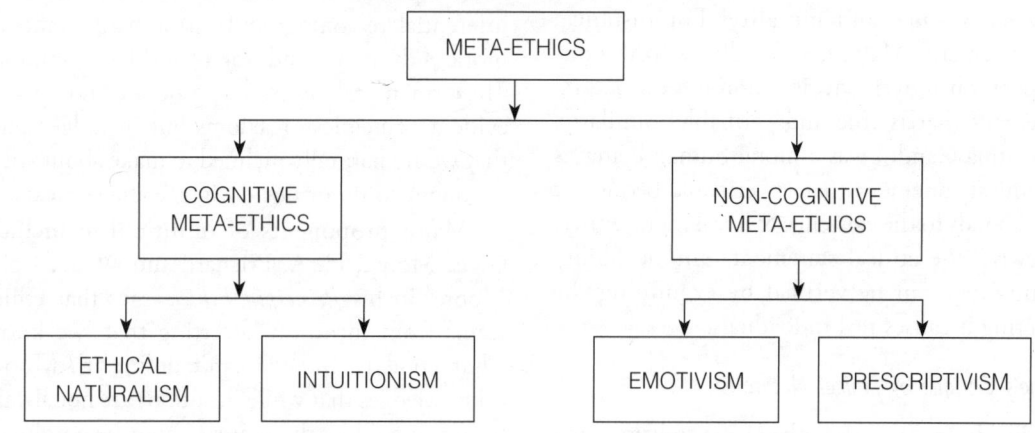

Figure 2.2: Classification of meta-ethics

Source: Created by authors.

Cognitive Meta-Ethics

Cognitive meta-ethics focuses on the mental or cognitive processes underlying ethical inquiry and knowledge, and is concerned with how humans come to acquire, process and understand ethical information. It studies the ways in which knowledge formation takes places about the ethical aspects of the descriptive world, involving living and non-living entities. Cognitive meta-ethics specifically involves the brain and mental processes, and aims to provide objective knowledge based on realism and reason, rather than emotions and volitions. Cognitive meta-ethics can be further divided into *ethical naturalism* which posits that moral facts and values exist as objective entities independent of the mind, and *intuitionism* which posits that moral knowledge is derived from intuitions or rational insights of the mind.

Ethical Naturalism

Ethical naturalism is grounded in realism, a philosophical perspective that posits that the physical world and its objects exist independent of the mind and its perceptions; they are not creations of our mind. Ethical naturalism asserts the existence of moral entities, maintains that moral statements and truths are verifiable in the real world, and that morality is factual and objective. Moral naturalism encompasses moral realism, metaphysical naturalism and epistemic naturalism.

According to F. H. Bradley, a principle proponent of ethical naturalism, a moral statement is factual and meaningful if it can be verified empirically like other statements or propositions. This implies that ethical statements express propositions that can be objectively verified as true or false in the external world. Unique moral statements may be derived by searching for appropriate genuinely existing moral entities, and hence are verifiable. The source of moral statements is not the mind, Bradley asserts, arguing that there exists an objective moral reality beyond space and time, although people may not always recognise this objective moral world as such.

Bradley draws a parallel between empirical knowledge in science (e.g., physics) and ethical knowledge, asserting an intrinsic connection between science and morality. For instance, the statement 'Mahatma Gandhi led the non-cooperation movement' is a non-ethical natural statement that is true and verifiable. Similarly, 'Mahatma Gandhi was a moral human being' is an ethical statement that is verifiable because it corresponds to the existence of a real moral entity. Likewise, the ethical statement 'untouchability is immoral' can be verified by examining the suffering it causes real individuals.

Hume's Critique of Ethical Naturalism

David Hume critiques ethical naturalism using his famous 'is-ought' distinction, or the idea that one cannot derive normative or prescriptive conclusions from purely descriptive premises. In simpler words, the fact that something *is* the case does not necessarily imply how it *ought* to be. Hume argues that statements describing what *is* the case in the world are fundamentally different from statements prescribing what *ought* to be done or what is morally right. Ethical naturalists mistakenly treat moral statements as objective, he argues, and fail to recognise that the statements they attempt to verify as moral are in fact subjective. Moral statements, being general and non-verifiable, are distinct from factual verifiable statements. For example, 'Mahatma Gandhi was a good human being' is a factual statement, while statements like 'The political thought of Mahatma Gandhi is moral' or 'We ought to follow the political thought of Mahatma Gandhi' introduce non-verifiable moral principles. Hume thus challenges the claim that morality is based on realism.

Intuitionism

Some of our knowledge is acquired directly through mental processes and does not rely on sensory experiences, as is the case with realism. The objects of such knowledge may include moral principles, specific moral duties in particular situations, and concepts of space and time. Intuitive knowledge can manifest in three potential forms: (i) as a self-evident truth; (ii) as the product of a distinct moral sense separate from the five senses, rather than inferential reasoning; and (iii) as a spontaneous moral judgement, and not a considered opinion. The term 'moral intuition' is grounded not in self-evident principles or axioms but in judgements that we are naturally inclined to make about what we ought to do or not do in specific contexts.

Major proponents of intuitionism include G. E. Moore, H. A. Prichard and W. D. Ross. Moore, in his *Principia Ethica*, says that ethics stems from intuition, asserting that 'we know what good is, but we can't define it'. Moore acknowledges that while intuitions are not always true or infallible, the senses cannot be employed to determine whether something is good or bad, and asserts that morality is invariably based on correct intuitions.

Prichard expands on Moore's work by differentiating between general and moral thinking. General thinking involves reasoning to assess the facts of a situation, while moral thinking relies on a sudden intuition about the right course of action in a specific situation.

Ross contends that we can never know all the facts about a given situation because all knowledge is inherently incomplete and partial, so we are compelled to rely on intuition for making moral judgements.

Non-Cognitive Meta-Ethics

Non-cognitive meta-ethics explores the nature and meaning of ethical statements through the expression of feelings rather than by describing the world. Unlike cognitive meta-ethics, which seeks to understand the truth conditions and knowledge associated with ethical propositions, non-cognitive meta-ethics focuses on the non-descriptive aspects of ethics, such as emotions, attitudes and expressions. Ethical statements are considered subjective, i.e., not objectively true or false.

Non-cognitive meta-ethics emphasises the subjective and emotive nature of ethical language, suggesting that ethical statements convey personal attitudes and feelings rather than making objective claims about the world. It shifts the focus from the truth conditions of ethical statements to their expressive and prescriptive aspects, and thus can be categorised under emotivism and prescriptivism.

Emotivism posits that descriptors like good or bad express emotions and are rooted in an individual's upbringing and environment. A. J. Ayer, a major philosopher associated with emotivism, asserts that terms like good, bad, right and wrong have no factual meanings but simply represent expressions of approval or disapproval. They are just emotional responses to situations. This theory is also known as the Boo-Hurray Theory.

Prescriptivism is about imposing our moral thoughts on others. According to R. M. Hare, when I say something is right or moral, I am trying to make others think the same. Hare aims to integrate meta-ethics and normative ethics, especially teleological ethics, and highlights that Kantian deontology and teleology can find common ground through a shared universal prescriptivism. Hare further unifies deontology and traditional teleology, and suggests that in most cases involving ethics, people could follow intuitionism or the deontological tradition, while the rare instances with a low possibility of occurrence could be addressed by utilitarianism with some flexibility.

APPLIED ETHICS

Applied ethics is the practical application of ethical principles to address everyday real-life issues and questions such as:

1. Is it ethical to grant legal permission for euthanasia?
2. Is it ethical for civil servants to engage in part-time business?
3. Is it ethical to award capital punishment?

As a multidisciplinary field, applied ethics encompasses diverse professional domains, and disciplinary and practical aspects of human life, including medical ethics, legal ethics, bioethics, business ethics and much more. While early twentieth-century analytic philosophers were less inclined toward normative or practical ethical inquiries, the latter half of the century saw a shift as moral discussions increasingly focused on complex issues like pollution, human rights abuses, human cloning and abortion.

Because of the complexity of each ethical dilemma, philosophers often find themselves delving into fundamental questions of meta-ethics and normative ethics. Utilitarian and deontological approaches prove to be particularly valuable in applied ethics. A contemporary strategy to navigate the sometimes indistinguishable aspects of deontology and utilitarianism involves case-based reasoning, a method known as casuistry.

Casuistry

Casuistry is an approach to solving ethical cases through reasoning. In involves applying multiple dimensions of ethics (discussed earlier) to particular situations while considering specific ethical obligations in order to reach a conclusion. It takes into account all the current facts of a real and precise case. Casuistry does not adhere to any specific ethical principle like deontology, consequentialism or virtue ethics, and is not biased for or against any ethical theory. Instead, it generalises the theory on a case-by-case basis, and the maxims so constructed become general rules but not universal, because they are case-specific. Like other ethical theories, casuistry takes moral intuitions into account.

Casuistry is based on an inductive approach, taking specific cases one by one and drawing general maxims by inductive reasoning. It is thus considered more a science rather than mathematics as it is knowledge based on inductive rather than deductive reasoning.

Casuistry started with the construction of a precise methodology that would include moral intuitions while drawing generalised rules from given specifics in order to reach reasoned ethical conclusions. A former Jesuit priest, Albert Jonsen, along with Stephen Toulmin formulated a system based on anti-theory and opposition to principlism that subjects particulars to universal maxims. In their book *The Abuse of Casuistry* (1988), Jonsen and Toulmin define casuistry as: 'the analysis of moral issues, using procedures of reasoning based on paradigms and analogies, leading to the formulation of expert opinions about the existence and stringency of particular moral obligations, framed in terms of rules or maxims that are general but not universal or invariable, since they hold good with certainty only in the typical conditions of the agent and circumstances of action.'

Casuistry is prevalent in bioethics. Bioethics evolved to delink itself from ethical theories, adopting a method based on induction, as opposed to the deductive method from universal principles. Casuistry achieves this using a process that involves three steps:

1. A contextually prominent case is described, highlighting the key points of ethical dilemma.
2. This case is classified, and analogical reasoning is applied to relate it to past paradigms in order to categorise the homogeneity and heterogeneity of the cases versus their paradigms.
3. Inductive reasoning is applied by incorporating moral intuition, then converging to a point taking into consideration past occurrences and the influence of current socio-cultural values, to finally obtain a moral judgement.

The new paradigm is then established by replacing the older cases in the abovementioned manner every time.

Business Ethics

Business ethics involves an inquiry into the moral principles and issues associated with honest business practices. It is widely acknowledged that resources collectively belong to the community, and those who own resources do so merely as their trustees. Many businesses, especially public limited companies, expand using public funds, making it crucial to establish ethical guidelines to regulate business behaviour for the benefit of customers, business owners and employees. The evolving demand for conscience-centric markets presents a challenge to ensure ethical practices in business activities. With the growing emphasis on public satisfaction in business, firms are under immense pressure to integrate ethics into their business practices.

Some ethical issues related to business activities include concerns related to safety standards (especially in hazardous work), surveillance and privacy, discrimination, harassment, child labour, gender-safe work environment, and so on. Business ethics can be either normative or descriptive. *Normative* business ethics implies that corporate practices should align with legal norms and guidelines, while *descriptive* business ethics considers non-economic social values. Most major corporate firms today emphasise the promotion of non-economic social values under different headings, like ethics codes and corporate social responsibility. In some cases, corporations have redefined their core values in light of business ethics considerations, or they project that they have, through corporate advertising, e.g., a mineral water bottling company's claim that 'we add more water than we use'.

Business ethics also addresses ethical questions in marketing, accounting, labour practices including child labour and abusive labour practices, human resource management, political contributions, business acquisitions such as hostile takeovers, production and use of toxic materials, insider trading, misuse of intellectual property rights and other relevant areas.

Legal Ethics

Legal ethics refers to an ethical code that regulates the conduct of those engaged in the practice of law. In India there are provisions for Bar Associations in both lower and higher courts, and they have promulgated model rules which have significantly impacted many jurisdictions. These model rules address various aspects of legal practice, including the client–lawyer relationship, the lawyer's interactions with persons other than the client, a lawyer's duties as an advocate in adversarial proceedings, public service in accordance with constitutional obligations, and preserving the integrity of the legal profession. Notable features of legal ethics include respecting client confidences, truthfulness in statements, and the importance of professional independence.

Environmental Ethics

Environmental ethics is a branch of environmental philosophy that examines the relationship between humans and the natural environment. This field draws on a wide range of disciplines, including law, sociology, theology, economics, environmental science and geography. Some of the key topics within environmental ethics are global warming, ozone layer depletion, deforestation, pollution, and their interconnectedness with issues such as poverty, sustainability and economic and social justice. Furthermore, since environmental problems often transcend national borders, these issues are closely linked to the realms of international relations and global governance, involving entities like the United Nations and programmes such as Conference of the Parties (COP).

Medical Ethics and Bioethics

Medical ethics is the study of moral values and judgments within the realm of medicine. It has evolved as a distinct discipline within the field of medical science, gaining prominence in the modern world where research and medical practices often raise ethical questions. As medical science has progressed throughout history, the need to define the scope of experiments and practices in this domain became apparent. Medical ethics extends to various subsidiary branches, including nursing ethics, the use of nutritional supplements and ethical considerations in health care business practices, especially during crisis periods.

The earliest instance of medical ethics can be seen in the well-known historical document known as the 'Hippocratic Oath'. The most ancient ethical obligation for physicians, it was written by Hippocrates, a Greek physician (460–370 BCE). This oath stipulates a range of duties for physicians while treating patients, covering aspects such as patient privacy, the preservation and advancement of medical science, and the passing on of knowledge to future generations. There are many versions of the Hippocratic Oath. Ludwig Edelstein's classical translation from the original Greek is one of the well-known versions.

The other famous classical version is a translation from the Greek by W. H. S. Jones. The classical version of the Hippocratic Oath is based on a religious oath taken in the name of the Greek god Apollo and others. It was opposed by secular thinkers, and later a secular oath was crafted to give it more acceptability. A modern version of the Hippocratic Oath was written in 1964 by Louis Lasagna, Dean of the School of Medicine at Tufts University. An excerpt from this is quoted below.

> ### An Excerpt from the Modern Version of the Hippocratic Oath
>
> I swear to fulfil, to the best of my ability and judgment, this covenant:
>
> > I will respect the hard-won scientific gains of those physicians in whose steps I walk, and gladly share such knowledge as is mine.... I will apply, for the benefit of the sick, all measures which are required, avoiding ... overtreatment and therapeutic nihilism. I will remember ... that warmth, sympathy, and understanding may outweigh the surgeon's knife or the chemist's drug.
> >
> > I will not be ashamed to say 'I know not,' nor ... fail to call in my colleagues when ... needed....
> >
> > I will respect the privacy of my patients ... treat with care in matters of life and death.... Above all, I must not play at God....
> >
> > I will prevent disease whenever I can ... remember that I remain a member of society, with special obligations to all my fellow human beings, those of sound mind and body as well as the infirm....

> ### Classical Version of the Hippocratic Oath
>
> I swear by Apollo Physician and Asclepius and Hygieia and Panacea and all the gods and goddesses, making them my witnesses, that I will fulfil according to my ability and judgment this oath and this covenant:
>
> > To hold him who has taught me this art as equal to my parents and to live my life in partnership with him, and if he is in need of money to give him a share of mine, and to regard his offspring as equal to my brothers in male lineage and to teach them this art—if they desire to learn it—without fee and covenant; to give a share of precepts and oral instruction and all the other learning to my sons and to the sons of him who has instructed me and to pupils who have signed the covenant and have taken an oath according to the medical law, but no one else.
> >
> > I will apply dietetic measures for the benefit of the sick according to my ability and judgment; I will keep them from harm and injustice.
> >
> > I will neither give a deadly drug to anybody who asked for it, nor will I make a suggestion to this effect. Similarly I will not give to a woman an abortive remedy. In purity and holiness I will guard my life and my art.
> >
> > I will not use the knife, not even on sufferers from stone, but will withdraw in favour of such men as are engaged in this work.
> >
> > Whatever houses I may visit, I will come for the benefit of the sick, remaining free of all intentional injustice, of all mischief and in particular of sexual relations with both female and male persons, be they free or slaves.
> >
> > What I may see or hear in the course of the treatment or even outside of the treatment in regard to the life of men, which on no account one must spread abroad, I will keep to myself, holding such things shameful to be spoken about.
>
> If I fulfil this oath and do not violate it, may it be granted to me to enjoy life and art, being honoured with fame among all men for all time to come; if I transgress it and swear falsely, may the opposite of all this be my lot.

Medical ethics is commonly perceived as a specialised branch of applied professional ethics, focusing on the ethical considerations within the field of medicine. In contrast, bioethics encompasses broader concerns, delving into the philosophy of science, and offering critiques of biotechnology and life sciences. Bioethics seeks to explore the boundaries of scientific advancements, examining their implications for fundamental principles of creation. Despite their distinct scopes, these two fields frequently overlap, and any divergence is primarily a matter of methodology rather than professional consensus. Key topics addressed by both disciplines include abortion, cloning, euthanasia, eugenics among others.

Ethical Egoism

Human beings are inherently driven by self-interest, a characteristic known as egoism. Psychological egoism posits that each of us is motivated by the ultimate objective of our own welfare, and thus views all human actions including altruistic ones as being inherently self-interested. While rewards and punishments often motivate people to acts of sacrifice or generosity in self-interest, this narrow interpretation fails to account for genuine altruism. For example, a soldier sacrificing his life to save innocent civilians cannot be explained solely by psychological egoism's emphasis on rewards and punishments.

Ethical egoism asserts that individuals should maximise their self-interest but do so ethically. It posits that every human action is motivated by the idea of coexistence and cooperation based on quid pro quo: if we don't help others, we may not receive help in turn. So people may exhibit dispositions of sacrifice, altruism, generosity and cooperation so as to maximise chances of receiving the same from others. The idea of cooperation is acceptable under ethical egoism when the losses incurred are temporary, insignificant and can be compensated by long-term gains. While such cooperation may serve the interest of others, it is not altruism. Egoistic conduct underlines personal gain, while altruism entails benefitting another purely for the sake of benefiting them, not out of expectations of return benefit, or guilt or any other reason.

Ethical egoism distinguishes itself from other moral theories by prioritising actions that yield maximum payoff. Traditional moral theories, such as Kantian categorical imperatives and utilitarianism, emphasise maximum payoff irrespective of whether it benefits oneself or others.

Psychological Egoism

Psychological egoism asserts that every individual has an ultimate objective—their own welfare—and that all actions are geared towards fulfilling self-interest. This theory does not concern itself with making norms, defining morality, or with 'ought' and 'should'. Instead, it offers an explanation of actual human behaviour and suggests that we do not perform actions for the wellbeing of others, and any sacrifices we make are ultimately for our own benefit and good. For example, helping a friend is seen as an effort that will be reciprocated in future, aligning with one's self-interest.

Philosophers have largely supported psychological egoism, with only a few, such as Hobbes and Bentham, arguing against it. Hobbes contends that all actions are driven by the intention of securing one's own welfare, and voluntary actions are motivated by the pursuit of personal good. Bentham, supporting psychological hedonism, asserts that people are governed by pain and pleasure.

Joseph Butler contradicts psychological egoism, stating that all specific desires and passions exist for external things independently of the pleasure or pain they generate, and that any pleasure or pain experienced from the fulfilment of desires is a by-product of prior desires for things that bring pleasure.

Ethical versus Psychological Egoism

Ethical egoism and psychological egoism are closely related concepts, but they address different aspects of human behaviour and morality. *Ethical egoism* focuses on normative ethics, prescribing how individuals ought to behave, and it prescribes that they should act in ways that maximise their self-interest. Ethical egoism is a moral theory that offers guidelines for determining what actions are morally right or wrong based on self-interest and suggests that we should prioritise our own welfare when making moral decisions. While ethical egoism allows for actions that benefit others (altruism), it insists that such actions should ultimately serve the self-interest of the doer.

Psychological egoism focuses on descriptive ethics, describing how individuals typically behave in reality, and asserts that all actions are motivated by self-interest. It is not a moral theory but an empirical claim about human motivation. Psychological egoism suggests that, in reality, individuals act in ways that promote self-interest, even if it appears altruistic, and thus it views altruistic actions as manifestations of disguised self-interest rather than true selflessness.

In essence, ethical egoism prescribes how individuals should behave morally, emphasising actions that serve self-interest, while psychological egoism describes the observed tendency of individuals to act in ways that promote self-interest, whether overtly or covertly.

Moral Relativism

Some moral judgments are neither inherently true nor false; their justification is not absolute but relative to their spatio-temporal context, reflecting the traditions and culture of a society. Varied intuitions and moral prescriptions exist among individuals and societies, contributing to the wide spectrum of moral diversity. *Moral relativism* is the philosophical position that moral or ethical propositions do not reflect objective and universal moral truths, but instead, are dependent on cultural, individual or situational factors. In other words, it asserts that there are no absolute or objective moral standards that apply universally to all people at all times in all contexts.

The absence of factual and verifiable knowledge in moral arguments implies that no one perspective is inherently right or wrong. Instead, judgments are grounded in individual feelings. A more nuanced version of moral subjectivism is represented by emotivism. Moral relativism, discussed within both meta-ethics and normative ethics, finds endorsement in the works of philosophers such as Herodotus and Protagoras.

Moral relativism distinguishes itself from moral skepticism by acknowledging the existence and importance of moral judgments. Unlike moral skepticism, which denies the possibility of moral knowledge, moral relativism recognises diverse moral perspectives and acknowledges the multiplicity of moral viewpoints rather than outright rejecting them. For instance, the assertion that 'capital punishment is morally wrong' may be accepted by one society while another perceives it as abominable and brutal. Different societies have different standards of justification, and conflicting opinions lack a universally rational basis for resolution.

Advocates of moral relativism often emphasise tolerance and respect for diverse moral viewpoints, acknowledging that different cultures and individuals may have legitimate moral perspectives. It is important to note that moral relativism is a complex and fiercely-debated philosophical stance. Critics argue that it can lead to moral nihilism, where any moral perspective is considered equally valid, and it may undermine the possibility of moral progress or moral criticism. Proponents argue that it provides a more inclusive and tolerant framework for understanding and respecting diverse moral beliefs in a complex and changing world.

Moral Scepticism

Moral scepticism is a philosophical tradition that casts doubt on moral statements, questioning their validity and denying claims of moral knowledge. Moral scepticism entails challenging commonly held beliefs, particularly established categorical moral norms, rather than critiquing weaker or more ambiguous moral propositions. Various forms of scepticism exist, with one strand focusing on the human capacity to acquire moral knowledge, known as epistemological moral scepticism. Further, epistemological scepticism has two main traditions: Cartesian scepticism and

Pyrrhonian scepticism. Cartesian scepticism or Academic scepticism claims that man never knows or can know anything. This scepticism claims universally without describing much, and hence it is called dogmatic scepticism. On the other hand, Pyrrhonian sceptics neither make any claims nor deny any claims. They do not accept that some individuals can sometimes have concrete knowledge of what is morally right or wrong. Moreover, they do not claim that moral knowledge is possible.

Epistemological moral scepticism argues that moral statements, typically framed as 'ought' statements, do not offer genuine knowledge since they cannot be validated through verification. The scepticism regarding the truthfulness of moral knowledge arises from the assertion that moral statements lack a basis for being verified as either true or false.

It is essential to distinguish moral scepticism from moral nihilism and moral absolutism. *Moral nihilism* posits that there are no objective facts about right and wrong actions, underlining the absence of any inherent moral truths. *Moral absolutism*, in contrast, asserts that knowledge of right and wrong is both factual and valid, with moral facts existing independently of perspectives and opinions, and grounded in objectivity. Additionally, moral relativism diverges from moral scepticism by maintaining that actions are not objectively right or wrong but are context-dependent within cultural realms. Moral relativism states that the morality of an action is determined by individuals or groups and is inherently tied to cultural contexts.

The Golden Rule in Ethics

The Golden Rule is a moral principle or ethical guideline based on the ideas of reciprocity and mutuality that encourages individuals to treat others as they would like to be treated themselves. It is often expressed in various forms across different cultures, religions and philosophical traditions, but the underlying idea remains consistent—promoting empathy, compassion and fairness in human interactions. The essence of the Golden Rule is captured in phrases such as: 'Do unto others as you would have them do unto you'; 'Treat others the way you want to be treated'; 'Love your neighbour as yourself.'

This principle encourages people to consider the impact of their actions on others and to extend the same considerations, kindness and respect to others that they would desire for themselves. The Golden Rule serves as a foundational element in many ethical and religious teachings, underscoring the importance of empathy and a sense of shared humanity in ethical decision-making.

EVOLUTIONARY ETHICS

Evolutionary ethics aims at ascertaining the origins of ethics, human moral behaviour and principles in the biological theory of evolution and seeks to understand how moral norms, values and conduct evolved over time through the process of natural selection and other mechanisms of biological evolution. Emerging as a response to the theological underpinnings of ethics, it seeks to uncover the foundation of ethics within the framework of biological evolution. The rise of secularism during the nineteenth century led to the popularity of evolutionary ethics, prompting moral philosophers to move away from the divine commandment theory of ethics. Evolutionary ethics progressed in three phases. Charles Darwin (1809–1882) and Herbert Spencer (1820–1903) were the first to propound ideas initiating the exploration of morality's roots in the theory of evolution, followed by subsequent phases in the early twentieth century and the modern era.

Darwin contended that any species capable of developing intelligence akin to humans would adopt moral behaviour. As human intelligence expanded, he postulated, individuals experienced emotions tied to pleasure and pain, compelling them to live in groups rather than in solitude. Over time, a moral faculty emerged from these emotions, contributing to the sustainable survival of human beings in communities. Each group formulated moral ideas that served as the foundation for human development. Spencer, in his work *Social Statics* (1851), emphasised individual free will within the bounds of not infringing upon the freedom of others. In *Principles of Ethics* (1879–1893), Spencer expounded on the idea of maximising pleasure and minimising pain, asserting that this propelled the biological evolutionary process, developing under the inheritance of acquired characteristics.

Spencer viewed evolution as a teleological process geared towards creating greater human superiority through progressive evolution, aimed at achieving a more evolved 'totality of life' encompassing advanced thoughts, feelings and actions, ultimately resulting in longer human life. While Darwinism rejected Spencer's teleological theory, emphasising reproductive fitness, Spencer's theory portrayed the evolution of humankind from unethical to ethical attitudes. Evolutionary ethics endeavours to elucidate human moral sense through the lens of natural sciences, explaining morality as a natural adaptation that enhances human fitness for survival, providing a selective advantage.

Edward O. Wilson (1929–2021) suggested that the ownership of morality be transferred from philosophers to biologists, highlighting that human morality is rooted in the social instinct. As human intellectual faculties developed, individuals could reflect self-interests on past actions, forming traits to approve or disapprove certain actions. This conscience regarding right or wrong stemmed from the biological evolution of human beings. Darwin regarded happiness as the criterion for determining right or wrong, positing that an action is deemed right or good if it maximises happiness by increasing pleasure or decreasing pain. Darwin held that the choice of good or right is driven by the pursuit of an advantage in the struggle for existence. Individuals exhibit morality, altruism, cooperation and sympathy as adaptive strategies for survival.

The theory of evolution offers a satisfactory response to David Hume's 'is-ought distinction' which posits that normative rules (*ought*) cannot be derived from empirical facts (*is*). Darwin and Spencer, however, do derive norms from facts. Darwin asserts that happiness is an integral part of the general good, and morality should promote happiness, thus bridging the normative claim of duty with the empirical fact of happiness.

G. E. Moore critiqued evolutionary ethics on the grounds of the *naturalistic fallacy*—a challenge that has persisted since Moore's time. The fallacy is often associated with attempts to derive ethical or evaluative conclusions from purely natural, descriptive or empirical premises without providing an additional ethical premise. The term 'naturalistic' refers to the idea of grounding ethics in the natural world or observable facts. For instance, if someone argues that because a particular behaviour is natural or commonly observed in the animal kingdom, it is morally acceptable for humans, they would be committing the naturalistic fallacy. The fact that something is a certain way in nature does not necessarily make it morally right or wrong.

Despite this, evolutionary ethics has continued to evolve, especially with the advent of *sociobiology*, defined as the systematic study of the biological basis of all social behaviour in human beings.

LYING AND ETHICS

Lying is the deliberate act of expressing falsehood with the intention to mislead others. It takes the form of baseless, fabricated, unreal and exaggerated speech or writing. Lying is a very common behaviour, and we often hear it said that lying is always and inherently wrong, except when it is told for a good reason. A lie typically has three essential components:

1. Communication of some information
2. Intention to deceive
3. Strong conviction that the information being conveyed is untrue

The philosopher Sissela Bok defines a lie as 'an intentionally deceptive message in the form of a statement'. Lying is generally considered unacceptable because it is fundamentally immoral and corrupts the mental faculty of the liar, fostering a habit of dishonesty. It erodes trust between individuals, leading to scepticism about the sincerity of others' speech and intentions. This in turn complicates the acquisition of knowledge because *shabda* (sound) or speech as verbal testimony is an important source of human knowledge and understanding. Lying is employed to achieve specific ends, using others who are deceived by the lie as means to desired ends, which goes against human dignity.

A lie harms both the liar and the recipient of the lie. The one who is told a lie is deprived of the ability to make informed decisions based on accurate information, leading to feelings of being cheated, manipulated and undeserving of the truth. The liar, too, faces the challenge of sustaining additional lies to maintain consistency with previous falsehoods. The Quran says: 'Do not conceal testimony, for whoever conceals it his heart is indeed sinful' and further advises: 'Do not mix the truth with falsehood or conceal the truth while you know it.'

The question of whether lying always produces negative effects or if it is acceptable in certain cases is a fundamental inquiry in philosophy. Some religious texts, such as the Bible and the Quran, suggest that lying may be acceptable in certain situations, such as protecting the innocent or during times of war. Hinduism also provides nuances regarding when lying might be permissible. In the *Mahabharata* (*Adi Parva*), it is mentioned that lying may be acceptable in certain situations, such as to protect life, preserve wealth, appease the wife or in the context of telling a joke. If one's speech does not cause harm to any living creature, even if factually incorrect, it is considered a form of truthfulness. Lying may also be used as a strategy to boost the self-confidence and morale of broken people. The *Mundaka Upanishad* declares, '*Satyameva Jayate*' (truth alone triumphs), which was later adopted as the official motto of the Indian government. Tamil poet Thiruvalluvar suggests that lying is permissible when it might attain the value of truth, when it serves the greater good and produces the least harm. Sankaracharya states that while one who lies habitually is untrustworthy, on occasions where protecting righteousness is paramount, even a lie may be considered sinless.

Plato discusses the idea of the 'noble lie' in *The Republic*, suggesting that statesmen may use lies as instruments of statecraft or education under specific situations. Several philosophers provide rational explanations for lying and truth. Benjamin Constant makes an interesting and nuanced argument and says: 'The morality which advocates telling the truth as a duty would make the sustenance of any society impossible if truth is taken in absolute and isolated terms. Duties and rights are complementary to each other. No one can imagine a duty without any related right. Truth can be conceived as a duty for those who are entitled to the truth. But no man has a right to the truth that jeopardizes others.'

In contrast, Kant however staunchly maintains that lying is always morally wrong in all forms in all contexts, and it is doubly wrong as it corrupts human moral capacity and violates human dignity. According to Kant, every human possesses intrinsic value, namely human dignity, which comes from the human property of rationality and the ability to make independent decisions exercising free will. Lying obstructs others from acting rationally and freely in making accurate and informed decisions, thus undermining their dignity. Kantian ethics and absolute rejection of lying complies with his philosophy of moral formalism.

Virtue ethics maintains that lying is wrong, but it does not take a stand as firm as that of Kant. It emphasises the inculcation of honesty and truthfulness as key virtues essential for holistic moral development, and the pivot of all other moral behaviour.

Utilitarians assess lies and truth based on the sum balance of benefits and losses. If a lie is deemed more advantageous than the truth in a given situation, utilitarianism would justify the lie for maximising benefits. However, accurately predicting the consequences of a lie poses a big challenge for utilitarianism.

In situations where lying seems unavoidable, individuals must explore the possibility of a truthful alternative, seek any moral justifications for the lie and consider public opinion on the matter.

QUESTIONS

1. How is ethics based on means different from ethics based on ends? How are these two methods applied to design norms? Explain with the help of examples.
2. Intuition is a source of morality: comment.
3. Ethics is related to 'ought', not 'is': comment.
4. Virtue ethics can be considered the essence of morality: critically evaluate.
5. Nothing is inherently good or bad but our thinking makes it so: critically evaluate.
6. Explain procedure established by law and due process of law in the light of ethics and morality.
7. Without God there is no morality: critically evaluate.
8. With regard to the morality of actions, one view is that means is of paramount importance and the other view is that the ends justify the means. Which view do you think is more appropriate? Justify your answer. (UPSC 2018)
9. 'The true rule, in determining to embrace or reject anything, is not whether it has any evil in it, but whether it has more evil than good. There are few things wholly evil or wholly good. Almost everything, especially of governmental policy, is an inseparable compound of the two; so that our best judgement of the preponderance between them is continually demanded.' Analyse this statement by Abraham Lincoln. (UPSC 2018)
10. What is 'environmental ethics'? Why is it important to study? Discuss any one environmental issue from the viewpoint of environmental ethics. (UPSC 2015)

3

ETHICS IN PRIVATE AND PUBLIC RELATIONSHIPS

> **KEY CONCEPTS**
>
> What, Why, How; Types of Conduct; Evolution and Emergence of Morality; Public and Private Relationships; Legal Intervention in the Realm of the Private

Ethics revolves around human conduct and a philosophical assessment of the moral value of conduct that also aims to ascertain the principles forming the basis for this assessment. Moral conduct or a moral lifestyle has two main dimensions: one pertains to the fulfilment of objective or purpose; the other is related to nature and human society. The first dimension includes internal factors like ideas, emotions, experiences, ideals, purposes, intentions, assessments and choices, while the second dimension involves external factors related to our social existence.

To progress, ethics must explore both *internal* and *external* dimensions simultaneously. First, it must study the internal processes influenced by changing external situations. Second, it must take into account our external behaviour or social conduct as determined by the objectives of our internal life. These internal objectives of life fall under the domain of psychology, addressing the standards that determine how the rights of others are affected in the pursuit of our personal objectives and whether such actions are deemed right or wrong. The discovery of moral principles thus provides a pathway that helps us resolve complex problems in life concerning ourselves and others.

WHAT, WHY, HOW

The question of ethical criteria has been central to philosophical inquiry. We often ask '*what* ought to be done' in a given situation, or '*what* is our intent' in doing something. We also ask *why* and *how* something should be done. These two aspects can be regarded as 'matter or content' (*what*) and as 'form or attitude' (*why, how*), respectively. If we focus on the *what*, two aspects emerge: the *what* may be of a higher or lower degree, and though the determination of this degree is not discussed here, it is generally accepted.

When we consider the *how*, it becomes crucial to differentiate between *right* and *good*. While these two words may appear synonymous, in the context of ascertaining morality, they hold different significance and implications. Declaring an action as *right* implies accepting it as a moral standard and giving consent to establish it as a moral law to be followed by all. This standard commands our desires and passions. One who adheres to this law is deemed rational, sensible, self-regulated and a strict follower of moral ideals. On the other hand, when we discuss *good*, we emphasise values. What we consider good or desirable has no bearing on moral rules or laws but is influenced by the potential outcomes of our actions and choices. We should not be controlled by the things we desire and choose; moral actions should stem from honour for ethical principles and a sense of duty rather than fear of punishment or desire for rewards. According to Aristotle, the emphasis in moral conduct is not just on doing the right thing but also how it should be done.

TYPES OF CONDUCT

Conduct may be divided into three types. The first type comprises actions that stem from human instinct and fulfilling basic needs, which include food, clothing, shelter, sex, as well as aspects like dignity, recognition and self-actualisation. While these actions generally align with moral laws, they may not necessarily be driven by moral commands.

The second type of actions is guided by societal standards and conscience, aiming to achieve social welfare. They prioritise overall social good or happiness over personal well-being and are characterised as *group morality*. Such actions arise either out of habit, suddenly, or due to rational deliberation.

The third type of actions is guided by standards established through societal consensus and rationality, and are not only aligned with the goals of individuals but are also considered as commonly shared values. We choose and perform these actions freely because they are both *right* and *good*, and are accepted by others as such, causing no difficulty in their selection.

EVOLUTION AND EMERGENCE OF MORALITY

The Family: The institution of family life is a product of innate human instincts and the forces of natural selection. Instincts such as attraction between males and females, the realisation of maternity and paternity and the accumulation of wealth contribute to the formation of social groups. The robust constraints imposed by religion, society and morality play a crucial role in maintaining the stability of family life, acting as deterrents against deviant behaviour among both men and women. The familial bond is further strengthened by parental care, a significant factor that emerges as a connection between parents. The vulnerability of children and extended period of adolescence necessitate the provision of parental care, giving rise to the moral value of parental love.

The Group or Community: The natural forces of instinct create bonds between individuals, leading to the development of *group morality* aimed at sustaining the social group. This group morality is further manifested in the form of traditions, commonly referred to as *customary morality* or *traditional morality*. Actions approved under this customary morality give rise to distinct cultural norms and traditions that are passed down from generation to generation, becoming ingrained habits within the social group. These norms are deemed essential for social welfare, and any deviation is met with strong societal disapproval.

Traditions: The guardians of traditions, including elderly members of society, religious leaders and community chiefs play a pivotal role in upholding and reforming traditions. These traditions are disseminated through education, restrictions and social regulations. Initially, there may be no universally accepted standards for newly conceived traditions, and decisions are made by group leaders on various occasions. But over time, a general morality emerges based on precedents, and legal traditions take shape.

The complete emergence of morality takes place when all members begin to freely recognise the *right* and voluntarily choose the *good* while earnestly considering the progress of societal development. Group morality sets standards through its agencies, but it is not necessary that every member of society adheres to these standards as part of their individual value system. Conflicts often arise between the authority and interests of the group, or between public and private interests, leading to tensions between status-quo and progress, and between habits and reforms.

Individuals hold personal opinions and beliefs in pursuit of their freedom and personal interests. True virtue is associated with self-sacrifice and altruism, yet egoism and selfishness are not easily curbed, especially in the present age. Moralities often result from a compromise between sacrificing the self to accommodate others and expressing the self, especially in the pursuit of professional success. Recent discussions highlight the notion that moral judgments are based on the expression of the individual's self, incorporating the selves of others. Individuals typically act driven by personal motivations and objectives, which may be partly selfish and partly unselfish. Morality serves to establish a common social order by recognising the selves and interests of others. Morality in essence is the 'knowledge of egoism', a means to achieve happiness by acknowledging others and our duties towards them, and by putting rational, ethical constraints on selfishness, thus bringing conflicting tendencies into compromise and resolution.

PUBLIC AND PRIVATE RELATIONSHIPS

We form various types of relationships with others which are shaped by the degree of affinity and trust granting others access to our privacy. The level of access can fluctuate based on the nature of the relationship, personal needs or motivations and the context. Sometimes one may choose to discuss personal matters with an outsider over a close friend or family. Understanding the dynamics of human relationships can be complex, often leading to significant mistakes in managing them. Philosophically, relationships are grounded in morality, social contracts and the prevailing laws and regulations; for instance, the private relationship of marriage for a Hindu couple is governed by the Hindu Marriage Act.

Relationships may be broadly categorised into public and private relationships. *Public relationships* are formal, and based on specific well-defined duties and a mechanism of quid pro quo; for example, those between teacher and student, between customers and service providers, or between a public servant and citizens. *Private relationships*, in contrast, are informal, can often be altruistic in nature and have no well-defined duties or boundaries. In private relationships, the notion of creating legal obligations through transactions is not strongly emphasised. For instance, an elder brother or sister's contributions towards the nurture and upbringing of younger siblings do not create a legal obligation. Private relationships do not seek validation from a legal entity, which suggests that they can be managed more casually, while public relationships require more careful transaction.

How do we identify a relation as public or private? They can be distinguished by the nature of the relationship and by the regulating authority. Public relationships are regulated by a legal authority according to established law, whereas private relationships are regulated by personal and moral obligations. Transactions between an office-bearer and a beneficiary are based on legal accountability, whereas interactions between a father and son are based on affection and moral responsibility. The former is a legal obligation, and more inclined towards deontology, while the latter is a moral obligation, based on teleology.

Public relationships are extremely significant and central to the life of a public servant as they involve interactions with the general public in their day-to-day activities. Public servants are expected to follow certain guidelines and rules when engaging in public relationships, as provided in the civil services conduct rules. These rules clearly delineate expected behaviours from public servants in their daily public lives, a topic we will discuss in detail in subsequent chapters. For example:

1. A public servant must never treat a public relationship as a private one as this can jeopardise public service values like impartiality and non-partisanship.
2. A public servant must avoid establishing private relationships with subordinates, which does not imply isolation but underlines the need to maintain appropriate professional boundaries guided by emotional intelligence.

Although private relationships are rooted in morality, they are also subject to minimal legal enforcement for effective societal regulation. For instance, the parent–child relationship is deeply personal; but if a parent neglects to provide education and forces the child into labour, legal issues may arise. Similarly, if a spouse fails to fulfil the physical needs of their partner, legal recourse can be sought to restore conjugal rights. There are many examples where legal authorities have intervened in private relationships that have become irreparable or harmful for the affected individuals. Generally, there are no stringent provisions for resolving such disputes, and counselling is often used to guide the concerned parties, except in specific cases.

LEGAL INTERVENTION IN THE REALM OF THE PRIVATE

Now we must ask: how far is legal scrutiny and intervention ethical in private relationships? What are the ethical implications thereof? There are no clear-cut guidelines in this regard. Most often it is the socio-cultural norms and the common ethos of the concerned society, collectively forming a 'social contract', that provide solutions to such issues. However, there is always potential for the violation of minority rights, particularly when a minority holds a divergent view on a specific private relationship. Issues like gay rights, Section 377 of the Indian Penal Code (IPC), Triple Talaq, adultery or Section 497 of the IPC, and the Surrogacy Act are examples of topics related to this notion.

Varied opinions exist in different countries regarding public and private morality, especially concerning issues like abortion, adultery and homosexuality. India is one of more than 60 countries to recognise women's rights to terminate unwanted pregnancy. Abortion is legal under specific, well-defined circumstances as per the Medical Termination of Pregnancy (MTP) Act of 1971, and the (Amendment) Act of 2021 which extended the upper limit for abortion from 20 to 24 weeks. The Supreme Court of India unanimously struck down Section 497 IPC and decriminalised adultery in 2018, in the case of *Joseph Shine vs Union of India*.

Homosexuality was considered a criminal offence in India under Section 377 of the Indian Penal Code, carrying a provision of 10 years' imprisonment, which lasted 157 years from 1861 to 2018. In 2009, the Delhi High Court declared Section 377 unconstitutional in the case of *Naz Foundation vs Govt of NCT of Delhi*, stating that punishing homosexuality is a violation of privacy and personal freedom granted under Article 21 of the Indian Constitution. Furthermore, it contravened Article 14 (Right to Equal Treatment) and Article 15 (Prohibition of Discrimination). In 2018, a divisional bench of five judges of the Supreme Court of India gave a historic ruling, declaring the law treating homosexuality as a criminal offence null and void.

Moral standards in any given society are influenced by its social, economic and spiritual development, which in turn shape the ethical and legal norms established by its state or government. These standards evolve differently in different countries due to various social, cultural, political and economic factors. Sometimes these may conflict with prevailing international systems. For example, German law mandates compulsory schooling for children aged 6 to 18, and homeschooling is not permissible. Two German Supreme Court rulings have granted the state equal authority to parents over children's education, emphasising that children should receive appropriate socialisation. But this law directly contradicts the International Covenant on Civil and Political Rights (ICCPR), which Germany has signed. The ICCPR recognises parental liberty, stating: 'States parties...undertake to have respect for the liberty of parents...to ensure the religious and moral education of their children in conformity with their own convictions.' This liberty includes the right to homeschooling. In addition, Germany is a signatory to the International Covenant on Economic, Social, and Cultural Rights (ICESCR), which recognises parental liberty to choose schools for their children which conform to minimum educational standards. However, Germany is also a party to the European Union Convention on Human Rights, which is less sympathetic to parental choice. In the Konrad case (2006), the European Court of Human Rights ruled against a German homeschooling family.

> The International Covenant on Civil and Political Rights (**ICCPR**) was adopted by the United Nations General Assembly on 16 December 1966, and came into force on 23 March 1976. The Covenant further extends the civil and political rights and freedoms listed in the Universal Declaration of Human Rights.

The Case of Konrad versus Germany

In the Konrad case, four applicants—Fritz Konrad, Marianna Konrad, and their children Rebekka and Josua—filed an application against Germany in the European Court of Human Rights. Residents of Herbolzheim city, they are Christians who maintain a strong bond with the Bible, and do not endorse any form of state-run schooling. The Konrad couple contended that school education contradicts their faith and beliefs, citing issues such as sex education and the study of mythological gods, which they argue induce psychological violence in school-going children.

The Konrad couple submitted an application on behalf of their children, seeking an exemption from compulsory school attendance and the opportunity for homeschooling. But the school administration rejected their application, and in July 2001, the Freeberg Administrative Court also ruled against it. While acknowledging that fundamental laws grant parents the right to freedom of religion and education based on their religious and philosophical beliefs, the court noted that removing children from school might expose them to certain risks. Bound by the duty of compulsory education, the state curtails such freedoms. The court argued that home education, within the protected confines of the home, would also deprive children of direct social interaction and experiences in society, and the state serves the interests of children better through school education. Given children's immaturity, the state must protect their educational rights, the court asserted.

Fritz and Marianna Konrad pursued their case before the Federal Court and Constitutional Court, both of which rejected their application. In November 2003, they brought their application before the European Court of Human Rights, citing violations of their rights under Articles 2, 8 and 9 of Protocol 1 of the Human Rights Act. Specifically, they argued that in denying them the right to homeschool their children, their parental rights under Article 2 of Protocol 1 had been violated. The article states: 'In the exercise of any functions which it assumes in relation to education and teaching, the State shall respect the right of parents to ensure such education and teaching in conformity with their own religious and philosophical convictions.'

Germany is a liberal democracy. Yet the state's action in this instance is antithetical to democratic principles. While the government should have the ability to monitor children's education, it should not exert complete control. Parents are above the state when it comes to deciding the future of their children. Education is not just about academics or a career; it involves life choices. It is also about parental choice concerning the inculcation of cultural, spiritual or religious values. In the absence of such educational freedoms, children can truly become 'prisoners of the state' and its pedagogy. Similar instances can be seen in Norway and other European countries.

Another notable example of government interference in private relationships is the Indian law, Maintenance and Welfare of Parents and Senior Citizens Act, 2007, which obliges progeny to provide maintenance and care for their elderly parents.

Transition between Public and Private

A change in the dynamics of a relationship, such as its scale, visibility, responsibilities or impact, can influence whether it is perceived as private or public. If the impact of a private relationship extends beyond its immediate participants and affects the larger community, it may be considered more public. A private relationship may acquire legal recognition or involve legal contracts (e.g., marriage), moving it into a more public domain. The distinction between private and public relationships can be fluid and context-dependent, varying across cultures, legal systems and societal norms, and what is considered private or public may evolve over time.

There are also instances where private and public relationships encroach upon each other and their boundaries become blurred, making it difficult to maintain a clear distinction between them. Overcoming such situations often requires self-restraint and sacrificing one's desires and pleasures. For example, it is advisable for a public servant to avoid having a romantic relationship with a subordinate if there is no intention of marriage; likewise, for a doctor and patient, or for a teacher and student. There are any number of situations where such guidelines become crucial for human behaviour.

Gandhi challenged the existence and practice of two levels of morality—one for our private life, and another for our public life. *Private morality* pertains to our personal and private conduct. *Public morality* pertains to collective social conduct and political life on a broader scale. This is known as the 'doctrine of double standards', which Gandhi rejected. He argued that a society governed by this doctrine is self-destructive and exploitative. Gandhi believed public and political morality must be reconciled with the personal and private, and extended to all individuals in all walks of life. Although Gandhi viewed politics as impure and sinful, he also firmly believed that it can and must be purified. And the first step in this process, he said, is to get rid of the discriminatory meanings of public and private morality, or political and personal morality, and to eliminate the distinction between them.

QUESTIONS

1. Explain ethics in private and personal relationships with the help of suitable examples.
2. The ethical division between private and public relationships poses challenges in the making of laws and legal intervention. Explain with the help of suitable examples.
3. Civil servants should be aware of the continuum of private and public relationships in order to preserve the integrity, probity and accountability of their public office. Explain with the help of suitable examples.
4. Do you agree that the state should control people's private lives? If yes, what should be the guiding principles which should be considered by the state? If not, explain why.

4

HUMAN VALUES

> **KEY CONCEPTS**
>
> What are Values?; Hierarchy and Classification of Values; Value Theory of Milton Rokeach (1918–88); Value Theory of Clare W. Graves (1914–86); Choosing Personal Core Values; Role of Family in Inculcating Values; Role of Society in Inculcating Values; Role of Educational Institutions in Inculcating Values

WHAT ARE VALUES?

Values are described as the worth, utility, merit, desirability and standards of an object. In terms of human values these objects are in the form of thoughts, words and actions. Different people have different standards while choosing their thoughts, words and actions. Thus, we can say that values are akin to preferences or choices. Some regard materialistic values as more important than moral and spiritual values, and this preference is highly dependent on individual attitudes and aptitudes. The formation of values involves factors which are more psychological than cognitive and is a dynamic process which changes with choices and preferences. For example, a student may value his books over and above everything else during examinations, but once examinations are over, these books may become less valuable. This illustrates how circumstances and desires influence our values. While some values may be considered as universally accepted, in exceptional cases they can become avoidable when taken to extremes. For example, maintaining hygiene and cleanliness is universally considered a positive value for personal health and societal wellbeing. However, if an individual becomes excessively obsessed with cleanliness to the point of developing an anxiety disorder where they constantly fear germs and contamination, this extreme adherence to cleanliness becomes detrimental to their mental health and quality of life.

When it comes to human values, the personal *core values* guide our conduct in everyday life and are in fact decisive factors in determining how we want to live and what sort of person we want to be in this world. Every decision we take is influenced by our internal values, which provide the objective as well as the criteria to take a particular decision in a particular way. The amount of satisfaction or discontent one experiences is largely influenced by one's personal value system because motivation and conduct are aligned with the ambition of what type of person one wants to be in life.

Personal core values also play a crucial role in professional life and at the workplace. For the success of any organisation, the values of those who work there are central. Researchers have focused on the values underlying the social behaviour of individuals, and consider them to be strong motivations that guide attitudes and provide justifications for such attitudes. Every organisation develops its own value system, and these organisational values manifest its objectives and priorities. Ultimately, values have the potential to effect major change in society. Researchers have established a link between values and organisational characteristics such as commitment, customer satisfaction and work culture. Various tools have been developed to gauge and estimate organisational culture. One notable effort was made by Polish-American psychologist Milton Rokeach in 1973. The 36 values Rokeach identified cover a wide range of individual and organisational values, as we shall discuss.

HIERARCHY AND CLASSIFICATION OF VALUES

Long-term research has focused on values as crucial to understanding social behaviour. They are considered abstract principles acting as motivations that guide, describe and justify norms, attitudes and views. Each individual and organisation possesses its own unique value system or value hierarchy, and prevailing values differ across societies. Values have predictive and explanatory potential at the individual, organisational and societal levels. Values play a central role in public discourse today, and can bring about major social change in societies and across nations.

According to Shalom H. Schwartz: (i) values are beliefs related to desirable behaviour or ends, and motivate action; (ii) they transcend specific circumstances; (iii) they guide us in the evaluation and selection of our preferences based on their possible outcomes; and (iv) values follow a definite *hierarchy* or order of importance and priorities relative to each other, that are specific and unique to everyone.

Ian C. Woodward and Samah Shaffakat posit values as abstract standards and guiding principles that are inculcated, learned and acquired in the form of beliefs; that influence choice; that function in a hierarchy; and are sustained over time. Values play a key role in determining behaviour and are themselves highly influenced by the external environment.

The Value System

Generally, both individuals and organisations adopt several interrelated values, instead of one specific value; this comprises the *value system* of that individual or organisation. A value system is conceived as a set of values ranked by priority or importance for an individual, group or a society at large. It is a preferential and hierarchical framework of standards, principles and criteria related to ethics, quality, commitment and so on. While everyone has their own value system, mere possession of the 'right' values does not suffice—their correct placement in the hierarchy is crucial for those values to effectively determine the desired behaviour and goals.

Values placed at higher levels of importance, or *core values*, are more influential in determining choices and behaviour than those at lower levels. Core values have the highest impact on behaviour, over and above other values in the value hierarchy. The same applies to organisational value systems: core organisational values occupy the highest level in the hierarchy and are more influential with respect to the behaviour and actions of the organisation as a whole. An organisation may comprise different groups, and the values of each group must align with that of the organisation. Every member of an organisation contributes certain values to it, and if a member's values do not align with the organisational values, it results in a misfit.

Organisational Values: An organisation's values are closely associated with its preferred leadership, the growth of organisational culture and the motivation level of its employees. Before the 1990s, organisational culture and values were treated as resources that helped stay in competition. Today, values are seen as crucial for organisational survival, and for understanding and inculcating leadership. Levels of employee motivation and commitment to work culture directly impact the organisation's value system and success. An individual's values ultimately determine whether or not they become a leader. Hard work, skills and merit are considered ineffective in absence of the right value system. It is impossible to lead people today by ignoring values, group or individual.

Levels of Classification

There are many interpretations and definitions for the term *value*, reflecting its multidimensional nature, and hence value systems are also many. In trying to understand, describe and classify different kinds of values and value systems, researchers have constructed models that classify values at multiple levels. Rokeach categorises values into *instrumental* and *terminal* levels; Barry Z. Posner and Warren H. Schmidt differentiate between *individual* and *organisational* levels; Geert Hofstede classifies values under *occupational*, *organisational* and *national* levels. These different models reveal the links between different kinds of values across multiple levels of human social organisation.

Rokeach lists 36 terminal and instrumental values; Shalom H. Schwartz describes 56 values, grouped into 10 motivational value types under four categories; Dennis T. Jaffe and Cynthia D. Scott list 40 values under six categories; Paul McDonald and Jeffrey Gandz mention 21 values; and Hofstede names 36 values. These models attempt to provide a broad list of values, expressed in order of importance, for individuals and organisations. The different value levels show which individual value coincides with values held by others at either the organisational or national level. When employees collectively feel they share in the values of the organisation, the organisation successfully creates an 'identity' for itself, and differences between the two can be smoothly overcome.

VALUE THEORY OF MILTON ROKEACH (1918–88)

Milton Rokeach posits that, 'Values are persistent beliefs regarding a particular way of conduct or end goal which are preferred over contrary ideas.' He defines values as: 'An enduring belief that a specific mode of conduct or end-state of existence is personally or socially preferable to an opposite or converse mode of conduct or end-state of existence.' Rokeach asserts that once values are inculcated, they become an integral part of the value system, operating in a self-automated manner to resolve conflicts and helping critical decision-making. Rokeach introduced two kinds of values: terminal and instrumental.

Terminal values comprise desirables and final objectives representing the end-states or end goals that a person would aspire to achieve during their lifetime. These end goals vary for different people and societies, and across time. Terminal values include: prosperity, security, peace, equality, liberty, salvation.

Terminal values are further categorised as social and personal values. *Social* terminal values are inculcated by focusing on others and concern the community at large. These are: a world at peace, a world of beauty, equality, family security, freedom, mature love, national security, social recognition and true friendship. *Personal* terminal values are self-oriented and focused on achieving intended goals in one's life. These are: a comfortable life, an exciting life, a sense of accomplishment, happiness, inner harmony, pleasure, salvation, self-respect and wisdom.

Instrumental values are the preferred means of achieving terminal values and involve specific desired modes of behaviour geared to attain end goals. Most instrumental values are formed by an individual's personal character traits. Instrumental values include: courage, honesty, intelligence, ambition, hard work, broadmindedness, rationality.

Instrumental values are further divided into moral and competence values. *Moral* values focus on morality and relationships, such as being broadminded, forgiving, helpful, honest, loving, cheerful, obedient, polite and responsible. *Competence* values focus on developing capability, such as being ambitious, capable, clean, courageous, imaginative, independent, intellectual, logical and self-controlled.

Table 4.1: Rokeach's terminal and instrumental values

Terminal values	Prosperity, Luxury, Beauty, Peace, Equality, Liberty, Wisdom, Salvation, Family security, National security, Self-respect, etc.
Instrumental values	Courage, Forgiveness, Honesty, Politeness, Obedience, Intelligence, Ambition, Hard work, Broadmindedness, Effectiveness, Rationality, etc.

Source: Created by authors.

Terminal and instrumental values are functionally interconnected as instrumental values serve to achieve terminal values. Individual behaviour based on instrumental values may be used to attain one or more terminal values, and a group of instrumental values may achieve a single intended terminal value. However, the decisive factor is not the values alone but their position and importance in the hierarchy of values. This hierarchy is influenced by an individual's experiences, gender, culture, family, education, etc. It can be said that while instrumental values may be altered at the organisational level, terminal values are more or less unaffected.

Rokeach's classification of values, developed almost 50 years ago, remains a basis for many modern studies. His 'Value Survey', conducted in 1973, is still recognised and widely used as a research tool. His list of 36 values, individual and organisational, is still considered valid and essential.

Table 4.2: Difference between instrumental and terminal values

Instrumental values	Terminal values
1. These are personal core values, comprising individual character traits.	1. These are desired end goals that one considers most important and aspires for.
2. Include preferred modes of behaviour, like honesty, sincerity, ambition, rationality, etc.	2. Include happiness, freedom, self-respect, security, recognition, etc.
3. Serve as a means for achieving life's end goals and terminal values.	3. Signify the ultimate things a person seeks to achieve through their behaviour.
4. Difficult to change.	4. Can be changed.

Source: Created by authors.

Bruce M. Meglino and Geert Hofstede argue that an individual's instrumental values can be changed at the organisational level, and that therefore, terminal values don't allow a description or comparison of organisational values. Päivi Korvajärvi says that gender must be given adequate place in the study of organisational values as it forms the basis for determining human behaviour and functions, and because patterns of relationship between individual values and organisational culture vary for men and women. Values can vary according to a respondent's gender, work status and length of work experience.

VALUE THEORY OF CLARE W. GRAVES (1914–86)

Clare W. Graves proposed that human values constitute a set of psychological mechanisms that thrive and evolve over time to enable individuals to cope with and navigate their external environment. He explained the evolution of the value system in a model where values at new levels emerge progressively over time by assimilating values at the preceding levels. The transition from one level to the next is not a linear progression, but rather a two-dimensional movement between *egocentrism* on the one hand and *community-centrism* on the other, and vice versa. This traversal may follow different routes in individuals based on their varying degrees of inclination towards egocentrism and community-centrism.

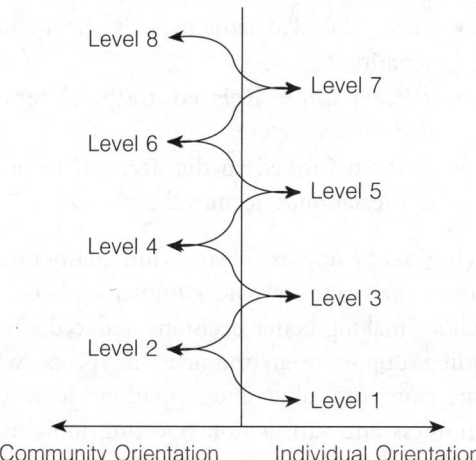

Figure 4.1: Graves' Value System

Source: Created by authors.

Graves identified eight levels in his value system, classifying four levels under the individual or egocentric orientation, and four levels under the community orientation, as shown in Figure 4.1.

Level 1/*Survival*: Pertains to individual orientation; values are animalistic and reactive.

Level 2/*Tribal*: Pertains to community orientation; values are loyalty, inclusivity and allegiance.

Level 3/*Power*: Pertains to individual orientation; values are domination and control.

Level 4/*Justice*: Pertains to community orientation; values are truth, duty and equilibrium.

Level 5/*Achievement*: Pertains to individual orientation; values are success, materialism, victory and prestige.

Level 6/*People*: Pertains to community orientation; values are equality, fairness and belongingness.

Level 7/*Systemic*: Pertains to individual orientation; values are wisdom, ambiguity and being non-judgemental.

Level 8/*Global*: Pertains to community orientation; values are globalism and universal wholeness.

CHOOSING PERSONAL CORE VALUES

Our life choices and behaviour reflect our personal core values, which are based on factors such as personal vision and core beliefs. Core beliefs supply core values, determining how we choose to live our lives. Individual value systems are shaped and formed during childhood, influenced by parents, teachers, friends, mentors, inspirational figures, education, the physical and social environment, key life events (good and bad), with early life experiences playing a crucial role.

Personal core values direct our daily decisions in personal and professional life, determining one's future. They serve as guides for living a meaningful, happy and content life. While personal value systems are subject to change and evolve with later life experiences as an adult, they are relatively stable, do not change quickly and persist. Deliberate inculcation and practice of core values provide numerous benefits, such as better decision-making, conflict resolution and reduced stress levels.

Our choice of personal core values both critically determines and hugely impacts how we live our life and who we aspire to be. They provide objectives and criteria that influence our personal decisions within the network of interweaving choices. Aligning our motivations, choices and actions with the kind of human being we want to be brings a sense of contentment. Whether consciously chosen or not, all individuals possess a set of implicit personal core values that help negotiate discontentment, conflict, frustration and lack of fulfilment.

How and what core values we choose are subjective depending on what we want in life and how we want to live it. When selecting, it is important to consider criteria such as our personal vision, mission and core beliefs. Other vital factors include:

- *Inspiration and guidance*: Personal core values should inspire and motivate you to pursue your larger life goals, and also guide you in your daily life, decisions and relationships.
- *Uniqueness*: Values can certainly be adopted or borrowed from others, but your personal core values must speak uniquely to you, reflect your identity, core beliefs and priorities in life, and they should emphasise your strengths while addressing your weaknesses.
- *Meaningful and rewarding*: Your core values should guide your actions, enabling you to live a meaningful and rewarding life.
- *Long-lasting*: Personal core values evolve and mature lifelong with individual growth through personal experience, but do not change overnight. If they do, they are not core values.
- A clear understanding of the reasons and basis for our choice of core values is crucial for refining them based on newer life experiences and learning, which are often the best teachers. Recognising that our understanding of our life experience can also be mistaken sometimes, especially during childhood, is also important.

Typically, individuals may expect to identify five to nine values that persist and evolve with time. Clarity about what constitutes our core values, and why, also enables us to unambiguously communicate them to others. Examples of personal core values include:

- *Love*: Encompassing compassion, patience, forgiveness, faith, generosity, selflessness.
- *Integrity*: Including honesty, truthfulness, responsibility, consistency, decency.
- *Stewardship*: Including resourcefulness, leadership, benefaction, charity.
- *Wisdom*: Encompassing rationality, understanding, intelligence, vision, perception, experience, intuition, maturity.
- *Freedom*: Comprising independence, free will, autonomy, self-determination.
- *Achievement*: Pertaining to success and accomplishment.
- *Happiness*: Including joy, contentment, pleasure.
- *Peace*: Linked to harmony, unity, tranquility, serenity.
- *Perseverance*: Related to persistence, dedication, determination.
- *Respect*: Linked to dignity, self-respect, appreciation, esteem, value.

Living according to clearly and deliberately chosen core values provides numerous benefits, such as: making better decisions, reduced stress, finding supportive environments and people who share your core values and aspirations, increased happiness and satisfaction boosting individual growth and development, greater clarity in times of conflict or confusion, increased social recognition and value, and providing motivation. People with similar values attract each other, drawing mutual strength and motivation from one another, leading to satisfaction and joy in life.

ROLE OF FAMILY IN INCULCATING VALUES

The family is regarded as a social system that evolves naturally while reconciling and adapting to changes in social conditions. The influence of family is seen both directly and indirectly in individual value systems. The ways that a family conducts its affairs seldom change, relying on customs and habits, subordinated to values and norms accepted in a given society. These interactions tend to reinforce the self-reproduction of societal value systems rather than transform them. The institution of family is considered to be the most stable creation of our civilisation. The present societal orientation significantly affects the family. Scientific and technological advances have drastically transformed family life. Modern values like cultural and religious tolerance, gender parity and openness influence a family positively, but negative values have also entered, with several degenerative effects.

In the post-modern world, despite economic development, society has become unable to address important matters related to human needs and satisfaction. Modern luxuries, information and communication technologies, material pleasures, wealth and consumerism have introduced conflict and discord into family life as the goals of life have been blurred and replaced by the demands of luxury. Families now suffer from frequent breakdowns, manifest in the growing distances in relationships, emotional as well as spatial, trust deficit between family members, and doubts about the necessity of marriage and family. Most factors contributing to these problems are generated outside rather than within the family. Pressures from the outside world as well as increased career opportunities away from home have contributed much in this direction. Despite all these challenges, most people still acknowledge the importance and centrality of good family life in providing happiness, security and the strength necessary to cope with life's challenges.

The initial schooling of any child starts at home with parents, who usually become the first role models for their children. Parents play a vital role in nurturing and preparing the future citizenry. Children pay close attention to and imitate their parents, making it essential for parents to act as moral agents for their children, setting examples for them to emulate. Parents should strive to teach children good human values and virtues that contribute to the greater good of society. Unfortunately, many parents fail in the task of good parenting, sometimes producing individuals who have negative and harmful impact on society.

For children, the family is where they receive the supportive environment necessary for growth. Family values strongly influence a child's life, shaping their character and conduct throughout life. The first values are most often taught at home rather than outside or in educational institutions. The values of a family are determined by its members. It is crucial for individuals to invest quality time in the family to raise children as good citizens. Parents are generally the first to impact a child's value system. Children learn, prioritise and determine the hierarchy of values from their parents and grandparents. Parents must be vigilant as their children closely observe their speech and conduct, continuously building their value system.

Great personalities, patriots, reformers and leaders were products of their family values imparted in childhood. For example, Mahatma Gandhi was deeply influenced by his parents, especially his mother Putlibai, who laid the spiritual foundations of his life. His mother's daily life, her words and conduct had a profound impact on his young mind. Gandhi writes: 'The outstanding impression my mother has left on my memory is that of saintliness. She was deeply religious. She would not think of taking her meals without her daily prayers.'

An instance from his life illustrates how parental conduct shaped his core values and philosophy. Gandhi recalls that as a child he stole some gold from his brother's bracelet, but couldn't bear to keep it a secret from his father due to the agony of breaking his father's trust. He decided to confess, and wrote a letter to his father. Reading the letter, his father's eyes were filled with tears, and Gandhi found himself in the same emotional state. Reflecting on this incident later, Gandhi writes in his autobiography: 'A clean confession, combined with a promise never to commit the sin again, when offered before one who has the right to receive it, is the purest type of repentance.... This was for me, a lesson in Ahimsa. Then, I could read in it nothing more than a father's love, but today I know that it was pure Ahimsa. When such Ahimsa becomes all-embracing, it transforms everything it touches. There is no limit to its power.'

ROLE OF SOCIETY IN INCULCATING VALUES

One determines one's life goals and, broadly, the moral life one intends to lead as shaped by values derived from social institutions. The social environment shapes and contributes to the development of the individual self, identity, values and conscience. The social universe is thus appropriately placed higher than the individual universe because the individual self is incomplete without it; realisation of this 'self' requires a comprehensive wholeness which can only be achieved within a social matrix. An individual cannot thrive in isolation; growth is possible only within this social wholeness.

The rules for the existence of a society dictate punishments and rewards for its members. The pleasure and pain experienced by individual members of society contribute to the development of values and ideals. One cannot independently establish values that support positive social progress; hence the values determined by all members of society through consensus should be applied universally. The moral principles established by society are accepted as 'ought' or moral obligations. These obligations compel our *ideal* self to impose constraints on our *actual* self. Since the ideal self is rational and cannot be realised in isolation, it can only be realised within human society.

All members of society are provided with opportunities for growth within a just social arrangement. Rules and laws are formulated to ensure that no member of society is deprived, unprivileged, destitute or impoverished. If some act unruly, they are deprived of the protection of the law. Therefore, people must be instilled with good habits and virtues in thought and conduct.

Public opinions evolve gradually, and a large part of society may remain unaware of them. To address this, a powerful agency needs to be created to enforce rules and establish uniform morality in society. Initially, individuals may act out of the fear of law or punishment; but over time, as they come to understand and internalise the meaning and value of moral principles, this behaviour becomes habitual and natural, not enforced. They act morally in accordance with their own free, conscientious and voluntary will. The process begins with the establishment and enforcement of laws, followed by the inculcation of moral conduct, and ultimately, the establishment of virtues as part of core values.

There are several ways of fostering cohesion among people by keeping them connected through various social groups and institutions, such as family, the workplace, civil communities, religion, friendships, the state, the nation and more. Social institutions that foster cohesion through moral ideals or values vary in nature and serve different objectives at different stages of social development. For instance, the 'Ten Commandments' were considered moral codes by Jews, Greeks placed emphasis on virtues, and Romans saw the establishment of social and political institutions as essential for human progress. The values of a society continuously evolve with time. It is essential to engage with others in order to cultivate our own values. The social development and enculturation of an individual are shaped by their social environment. We can discern the social background of people by observing their values and behaviour. The social milieu transforms an individual into a moral being based on the prevailing value system of that society, serving as a yardstick for its members to assess virtues and vices, good and evil. Values are not innate but drawn from the social milieu. Rationality alone cannot discern between right and wrong, good and bad, just and unjust; it requires the assistance of values. Values are the motivating force driving human behaviour, passed on from generation to generation.

It is society that establishes standards for the acceptance and rejection of social behaviour among its members. Society creates a checklist of human values for its own benefit, thereby assuming the responsibility of instilling values in its members. Currently, society is grappling with pervasive unrest, disturbance and an unstable, fragmented way of life. In contemporary society, fundamental human values, particularly among the youth, are undergoing a decline. This predicament is a result of the swift erosion of morality from human life. While globalisation and westernisation have brought positive change, they have also introduced social ills disguised as global values. The goodness of a society is contingent on how it defines its core values and ensures their transmission from one generation to the next. Public policies should also integrate core values in developmental and legal norms.

ROLE OF EDUCATIONAL INSTITUTIONS IN INCULCATING VALUES

The progress of any nation hinges on the values instilled in its citizens. A significant portion of a person's formative years is spent under the influence of educational institutions. Education plays a crucial role in fostering the all-round development of individuals, encompassing the inculcation of values and character. But educational institutions are not meant solely for imparting skills and knowledge geared for achieving success—a vital aspect is also to teach and nurture human values and ideals. A good education must mould individuals into responsible and humane members of society.

Albert Einstein's statement 'Try not to become a man of success but rather try to become a man of value' underscores that education bereft of human values is meaningless, and may transform an individual into a clever monster. Value education contributes to the transformation of an individual's personality, fostering awareness of what is right and good, and cultivating empathy. It connects knowledge with humanism, emphasising that knowledge should strive to bring prosperity, equality, justice and wellbeing for all. Value education is indispensable for providing direction to one's life and training individuals to contribute to making the world a better place.

The writer C. S. Lewis believed education must be firmly anchored in absolute and transcendent human values, for without human values, no matter how 'useful' an education may be, it only makes man 'a more clever devil'.

Educational institutions are the principal source of value education. Children learn at school what is right and wrong both inside and outside the classroom. A value-based education imparts knowledge of good and bad, fair and unfair, and teaches values like trustworthiness, honesty, responsibility, generosity, cooperation, truthfulness, integrity, justice, courage and more. Students study, work, learn both individually and together from each other as well as compete. They are taught etiquettes of speech, behaviour and work. They participate in co-curricular activities including sports and cultural events by which they learn the importance of teamwork, coordination, competition, discipline, hygiene, punctuality, equality and togetherness. They also learn to appreciate the values of friendship, sharing, inclusiveness, accommodation and respecting differences.

Schools organise various camps and events related to social and voluntary work where students learn the importance of the dignity of labour and about those less privileged than themselves. Co-education schools provide a healthy open environment where boys and girls study together, compete on par and are treated equally. All school activities happen as per predetermined schedules which are followed by all, which instils the importance of punctuality and discipline.

The University Education Commission (1948–49) gave special emphasis on inculcating values of loyalty, courage, discipline, self-sacrifice and spirituality in its recommendations, while the Secondary Education Commission (1952–53) emphasised character-based values like efficiency, cooperation, integrity and discipline. The Education Commission of (1964–66) observed regarding the Indian education system that, 'A serious defect in the school curriculum is the absence of provision of education in social, moral and spiritual values.' Value education has the potential to transform an indifferent or troubled or negative mind into one that is fertile and humanitarian, fostering positive growth. The Kothari Commission (1964–66) explicitly declared that education did not have much to do with imparting knowledge or skills, but plays a crucial role in raising curiosity, developing interest, evolving values for harmonious coexistence and the right attitude in modern society. The National Policy on Education (1986) noted that, 'The growing concern over the erosion of essential values and an increasing cynicism in society has brought to focus the need for readjustment in the curriculum in order to make education a forceful tool for the cultivation of social and moral values.'

In Indian society the teacher-disciple tradition (*guru-shishya-parampara*) is deeply rooted. The teacher plays a central role in shaping future society. The primary function of educational institutions is to produce ethical citizens of sound character and a healthy mindset. Values must be inculcated in the young with care and caution, for they can last a lifetime. Moral education must be part of the curriculum as a compulsory subject across streams. Essential values like respect for elders, compassion towards the weak and the marginalised, respect for difference and diversity, and tolerance can be instilled through value education. Interpersonal relations, religious and cultural tolerance, cooperation, team spirit, etc. are developed through sports, cultural activities, NCC, Scouts and Guides, group studies, and through academic debates and seminars. Celebration of national festivals, birth and death anniversaries of great leaders and visionaries provide occasions for instilling values like nationalism, patriotism, secularism, self-sacrifice, unity and diversity in young minds.

QUESTIONS

1. Some people feel that values keep changing with time and circumstances, while others strongly believe that there are certain universal and eternal human values. Give your perceptions in this regard with due justification. (UPSC 2013)
2. In the context of defence services, patriotism demands the readiness to lay down one's life in protecting the nation. According to you, what does patriotism imply in everyday civil life? Explain with illustrations and justify your answer. (UPSC 2014)
3. 'Human beings should always be treated as ends in themselves, and never merely as means.' Explain the meaning and significance of this statement, giving its implications in today's modern techno-economic society. (UPSC 2014)
4. 'Social values are more important than economic values.' Discuss this statement with examples in the context of a nation's inclusive growth. (UPSC 2015)
5. Our attitudes towards life, work, other people and society are generally shaped unconsciously by the family and by the social surroundings in which we grow up. Some of these unconsciously acquired attitudes and values are often undesirable in the citizens of a modern democratic and egalitarian society.
    a) Discuss such undesirable values prevalent in today's educated Indians.
    b) How can such undesirable attitudes be changed? How can the socio-ethical values considered necessary in public services be cultivated in aspiring and serving civil servants? (UPSC 2016)
6. The crisis of ethical values in modern times is traced to a narrow perception of the good life. Discuss. (UPSC 2017)
7. Without commonly shared and entrenched moral values and obligations, neither the law, nor a democratic government, nor even the market economy

will function properly. What do you understand by this statement? Explain with illustrations from contemporary times. (UPSC 2017)

8. 'If a country is to be corruption-free and become a nation of beautiful minds, I strongly feel there are three key societal members who can make a difference. They are the father, the mother and the teacher.' —A. P. J. Abdul Kalam. Discuss and analyse. (UPSC 2017)

5

LESSONS FROM THE LIVES AND TEACHINGS OF GREAT LEADERS, REFORMERS AND ADMINISTRATORS

> **KEY CONCEPTS**
>
> Mahatma Gandhi; Sardar Vallabhbhai Patel; Jawaharlal Nehru; Dr Bhimrao Ambedkar; Napoleon Bonaparte; Abraham Lincoln; Swami Vivekananda; Raja Rammohan Roy; Nelson Mandela; Martin Luther King Jr; George Washington; Deendayal Upadhyaya; Rammanohar Lohiya; Swami Dayananda Saraswati; Tulsidas; Kabir; Guru Nanak; Guru Ravidas; Sri Ramakrishna Paramhans; Sri Narayan Guru; Maulana Abul Kalam Azad; Rabindranath Tagore; Mother Teresa; A. P. J. Abdul Kalam

Our values have a direct bearing on our beliefs, and vice versa. Beliefs motivate a person to think and act in certain ways guided by certain reasons and thus shape the value system. The values we inculcate may also be influenced by the lessons learnt from the lives and teachings of great public figures, leaders, social reformers and administrators. We will discuss the lives of some important historical figures, reformers who brought change and gave society a direction, and administrators who are recognised for their transparency, integrity and exemplary decision-making.

MAHATMA GANDHI

Gandhi is known for his moral greatness, lived a life anchored in moral principles and consistently practised what he preached. As an exemplary practitioner of morality across politics, religion and personal life, Gandhi explored multiple dimensions of moral conduct. We will discuss some of these which have relevance for both civil servants and leaders.

One of his primary concerns was the purification of politics, advocating for the infusion of values and principles as moral commitments. Gandhi grounded his understanding of morality in the inherent nature of human beings and in human conscience. *Satyagraha*, his formidable weapon and philosophy of truth, played a pivotal role in his life. Gandhi also underscored the importance of *ahimsa* (non-violence), considering it a central tenet of ideal human existence. He masterfully deployed the interdependence between *satya* and *ahimsa* in leading India's political struggle for *swatantrata* (independence) and *swarajya* (self-rule). A closer examination of these Gandhian tenets is thus warranted.

In Gandhi's worldview, the prevalence of evil in the world is attributed to *maya* (illusion), *moha* (affinity and attachment), delusion and glamour. Humans continually chase these illusory pursuits, driven by their inability to attain lasting satisfaction. Gandhi viewed these as having an intoxicating and temporary but pervasive influence in human lives.

Gandhi attributed the current degradation of civilisation to the soullessness of politics and its hunger to seize power at any cost. He appears to endorse the Hobbesian theory that underscores the pursuit of power as a primary human motivation and tendency, and acknowledges that the interplay between this pursuit and morality gives rise to various evils within the political arena.

Politics and Religion

Gandhi acknowledges the inevitability of politics and its inseparability from life but contends that politics must align with religion; otherwise, it becomes akin to a lifeless body fit for cremation. Here, religion encompasses a broader meaning beyond the conventional understanding of religiousness. For Gandhi, it involves adhering to one's conscience, intuition and personal faith and values. Gandhi advocates for politicians to embrace the voluntary abandonment of property, aligning with the views of Plato. He asserts that one cannot be deemed religious unless one becomes a part of the entire human race, through political engagement. Gandhi views politics as an avenue for societal and moral progress, emphasising that political power must serve as a means to enhance people's wellbeing, and not as an end for the politician's self-interest. Gandhi holds that religion, in its truest purest sense, transcends sectarianism and all religions including Hinduism, Islam and Christianity; rather, it is 'a belief in the ordered moral government of the universe.'

Gandhi strongly opposed the establishment of a state religion, championing the individual's right to choose and practise their own religion as a deeply personal matter. In stark contrast to Vivekananda's views on politics and religion, Gandhi invoked and rallied all religions against the notion of a state religion. Gandhi also sparked a controversy with Tilak, who argued in a letter to Gandhi that politics should not be driven by religious considerations as politics was for ordinary worldly people, not saints.

Gandhi firmly believed that true power does not stem from instilling the fear of punishment in others, but from renouncing power and dedicating oneself to the service of humanity. Such an approach yields far greater influence than holding a position in the government. He envisioned a future where people would yearn for a leader who serves them genuinely, surpassing the desire for anyone else to wield power over them. Gandhi emphasised that power should be wielded constructively for the greater social good (*sarvodaya*) and employed peacefully to protest unjust laws and state oppression.

Gandhi rejected the separation of politics and religion, embodying a purely subjective and mystical approach to his own faith. He confronted the existence of two levels of morality: one governing an individual's private life and the other their public life. The first focuses on personal conduct, while the second encompasses social conduct and political life, a concept known as 'the doctrine of double standards.' Gandhi adamantly denied this doctrine, asserting that a society adhering to it is inherently self-destructive and exploitative. He advocated for the reconciliation of political and personal morality, extending this unified moral standard to all individuals across diverse aspects of life. Despite perceiving politics as impure and sinful, Gandhi maintained a steadfast belief in its potential for purification. The initial step in this transformative process, according to him, involves discarding the discriminatory distinctions between public and private morality or political and personal morality.

Dharma

In his work *Ethical Religion: Neethi Dharma*, Gandhi stated that a truly religious or moral individual is one who is free from hatred and selfishness, leading a life purely dedicated to selfless service for humanity. Morality is not about adhering to rigid rules, he asserted, but is about remaining flexible to the needs of the situation. Morality must be voluntary and intuitive, not mechanistic. A moral action must be guided naturally by conscience, and not performed under any form of fear or coercion, or for any kind of reward. Consistency, for Gandhi, involves adhering to the truth over time, even if it contradicts one's previous actions. For Gandhi, *dharma* (duty) is the highest human value, with *artha* (wealth), *kama* (pleasure) and *moksha* (liberation) being of secondary importance. And the true meaning of Gandhian *dharma* lies in serving mankind.

Gandhi asserts that people must liberate themselves from all types of passions and biases that they have acquired in the past. In *Ethical Religion*, he states: 'A man is but the product of his thoughts; what he thinks he becomes.' An individual's behaviour thus aligns with how they see themselves. 'A man who broods on evil is as evil as a man who does evil, if not worse.' Gandhi, like Kant, follows a wholly deontological approach, and aligns with the *Gita*'s categorical imperative of doing one's duty or dharma above all else. Dharma should be performed for its own sake, and spontaneously and naturally, rather than through strenuous effort. The virtue of dharma is universal, transcending specific individuals. Gandhi believes in the paramountcy of the moral law in the universe, urging us to grasp the fundamental principles of morality. He emphasises that 'A principle is a principle, and it should never wither because of our inability to live it in practice. We ought to endeavour to achieve it consciously and deliberately.'

Conscience

Gandhi declares conscience to be the voice of God within humans that guides us on the rightness or wrongness of every thought and action. He said, 'Sometimes you have to follow a call which is the greatest of all, the voice of conscience, even though such commitment to that voice may cause trouble, abandonment of nears and dears, your place, and everything you consider very close to your heart and equal to your life.' He further adds, 'The law of the majority has no significance in front of the voice of conscience; the court of conscience supersedes all courts.' Gandhi rejected the notion that wilfulness is conscience, asserting that conscience is the ripe fruit of hard discipline, thriving only in a delicately tuned heart. Unlike Émile Durkheim's concept of a collective conscience legitimising coercion for the moral purpose of society, Gandhi believed that conscience makes individuals humble, compromising, receptive and consentaneous.

Gandhi strongly believed that ethical dilemmas in political matters are not solely about making urgent decisions but, more importantly, about finding solutions that address the issue beyond immediate practicality. He advocated for instructing oneself with positive exhortations rather than providing negative incitements to others, emphasising that setting an example is more convincing than designing moral codes. The key, Gandhi said, is not merely to teach others about morality or make them aware of their wrongdoings—it is about inspiring them to act on what they already know they should do.

Gandhi's Seven Sins

The dichotomy between means and ends is a common theme in ethical discussions. Those supporting this idea argue that means should never overlook the moral implications and must align with the final consequences or ends. Gandhi, however, stands out as an exception among political and moral thinkers. He refutes the dichotomy of means and ends, stating, 'For me, it is enough to know the means; means and ends are convertible terms in my philosophy of life. We always have control over means but not over ends. I feel that our progress towards the goal will be in exact proportion to the purity of means.' Gandhi asserts that there are seven things that spoil human beings, connected with their social and political behaviour. He identifies these as the 'seven deadly sins' and underlines the necessity of avoiding them under any circumstances.

1. Wealth without work
2. Pleasure without conscience
3. Knowledge without character
4. Commerce (business) without morality
5. Science without humanity
6. Religion without sacrifice
7. Politics without principles

Gandhi's moral philosophy is centred around and motivated by the care and wellbeing of the weak and disenfranchised. He famously said:

> I will give you a talisman. Whenever you are in doubt or when the self becomes too much with you, apply the following test. Recall the face of the poorest and the weakest man or woman whom you may have seen, and ask yourself, if the step you contemplate is going to be of any use to him or her. Will he or she gain anything by it? Will it restore him or her to a control over his or her own life and destiny? In other words, will it lead to 'swaraj' for the hungry and spiritually starving millions? Then you will find your doubts and your self melt away.

SARDAR VALLABHBHAI PATEL

Sardar Vallabhbhai Patel was an exceptional leader and devoted patriot who played an active role in India's freedom movement. His enduring legacy lies in his unparalleled contribution to integrating the nation after Independence. Patel firmly believed that religion and patriotism were inseparable as both were deeply rooted in matters of faith. For Patel, religion encapsulated patriotism through sentiments and a strong bond with the nation; and patriotism represented the highest form of religion.

Patel held a steadfast faith in the power of rural communities and successfully mobilised them in India's long struggle for independence from colonial rule. A vocal critic of the purdah system in Indian society, Patel recognised the need for women to engage in public life and actively encouraged the women of Bardoli in his home state Gujarat to participate in the freedom movement. Patel's vision and leadership continue to inspire generations in the collective memory of the nation.

Democracy

Sardar Patel believed that in a democracy, rulers can only govern effectively if they have the people's trust. The government must act as a trustee for the entire populace, without any discrimination based on religion, region, caste or creed, Patel asserted, for only a government that does not discriminate has the right to rule the nation. Rulers are servants of the state and have a duty to serve the state. The government must see all citizens as their children, and themselves as guardians. Public welfare should be their primary objective. Patel advocated for progress and innovation in administration, urging leaders to step out of their comfort zones for the greater good of the public. He argued that mutual understanding between rulers and the ruled should be based on common interests. As a staunch advocate of democracy, Patel equally recognised the importance of a robust opposition in the legislature for the stability and progress of the nation. These perspectives reveal Patel as a staunch supporter of the socio-political advancement of Indian citizens through a democratic system of governance in a constitutional manner.

While emphasising the government's role in relation to the people, Patel also highlighted the duties of citizens towards their nation. He stressed that people should be aware of their responsibilities and show allegiance to the state, should maintain unity, promote harmony, tolerance, fraternity and inclusiveness. The people and the state must both shun divisiveness based on religion, region, caste or creed, and must not allow anyone to instigate hatred against fellow citizens.

Bureaucracy

Patel had great faith in the Indian bureaucracy and strongly opposed political interference in civil services within a democratic environment. He warned against the devastating effects of such interference, urging bureaucrats to contribute to the growth of democracy. He emphasised that administrators should not misuse their authority and powers, and warned politicians against maintaining negative relations with bureaucrats as unwarranted criticism can adversely affect efficiency.

Drawing from his vast experience in civil services during his tenure as the president of Ahmedabad Municipality, Patel was acutely aware of the need for experienced and capable civil servants to efficiently run the newly independent country and meet its manifold complex challenges. Unlike many Indian leaders who doubted the motivations, suitability and capabilities of colonial-era civil servants, particularly Nehru, Patel endorsed their vital role in India's stability, integration and nation-building, when the reins of government passed from British to Indian hands in 1947.

Patel played a key role in reorganising and motivating the Indian bureaucracy. In his address to the probationers of the Indian Administrative Service at the All India Administrative Service Training School on 20 April 1947, Patel said, 'You are pioneers in the Indian service, and the future of this service will depend much upon the foundation that will be laid down by you, by your character and abilities, and by your spirit of service.' In a parliamentary address on 10 October 1949, he acknowledged the crucial contribution of civil servants, stating, 'I wish this to be recorded in this house that during the last two or three years, if most of the members of the services had not been serving the country efficiently, practically the union would have collapsed.' Despite initial scepticism from leaders like Nehru, Patel eventually convinced them of the value of retaining the services of experienced officers from the colonial government.

Known for fostering a friendly working atmosphere as a minister, Patel considered his secretaries as friends rather than subordinates. He encouraged open communication and honest advice, ensuring that his secretaries felt free to express views opposed to his. Patel was unique in recognising the challenges faced by civil servants, and provided constitutional safeguards to empower them in fearlessly and honestly executing their duties.

Education

Patel believed in the power of education to uplift rural India. In his view, contemporary education resembled teaching a parrot, focusing solely on rote memorisation without fostering a meaningful connection between body and mind, between knowledge and learning. He advocated for an education system that harmoniously developed both the mind and body, contributing to the positive and holistic evolution of the soul. Patel asserted that the impact of education extended well beyond the school. If the home environment failed to support the child's educational journey, knowledge gained at school would fade away upon returning home, leaving the child blank the next day. He envisioned education as a means to integrate urban schools with villages in a symbiotic relationship. Expressing concern for the current state of villages, Patel asserted that without a transformative approach, neither the children in the cities nor the residents of villages would receive a meaningful education. Thus, he advocated for an education system that bridged the gap between urban schools and villages, ensuring holistic development for individuals in both contexts.

JAWAHARLAL NEHRU

A prominent statesman, scholar and the first prime minister of the world's largest democracy,

Pandit Jawaharlal Nehru was a staunch believer and adherent of socialism who drew inspiration from the ideas of Marx and Lenin. 'I am a socialist as well as republican,' he proclaimed in his speech on the banks of river Ravi.

Democratic Socialism

Nehru wasn't merely a political philosopher; he was a man of action. Propounding the idea of democratic socialism as central to India's development, he viewed democracy through the lens of religious and cultural tolerance, civil liberty, freedom of expression and dissent, inclusivity, community, self-discipline, good governance, accountability and strong pro-people values. He held that only a government aligned with the needs and desires of the people exemplifies democratic governance. Advocating for civil liberty as crucial for holistic individual development, Nehru asserted that its realisation is achievable within the framework of democracy.

Despite the transformative changes in Indian governance post Independence, remnants of the British administrative structure such as the paramilitary and civic bodies persisted in free India. Although inheriting institutions from the British era, Nehru, unlike Patel, staunchly opposed retaining civil servants from the colonial bureaucratic system.

While recognising the contradictions inherent in incorporating capitalism for economic prosperity, he strongly emphasised the proactive role of a socialist welfare state in bridging the glaring and deep socio-economic divides in Indian society. The welfare state under Nehru's leadership and vision was committed to people's all-round welfare through developmental initiatives like schools, public universities, hospitals and public healthcare facilities, dams, canals and farming subsidies, alongside modernisation and industrial, scientific and technological advancement. Nehru asserted that democracy and socialism must be complementary, with socialism addressing socio-economic aspects and democracy handling the political sphere. He strongly believed that a democracy guided by socialist principles and nationalism must coexist for India to prosper and advance.

The Non-Aligned Movement

Known for authoring the five influential principles of *Panchsheel*, Nehru declared India's political non-alignment with any major power bloc at the height of the Cold War, and was one of the leading figures of the global Non-Aligned Movement (NAM). Nehru was instrumental in shaping the principles and objectives of NAM. His commitment to the ideals of non-alignment, anti-colonialism and independence for newly emerging nations contributed significantly to the movement's foundation.

> **Panchsheel** or the Five Principles of Peaceful Coexistence as enunciated on 29 April 1954 comprise:
> 1. Mutual respect for each other's territorial integrity and sovereignty
> 2. Mutual non-aggression
> 3. Mutual non-interference
> 4. Equality and mutual benefit
> 5. Peaceful coexistence

The Non-Aligned Movement was initiated by a group of nations who sought to remain independent and neutral during the Cold War. It officially began with the 1955 Asian-African Conference or the Bandung Conference in Indonesia. Key figures included Nehru of India, Sukarno of Indonesia, Gamal Abdel Nasser of Egypt, and Josip Broz Tito of Yugoslavia. They aimed to create a group of nations that were not aligned with either the Western bloc led by the United States or the Eastern bloc led by the Soviet Union, to promote common shared goals of peaceful coexistence, non-interference in the internal affairs of other nations, mutual respect for sovereignty, and maintain neutrality during the Cold War. In the aftermath of the unprecedented devastation and uncertainty caused by two World Wars, this was also a joint effort to de-escalate the potential threat of a Third World War that loomed large.

Secularism

Nehru was a firm and dedicated proponent of secularism, advocating for its implementation in India throughout his lifetime. His commitment to secular ideals was evident in both his thoughts and actions. Nehru stressed the importance of fostering a rational, scientific temperament devoid of superstition and religious dogmatism among all Indians. Like Gandhi, he believed religion was a personal matter for citizens, and the state must refrain from interference. Nehru expressed his disillusionment with the perpetual conflict between nation, state and religion. His vision was to establish a free secular state where every religion could coexist, thrive and receive equal opportunities with respect and dignity.

Nehru strongly advocated for a state that maintained an unbiased and neutral stance on religious matters and treat all religions equally. He viewed religion as an impediment to national integration and nation-building as it hindered free, rational, critical thought, leading to bias and prejudice. Nehru perceived secularism as a dynamic idea that evolves and refines over time, and becomes naturally ingrained in the national attitude. It is important to note that secularism for Nehru is *not* a rejection of religion or faith, but an adoption of noble values such as love, sacrifice, truth, compassion, humanity, mutual respect and cooperation, love for the nation and a rational temper.

Nehru's views on secularism were not confined to narrow nationalism but were part of his broader internationalism. Nehru was a prominent advocate for world peace during his era, emphasising the necessity of internationalism for the prosperity of humanity. While Nehru acknowledged the importance of non-violence and found it appealing, he did not express complete faith in it. Nonetheless, he believed that non-violence was an essential way of life in the Indian context and could be practised not only by great men like Mahatma Gandhi but also by common citizens. Nehru distanced himself from extremist ideologies like Nazism and fascism, condemning their inherently violent, reactionary, regressive, fundamentalist and exclusionary nature.

Nazism, from German *Nationalsozialist*, was the ideology associated with the National Socialist German Workers' Party (NSDAP) under Adolf Hitler's leadership in Germany in the 1920s. Nazism promoted the notion of Aryan racial supremacy and extreme nationalism; anti-Semitism leading to the genocide of 6 million Jews; a totalitarian state that controlled all aspects of German life and economy; an authoritarian leadership where all power was concentrated in Hitler. The Nazis built concentration camps where Jews, minorities, dissidents and anyone considered 'enemies of the state' were mass exterminated. Nazism arose as a response to Germany's defeat in World War I, and the emergence of fascism. The defeat of Nazi Germany in 1945 marked the end of this dark chapter in history.

Fascism is an extreme right-wing political ideology, movement, and totalitarian regime similar to Nazism, characterised by authoritarian power, dictatorial control, extreme nationalism, aggressive militarisation, and rejection of civil liberties, political dissent and democracy. It emerged in early 20th-century Europe, particularly in Italy under Benito Mussolini and Germany under Adolf Hitler, but variations of fascist movements have also appeared in other countries.

DR BHIMRAO AMBEDKAR

Babasaheb Bhimrao Ramji Ambedkar was an eminent Indian jurist, scholar, social reformer and politician who dedicated his life to fighting tirelessly against the social discrimination, oppression and untouchability faced by Dalits. He campaigned for their social and political rights, and worked towards eradicating caste and caste-based discrimination through socio-political movements. He was a strong proponent of affirmative action and reservations for Dalits in educational institutions and government jobs. He led the Mahar Satyagraha in 1927, where Dalits demanded access to water from a public tank in Mahar, Maharashtra, which was traditionally prohibited for them by Hindu Brahmins and upper castes.

Despite facing social discrimination himself as a Dalit, Ambedkar pursued higher education and earned multiple degrees, including a doctorate in economics from the London School of Economics and a law degree from the University of London. He went on to serve as independent India's first Law Minister in the government led by Nehru. As chairman of the Drafting Committee of the Constituent Assembly in India, Ambedkar played a central role in drafting the Constitution of India, which was adopted on 26 January 1950, and he is thus often referred to as the 'Architect of the Indian Constitution.'

Disillusioned with the entrenched caste system in Hinduism and its discrimination against Dalits, Ambedkar embraced Buddhism along with thousands of his followers in a mass conversion ceremony in 1956. He is widely respected for his contributions to social justice and equality, and the framing of India's Constitution. His powerful and cogent ideas continue to influence social and political discourse in India, and he is a revered and iconic father figure, especially among Dalits. Ambedkar's legacy endures through his writings, speeches, and the initiatives he championed for the upliftment of marginalised communities in India.

Morality and Religion

A distinguished scholar in law, economics and political science, Dr Ambedkar often drew inspiration from the ethical studies of the American philosopher John Dewey. Personally, Ambedkar regarded morality as a fundamental necessity for the wellbeing of society. He critiqued religion for alienating morality in both its original form and its efficacy, and preferred to instead define morality using the term *dhamma* from Buddhist philosophy.

> **Dhamma**, Prakrit form of the Sanskrit word *dharma*, is central to Buddhist philosophy which upholds the natural order of the universe. King Ashoka popularised the term, which includes the following principles:
> 1. Non-violence and truthfulness
> 2. Treating slaves and servants humanely
> 3. Mutual tolerance amongst all religious sects
> 4. Obedience to parents and respectfulness to teachers
> 5. Abolition of death sentence
> 6. Discouraging inappropriate religious practices, animal sacrifice and superstitions
> 7. Kindness towards humans as well as animals
> 8. Provisions for the poor and elderly

Ambedkar was deeply concerned with individual moral development that necessitated a shift from collective customs, traditions and habits to those based on individual reflection and conscience. He challenged the caste system, rooted in group-based collective morality which hindered the evolution of individual conscience, and asserted, 'Man's life is generally habitual and unreflective.' Ambedkar argued that reflective thoughts, generated through continuous, active contemplation based on reality and experience, play a crucial role in resolving ethical dilemmas.

Emphasising reflective morality, Ambedkar highlighted the need for rational critical inquiry into customs, habits, and the definition of good and bad. Conscience, he argued, must replace customs and rules with principles, as principles provide intellectual direction while rules are practical and subject to varying with situations. Ambedkar criticised the formalistic nature of many religions and advocated for the total dismantling of age-old entrenched Hindu habits such as the caste system and rituals.

Ambedkar believed that reform begins with individual opinion or conscience challenging group interests. The survival of such reforms depends on the group's receptiveness and tolerance. In addressing the upliftment of depressed classes, Ambedkar proposed two approaches. The first focuses on the conduct of the individual, attributing their suffering to personal sins and vices. Efforts under this approach aim to instil personal virtues through education and the promotion of temperance. The second approach recognises that individual destinies are shaped by their circumstances and social environments, and that addressing their suffering requires positive changes in unfavourable environments.

Ambedkar said the Anti-Untouchability League should not focus on individual cases but should concentrate on a programme that can bring about positive change in the social environment of such people as a whole. He advocated for the 'rationalism of enlightenment' which includes the following tenets:

1. Valid knowledge is based on scientific methods, employing both empirical and deductive approaches.
2. Rational morality is based on utilitarianism, emphasising the egalitarian distribution of well-being, happiness and equal justice.

> The **All India Anti-Untouchability League**, later renamed Harijan Sevak Sangh, was founded by Mahatma Gandhi in 1932 to eradicate untouchability from Indian society.

Ambedkar outright rejected the need for the present form of religion, and replaced it with 'dhamma', declaring, 'Morality is dhamma, and dhamma is morality.' He argues that morality is not inherent to religion, but merely incidental. Ambedkar asserted that while religion describes the role of man with respect to God, morality explains the role of man in relation to other humans. He contended that every religion preaches morality, but morality is not rooted in religion; it preserves its own separate identity, free from religious associations.

NAPOLEON BONAPARTE

Napoleon Bonaparte, a French statesman and military general who later became emperor of France, was a visionary leader known for his military prowess and ambition to conquer the whole European continent. His strategic brilliance and determination played a crucial role in establishing a powerful state in France. Napoleon asserted that great ambition was the attribute of a strong character, and those endowed with ambition could undertake both commendable and condemnable actions, depending on what principles they were guided by. He said, 'There are only two forces in the world: the sword and the spirit; in the long run the sword will always be conquered by the spirit.'

His military tactics were unmatched, and his leadership qualities teach us that effective leadership demands a clear vision before leading others. Napoleon had the ability to garner the loyalty and affection of his people. He knew each of his soldiers by name, fostering strong bonds with his troops. He believed perseverance was a key to success, as evidenced by his multiple comebacks in France, highlighting his tenacity and commitment to achieving desired goals against the odds. His famous words, 'Impossible is a word to be found only in the dictionary of fools' underscored his unwavering determination and refusal to accept failure.

Napoleon recognised the importance of adequately providing for soldiers, knowing that a healthy, strong, well-fed soldier is crucial for victory in battle, because 'An army marches on its stomach.' He believed that 'The first virtue in a soldier is endurance of fatigue; courage is only the second virtue.' An advocate of effective logistics, he also displayed a keen understanding of financial responsibility, often rejecting extravagant bills associated with the construction of his palace. His philosophy on wealth resonated with the idea that 'Riches do not consist in the possession of treasures, but in the use made of them.'

Some famous quotes by Napoleon:

> The truest wisdom is a resolute determination.
> A leader is a dealer in hope.
> A true man hates no one.
> Imagination rules the world.
> Victory belongs to the most persevering.
> Take time to deliberate, but when the time for action has arrived, stop thinking and go in.
> It takes more courage to suffer than to die.
> Never interrupt your enemy when he is making a mistake.
> When small men attempt great enterprises, they always end up reducing them to the level of their mediocrity.
> Four hostile newspapers are more to be feared than a thousand bayonets.
> There are only two forces that unite men—fear and interest.
> The people to fear are not those who disagree with you but those who disagree with you and are too cowardly to let you know.
> Nothing is more difficult and therefore more precious than to be able to decide.
> Until you spread your wings, you will never know how far you can fly.

ABRAHAM LINCOLN

Abraham Lincoln, the 16th President of the United States of America (from March 1861 until his assassination in April 1865), widely regarded as one of the greatest American presidents, played a key role in the American Civil War and the abolition of slavery in America. Before entering politics, he worked as a lawyer. His leadership during the Civil War and his efforts to preserve the Union had a profound impact on American history. In his famous Gettysburg Address in 1863, he underscored the principles of equality and democracy. Lincoln's legacy includes his contributions to ending slavery, his leadership during a critical period in American history and his enduring impact on the principles of democracy and equality.

Lincoln's life and leadership—deeply rooted in his moral principles of liberty, equality and fraternity—offer valuable lessons. Lincoln not only espoused these as fundamental life values but also translated them into concrete actions. On one occasion he said, 'Let us have faith that right makes might, and in that faith, let us, to the end, dare to do our duty as we understand it.' As a leader Lincoln demonstrated effective planning, proactive action and timely execution, emphasising that nothing which can be done today should be left for tomorrow. His law partner William Herndon described Lincoln as 'a little engine that knew no rest.'

Lincoln recognised the importance of collaboration and understood that achieving larger goals often requires collective efforts. He underscored the value of building strong relationships and maintaining trust with allies, and said, 'Stand with anybody that stands right. Stand with him while he is right and part with him when he goes wrong.' Known for his eloquence and powerful oration, he was both an outstanding speaker and an impressive writer. Lincoln consistently advocated for the value of speaking less but meaningfully, and once remarked, 'I am rather inclined to silence, and whether that be wise or not, it is at least more unusual nowadays to find a man who can hold his tongue than to find one who can't.'

The following quote, popularly attributed to Lincoln, is said to be from a letter he wrote to the headmaster of his son's school, requesting him to teach his son good human values.

> 'Teach him, if you can, that a dollar earned is of far more value than five found, teach him to learn to lose and also to enjoy winning. Steer him away from envy, if you can. In school, teach him it is far more honourable to fail than to cheat. Teach him to listen to all, but also to filter all he hears on a screen of truth and take only the good that comes through. Let him have the courage to be impatient, let him have the patience to be brave. Teach him always to have sublime faith in himself, because then he will always have sublime faith in mankind.'

Lincoln possessed the following qualities that made him a great leader:

1. Listening to contrasting views.
2. Learning from past experiences.
3. Sharing credit for success with associates.
4. Accepting responsibility for failure.
5. Acknowledging weaknesses.
6. Emotional intelligence.
7. Leading from the front.
8. Ability to communicate vision and mission.

World renowned Russian writer and humanist Leo Tolstoy, famous for his book *War and Peace*, said Lincoln's greatness lay in 'the integrity of his character and the moral fabric of his being.'

SWAMI VIVEKANANDA

Swami Vivekananda was an Indian saint and philosopher. He advocated for the assimilation of Western rationalism and scientific temper in Indian religion but not in a radical manner. He emphasised the importance of educating the youth. He believed that values are crucial components of a civil society, not necessarily tied to high-profile individuals or historical heroes. Vivekananda strongly believed in the eventual convergence of science and religion, envisioning a complementary relationship between history and philosophy. He asserted that our attitudes and actions towards objects are regulated by values, which are best realised in the pursuit of specific goals. Values are not merely acquired through reading or listening but are ingrained during the process of striving to achieve defined objectives. Therefore, he underscored the significance of incorporating values into education.

Vivekananda proposed that worldly prosperity should align with the principles of *dharma, artha, kama* and *moksha*. Artha (economic value) and kama (psychological value) should both be pursued under the guidance of dharma (moral value) to ensure that they contribute to societal happiness. Dharma, as a moral force, prescribes guidelines and duties for society. Finally, moksha or spiritual value is attained with the support of the other three values—dharma, artha and kama.

Vivekananda emphasises love as 'the only law of life; he who loves lives, and he who is selfish is dying'. According to him, religion is not about dogmas but concerns conquering the inner self, understanding the subtle workings of the human mind; while science deals with the knowledge of laws governing the external world. In his perspective, religion and science therefore become complementary. Vivekananda expressed serious concerns about society's shift towards materialistic values. He viewed education as a tool for instilling positive values in individuals, stating, 'The ideal of all education should be man-making. Education is not merely pouring information into the brain; it should be absorbed and applied, shaping a person's character for a lifetime.'

Vivekananda placed great emphasis on the concentration of the mind, highlighting its role in developing innate qualities like fearlessness, courage, love and compassion. He believed that these qualities remain dormant unless consciously emulated and habitually practised. According to him, focused concentration is what sets humans apart from animals and even distinguishes one individual from another.

RAJA RAMMOHAN ROY

In the words of Mahadev Govind Ranade, 'Rammohun Roy was at once a social reformer, the founder of a great religious movement and a great politician. These three activities were combined in him in such a way that they put to shame the performance of the best amongst us at the present time.'

Raja Rammohan Roy, considered one of the heroes of humanity and a harbinger of social reform and women's emancipation, is often referred to as the father of the Indian renaissance. Through his study and analysis of the Indian society's condition, he advocated for modern education and liberal ideas, steering away from outdated traditions. Proficient and well-versed in important Hindu scriptures such as the Vedas, Upanishads and the *Gita*, Roy emphasised that knowledge of the divine is attained through internal purity of the soul rather than external compliance and rituals. He believed that the path to the Supreme Being lies in selfless service to mankind.

Roy asserted that religious and social reforms alone were insufficient for social upliftment—a radical shift in values and attitudes, through education and awareness, was equally crucial for actual reform. Emphasising *gyanmarga* (the path of knowledge), he upheld values of truth, reasoning, justice and philanthropy. Rejecting sectarianism, he saw religion as a concept of universalism, present in the form of knowledge in Hinduism, monotheistic zeal in Islam and ethical guidance in Christianity. While a follower of Vedanta philosophy, he expressed dissatisfaction with the theoretical idea of falsehood presented by Advaita (non-dualism) Vedanta, as it could mislead the youth into considering worldly things as illusions.

Rammohan Roy's religious beliefs centred on the worship of one true God under the concept of a universal religion, aimed at dispelling superstitions and hatred from humanity. Synthesising nationalism with internationalism through rationalism, his philosophy was grounded in reason, truth and compassion, paving the way for the renaissance in Indian society. He advocated for values such as liberty, freedom of expression and an open, questioning mind.

NELSON MANDELA

Nelson Mandela, a legendary and inspirational figure who fought against apartheid and for the rights of black South Africans, sacrificing many years of his life in prison, is known for his leadership style and devotion to humanity. Mandela said, 'Men and women who fight the suppression of the human voice, who fight disease, illiteracy, ignorance, poverty, and hunger, some are known, others are not. Those are the people who have inspired me.' He never compromised with his values and principles, refusing offers of his release from prison on a conditional basis many times. He never allowed himself the emotions of retaliation and bitterness against whites and urged his followers to refrain from violence.

Mandela believed change can be brought about by any one irrespective of who they were. Even a small but kind effort that can restore harmony and make room for leading a dignified life for the people is laudable. From Mandela's life we can learn the values of courage of conviction and fearlessness. He also teaches us the values of forgiveness, compassion towards the deprived and weaker, and inclusiveness. Mandela was honoured with India's highest civilian award, the Bharat Ratna, in 1990. The UN General Assembly unanimously declared 18 July, his birthday, as Nelson Mandela International Day.

Mandela never strayed from his high moral principles and worked incessantly for his people. He won the battle against apartheid with his powerful moral leadership, determination, exemplary character and conduct. Mandela's political values were based on democratic leadership. He had a strong conviction that the solution to the long battle against racial discrimination and apartheid lies in democracy. He emphasised a parliamentary system, fundamental rights, separation of power and an independent judiciary in independent South Africa, asserting that 'a minority was not to be annihilated by the majority.' He said, 'I have nurtured the ideal of a democratic and liberal society', adding that 'I should live for such an ideal. But my lord, if circumstances arise that I have to put my life for an ideal, I would be prepared to die.'

Mandela said, 'Do not judge me by my success, judge me by the number of times I fell down and raised myself again and again.' He advises making friends with people who have a multidimensional vision and a critical attitude towards the problem at hand. 'I love those people to be my friends who are of free minds so that they can make me think of the solutions to the problems from every angle.' Mandela had a strong conviction that greatness comes with hardship, and believed that 'Difficulties break some people but make others. No axe is sharp enough to cut the spirit of a man who fights with the hope that eventually he would rise.' Mandela sees education as the most powerful weapon that can be used to transform the world. He emphasises intelligence but with compassion, for 'A good head and a good heart are always a formidable combination.' He believed, 'People must learn to hate; once they are trained in this, they can be taught to love. Love comes more naturally to the human heart than its opposite.' Mandela won the hearts and minds of people by his immense love, his generosity, nobility and sheer tenacity of spirit.

MARTIN LUTHER KING JR

Martin Luther King Jr was one of the most influential leaders of 20th century, known for his moral leadership, which was deeply influenced by Christian thought and the teachings of his parents, and further shaped by his experiments with personal values. King advocated for the protection of the dignity of every individual, asserting that a person should not be disgraced even if they have committed a wrong, and if such injustice occurs, one should raise their voice against it. Having witnessed apartheid and racial discrimination commonly as a black man, King personally experienced racial segregation when asked to give up his bus seat for white passengers, leading to a lasting memory of indignation and humiliation.

The son of a priest, King followed the Church throughout his life, and his faith in God played a crucial role in shaping his convictions. He believed in the omnipotence, omnipresence, and moral love of God. King's powerful oratory abilities, commitment to non-violence and adherence to Christian doctrines were pivotal in shaping his greatness as a leader. He recognised that the civil rights movement's first responsibility was to make white people realise their guilt and inhumanity. King strongly opposed the Vietnam War, emphasising his faith in a moral order and the belief that the moral universe bends towards justice. He felt that leaders had a moral responsibility to eradicate all forms of injustice, not limited to racial discrimination.

Love was the primary human value for King, and he considered it the source and strength of his leadership. His concept of love was rooted in the highest form of love for the divine. King's leadership of the struggle against race significantly contributed to the elimination of racism and sexism from America. His unforgettable and historic speech, 'I have a dream' is considered one of the most acclaimed and inspiring speeches of the 20th century.

Some quotes from 'I have a dream':

'... we refuse to believe that the bank of justice is bankrupt. We refuse to believe that there are insufficient funds in the great vaults of opportunity of this nation. So we have come to cash this check ... that will give us upon demand the richness of freedom and security of justice.'

'There is no time to engage in the luxury of cooling off or to take the tranquilizing drug of gradualism. Now is the time to make real promise of democracy.'

'No, no, we are not satisfied and we will not be satisfied until justice rolls down like waters and righteousness like a mighty stream.'

'Now is the time to rise from the dark and desolate valley of segregation to the sunlit path of racial justice.... I have a dream that one day this nation will rise up and live out the true meaning of its creed.... I have a dream that my four little children will one day live in a nation where they will not be judged by the color of their skin but by their character.... With this faith we will be able to transform the jangling discords of our nation into a beautiful symphony of brotherhood. With this faith we will be able to work together, to pray together, to struggle together, to go to jail together, to climb up for freedom together, knowing that we will be free one day.'

GEORGE WASHINGTON

George Washington, a man of character and integrity, and a true servant of his country, is often exemplified by the famous story of his childhood, the tale of George and the cherry tree, which symbolises his strong moral foundation. While the story might be fictional, its essence, depicting the sound character of a mature Washington, leaves no doubt about his moral integrity. His moral wisdom and beliefs were significantly influenced by his mother. Washington credited his success in life to the moral, intellectual and physical education imparted by his mother, whom he considered the most beautiful woman he ever saw. Known for being beyond the reach of temptation, Washington maintained his integrity in all respects, aspiring to be known as an honest man. He inherited his sense of morality from Christianity and his faith in God, emphasising the duty of all nations to acknowledge the providence of Almighty God and obey His will.

Washington believed in the everlasting connection between virtue and happiness, duty and benefit, and the genuine maxims of an honest and grand policy. He saw human happiness as contingent upon exercising moral duty, with virtue naturally emerging from popular government. Washington recognised the importance of virtue in enhancing talents, asserting that even the finest talents and greatest achievements lack value without the association of virtue and integrity. He considered good sense and honesty as rare and precious qualities, essential for making individuals great and nations happy. Washington stressed the need for a little more than common sense and common honesty in societal transactions to foster greatness and national happiness. Emphasising alertness and dutifulness in office, he declared his commitment to not letting personal convenience influence his official duties.

DEENDAYAL UPADHYAYA

Pandit Deendayal Upadhyaya is known for his right-wing Hindu ideology, particularly his philosophy of integral humanism, which holds a broad social dimension. According to him, human beings consist of four elements or *tatva*s: body, mind, intelligence and soul. These elements are equally important and integrated, and the absence or imbalance of any can affect one's personality. A complete human being, in his view, is an integrated being who is continuously evolving in the pursuit of self-realisation. Upadhyaya emphasises the satisfaction and nurturing of all four elements to achieve overall individual development. He views humans as both materialistic and spiritual, possessing elements of both. This perspective aligns with other major modern Indian philosophers like S. Radhakrishnan and Sri Aurobindo, with slight differences. While Radhakrishnan sees man beyond matter, soul or mind, Sri Aurobindo envisions humans reaching their highest development and becoming superhuman.

Delving into human nature, Upadhyaya identifies bipolar continuums between *asuri-bhav* (demoniac disposition) and *devi-bhav* (divine disposition). Asuri-bhav inclines towards self-interest, while devi-bhav leans towards selfless service. Similar to Sri Aurobindo, Upadhyaya stresses the evolutionary process that refines inherent imperfections, leading to a higher level of consciousness transcending material reality. He advocates selfless service as the path to self-perfection, obligating individuals to fulfill duties towards all creatures, not just human society.

Upadhyaya explores the pursuit of happiness, categorising it into fourfold aspirations related to body, mind, intellect and soul. He distinguishes *rajasukh* (mundane pleasure) from divine feeling-derived pleasure, highlighting the importance of sacred objectives. He considers physical, mental and intellectual pleasures, with the prime status given to the happiness of the soul. He introduces the concept of *purushartha*, which includes *dharma* (conduct for societal sustenance), *artha* (means for physical needs), *kama* (satisfaction of natural desires) and *moksha* (culmination through detachment). While emphasising the importance of all purusharthas, Upadhyaya distinguishes dharma from religion, viewing it as a notion focused on societal conduct.

Integral Humanism

Upadhyaya sees the individual and society as complementary, asserting that societal efforts contribute to the happiness and pleasure enjoyed by individuals. He advocates ensuring work for all to maintain societal balance and emphasises the interdependence of individual and societal pursuits of happiness. His philosophy of integral humanism aims to address the incompatibilities in political, religious and economic ideals. Deeply rooted in Indian culture and Hinduism, his philosophy neither dismisses nor rejects Western culture but distinguishes itself from Western 'isms' that prioritise the individual over society. He critiques Western 'isms', asserting that they emphasise personal freedom and rights stemming from materialism, while perceiving the individual as inseparable from society.

Upadhyaya liberally employs phrases like nation, glorious past, national self-respect and national character to connect individuals to humanity. He defines a nation as a collective of individuals pursuing a goal, ideal or mission, revering their land as a motherland. Emphasising the collective society or integral being missing in the capitalist system, he advocates considering the use of manpower and enjoyment in the context of the entire human community. Critiquing socialism, Upadhyaya acknowledges it as a reaction against capitalism but contends that it also fails to accord proper importance to the human being. He highlights socialism's tendency to shift capital ownership to the state, pointing out its shortcomings in prioritising individual wellbeing within the collective framework.

RAMMANOHAR LOHIYA

Rammanohar Lohiya, a prominent Indian freedom fighter, was a charismatic personality and leader of his time. He was a follower of Gandhi and Gandhian philosophy, but also differed from Gandhi on many issues. Lohiya possessed values of courage, love, humbleness and compassion for the weaker sections of society. He was a persuasive influencer who could convince people through his strongly argued rational views. Despite his strong socialist inclinations and commitment, Lohiya preferred not to be labeled as one, emphasising the necessity and inevitability of struggle in order to usher change and attain something new.

A vocal critic of Nehruvian policies, Lohiya advocated for the decentralisation of power, promoting self-regulation in villages and empowering villagers to create their own indigenous plans. Waging war against social and political evils, he introduced slogans like 'Contain Prices', 'Destroy Caste', 'Bhoomiseva', 'Lokbhasha' and 'Save Himalaya'. Lohiya strongly opposed the English language, advocating for Hindi as the principal language of the nation. He attacked the caste system, proposing a reservation of at least 60 per cent of jobs for the downtrodden, including women and backward communities.

Lohiya's philosophy can be broadly summarised by the following principles, famously known as the 'seven revolutions' through which Lohiya articulated his philosophy and values.

1. Equality between men and women.
2. Struggle against discrimination based on skin colour.
3. Struggle against the hereditary caste system, advocating provisions for the backward classes.
4. Struggle against capitalism, promoting planned social and economic equality.
5. Liberty to live a private life without state encroachment under a democracy.
6. Opposition to armed struggle, favouring the use of satyagraha.

SWAMI DAYANANDA SARASWATI

Swami Dayananda Saraswati was an Indian social reformer and philosopher who espoused the

Vedanta philosophy, rejecting rituals prevalent in Hinduism such as idolatry, the concept of multiple gods, pilgrimage, etc. He also denounced regressive societal practices like child marriage, discrimination against women, the caste system, and offerings to religious places. Drawing inspiration from the *Bhagvad Gita*, he introduced the term *swaraj* and emphasised the importance of *jnanam*, understood as value or knowledge, a state of mind reflecting universal values and ethical attitudes, that also facilitate self-knowledge. Jnanam is not knowledge of the self but the means to it.

Dayananda highlighted 20 values of jnanam mentioned in the *Gita*, some of which are particularly relevant for civil servants:

1. Absence of self-worship
2. Absence of pretence
3. Non-injury
4. Straightness
5. Steadiness
6. Mastery over mind
7. Absence of egoism
8. Absence of sense of ownership
9. Constant even-mindedness in the presence of the desirable and the undesirable
10. Constant application of the knowledge of self
11. Keeping in view the purpose of knowledge of truth

Dayananda explains 'value' as regard for an object which is precious for an individual for reasons specific to that individual. He expounded on ethical values or dharma, describing it as a standard of conduct defining acceptable or desirable behaviour within an individual and towards others. He acknowledged the relativity of ethical values, stating that 'Ethical values are universal in content but relative in application.' For example:

> I wish my children should respect me.
> I don't wish that my children disrespect me.
> Respecting parents is dharma for me.
> Disrespect of parents is adharma for me.
> Religious texts also confirm that respect of parents is desirable conduct.
> Religious texts denounce disrespect and declare it undesirable.

While ethical values are relative, he argues, ethical norms are not arbitrary; they emerge from the reconciled self-interests of all members of society, which makes ethical standards natural and universal but not absolute. Something that is ethical for one is unethical for another and vice-versa. Ethical standards are defined by a consensus about acceptability of behaviour but this consensus is situation-specific. In general, people tend to exercise and apply their values more consistently in the case of others than themselves. Further, Dayananda explains one cannot evade exercising values because it is inherently difficult to escape relationships based on the concern that what is valued may be hurt or diminished or disturbed. Additionally, Dayananda stressed the desirability of values to minimise conflicts in the mind, overcoming by-products such as regret, guilt, self-doubt and self-confidence.

In exploring the pursuit of ethical values, Dayananda also emphasised the value of the value itself, asserting that its pursuit is driven by its perceived value. He contended that the expression of an individual's life reflects a well-assimilated value structure, with actions dependent on what is valuable to them. Dayananda warned against unassimilated values, considering them more susceptible to compromise and conflict, and emphasised the need for reasoning to assimilate values into one's personal value structure. Once assimilated, these values become spontaneous and habitual in one's life.

TULSIDAS

Tulsidas was a great composer and grammarian proficient in Sanskrit and Awadhi. His notable work, *Ramcharitmanas*, is an epic that depicts the personality of Lord Rama, highlighting the grandeur of moral character and ideal social behaviour. Among his other literary marvels are

Vinaya Patrika, Gitavali, Kavitavali, Dohavali, and *Vairagya Sandipani*. In his *Vinaya Patrika,* Tulsidas attempts to interpret the term *vinaya,* describing it as an attitude of a leader or hero, embodying the attributes of modesty, bashfulness and demureness. Tulsidas suggests that, like an organ composed of several organs and an element composed of several elements, devotion is also composed of modesty (*vinaya*). Without possessing the attitude of vinaya, a seeker cannot attain devotion.

Tulsidas emphasises that if the formless one without attributes and qualities (*Nirguna*) did not exist, the one with qualities (*Saguna*) would not have come into being and would not have had any utility, and sees the Nirguna and Saguna as complementary to each other.

KABIR

Kabir, a mystic poet from the 15th century AD, was a follower of 'Nirguna Brahma'. His significant work, *Beijak* (the seedling), comprises a collection of poems known as *Sakhi*. Kabir vehemently opposes the prevailing evils in both Hinduism and Islam. He was particularly concerned about the exploitation of the poor, downtrodden, despised and oppressed individuals who were often victims of religious and social dogmas. Being a monist, Kabir aligned with Vedantic philosophy and rejected idolatry. He believes that God resides within each of us, likening the Divine to the fragrance of *kasturi* (musk) present within a deer itself, yet the deer wanders, seeking it elsewhere.

Kabir also stresses the importance of self-knowledge and self-scrutiny instead of focusing on others' faults. He expresses that when he examines his own heart, he finds himself to be more blameworthy than everyone else, as encapsulated in his saying:

> *Bura jo dekhan mein chala bura na milya koye,*
> *jo dil dhoonda aapna mujhsa bura na koye.*

Kabir vehemently denounces the determination of wisdom based on someone's caste, for knowledge is not the slave of high-caste people and a saint or a scholar should not be asked his caste; rather he should be asked for knowledge. He expresses this as:

> *Jati na puchho sadhu ki puchh lijiye gyan,*
> *mol karo talwar ka padi rahan do myan.*

It means that the sword should be valued rather than its cover. Kabir considers truthfulness as the greatest virtue, and lying as the greatest sin. God belongs to them who speak the truth. He explains this as:

> *Saanch barabar tap nahi jhoot barabar pap,*
> *jake hriday saanch vaa ko hein aap.*

Kabir considers quality of speech to be important as sweet and sober words have a positive effect on both speaker and listener. He says:

> *Aisi vaani boliye mann ka aapa khoye,*
> *Auran ko sheetal kare apao sheetal hoye.*

Kabir's teaching on renunciation of greed and contentment is important in the life of a civil servant. He says, one should ask for that much which is sufficient for nurturing and feeding family and guests.

> *Sayi itna dijiye jamein kutumb samaye,*
> *Mein bhi bhukha na rahun sadhu na bhukha jaye.*

GURU NANAK

Guru Nanak, the founder of Sikhism and the first of the ten Sikh Gurus, was born on 15 April 1469 in a devout Hindu family near Lahore. His teachings emphasise the unity and oneness of God, the importance of leading a spiritual life while remaining a social being (without the need to be a *sanyasi*), and the need to promote equality among all human beings. Unlike the concept of original sin in Christianity, Guru Nanak asserted that no man or woman is a fallen soul, and everyone is eligible to lead a moral life. He identified five human tendencies as obstacles to virtuous living: lust, greed, attachment, anger and pride, which could be overcome through chanting the name of God. Rejecting religious rituals and priesthood, he deemed them false and unproductive. Guru Nanak also dismissed the four traditional phases of life in Hinduism—*brahmacharya*, *grihastha*, *vaanaprastha* and *sanyas*—while emphasising the eightfold path given by Buddha with a positive outlook towards life.

According to Nanak, the Supreme Being is shapeless and profound, consistently showering grace upon humanity. He outlined the five phases of the spiritual journey of man. The initial phase involves leading a moral life (*dharma khand*), wherein morality involves following the common principles of traditional morality that are inherent in all religions. The subsequent phases include divine knowledge (*jnankhand*), the unfolding of the aesthetic experience of spirituality (*saramkhand*), achieving divine grace intended for limited seekers, and finally, acquiring knowledge of eternal truth in the form of self-actualisation and consciousness.

Guru Nanak's cardinal values encompass non-violence, truth, honesty, love, virtue, equality and theism. Virtue, in his teachings, involves adhering to morality in daily life, including the pursuit of the highest standards in family affairs. Nanak asserted that God is omnipotent and omniscient, observing our deeds, and meting out consequences according to our actions. He emphasised respecting the rule of law and the will of society, advising rulers to embrace democratic ideals for lasting reign, as democracy reflects the divine order. Denouncing oppressive wielding of power, he believed that heaven on earth could be realised by granting freedom and voice to society. Nanak contended that continuous remembrance of God cultivates altruism, leading to selflessness. A selfless individual influences others, fostering a society that lives in peace and harmony. The Guru's spiritual compositions, recorded in the *Guru Granth Sahib*, continue to guide and inspire millions of Sikhs around the world.

GURU RAVIDAS

Guru Ravidas was an important saint of the Nirguna Bhakti Dhara during the medieval period of Indian history. He advocated for a simple path to attain Brahma that was accessible to all, regardless of their religious or caste affiliations. Guru Ravidas strongly opposed prevalent social evils in Indian society during his time, condemning all religious rituals and grandiosity as artificial and futile. He particularly criticised the deeply entrenched caste system, which perpetuated social discrimination and untouchability, hindering the progress of Hindu society.

Guru Ravidas' teachings emphasise the paramount importance of a guru or teacher in its highest form. The guru, according to him, plays a crucial role in introducing followers to the pure *Brahma* or *Parmatma*. Ravidas believed that the guru's position is close to God because only the guru can dispel illusions, eradicate false knowledge and illuminate the minds of disciples with the right kind of wisdom and knowledge. He expresses this as:

> *Guru gyan deepak diya, baati dayi jalaye.*
> *Ravidas hari bhagati kaarne, janam maran bilmaye.*

It means that a guru illuminates the path of prayer and devotion to reach God, enabling one to break out of the endless cycle of birth and death. Ravidas emphasises that individuals are influenced by their social environment and the company they keep. If one wants to achieve spiritual progress, one must choose friends wisely.

> *Jo jan dusht kumaargi, baithai nahitinh paas.*
> *Jo jan san sumaargi, tin payan lago Ravidas.*

SRI RAMAKRISHNA PARAMHANS

Sri Ramakrishna Paramhans was born in 1836 in the village of Kamarpukur in the Hooghly district of West Bengal, and belonged to a poor family. Serving as the priest at Dakshineswar Temple, he communicated his teachings in the form of mystic parables and metaphors, which were later compiled by his disciples and published in English in 1942 as *The Gospel of Sri Ramakrishna*.

According to Ramakrishna, the ultimate goal of human life is the realisation of God—the absolute and only reality. He embraced the unity of God in both *Saguna* and *Nirguna* forms, expressing a strong belief in the truth of all religions, each guiding the way to the ultimate reality. He emphasised the purification of the mind by overcoming passions like lust and greed, asserting that purity of mind is essential for attaining God. Egoism, born out of ignorance, was seen as the source of all suffering.

Ramakrishna said that the eligibility for Brahma knowledge requires liberation from the three *guna*s: *satva*, *rajas* and *tamas*. Among these, rajas and tamas were considered particularly perilous. Rajas creates attachment to worldly objects, entangling individuals in mundane activities, while tamas instils violent and destructive tendencies. Satva, although positive in worldly matters, can also be an obstacle to salvation. To attain pure Brahma, all three gunas must be eradicated, Ramakrishna asserted.

Ramakrishna categorised people into four groups: i) prisoners of the world; ii) seekers with a strong desire for liberation; iii) liberated souls; and iv) the ever-free. Prisoners are entangled in worldly affairs, seekers may or may not achieve liberation, and liberated souls have attained a higher state. He asserted that true knowledge lies not in knowing all religious texts but in navigating the river of the world. Ramakrishna emphasised that God is the only reality, and the world is false and illusory (*maya*). Vanity and egoism lead to destruction, while faith can work miracles in times of crisis. Surrendering to God and maintaining unwavering faith leads to a life filled with miracles and peace.

SRI NARAYAN GURU

Sri Narayan Guru was one of the great saints, and social and religious reformers of twentieth-century India. His mission aimed at eradicating the pervasive evils of untouchability, social inequality and gender discrimination that plagued Kerala's society. Seeking inspiration from Shankara's spiritual monism of *advaita*, Sri Narayana Guru propagated the idea of social unity with his famous slogan: 'One God, One Religion, One Caste.'

Born in Thiruvananthapuram into the Ezhava caste, traditionally considered untouchables by the Namboodari Brahmins, Sri Narayana Guru initiated a movement to challenge these social hierarchies. His approach was deeply influenced by the concept of 'dharma', not in the sense of Hindu Sanatana dharma, but rooted in modernity and emotional appeal. Sri Narayana Guru authored several treatises in Sanskrit, Malayalam and Tamil, including *Atmaupdeshshatkam*, *Darshanmala* and *Sri Narayan Smriti*. He emphasised that all religions serve as powerful sources of faith and belief for their followers. While religious texts from various traditions describe the origin of the universe and the evolution of life, Hinduism, according to him, stands out with its depiction of societal divisions into castes. He argued that the caste hierarchy in Hinduism was a result of specific groups exploiting the system for social, economic and political advantage.

MAULANA ABUL KALAM AZAD

Maulana Abul Kalam Azad, a prominent freedom fighter and leader in India's struggle for independence, dedicated his life to opposing colonial rule. Breaking free from the traditional religious doctrines of Islam, Maulana Azad asserted that the connection between the human mind and the physical world exists on intellectual and moral grounds rather than emotional or imaginative ones. His courageous stance against his parental values reflected his conviction.

A strong advocate for scientific knowledge, Maulana Azad believed that true education encompasses the study of science, philosophy and literature. He opposed the restrictive nature of *taqlid*, emphasising that moral and spiritual development is hindered by such constraints. Influenced by the religious writings of Syed Ahmad Khan, he emerged as a follower of Islam free from the interpretations imposed by the Ulemas. Rejecting the tradition of *piri* and *muridi*, he interpreted Islam as a liberal and egalitarian system that upholds freedom and democracy. According to him, Islam teaches that the highest right is just right, not might. Maulana Azad asserted that freedom is a gift from God to humanity, and no individual or country has the right to subjugate others, whether under the guise of benevolence or renaissance. While he admired the virtue of multiculturalism, he opposed the tendency of different cultures to exclusively revive their past, neglecting the rich heritage of a common culture.

RABINDRANATH TAGORE

Rabindranath Tagore, a Nobel laureate in literature, was an eminent writer, poet, painter and musician. According to him, a person's character is the by-product of their spiritual and moral values, and individuals have the potential to attain godliness through spiritual and moral perfection. Tagore perceives God and humanity as identical. He defines humanism as the feeling of being human, bringing joy. The human mind is the means through which the purpose of things is revealed, and things are as they are perceived.

In Tagore's philosophy of spiritualism, self-realisation is a pivotal idea. He distinguishes self-realisation as soul consciousness rather than self-consciousness, where the 'self' represents the egoistic existence of an individual, and the soul signifies the individual's existence in a universal context. According to him, 'Man is proceeding from era to era towards the complete realisation of his soul, which is higher than worldly objects, actions, and principles.' The history of humanity, in Tagore's view, is a journey in quest for the immortal soul.

Tagore sees love and sacrifice as complementary. True love, for him, does not claim possession but gives freedom, following the principle of 'give and give'. He emphasises that power claims ownership and is imprisoned on a throne, while love declares that it belongs to the world and is granted the freedom of its house by the world. Tagore underscores the importance of education, stating that it enables the mind to attain the ultimate truth. This truth, he believes, liberates us from bondage, bestows enlightenment over wealth and promotes love over power.

MOTHER TERESA

Mother Teresa was born in Skopje, Macedonia, and dedicated her life to serving the weaker sections, sufferers and individuals rejected by society due to various reasons such as illness and deprivation. After leaving her family, she joined a missionary and eventually came to India, spending her entire life in Bengal serving the people. She expressed her calling, stating, 'I came to know that I had the call to serve the hungry, the naked, the homeless, the crippled, the blind, the lepers, all those people who feel unwanted, unloved, uncared for in the society, people that have become a burden to the society and are shunned by everyone.'

Mother Teresa highlighted the hunger for love in humanity, stemming from pain and seclusion. Recognising and addressing this scarcity of love is crucial, and she emphasised that this hunger is even greater than the need for bread. Poverty, she believed, doesn't only affect the economically poor but also those who feel undesired, unloved and unattended. She advocated for addressing this issue starting from one's home, promoting selflessness in conduct, which she considered one of the greatest human values. Acknowledging the limitations of resources, Mother Teresa provided a practical approach—instead of worrying about everyone at once, start by helping one person closest to you and gradually reach out to others.

She stressed the importance of giving quality time to one's family, which she believed in turn contributes to global peace in a collective sense. She says, 'Everybody today seems to be in such a terrible rush, anxious for greater development and richness. Children have very little time for parents, parents have very little time for each other, and at home begins the disruption of the peace of the world.'

Mother Teresa considers silence to be more significant than speech. According to her, silence is the foundation of spirituality. She said:

> The fruit of silence is prayer,
> The fruit of prayer is faith,
> The fruit of faith is love,
> The fruit of love is service.

Some significant thoughts of Mother Teresa that should be kept in mind by every civil servant in relation to public service, although she expressed these for everyone, include:

> People are often unreasonable and self-centred. Forgive them anyway. If you are kind, people may accuse you of ulterior motives. Be kind anyway. If you are honest, people may cheat you. Be honest anyway. If you find happiness, people may be jealous. Be happy anyway. The good you do today may be forgotten tomorrow. Do good anyway. Give the world the best you have, and it may never be enough. Give your best anyway.

A. P. J. ABDUL KALAM

A. P. J. Abdul Kalam was a prominent scientist and the driving force behind India's space programme and missile technology. Popularly known as the 'missile-man', he also served as the 11th President of India, dedicating his life to the nation. Revered for his values, inspirational speeches and nation-building efforts, Kalam inspired diverse groups of individuals, including politicians, bureaucrats, scientists, the general public and children. He consistently encouraged children to dream, firmly believing that dreams are the foundation of turning aspirations into reality. According to him, 'You have to dream before your dream would come true.'

Kalam placed a strong emphasis on the role of a trained mind, advocating that such training must incorporate values. He believed that parents and teachers bear the responsibility of shaping young minds. In his words, 'If a country is to be corruption-free and become a nation of beautiful minds, I strongly feel there are three key societal members who can make a difference. They are the father, the mother, and the teacher.'

Addressing the youth, Kalam encouraged them to have the courage to think outside the box, adopt rigorous paths, and find solutions to challenging problems. He defined leadership as the ability to fearlessly confront difficult situations, possessing the vision and vigour to overcome them while maintaining integrity in conduct. Kalam viewed difficulties as an essential part of life that provide a sense of ecstasy when their solutions are discovered. He believed that God helps those who are industrious and ready to face problems, asserting that a dreamer and hardworking individual is always assisted by good fortune, with the entire universe conspiring to offer the best outcomes.

QUESTIONS

1. Given below are three quotations of great moral thinkers/philosophers. For each of these quotations, bring out what it means to you in the present context. (UPSC 2013)
    (a) 'There is enough on this earth for everyone's need but for no one's greed.' —Mahatma Gandhi
    (b) 'Nearly all men can withstand adversity, but if you want to test a man's character, give him power.' —Abraham Lincoln
    (c) 'I count him braver who overcomes his desires than him who overcomes his enemies.' —Aristotle
2. Which eminent personality has inspired you the most in the context of ethical conduct in life? Give the gist of his/her teachings. Giving specific examples, describe how you have been able to apply these teachings for your own ethical development. (UPSC 2014)
3. Current society is plagued with a widespread trust deficit. What are the consequences of this situation for personal wellbeing and for societal wellbeing? What can you do at the personal level to make yourself trustworthy? (UPSC 2014)
4. Discuss Mahatma Gandhi's concept of seven sins. (UPSC 2016)

5. 'Corruption causes misuse of government treasury, administrative inefficiency and obstruction in the path of national development.' Discuss Kautilya's views. (UPSC 2016)
6. 'Great ambition is the passion of a great character. Those endowed with it may perform very good or very bad acts. All depends on the principles which direct them.' —Napoleon Bonaparte. Giving examples, mention the rulers
   (i) who have harmed society and country.
   (ii) who have worked for the development of society and country. (UPSC 2017)
7. 'Anger and intolerance are the enemies of correct understanding.' —Mahatma Gandhi. Discuss and analyse with examples. (UPSC 2018)
8. 'In looking for people to hire, you look for three qualities: integrity, intelligence and energy. And if they do not have the first, the other two will kill you.'—Warren Buffett. Discuss and explain.
9. 'A man is but a product of his thoughts. What he thinks he becomes.' —M. K. Gandhi. Discuss and critically analyse. (UPSC 2019)
10. 'Where there is righteousness in the heart, there is beauty in the character. When there is beauty in the character, there is harmony in the home. When there is harmony in the home, there is order in the nation. When there is order in the nation, there is peace in the world.' —A. P. J. Abdul Kalam. Discuss and elaborate. (UPSC 2019)

6

ATTITUDE

> **KEY CONCEPTS**
>
> What is Attitude?; Components of Attitude: The Tripartite ABC Model; Implicit and Explicit Attitudes; Measuring Attitude; Behaviour, Intention, Beliefs and Goals; Functions of Attitude; Attitude and Behaviour; Attitude Formation and Attitude Change; Factors Controlling Attitude Change; Methods of Attitude Change; Goals and Attitude Change; Moral, Political and Bureaucratic Attitudes; Persuasion as a Model of Belief Correction for Attitude Change

WHAT IS ATTITUDE?

Attitude is generally understood as a way of thinking, feeling or behaving that reflects a complex state of mind involving beliefs, feelings, values and dispositions to act in certain ways. It refers to a tendency or predisposition to evaluate and respond to people, situations, events and objects in specific ways. Attitudes can be positive, negative or neutral, and they influence how we perceive and interact with the world around us. Attitudes may be formed through personal experiences, social influences and cultural factors, and they play a vital role in shaping our thoughts, emotions, actions, decisions and judgments.

Attitude is directly related to the study of human psychology and social behaviour. In psychology, attitude is described as a predisposition in response to an object based on knowledge about that particular object, and a stance regarding liking or disliking it. The former, knowledge-based attitude, is related to *cognitive psychology*, while the latter is rooted in *biological psychology*. Generally, we learn attitudes from others, except in cases of genetically predisposed attitudes, making it a subject of social psychology and social pressure. Over time, persistent social pressure can transform behaviour into lasting attitudes towards specific objects. The study of persuasion thus becomes crucial when examining attitudinal change. Attitude was first examined with respect to reaction time for a given object by W. James and C. Lange in 1888.

The **James-Lange theory of emotion**, proposed independently by psychologist William James and physiologist Carl Lange in the late nineteenth century, suggests that emotions are the result of physiological reactions to stimuli in the environment. According to this theory, an event or stimulus triggers a physiological response in the body, and it is the interpretation of this physiological response that leads us to experience emotion. In other words, the theory suggests that you feel an emotion because of a specific physiological response, such as changes in heart rate, breathing or other bodily reactions. While the James-Lange theory has contributed much to our understanding of the relationship between physiological processes and emotions, it has also evolved over time. Many contemporary theories propose that both physiological responses and cognitive appraisals play important roles in the experience of emotions.

The target or subject matter of an attitude can be any entity such as an object, a person, a group or an idea. Attitudes towards objects involve applications of social psychology in daily life, including eating habits (attitudes towards food), marketing (attitudes towards products), advertising (attitudes towards advertisements), political behaviour (attitudes towards political ideologies, candidates, parties or voting behaviour), health concerns (attitudes towards physical exercise, new medications or the health system) and more. Attitudes towards individuals or groups are often explored within the realm of interpersonal likes and biases. Values play a role in maintaining attitudes towards abstract ideas, and may involve judgments on freedom, equality or justice as per the needs of the hour.

Attitudes also vary in terms of specificity versus generality. An attitude towards a leader is specific (e.g., in response to his/her speech), but many attitudes are general, for example, some individuals hold relatively positive attitudes towards all objects, while others dislike most things, people and ideas. Further, attitudes concerning an object can exhibit different degrees of specificity in different temporal and spatial contexts (Ajzen and Fishbein 2005; Fishbein and Ajzen 1975). For example, saving money may not be a priority for a recently employed person, unlike someone who has been working for some years and is now considering marriage. Similarly, a person who has to catch a train and is short of time may not show a positive attitude towards their favourite food as eating it could make them miss the train.

COMPONENTS OF ATTITUDE: THE TRIPARTITE ABC MODEL

Where do attitudes come from? Research suggests that attitudes can be based on three different sources or components, namely: the affective component, the behavioural component and the cognitive component. This tripartite model is also known as the ABC model of attitude, taking the first alphabets of these three attitudinal components (see Figure 6.1).

The *affective* component refers to feelings, moods and emotions associated with the object of attitude. Consider for example someone who likes jogging and has a positive attitude towards physical exercise. The feelings of invigoration experienced while jogging serve as the affective basis of this person's attitude. The affective component thus involves the emotional aspect of the attitude towards an object. The *behavioural* component refers to how this person has acted or will act in the future with reference to the object. If this person consistently jogs or goes to the gym, these activities serve as the behavioural basis. Finally, the *cognitive* component refers to the overt thoughts or beliefs the person has in regard to the target object. If the person believes jogging is good for health, such thoughts constitute the cognitive component of their attitude.

In the aforementioned example of jogging, the affective, behavioural and cognitive components of the person's attitude are all positive, which suggests that s/he is likely to hold an overall positive attitude towards jogging, i.e., the attitude object. However, these three components will not necessarily always be consistent. For instance, a person may think chocolate cake tastes wonderful (affective) and may eat chocolate cake often (behavioural), but may also think that it is calorie-heavy and hence harmful to health (cognitive). In this situation the attitude formation would be complex and will definitely involve other factors. Also, in such situations, attitude may affect all three components at various levels.

Figure 6.1: The tripartite or ABC model of attitude

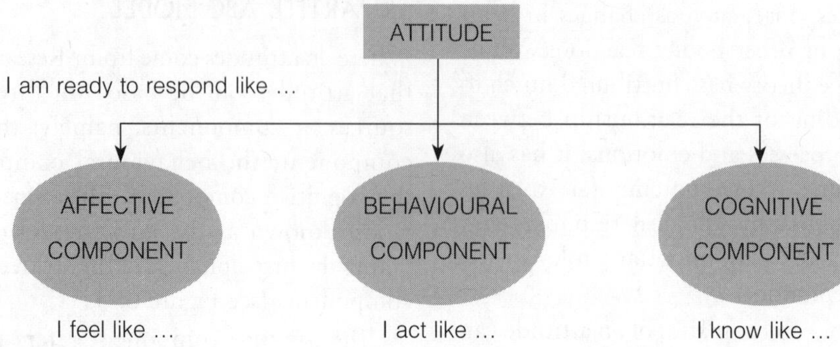

```
                        ATTITUDE
    I am ready to respond like ...
         ↓                 ↓                 ↓
    AFFECTIVE         BEHAVIOURAL        COGNITIVE
    COMPONENT         COMPONENT          COMPONENT

    I feel like ...    I act like ...    I know like ...
```

Source: Created by authors.

How this tripartite ABC model works in the life of a civil servant and influences his/her decisions can be illustrated through an example. Suppose you have just been appointed a district magistrate, and have received multiple applications for arms licences, how you decide on these applications will depend upon the interplay between the ABC components of your attitude. If the sight of a gun has made you fearful since childhood, this fear towards the gun (object of attitude) is an emotion and considered the affective component of your attitude towards the gun. You have also witnessed several cases of suicide involving licensed guns, and possess a strong conviction that guns are often misused in situations that have nothing to do with self-defence—this represents the cognitive component of your attitude. Therefore, you decide to reject all the applications for arms licences, reflecting the behavioural component of your attitude towards guns.

Alice H. Eagly and Shelly Chaiken (1993) described how attitudes function under the influence of these three components, and held that our emotions, behaviour and cognition not only guide and shape our attitudes but may also be driven or influenced by those attitudes in turn. Thus the components of the tripartite ABC model can be conceptualised in terms of both the antecedents and the consequences of their associated attitudes; in other words, there is a clear feedback mechanism between attitudes and their respective components or sources.

Features of Attitude

Attitudes may be characterised by four basic features: valence, extremeness, simplicity and centrality. *Valence* is defined as inclination or deflection with respect to the attitude object and is positive as well as negative in nature, hence termed positive and negative valence respectively. The *extremeness* of a particular attitude is defined in terms of how positive or negative it is towards a given object. Figure 6.2 shows an example of valence towards the attitude object of plant-based food. Here plant-based food is an object for which one may show positive valence, but at the same time different valences may be expressed for the different properties (adjectives) of plant-based food, like its taste, price, texture, etc. In the Likert scale (Figure 6.2), ratings 1 and 2 show negative valence, 4 and 5 show positive valence, and rating 3 represents neutral valence. Ratings 1 and 5 reflect extreme attitude whereas rating 3 shows neutral attitude. In the example in Figure 6.2, the attitude towards plant-based food is positive with respect to its taste and healthiness while the attitude towards its price is neutral.

There can be a number of smaller differing attitudes inherent within a larger attitude. For example, an individual with a broadly positive attitude towards plant-based food also exhibits different attitudes within it. This broader attitude is known as an *attitude system*, and the multiple attitudes contained within it are known as its *member attitudes*. An attitude system having multiple member attitudes shows *complexity*, while one with a smaller number of member attitudes shows *simplicity*. Each of these member attitudes also possess A-B-C, that is, affective, behavioural and cognitive components. *Centrality* is defined as the amount of influence exerted by an attitude to control other attitudes of an attitude system. For example, the attitude concerning healthiness of plant-based food shows greater centrality as shown in Figure 6.2.

IMPLICIT AND EXPLICIT ATTITUDES

If attitude is the result of various external factors (cognitive knowledge of the outer world) and internal biological constructs, then we may ask: is it possible to measure attitude? Measuring attitudes also enables us to distinguish between different kinds of attitudes. Developing attitude measurement techniques has, for instance, enabled researchers to evaluate attitudes indirectly rather than relying exclusively on explicit ratings of liking or approval. Such indirect measurement of attitudes, referred to as *implicit*, is helpful in assessing automatic evaluations that are generally challenging to gauge using only *explicit* self-reports. The effectiveness of implicit measures is suggested by evidence showing that they often diverge from general attitudes and predict different outcomes than self-reported or explicit attitudes.

Implicit attitudes are the responses of earlier, spontaneous, affective processes, whereas *explicit* attitudes reflect more deliberate adjustments based on current goals or social desirability concerns. Some scholars have even questioned whether attitudes can be regarded as stable entities, or if they are instead constructed only on encountering an object that is variable. The divergence between implicit and explicit attitudes has commonly been interpreted as evidence suggesting that they measure two distinct cognitive processes—namely, *unconscious* (automatic evaluation) and *conscious* processes (controlled evaluation), respectively. The lack of inter-correlation between implicit and explicit attitudes has been used to suggest that each measure captures *upstream* and *downstream* processes, specifically automatic responses and intentionally self-edited judgments or responses related to the same attitude.

The correlation between implicit and explicit measures varied as a function of the amount of cognitive efforts used during explicit self-report tasks, suggesting different transformations of a single evaluative response. Neuro-imaging studies have observed similar differences between implicit and explicit attitudes (Corlett and Marrouch 2018). For example, the brain structures involved during automatic evaluations were found to include the amygdala, the insula and the orbitofrontal cortex (Cunningham et al. 2003, 2009; Cunningham, Raye and Johnson 2004). In contrast, those involved during controlled evaluations were found to include regions of the anterior cingulate cortex, including the dorsal anterior cingulate cortex (Cunningham et al. 2003; Cunningham, Raye and Johnson 2004).

MEASURING ATTITUDE

If attitude plays such a crucial role in determining an individual's performance in personal and professional life, it becomes essential to develop methods for its assessment. Researchers have developed a variety of tools to measure attitudes. Two most commonly used techniques are the Likert scale and the semantic differential scale. Figure 6.2 shows participants reporting attitudes on a Likert scale when asked to indicate the extent to which a variety of statements characterise them. Similarly, Figure 6.3 shows participants reporting attitudes on a semantic differential scale when asked to indicate how a set of properties or adjectives defined the attitude object. In both cases, the participants were provided with various items to complete the exercise. The scores from

Figure 6.2: Likert scale

Please indicate the extent to which the following statements are or are not characteristic of you:	
1 = very uncharacteristic of me	
2 = somewhat uncharacteristic of me	
3 = neither characteristic nor uncharacteristic of me	
4 = somewhat characteristic of me	
5 = very characteristic of me	
1. Plant-based food is healthier	5
2. Plant-based food tastes good	5
3. Plant-based food is cheaper	2
4. Plant-based food is pleasant	5
5. Plant-based food is messy	3

Source: Created by authors.

Figure 6.3: Semantic differential scale

Plant-based food						
Healthy	...✓...	......	......	.....	......	Unhealthy
Good-tasting	...✓...	......	......	.....	......	Bad-tasting
Expensive	......	......	......	...✓...	......	Cheaper
Pleasant	...✓..	......	......	......	......	Unpleasant
Messy	......	......	...✓...	......	......	Clean

Source: Created by authors.

these items were then combined to generate an overall measure of the person's attitude toward the target object, here plant-based food.

There are several guidelines that researchers can follow to minimise errors when attempting to assess a person's attitude. One is to employ reverse coding for some items by framing them negatively, as done in the third and fifth items in Figures 6.2 and 6.3. This serves two purposes. First, it reduces the likelihood that a respondent will simply check the leftmost or rightmost box down the entire set-up in attempts to save time or cognitive resources. Respondents are less likely to do so if they recognise that various items are indeed reverse coded. Similarly, if only the leftmost or rightmost boxes are checked throughout the set-up, the researcher can identify this pattern and interpret the findings accordingly. Further, some research suggests that providing respondents with five to seven options to choose from yields the most valid data. Scales with fewer than five options lack the precision necessary to measure attitudes accurately, while scales with more than seven options tend to introduce additional noise without gaining additional precision or information.

Students commonly use the Likert scale to evaluate their professors at the end of a semester, and departments and universities use this data, in part, to make personnel decisions. Companies also use such techniques to gauge customers' attitudes towards their products and services. By identifying which aspects customers like or dislike, managers can allocate resources to improve deficient areas in their companies. Preferences of an individual or a group of individuals, viewed as a uniform group, can be measured, enabling the prediction of the behaviour of individuals or groups based on attitude measurement.

BEHAVIOUR, INTENTION, BELIEFS AND GOALS

Behaviour, beliefs, intentions and goals are some crucial concepts that contribute to a comprehensive understanding of attitude, in addition to the psychological study of attitude. *Behaviour* is typically defined as the overt actions of an individual and generally considered to stem from their attitude. Several research studies suggest that the relationship between attitude and behaviour is inevitable, and that attitude is a reliable predictor of behaviour with a strong correlation.

Intention is the willingness to perform a specific behaviour. According to Icek Ajzen and Martin Fishbein, intention is rooted in the final objective or goal which encompasses broader and desirable end states. Intentions can be achieved through sustained behaviour and repeated efforts, often requiring external help or resources. These end results are often uncontrollable; for example, people may develop intentions to increase physical activity with the goal of losing weight, but executing the intended behaviour is not guaranteed, necessitating multiple repetitive efforts and external resources.

Belief, according to Fishbein and Ajzen, is the subjective probability of the occurrence of a relation due to the interaction of the object of belief with another object, and value systems, notions, or attributes. Beliefs affect people's understanding of themselves and their immediate environments. Beliefs differ from another closely related concept: *values*. Belief is a cognitive component of attitude and forms the foundation for attitude, while values encompass both beliefs and attitudes. Values are internalised as a compelling force and are associated with the imposition of an 'ought' after its formation in an individual's personality, perpetuating belief or attitude.

Goals, like attitudes, can be both specific and general. However, most of the research establishing the relationship between goals and intentions has focused on specific goals, such as the goal to quit smoking. Once a goal is set, it is followed by the intention to perform actions that support achieving that goal, like throwing away smoking-related paraphernalia or avoiding the company of friends who smoke. Here, the intention to quit smoking or achieving a similar goal serves as an excellent predictor of actual behaviour.

FUNCTIONS OF ATTITUDE

People hold different attitudes for varying reasons. Attitudes serve different functions in our life. Daniel Katz suggests four principal functions of attitude: adjustment, ego defense, expressing value and acquiring knowledge.

1. ***Adjustment Function***: An individual may hold contrasting attitudes regarding particular social institutions, such as the workplace, school or university, political and religious groups. To navigate conflicting situations, we often try to align our attitudes with societal norms. In other words, due to social pressures we may adopt attitudes which we think may be pleasing and acceptable to others. This reflects the utilitarian function of attitudes wherein individuals aim to maximise rewards and minimise punishments by adjusting and conforming to their social milieus.

2. ***Ego-Defensive Function***: Every individual has an innate propensity to protect their self-esteem. They also attempt to justify wrong actions as righteous to alleviate a guilty conscience, and project weakness or incapacity as strengths or choice to protect self-esteem. Essentially, individuals seek to shield themselves from self-criticism by adopting attitudes that function as a defense of ego. For instance, a person may harbour a strong inner desire to become a civil servant, but due to their inability or failure to achieve this goal they may develop a negative attitude towards the civil services. This function carries a psychological undertone, and such attitudes are inclined towards positivity to safeguard one's self-image. The underlying idea behind this is that attitudes play a mediating role between one's internal needs for self-expression and defending our ego, and the external world's requirements for knowledge and adaptability.

3. ***Value Expression***: According to Daniel Katz, attitudes reflect and express the core values of a person, and an individual doesn't have to exert much effort to articulate them while holding the corresponding attitude. In the life of a civil servant, numerous situations arise where their attitude provides others with sufficient information about how they will perform their duties.

Their attitude conveys not only who they are but also establishes their identity in terms of their personal values like integrity, patriotism, non-partisanship, transparency, etc.

4. ***Knowledge Function***: Attitude also helps in acquiring the right kind of knowledge based on requirement. In a world crammed with information, when confronted with an overload of data, individuals benefit significantly from an attitude that directs their focus towards particular subjects and aids them in filtering knowledge they can use. People's attitudes restrict others (senders or sources) from providing unnecessary information while encouraging them to give desired information. Certain attitudes thus contribute to make this world more knowable and predictable, and help us ascribe causes to events and direct our attention towards the characteristics of people and circumstances. For instance, stereotyping can be seen as an example of the knowledge function of attitude, as stereotypes are mental structures that allow us to predict the features of people and things in the world around us.

ATTITUDE AND BEHAVIOUR

Our behaviour, as mentioned above, is intricately linked to our attitudes. The extent to which behaviour conforms to attitude and their interrelationship has been a longstanding area of interest and research in social psychology. In the early 1930s, Richard LaPiere conducted several pioneering studies on this question, focusing on how ethnicity and race impact social norms and social psychology.

When Does Attitude Guide Behaviour?

We have seen that attitude and behaviour have some correlation, which depends upon certain factors. These factors are known as *moderating* factors because they moderate the relation between attitude and behaviour. Some of these moderating factors are: qualities of the attitude, behaviour, person, situation, time pressure and attitude accessibility.

Qualities of the Behaviour

The behaviour that a social psychologist might seek to predict based on knowledge of a person's attitudes can range from the very specific (e.g., deciding to provide an arms licence to Mr A due to his specific circumstances) to the very general (e.g., refusing to provide arms licences to anyone). In an influential analysis, Ajzen and Fishbein (1977) emphasised the importance of measuring attitudes and behaviour at an equivalent level of specificity. A specific behaviour is best predicted by an attitudinal question that is specific to the action in question, the target of the action, the context (e.g., a senior officer's personal recommendation to provide the arms licence in the case of Mr A), and the timing of the action (e.g., obtaining an annual confidential report from the senior officer who referred Mr A's case).

Conversely, a general pattern of behaviour is best predicted by a general attitude measure. In one study, the participants' overall attitude towards 'being religious' was used to predict the likelihood of their performing each of 100 specific religious behaviours (e.g., praying before or after meals, donating money to a religious institution, etc.), along with a general measure of engaging in religious behaviours that served as a composite measurement of the 100 specific religious behaviours (Fishbein and Ajzen 1975).

We will try to understand the correlation between attitude and behaviour with the help of Table 6.1. These correlations between the general attitude towards arms licences and any specific single action (special case of Mr A) will remain low. In contrast, the correlation between attitude and the general behaviour pattern (i.e., to reject all arm licence applications) will be high. On the other hand, the correlation between specific attitude (to grant very few licences in rare cases) and specific behaviour (to release the licence) will remain high.

Table 6.1: Attitude–behaviour correlation

Attitude	Behaviour	Correlation
General	Specific	Low
Specific	Specific	High
General	General	High

Source: Created by authors.

Qualities of the Person

In addition, certain individuals consistently exhibit greater attitude–behaviour consistency than others. Generally, two types of individuals are considered: those who know and are attuned to their internal emotions and are regulated by them; and those who regulate their behaviour based on cues in the external situation and then determine how they should behave. In general, people who are aware of their feelings tend to demonstrate greater attitude–behaviour consistency than those who rely on external situational cues, although this is a broad distinction. Any given behaviour can be guided both by an individual's internal feelings and by external cues.

Several personality scales have been developed and successfully used to assess whether a person tends to rely more heavily on one type of cue or the other. Although important differences exist among the personality traits that have been explored as possible moderators of the attitude–behaviour relation, each of them relates to this general distinction. The level of moral reasoning, for example, has been found to influence the relationship between attitudes and behaviour (Rholes and Bailey 1983). More progressive moral reasoning is characterised by ideals, principled thinking and morally responsible reasoning based on one's own moral principles. Inferior moral reasoning is bound by social and legal norms that emphasise the outcomes of actions. Individuals who rely on their own feelings, values and principles to make moral judgments tend to act more consistently with their attitudes towards moral issues than those who depend on external standards to determine what is moral.

The personality dimension that has received the most attention in the context of the attitude–behaviour issue is *self-monitoring*. Individuals who score low on the self-monitoring scale are seen to be regulated by inner feelings. They believe that their behaviour generally reflects genuine emotions, true attitudes and beliefs. On the other hand, high scorers on the self-monitoring scale view their behaviour as primarily stemming from a pragmatic concern with what is appropriate in each situation. They acknowledge that in different circumstances and with different people, they may act in completely different ways. These individuals monitor the impact they make on others and adjust their actions accordingly to fulfill others' expectations.

Multiple studies have shown that individuals with low self-monitoring tendencies tend to behave more consistently with their attitudes than those with high self-monitoring tendencies (Ajzen, Timko and White 1982; Snyder and Kendzierski 1982; Snyder and Swann 1976; Zanna, Olson and Fazio 1980). For example, in a study examining the relationship between attitudes toward affirmative action and judgments of liability in a simulated sex discrimination case, low self-monitors demonstrated a higher correlation (0.42) between their attitudes and judgments of liability. Conversely, among high self-monitors, the correlation was a negligible 0.03 (Snyder and Swann 1976). This suggests that people who are more focused on their internal selves are inclined to act in accordance with their attitudes. In contrast, individuals influenced and regulated more by external factors are less likely to act according to their attitudes.

Qualities of the Situation

Situational variables can also significantly influence the attitude–behaviour correlation, shaping how attitudes manifest in actual actions in different contexts. These variables incorporate different normative factors including societal norms, social pressure and time pressure to determine decisions. Understanding these situational influences is crucial for understanding the complex interplay between attitudes and behaviour since the dynamic nature of the situations in which individuals find themselves can impact behaviour over and above their attitudes. Some situational variables are discussed below.

1. *The effect of norms*: Norms or beliefs about how one should or is expected to behave in a given situation can exert a powerful influence on behaviour. Fishbein and Ajzen (1975) proposed a model (which we will discuss) that views norms as playing an important role in influencing behaviour. Much evidence has been found to support this view. People often behave in ways that they believe others expect them to behave. Norms can impose constraints on an individual's behaviour to the extent that it becomes unlikely that the person will display behaviour consistent with their attitudes. In fact, societal or group norms may be so strong and universally accepted that individuals may find it difficult to defy them, regardless of their personal attitudes. For example, someone may hold progressive views on gender equality but conform to traditional gender roles in a conservative family or the workplace.

2. *Time pressure*: Individuals are more likely to rely on their attitudes when making decisions under severe time constraints because their attitudes serve as a heuristic for faster decision-making. It appears that time pressure pushes people away from a careful examination of the available information and towards a greater reliance on their preexisting attitudes.

3. *Qualities of the attitude*: An attribute is an attitudinal quality that has been thoroughly imbibed during the process of attitude formation. Attitude formation can occur through direct behavioural experiences with the attitude object, or through indirect and non-behavioural experience with the attitude object. For example, a child may form an attitude towards a toy by playing with the toy (direct experience) or based on descriptions of the toy given by a friend or an advertisement (indirect experience). Attitudes formed through direct experience have been found to be more predictive of subsequent behaviour than attitudes formed through indirect experience. Certain types of attitudes seem to be stronger than others—here, 'stronger' indicates the magnitude of influence that such attitudes exert in guiding behaviour.

4. *Attitude accessibility*: The distinction between direct and indirect attitudes is attributed to the level and quality of accessibility of attitudes from memory. Accessibility here refers to the ease with which a particular attitude comes to mind. Some attitudes effortlessly come to mind without conscious effort, for example, on encountering a tiger, the immediate response is of fear, suggesting highly accessible attitudes stored as responses in our memory. However, considerable deliberation is needed to identify our attitudes towards certain objects, for instance, when asked about the best car or best film or best restaurant, we may need to think to determine our preference; in these cases, the attitude is not readily accessible from memory. Attitudes based on direct experience tend to be more accessible and are expressed more quickly from memory.

5. *Role and identity*: People may act in ways consistent with the expectations associated with their given roles in a particular situation, even if it contradicts their personal attitudes.

6. *Cognitive dissonance*: When individuals experience discomfort due to conflicting

attitudes and behaviour, they may adjust their attitudes to align with their actions. For instance, someone who engages in environmentally harmful behaviour might downplay the importance of environmental conservation to reduce the discomfort caused by the inconsistency.

7. *Availability of resources*: Due to situational constraints and availability of resources individuals may act in ways that are practical or feasible in a given situation.
8. *Immediate gratification vs. long-term goals*: Situational factors may influence individuals to prioritise immediate gratification over long-term goals. For example, someone may have positive attitude toward a healthy lifestyle but choose to indulge in unhealthy eating behaviour in the presence of tempting, easily accessible food.
9. *Environmental cues*: The physical environment and cues in a situation can trigger certain behaviours. For instance, a person with a positive attitude toward recycling may be more likely to do so when recycling bins are readily available and visible.

How Does Attitude Guide Behaviour?

Ajzen and Fishbein's Theory of Reasoned Action

Icek Ajzen and Martin Fishbein's 'theory of reasoned action' is based on the premise that behaviour is not strictly aligned with attitudes; rather, it represents an adjusted attitude shaped by reasoning, including norms, beliefs, and the motivation to possess the attitude in terms of ability. They elaborate that behaviour is propelled by intention, emphasising that people engage in a particular behaviour after a thoughtful consideration of the consequences associated with the intended action. The 'theory of reasoned action' posits that our actions related to social relevance are influenced by volitional control, and the intention to either perform or abstain from a particular behaviour serves as the immediate determinant of action. According to this theory, a person's behavioural intention stands as the single best predictor of their eventual behaviour. The theory delineates two factors taken into account by an individual in shaping their actions:

1. *Attitude towards the behaviour in question*: This is different from an individual's general attitude towards the concerned attitude object.
2. *Subjective norms pertaining to such behaviour*: This includes a person's belief about others' expectations with respect to specific actions s/he should perform and, most importantly, a person's motivation to follow the wishes of others. For example, in deciding for a love marriage, one may consider what their parents think about love marriage as well as how important it is to comply with their wishes.

Richard LaPiere's Study

Richard LaPiere aimed to test how people's attitude towards other races and ethnicities aligns with their behaviour. He sought to understand prejudice towards the ethnic Chinese diaspora in the USA during the 1930s when large-scale immigration triggered strong anti-Chinese prejudices among Americans. He encountered an incident when he, along with his Chinese student, checked into a hotel in a small California town, expecting to be refused accommodation. However, they were provided a room without any hassle. Months later, when LaPiere called the same hotel to inquire if they would provide a room for an important Chinese gentleman, he surprisingly faced a refusal. This incident prompted him to investigate the interplay between attitude and behaviour.

LaPiere, accompanied by his Chinese student and the student's wife, who spoke unaccented American English, embarked on several trips in the US. LaPiere did not disclose his research aims to the Chinese couple. The Chinese couple handled all reservation formalities. Out of 66 hotels they visited, only one rejected them accommodation, and they received good services in most places. They were also never refused service in the 184 restaurants in which they ate. Six months later, LaPiere sent questionnaires to the 251 hotels and restaurants that the Chinese couple and LaPiere had visited over the past two years, asking: 'Will you accept members of the Chinese race as guests in your establishment?' Out of 251, only 128 responded, and surprisingly, 92 per cent of them said 'No'.

The study revealed a significant contrast between what people said and claimed, and their actual behaviour. LaPiere concluded that appearance and self-confidence were more influential in impacting attitude than race. Despite claiming to be racist, the natural behaviour of white Americans towards the Chinese and those of other ethnicities was often contrary. Today, concerns focus more on the opposite pattern: hypocrisy. The key finding of this case study was that attitudes do not always align with actions. A major criticism of this study revolved around the questionnaire, which some felt may have been manipulated by the hotel managements to conceal the true attitudes of their staff. Further, LaPiere himself also concluded that questionnaires were relatively poor and unreliable predictors of how individuals actually responded to real-life people relative to prejudice and discrimination.

Richard LaPiere's study is considered seminal and pioneering even today and continues to be cited in current research by sociologists and social psychologists.

Fazio's Attitude-to-Behaviour Process Model

The theory of reasoned action says that attitudes guide behaviour through deliberate reasoning and considering the implications of actions. In contrast, the *process model* proposed by Russell H. Fazio posits that attitudes can guide someone's behaviour spontaneously, without conscious reasoning. For example, when confronted with a cockroach, we neither consciously consider our knowledge of its filthiness nor deliberate upon what others may think of killing the cockroach. If we engage in such reasoning, the cockroach may disappear before we can decide how to respond to it. In other words, the process model says that an individual's unconscious or spontaneous attitude towards a cockroach may lead them to perceiving the situation as nasty and prompt a response based on this perception.

According to the process model, the precursor of any behaviour shown by an individual is simply their interpretation of the event taking place. This interpretation varies from person to person, indicating two components during the interpretation of any event. The first component is the individual's perception of the attitude object in the current situation, and the second is the definition of the situation or event. The perception of the attitude object in a situation shapes the definition of that situation/event and assigns meaning to the impact of attitude. The process model views attitude as a bridge between the attitude object and an individual's evaluation of that object, determining the level of accessibility of the attitude from memory.

The strength of the connection between the attitude object and a person's evaluation of the object varies from case to case. The association is stronger when the evaluation is immediate and spontaneous upon encountering the attitude object. This model maintains that the attitude-to-behaviour process depends upon whether the attitude is activated from memory or not. An attitude with a robust object–evaluation linkage is highly accessible from memory and can be activated automatically without much effort upon seeing the attitude object.

The MODE Model: An Integration

We have discussed two different processes of attitude–behaviour interplay. One process emphasises deliberate, planned and reasoned action. The other process focuses on the influence of attitude that does not necessarily manifest as a conscious mental reflection but can stem from the impact of attitude on the perception of the attitude object and the immediate situation, subsequently influencing one's behaviour. The MODE (Motivation, Opportunity and Determination) model integrates both these processes within a single framework encompassing motivation and opportunity. The theory of reasoned action demands thorough cognitive engagement of the mind. This level of mental exertion always requires some motivation to entice individuals to participate in the reasoning process. Motivation becomes imperative in situations where behavioural actions will have significant outcomes. An individual is motivated to carefully engage in the reasoning process when a poor decision is likely to incur substantial costs. However, motivation alone is insufficient to compel an individual to embark on a cumbersome reasoning process; the opportunity to engage in such reasoning is equally crucial. The MODE model argues that the process expounded by the theory of reasoned action occurs when the situation motivates an individual to contemplate the impending action and also provides the opportunity to do so.

According to the MODE model, when an individual is highly motivated and also has the opportunity to deliberate with due care, s/he will pay close attention to the information received from the object of attitude. On the other hand, if the individual lacks sufficient motivation and the opportunity to reflect on the situation, s/he will likely behave based on his/her general attitude rather than under any influence. Results from various experiments align with the predictions of the MODE model. In general, when both motivational factors and opportunity for careful deliberation are high, an individual engaged in such endeavours needs to draw specific details from memory.

Experiments conducted on the MODE model demonstrate that decisions are made rapidly, and behaviour can be assessed based on the generally accessible apparent attitude. However, the accessible apparent attitude is not effective in predicting behaviour when reasoning and deliberation play a major role in decision-making.

ATTITUDE FORMATION AND ATTITUDE CHANGE

Attitude formation has remained a favoured subject among psychologists. Attitudes, as we have seen, are products of learning through diverse mediums of experience. In other words, the A-B-C components are constructed through various means of knowledge acquisition (direct or indirect) and interactions with others, and this process gives birth to a specific attitude. This process includes learning through association, reinforcement through rewards or punishment, observational learning (modelling), adherence to cultural norms (ethics) and gathering information about the object. The factors influencing attitude formation include:

1. Family and educational background
2. Reference groups
3. Personal experiences
4. Media

The process of attitude formation also paves way for attitude change. Attitudes that are nascent, immature and weaker are more susceptible to change than those that are stable or well established. There are three major theories related to attitude change:

1. Theory of Balance
2. Theory of Cognitive Dissonance
3. Two Step Theory

Theory of Balance

The theory of balance was propounded by Fritz Heider, who explained the concept through the 'P-O-X' triangle which depicts the three aspects of attitude. These are: the person P who is the subject of study for attitude, another person O and the attitude object X with reference to which O would study the attitude of P. The idea behind this study is related to the imbalance between attitudes that would take place during P–O, O–X and P–X interactions. Imbalance occurs when all three sides of the triangle P-O-X are in a configuration other than having all three sides positive or having two sides negative and one side positive.

Table 6.2: P-O-X Triangle

P–O	O–X	P–X	
+	+	+	Balanced
–	+	+	Unbalanced
+	–	–	Balanced
+	–	+	Unbalanced

Source: Created by authors.

We can understand this by an example of attitude towards firearms that is here represented by X (see Table 6.2). Let's say a person P wants to secure a firearms licence (P–X positive). He applies for this before an appropriate authority O who holds a negative attitude towards firearms (O–X negative). Characteristics of the attitude P–O and how the situation would achieve balance or imbalance in different conditions are explained below. Suppose authority O likes person P, then the following matrix would form. In this scenario, one of the three attitudes should change to bring about balance. This change could occur if P–X becomes negative (P starts disliking firearms), or O–X becomes positive (the licence issuing authority starts liking firearms). In other words, an attitude change may be caused due to all positive relationships, or two negative relationships and one positive relationship (in this case P's negative attitude towards firearms).

Theory of Cognitive Dissonance

This theory was promulgated by American psychologist Leon Festinger—widely recognised as the father of modern social psychology, akin to Sigmund Freud in clinical psychology and Jean Piaget in developmental psychology. The cognitive dissonance theory emphasises the importance of achieving consonance or rational, logical alignment between the different cognitive components related to an attitude. If any of these components show dissonance, there is a tendency for them to be brought into order through attaining consonance. For example:

> Cognition 1: Firearms may become the cause of suicide.
>
> Cognition 2: I like firearms.

To achieve consonance, one of the above two cognitions has to change. Thus, the balance theory and the cognitive dissonance theory are interrelated within the framework of cognitive consistency. Cognitive consistency asserts that components or aspects of an attitude must be aligned and logically supportive of each other. If this consistency is disrupted, individuals may experience mental discomfort and conflict and perceive that something is wrong. To alleviate this discomfort, efforts are made to establish logical consistency in order to attain cognitive consistency.

Two Step Theory

This theory was devised by Indian psychologist S. M. Mohsin, who proposed that attitude change takes place in two distinct steps. First, the target of change is identified with the source. Here *target* is the person whose attitude is to be changed, and *source* is the person whose influence will be used to effect this change. *Identification* implies that the target likes the source and should have positive emotions and affinity towards the source. Likewise, the source should also have a positive attitude and affinity towards the target, thus establishing a mutual liking between them.

In the second step, the source begins to exhibit a changed attitude towards the attitude object. This shift in attitude is then reflected in the target imitating the source as the target emulates the source's attitude towards the attitude object and alter their own perspective and behaviour in a manner similar to the source.

FACTORS CONTROLLING ATTITUDE CHANGE

The degree of change in attitude depends upon the characteristics of attitude, such as positive or negative valence, extremeness, simplicity and centrality of attitude towards the respective target object of change. It is relatively easier to induce change when a person holds a positive attitude as compared to altering a negative attitude in a similar situation. Extreme attitudes and those with greater centrality are more resistant to change, while attitudes characterised by simplicity are more susceptible to change.

Change in attitude also tends to follow the direction of the previously held attitude. In other words, if one holds a positive attitude about something, it is more likely to change in a favourable direction and become even more positive. This is equally true of negative attitudes, that is, a negative attitude may easily become more negative if the change moves in a favourable direction. This phenomenon is known as *congruent change* in attitude. However, attitude change may also be *incongruent* and occur in the opposite direction of the valence, but achieving this demands considerable effort.

Information provided in favour of the attitude object typically contributes to a positive change in attitude towards that object. However, information that induces excessive fear or revulsion may lead the recipient to disregard it altogether, resulting in little or no change. The *source* of the information or message plays a crucial role in attitude change. If the source is perceived as credible, reliable and attractive, the likelihood of influencing change increases. The *content* of the message also impacts the degree of change. The effectiveness of the message in influencing change is determined by its content—it must strike a balance between providing sufficient information without overwhelming or underwhelming the recipient. An ideal message incorporates both rational and emotional appeals to capture the receiver's attention. The *purpose* embedded in the message further influences the receiver's response. The *mode of communication* from source to receiver, whether direct or indirect, impacts the extent of attitude change. Generally, direct communication is more convincing and effective than indirect methods. The *nature of the recipient*, including persuasiveness, biases, self-esteem and rational capability, also shapes the degree of change in their attitude. Individuals who are reserved, rigid, not very open to other people or ideas, stubborn and highly logical are less susceptible to change as compared to those who are open, flexible and less governed by strict logic.

METHODS OF ATTITUDE CHANGE

Classical or Pavlovian Conditioning

Russian scientist Ivan Pavlov (1849–1936) dedicated his research to studying the digestive system of mammals, particularly dogs. Through meticulous observations, he documented the factors influencing canine salivation, a process vital for food digestion. While Pavlov initially focused on the physiological aspects of digestion, an intriguing psychological dimension emerged. He noticed that the dogs not only salivated in response to the presence of food, a natural unconditioned stimulus, but also displayed the same reaction when they saw the white lab coats worn by those who regularly fed them. This observation led to a groundbreaking experiment in behavioural science. In this experiment, Pavlov paired a neutral stimulus, a ringing bell, with the presentation of food. Remarkably, the dogs soon began to associate the ringing bell with food and started salivating in response to the bell alone.

This behavioural phenomenon, known as *classical conditioning*, prompted Pavlov to formulate his conclusions. He identified two types of stimuli: the *unconditioned stimulus* (food) and the *neutral stimulus* (bell). While the neutral stimulus, in isolation, did not elicit the unconditioned response of drooling, its consistent association with food taught the dogs to link the bell with the impending presence of food. Over time, the bell alone came to evoke salivation, a response termed *conditioned response*. Pavlov's experiment highlighted the distinction between unconditioned responses, which are innate and unlearned, and conditioned responses, which are acquired through repeated observations and associations.

Direct Experience

The construction and acquisition of knowledge relies on direct experiences perceived through the senses. Direct experience stands out as the most fundamental and explicit method for forming attitudes toward an object, and has a profound impact, capable of consistently evoking attitudes in the same manner as during the initial encounter with the object. In an experiment, participants engaged in playing puzzles for the first time, creating a robust direct experience. Conversely, another group was provided with puzzles previously solved by others, resulting in a weaker direct experience. When participants were later asked to rate the interest level of the puzzles, the findings revealed that attitudes formed through direct experience were stronger predictors of actual behaviour compared to those formed through indirect experience (Regan and Fazio 1977).

Fazio and his colleagues argued that the strong correlation between direct experience and behaviour arises because attitudes formed through direct experiences are more easily retrievable from permanent memory. While repeatedly expressing or reporting attitudes may appear analogous to direct experience, the latter does not contribute as strongly to attitude–behaviour correspondence when the bases for attitude and behaviour are not aligned. For example, an attitude formed based on the pleasure of playing video games may not necessarily translate into a career choice in designing video games.

Under similar conditions, direct experience stimulates the use of resulting attitudes as a foundation for future behaviour. However, direct experience may sometimes yield mixed evidence regarding the desirability of an object. In today's era of virtual reality, virtual experiences play an inevitable role. For example, individuals can explore computer-based imaging of different hairstyles without undergoing a haircut at a salon to form an attitude towards a particular hairstyle. Griffith and Chen (2004) highlight the impact of digital advertisements on products like movies and music, which, when presented in a digital format, can create an impact similar to that of direct experience.

Mere Exposure

Mere exposure is a phenomenon in which an attitude towards a given stimulus becomes more favourable with increasing frequency of exposure to that stimulus (Zajonc 1968). In the classic example of the mere exposure paradigm, native English participants were shown unknown Chinese characters from 0 to 20 five times. Participants liked the characters better when they were exposed to them more frequently (ibid.). In another study, participants subliminally presented with 10 different polygons were later asked to indicate which one of two polygons they had been shown earlier they preferred. Recognition of the polygons was just below chance (48%), but preference for old polygons was substantially higher (60%) than chance (Kunst-Wilson, Raft and Zajonc 1980).

Numerous studies have been conducted to examine the mere exposure effect. A meta-analysis summarising 208 empirical studies from 134 articles published between 1968 and 1987 (Bornstein 1989) obtained a moderate effect size. The mere exposure effect was seen to be true across a range of stimuli, including sounds, ideographs, nonsense words/syllables, photographs, meaningful words/names, polygons and real people/objects. The effect tended to be stronger when a heterogeneous versus homogenous pool of stimuli was presented, when exposure times were shorter, when there was delay between stimulus exposure and evaluation, and when participants were adults instead of children aged 12 or under. A more recent meta-analysis synthesised growth curves from 118 studies which yielded 268 curves. Their general finding across different models was a positive slope, suggesting that higher exposure frequencies were associated with increased liking, recognition and familiarity. In the overall model, this effect corresponded to an increase of 0.23 points on a scale of 0–100 for each additional exposure (0.17 points when liking was the only dependent variable). The same model also showed evidence of an inverted U-shaped curvilinear effect, suggestive of habituation effects that occur after many exposures. Whereas R. F. Bornstein (1989) found that the mere exposure effect was highest when participants were exposed to stimuli no more than 9 times, the maximum of the inverted U-shape in Montoya et al. (2017) was always larger than 10 and, across sub-analyses, more often fell between 20 and 75.

Various theories have attempted to explain the mechanisms underlying the mere exposure effect. One prominent explanation—the *perceptual fluency/misattribution account*—suggests that the ease of perceiving and processing previously encountered stimuli is misattributed as liking. This account is considered more parsimonious and widely accepted. According to it, individuals, when exposed to stimuli they have encountered before, may develop an increased liking for those stimuli due to the misattribution of perceptual fluency. If liking is indeed influenced by misattributed perceptual fluency, individuals should either discount or over-discount the impact of irrelevant fluency on learning the true source of the fluency. For example, participants have been seen to make negative adjustments in evaluating previously seen stimuli when led to believe that they have seen it before.

Recent research has, however, raised some scepticism on the perceptual fluency/misattribution account. Evidence suggests that people generally prefer stimuli that they recognise. The mere exposure process seems to involve at least some intentional cognitive processing. Nonetheless, a meta-analysis by Montoya et al. (2017) found that the mere exposure effect occurs even with exposure durations shorter than 16 ms, a time frame in which conscious recognition or intentional processes are not expected to occur. Moreover, evidence suggests that the effect extends to novel stimuli and positively affects mood, neither of which phenomena can be fully explained by the perceptual fluency/misattribution hypothesis, but can be explained by fluency more generally.

The Role of Fluency

The role of fluency in evaluative judgments is proposed to be potentially independent of intentional information processing. According to the *hedonic fluency model*, perceptual and/or conceptual fluency may or may not be consciously recognised. Fluency, combined with swift and effortless mental processing, leads to positive affect detectable even with physiological measurement. This positive affect may influence evaluative judgments of previously seen stimuli, new stimuli, self-reported affect and physiologically-measured mood.

A meta-analysis of 90 studies examining the effect of perceptual fluency on affective judgments revealed a medium effect size. The effect was moderated by participants' awareness of the experimental manipulation. Participants who were aware of this tended to discount fluency and relied on other inputs to form attitudes. Additionally, neutral and positive stimuli produced larger fluency effects than negative stimuli.

More recently, an embodied account has been proposed to explain the mere exposure effect, arguing that the fluency responsible for increased liking of repeated stimuli comes from specific motor responses associated with such stimuli. The idea is that specific sensory organs such as eyes, mouths, hands register and remember fluency when processing stimuli, and this embodied fluency is later activated to make judgments about the stimuli. Therefore, preventing people from registering embodied fluency and from retrieving it when they make judgments about the stimuli may decrease the mere exposure effect. For example, asking participants to perform a secondary oral motor task when repeatedly presented with names of actors decreases the mere exposure effect for those names. Chewing gum while evaluating stimuli eliminates mere exposure effects for words but not for visual characters (Topolinski and Strack 2009).

Evaluative Conditioning

Evaluative conditioning (EC) shares some similarities with Pavlovian or classical conditioning, which takes place when a conditioned stimulus (CS) is consistently present together with the unconditioned stimulus (US). However, EC differs from classical conditioning in several aspects. Classical conditioning demands sufficient awareness of both conditioned and unconditioned stimuli CS and US as well as their coexistence, while EC may take place with or without such awareness. For example, if an individual doesn't know that an electric shock always follows the ringing bell, they would not evolve a cringe response to the ringing bell. In contrast, EC may occur with or without such knowledge. Moreover, EC is said to be goal-dependent and may rely on the goals activated during the process. EC also differs from Pavlovian in terms of the sustenance of the CS-US pairing: classical conditioning diminishes once this coexistence is removed, while evaluative conditioning persists even after 5 to 10 repetitions of the CS without pairing with the US.

Social Judgment Theory

Social judgment is a process that involves adjusting one's attitude based on the attitudes prevalent in the surrounding social environment. Social judgment theory posits that attitude change occurs as a response to our perception of our social context. When a communication aligns closely with the recipient's existing attitude, individuals tend to move closer to the position advocated in the message, striving to harmonise their attitude with that of the communicator. Conversely, in cases of contrast, where the communication deviates significantly from their attitudes, causing a mismatch, people may abruptly shift their original position to adopt a more compatible attitude.

Various considerations come into play regarding the extent of attitude change allowed within the framework of social judgment. The degree of attitude change depends on the range of acceptance of the advocated communication within the social milieu. If the information falls within the accepted domain of an individual, the attitude aligns accordingly. However, in cases of contrast, where the information is outside the accepted domain, the attitude remains unchanged.

Selective Exposure

Selective exposure is a psychological hypothesis that refers to the propensity to endorse information or communication that complies with preexisting perceptions, while completely disregarding contrasting or unfavourable evidence. Also known as 'congeniality bias' or 'confirmation bias', this tendency leads individuals to selectively choose specific aspects of given information based on their objectives, attitudes, previous beliefs and past decisions with respect to the object of information. Despite the widespread availability of strong arguments and convincing evidence aimed at inducing attitude change, the process of selective exposure acts as a deterrent to change. It defends the original attitude by deliberately overlooking and ignoring information likely to challenge it, while actively seeking favourable information. This behaviour stems from people's search for internal congruence and satisfaction, and any incongruence causes dissatisfaction and disharmony.

Selective exposure suggests that individuals harbour a fear of altering their original beliefs about themselves, others and the world in general. This theory is closely related to the theory of cognitive dissonance, which emphasises that when confronted with contrasting and conflicting ideas, certain mental defence mechanisms come into play to defend preexisting beliefs and attitudes. These defence mechanisms work to establish harmony or cognitive equilibrium between personal mental images and information received from the social milieu.

Cognitive Dissonance

The theory of cognitive dissonance (discussed earlier), as proposed by Leon Festinger, provides the basis for understanding the process of selective exposure. Here, *dissonance* represents a psychological state of stress that individuals naturally strive to reduce, aiming to make life more comfortable and free of conflict. Festinger posits that the recognition of contrasting attitudes, information or beliefs leads to mental stress or discomfort. Individuals inherently seek to avoid any potential discomfort arising from conflicting information. The conflict between preexisting thoughts and new, contrasting information generates a state of psychological discomfort and self-threatening aversion that motivates individuals to reduce it through selective exposure to information. People tend to selectively prefer information that supports their original position and beliefs, and disregard information that contradicts it. Further, they may present selective information that confirms and supports their initial stance, actively working towards the goal of reducing cognitive dissonance. In simpler words, we usually see and believe what we ultimately *choose* to see and believe.

GOALS AND ATTITUDE CHANGE

Changes in original attitude or the formation of a new attitude are influenced by a variety of goals and motives. These goals may include the motivation to be correct and consistent, to have knowledge of a just world, avoiding uncertainty and ambiguity, and ultimately it is related to avoiding excessive involvement in cognitive exercises. These goals may be either specific or general. Once a specific goal is activated, it directs an individual's attention towards information that aligns with that goal. Individuals inclined to maintain status quo and adhere to their original stance prefer information that confirms and supports their existing attitude, while those motivated to challenge status quo prefer information that contradicts or challenges their existing stance.

In the case of general behavioural goals, once activated, they exhibit an astonishing and robust impact on attitude change. *General action goals* are goals with end states at the extremes of the continuum of activity level—either high or low motor and cognitive output. For example, people primed via subliminal or supraliminal exposure to action-related words like *move*, *go* and *walk* show higher levels of cognitive and physical activity, such as doodling, exercising longer, taking more nutrition and solving a larger number of mathematical exercises, as compared with those exposed to inaction-related words like *stand*, *still* and *calm*. The initiation of an action goal increases cognitive efforts when one is confronted by a persuasive message. The action goal facilitates the retrieval of the original attitude that may, in turn, resist the process of attitude change. People primed via general action goals are found to be agile and adept in conscious recollection of prior attitudes, hindering the process of attitude change.

MORAL, POLITICAL AND BUREAUCRATIC ATTITUDES

Moral Attitude

A moral attitude is an attitude or orientation towards a moral entity which determines how an individual is predisposed to fulfill a moral obligation. Like any other attitude, a moral attitude comprises three components: affective/emotional, cognitive/knowledge and behavioural. To illustrate, when faced with a situation where a beggar asks us for money, emotions like guilt, pity and empathy may arise, guided by humanitarian considerations, reflecting the emotional component. Simultaneously, our knowledge of laws against begging might deter us from helping, constituting the cognitive component. Lastly, the behavioural component could manifest in charity and contributing to NGOs working for the rehabilitation of beggars.

Moral attitudes are propelled by emotions like philanthropy, pity, guilt, love and aesthetic sense. They are also grounded in knowledge derived from deontology, teleology, meta-ethics, and are manifested through behaviours such as social service, sacrifice, altruism and charity for social causes. While moral attitudes are generally intrinsic, they may become extrinsic in ethical dilemmas. Moral attitudes are typically stable in individuals and do not change frequently, although variations may occur from person to person and case to case.

Political Attitude

Political attitude can be defined as an individual's political behaviour shaped by their knowledge of the political environment and emotional judgment of a particular political system. It serves as a crucial indicator for understanding the political functioning, performance and evaluation by citizens. The development of political attitudes in a nation and among its citizens is influenced by its political processes, such as the evolution of democratic, socialist or Nazi ideologies in various historical contexts like India, Russia, China and Germany.

Governments primarily function to provide goods and services to citizens, and the increasing choices in the quality of these offerings have raised political awareness among common citizens. Citizens now actively seek information about the political system's content, structure and processes to make informed decisions about their self-interest and choose appropriate political leadership. However, political awareness is not uniformly distributed, and a significant portion of the working population remains politically ignorant, lacking defined attitudes toward various political issues.

Philip E. Converse (1964) suggests that support for the Nazi party in Germany was largely among uneducated and illiterate peasants or uninformed citizens. Even in modern times, major political parties exploit the lack of political knowledge among certain demographics. Periodic elections provide citizens with the opportunity to replace a government that serves its own interests or is tyrannical. Normative models of democracy emphasise the importance of a politically well-informed and participatory citizenry. While individual citizens may lack political knowledge, small groups such as trade unions, pressure groups and civic associations contribute to creating political awareness. Although individuals may exhibit ignorance, rationality prevails in groups and citizens vote according to that rationality, irrespective of broader political perspectives. Political information and voting behaviour are influenced by both identity and rational choice. Citizens seek fulfilment of their orientation for a political party through identification, and powerful party bonds impact voting behaviour.

Joseph Schumpeter (1943) and E. E. Schattschneider (1942) rejected notions of the 'common good' and the 'will of the people' as romantic fallacies, and proposed the concept of a 'competitive elite democracy', arguing that citizens have a limited role in the political system and only exercise their influence through periodic voting. Competent elites, democratically elected by citizens, govern the state according to them.

Political Spectrum: It is a model that classifies political ideologies, political parties and their representatives in a two-dimensional way in order to delineate the differences between them. The political spectrum originated during the French Revolution when different political ideologies based on social, political and economic characteristics came to be prioritised, and the spectrum broadly represents these along the left and right axes, as seen in Figure 6.4.

Figure 6.4: Political spectrum

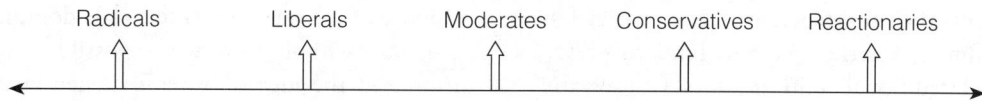

Source: Created by authors.

The left–right political axes were first observed during the meeting of the French National Assembly in Versailles in 1789. Revolutionaries sat on the left side of the assembly, forming one group, while supporters of the French king were grouped on the right. Leftists advocated for egalitarianism, while Rightists upheld traditional values and a hierarchical structure of administration. L. L. Thurstone made pioneering contributions to describing the political spectrum, drawing on the political environment of America. He outlined the axes as radicalism–conservatism and nationalism–internationalism, which were analogous to the early conceptualisations of the political spectrum.

German-British psychologist Hans Eysenck proposed a two-dimensional model of the political spectrum, with one axis representing a radicalism–conservatism spectrum (known as R-axis) and the other axis representing political tender-mindedness and tough-mindedness (known as T-axis). The T-axis was used to allocate levels of authoritarianism in which 'tough-minded' political agents may endorse the use of instruments associated with a totalitarian dictatorial regime, whereas the 'tender-minded' are more inclined towards libertarianism.

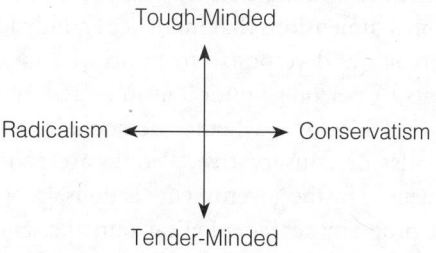

Figure 6.5: Two-dimensional model of political spectrum

Source: Created by authors.

Political Ideologies

Radicalism: A political doctrine adopted by socio-political movements that favour individual and collective liberty, radicalism advocates freedom from authoritarian regimes and hierarchical social structures. Radical political parties have played a principal role in establishing democracy in numerous countries. Radicalists reject the status quo and advocate for political restructuring by removing old and outdated political structures. It is important to note that radicalism is distinct from extremism as both refer to socio-political forces at the margins of liberal-democratic societies. Radicalists may use political violence pragmatically and limitedly, but extremists consider violence against those with opposing views as a legitimate political instrument. While radicalists don't oppose democratic ideals, extremists often don't associate with liberal-democratic societies.

Liberalism: A political ideology that holds liberty as its principal political view, liberalism places a high value on individual liberty, equality of opportunity and the rule of law. Liberals believe that humans are naturally free to decide their actions as rational individuals. A liberal state typically adopts the principles of a constitution and democracy. Liberals believe in protecting civil liberties, supporting democratic institutions and promoting social justice. Liberalism is often associated with the centre-left or centre-right of the political spectrum, depending on specific social and economic policy positions.

Moderate or Centrism: A political stance that rejects both radical and extreme (reactionary) views. Moderates occupy a central position on the left–right axes of the political spectrum, and are hence also called centrists.

Conservatism: In contrast to liberals, conservatives are right-wing anti-federalists. They prefer lesser government interference and tend to preserve old and traditional political values. Conservatives oppose progressive ideas such as multiculturalism, gay marriage and abortion.

Reactionary: Reactionaries are individuals who oppose political change and seek to restore previously existing traditional, usually regressive and outdated social and cultural values. Positioned on the extreme right of the political spectrum, reactionaries are described as extreme right-wing populists and ultra-nationalists.

Socialism: A system of social and political organisation in which the means of production and distribution of goods are owned and controlled collectively by the people or by the government. Socialism stands in contrast to ***capitalism***, which is an economic system where the means of production are privately owned, and the free market determines production of all goods and services, prices and distribution. In capitalism, profit is the primary determinant of all economic activity.

Communism: Communism espouses community ownership of property aiming for social equality through economic equality. Communism argues for a classless, stateless society free of exploitation, oppression and domination, where each individual owns their own labour and any profit produced by that labour belongs to the individual.

Fascism: A totalitarian political system under a dictator who forcefully controls a nation by total suppression of all liberties, regimenting all economic and social activities. Aggressive nationalism is a defining characteristic of fascism, and it stands in direct opposition to Marxist socialism.

Anarchism: A political ideology that questions state authority and emphasises civil liberty and freedom from all forms of state domination, embodying the idea of 'rule by no one' or non-rule. According to Mikhail Bakunin (1873), the existence of the state guarantees class domination and a state without slavery is impossible. Gandhi introduced the idea of an enlightened anarchy, asserting that the people's sovereignty is based on the pure moral authority of the individual. Gandhi's philosophy of anarchism is reflected in his concept of *satyagraha*, based on the 'law of conscience and truth' as above all laws, using which he challenged the British Raj.

The Formation of Political Attitude

Every society establishes a system of governance, to administer, maintain law and order and harmony. Political attitudes are formed through a process involving the history of nation-building, the development of political systems, and national values. In India, for example, individual political attitudes are significantly influenced by the roles of political parties and associated agencies in the freedom struggle, constitution-making processes and major historical events.

Political attitudes tend to be rigid and resistant to change, making it challenging to influence them through campaigns or allurement. The initial political orientation often begins in the family, and attitudes shaped in childhood toward a political ideology or party can persist into adulthood. This is evident in political families where political ideologies and attitudes pass from generation to generation, with rare instances of successors differing from their ancestors. Beyond the family, an individual's political leanings are influenced by their surroundings, including friend circles, social groups and the charisma of political leaders.

Political attitudes encompass both emotional and rational dimensions that influence an individual's approach and response to political issues and events. A person's political attitude reflects their political ideology, whether democratic, radical, socialist or conservative. People are generally influenced by the government's actions, its policies and programmes, ideological pursuits, and the response and views of the country's media, the intelligentsia and the international community. While few are experts at analysing the performance of the political leadership and government, many external factors shape the attitudes of the masses. Factors influencing the political attitudes of the masses play a crucial role in determining the next government and the nation's future leadership. Sometimes these attitudes become so intrinsic that predicting the future political scenario of a nation becomes challenging.

Mass media, social networking forums, newspapers, TV and radio are the major sources of political information. Accurate and informed adjustment of political attitudes depends much upon the honest role played by these agencies. People are also influenced by the political environment of the workplace, peer groups, functioning of the bureaucracy, and views expressed by political leaders. Additionally, religious groups, social activist groups, cultural groups and various interest groups representing specific communities, professions, businesses or activities also influence people's political attitudes.

In India majority of the population is deprived of information that could lead to informed political choices and attitudes. Many people are compelled by pressure groups to exhibit a specific political behaviour in a specific fashion. Women in India are often denied a congenial environment to discuss and form their personal political attitudes, with their voting behaviour frequently being decided by male family members. Similarly, backward and poor people, minorities and other vulnerable groups may be influenced and pressurised using financial and other aid, or by threats, and their political behaviour is greatly controlled and manipulated by those in power. Crowds gathered to hear the public speech of a politician are not always due to the people's motivation but because they are amassed and brought to the rally in the name of various allurements or pressures.

Functions of political attitude formation include the following:

1. Public political attitudes play a crucial role in maintaining a healthy and robust political culture in the state. They facilitate the transfer of political culture and values from one generation to the next, contributing to the continuity and evolution of societal norms.
2. Political attitudes, starting at the individual level, have the potential to shape the collective outlook of society, leading to major change. This is instrumental in fostering democratic values in the polity, and in keeping governments accountable and answerable to their citizens.
3. Political attitudes serve as indicators that reflect the need for change or the continuation of governing principles.
4. Political attitudes provide insight into public opinion and preferences, guiding decision-makers in evaluating the efficacy of existing governance structures.

Bureaucratic Attitude

The term bureaucracy is derived from the Latin word *bureau*, meaning desk, and the Greek word *cracy* or *kratia*, meaning rule. Bureaucracy may be defined as a hierarchical system where decisions are made at different levels based on the delegation of power according to established rules. The popular understanding of a bureaucracy draws heavily from the Weberian model. Max Weber compared a bureaucratic system to a machine, positing that administrative efficiency and effectiveness could be compromised unless the bureaucracy becomes neutral and emotionless like a machine.

According to Peter M. Blau, bureaucracy is a kind of 'organisation designed to accomplish large-scale administrative tasks by systematically coordinating the works of many individuals.' Bureaucratic attitude may be reflected as:

1. Consistent adherence to official business strictly as per the duties and powers assigned to each individual post.

2. Zero response to any requests that fall outside the jurisdiction of that official authority.
3. Maintaining a politically neutral attitude while working with political executives.
4. Conducting all business on the basis of written documents and file work.
5. Clear exposition of hierarchical authority and power.

Bureaucracy in India

Bureaucracy, particularly in India, is characterised as a traditional bureaucracy that draws heavily from the Weberian model. It is not designed to accommodate people's aspirations but rigidly follows rules and policies irrespective of the final outcome. There are various factors influencing such a modus operandi which are beyond the scope of this discussion. The most striking feature of a bureaucratic attitude is *red-tapism*: a fastidious system of administrative decision-making on paper following a strictly hierarchical file movement and strict adherence to rules and policies. Bureaucracy is committed to and prioritises procedure over and above goals. However, this attitude needs positive change to maintain checks and balances between political executives and the bureaucracy.

Bureaucrats often tend to resist change to protect their self-interest, especially when these changes threaten their extant work culture or compel them to acquire new skills. The failure of new initiatives in administrative reform is due to bureaucratic behaviour. This bureaucratic attitude is a by-product of the government's administrative system, influenced by political interests and various related constraints, micromanagement at different levels, and the myopic self-interest-driven attitude of bureaucrats themselves.

The bureaucratic attitude can be explained under two theories which provide the basis for understanding bureaucratic behaviour. The *first theory* describes bureaucracy by laying emphasis on rational decision-making within economic and organisational perspectives. This theory highlights bureaucratic attitude by considering the behaviour of individual bureaucrats rather than as a group. Individually, a bureaucrat operates based on bounded rationality, attempting to maximise self-interests within certain constraints and a complex professional environment. Here, self-interest pertains to the type of organisation bureaucrats work for and their personal values. Self-interest comprises factors such as salary and facilities, promotions, reputation, status, efficiency, impact, convenience, luxury, ease of government functions, low transparency and minimal political interference.

The *second theory* portrays bureaucracy as an institution and ethos primarily drawn from public administration literature. This theory defines bureaucratic attitude as exhibiting a sense of superiority, being a power centre and dictatorial behaviour. Bureaucrats often harbour a strong sense of being the controlling authority and decision-maker. In India, some IAS officers, for example, hold a conceited view of being in a superior service in terms of importance, status and authority. This attitude also prevails in other services where generalists consider themselves more important than specialists, irrespective of their performance and efficiency.

The roots of the Indian bureaucratic attitude can be traced to the colonial legacy of civil services. After Independence, the Indian Constitution introduced provisions to safeguard civil servants—a measure that was deemed essential for ensuring the fearless and efficient execution of administrative affairs and for maintaining political neutrality in making and executing decisions. Bureaucrats play a crucial role in assisting political executives in governance, and their political neutrality is vital for ensuring the just and equitable distribution of welfare across all sections of society. It is imperative for bureaucrats to have adequate safeguards in place to protect them from potential political interference in times of crisis and conflict. Article 309 to Article 323 of the Indian Constitution outline provisions to address this requirement.

In Britain, traditionally, a servant of the British Crown would remain in office at the pleasure of the Crown—also referred to as the 'doctrine of pleasure'. The Crown was not obliged to provide security of service or tenure to a public servant. However, the operation of the doctrine of pleasure was modified in modern governance. In India, the president appoints a public servant at the centre, and the governor appoints one at the state level. Legislative measures related to employment security, labour relations and social security have restricted the doctrine of pleasure. This shift has led to the introduction of safeguards for public servants against arbitrary actions, fostering a sense of fearlessness and ensuring bureaucratic neutrality and efficiency. However, the high degree of security afforded to established civil servants is occasionally susceptible to misuse, contributing to the growth of certain negative bureaucratic attitudes. The various Constitutional safeguards available to civil servants include:

1. Restrictions on the doctrine of pleasure.
2. Applicability of Article 311 to permanent as well as temporary public servants.
3. Exclusion of Article 311(2).
4. Provision of sovereign immunity through Article 300(1).

Article 311 provides civil servants effective protection against arbitrary actions that may lead to their dismissal from their post. Article 311(1) states: 'No person holding a civil post under the Union or the States shall be "dismissed", "removed" or "reduced" in rank except after an inquiry in which he has been informed of the charges against him and given a reasonable opportunity of being heard in respect of those charges.' While 'dismissal' and 'removal' are synonymous here, they have different legal consequences. In case of 'dismissal', one is completely debarred from future employment in the government, whereas in the case of 'removal', one is not debarred from future government employment. If a government servant is duly suspended by an appropriate authority, the suspension is not considered a punishment. Compulsory retirement has also become a means to evade departmental inquiry because compulsory retirement is not considered a punishment, and various pecuniary benefits of a civil servant being retired are protected.

Several provisions of the Criminal Procedure Code (CrPC)—including Sections 45(1), 132(1), and 197—restrict the jurisdiction of both civil and criminal courts in cases involving human rights violations committed by public servants or members of the Armed Forces while acting, or purporting to act, in discharge of their duties. Courts are barred from exercising their authority unless they receive prior approval from the government itself. The recently added Section 17(A) of the new Prevention of Corruption (Amendment) Act 2018 stipulates that: 'No police officer shall conduct any inquiry or investigation into any offence alleged to have been committed by a public servant under this Act, where the alleged offence is related to any recommendation made or decision taken by such public servant in discharge of his official functions or duties, without prior approval.'

PERSUASION AS A MODEL OF BELIEF CORRECTION FOR ATTITUDE CHANGE

Attitude change is a challenging phenomenon with an abysmally low success rate as it cannot be achieved simply by providing new information about the object of attitude. The prevalent understanding is that old existing attitudes strongly resist change, and persuasion often fails. What lies behind this stubborn persistence of old attitudes? Why do repeated attempts at persuasion, change and disownment frequently fail to rectify originally held attitudes and beliefs even when all evidence points to their wrongness? We will explore some issues pertaining to these questions. A simple example here is the belief in idol worship: despite accepting the concepts of *nirguna* and *nirakar brahma*, and despite belief in the essential formlessness, oneness and omnipresence of God, idol worshippers do not abandon their steadfast attitude towards idol worship. Persuasion or attitude change is a complex behavioural science that demands a high degree of precision, including considerations such as who is the persuader, the amount of information being conveyed, the content and intent of the message, and the exact timing for implementing persuasion.

An Example of Persuasion: Swachh Bharat Abhiyan

We will attempt to understand how persuasion works with the help of the Community-Led Total Sanitation (CLTS) programme as part of the Indian government's Swachh Bharat Abhiyan to eradicate open defecation, following the methodology devised by Dr Kamal Kar in Bangladesh. It is seen that adults are less likely to engage with an issue in the absence of prior information regarding that issue and its stated goals. Ziva Kunda (1990) suggests that people arrive at desired conclusions by constructing apparent and reasonable justifications for such conclusions. Humans are cognitive misers, requiring considerable motivation to adopt new cognitive mechanisms and change existing ones. The persuasion process unfolds in phases. First, defensive cognition processes actively guard the original attitude and belief, particularly when the self-protective motivation is high and motivation for accuracy is low. A higher, even unreasonable, evidential threshold is often required to modify deeply cherished attitudes and beliefs. Motivated cognition, however, is not the only process that explains the stubborn persistence of old attitudes and beliefs. According to Amos Tversky and Daniel Kahneman (1974), cognitive processes like *anchoring* and *adjustment* are important to understand the resistance and difficulty in changing attitudes and beliefs. The existing attitude and belief play a vital role in establishing an initial anchoring position, and correcting that belief requires an adjustment moving away from this initial position. The adjustment, in terms of deviation from the anchored position to the new correct position, needs confronting misinformation with accurate knowledge.

The process of persuasion towards attitude change unfolds in a phased manner and comprises three major components:

1. Content of persuasive information
2. Source of information
3. Recipient of information

The content of the intended message must be clear and organised to meet the requirement of deviating from the initial anchored position. The content should encompass values such as fear, anxiety, rewards, punishments, etc. The success of persuasion also depends on the volume or length of the message. Some psychologists argue that shorter messages have under-corrective potential, allowing room for auto-rationalisation by the receiver to correct their position, while others support the use of a plethora of over-corrective information, considering humans to be cognitive misers. Both *under-correction* and *over-correction* are possible because accurate adjustment requires rational and factual knowledge about the influence of misinformation. According to N. Epley and T. Gilovich (2006), under-correction or insufficient adjustment is more successful than over-correction because people tend to align gradually, starting with the inferior self-generated value, and culminate their adjustment once a plausible value is reached. Unless individuals are willing to search for a more accurate value, under-correction is likely to be the outcome, explaining the continued influence of misinformation. Past studies on judgment adjustment have mainly focused on under-correction. A recent study by M. J. Telch et al. (2013) found that both under-correction and over-correction are suggestive, depending on the type of information presented. For example, when it comes to corrective positive misinformation about open defecation, recipients overestimate how much correction is needed, which leads to an excessively negative attitude towards open defecation.

Cognitive Factors Influencing Attitude Change

There are various cognitive factors that contribute to the persistence of attitudes, including the generation of explanations about misinformation. The tendency to rationalise and justify the misinformation increases the persistence of the original attitude, whereas the generation of alternatives reduces its persistence. Counterarguments are generated based not only on opposing beliefs but also depend on meta-cognitive experiences that include the reasoning process. The ease or difficulty in processing information is one such meta-cognitive experience. People are more likely to believe in information that is easily accessible and can be brought to mind without effort. Arguments against prior belief are more effective when they are clear, lucid and fluent rather than difficult and non-interconnected. Another meta-cognitive experience involves the ease or difficulty in processing new information. Information that is incongruent or inconsistent with one's prior beliefs is processed less fluently than information that is consistent with one's belief. Fluency signifies congruency, and information that can be processed fluently appears more familiar and true, and solicits less scrutiny. People are more inclined to engage in confirmatory or positive hypothesis testing, favouring reasons for an assertion that might be true rather than false. Individuals are thus likely to elaborate on plausible premises even if they are false, and this confirmatory fallacy decreases our ability to edit past attitudes and beliefs. People are more likely to falsify attitudes and beliefs when supportive arguments are difficult to generate.

Old theories of thinking and reasoning shed light on the cognitive processes leading to revision. The mental model of reasoning states that people construct a web of mental models from which they can draw conclusions. As new information emerges, people may create new models or extend existing ones, but they often hesitate to set aside key information if no plausible alternative emerges to fill the gap. Therefore, providing a causal alternative or a fully explained mental model can facilitate belief revision.

Attitude change can be understood within a dual-process framework. The first process involves fast, instinctive and emotional reasoning, whereas the second process involves slower, more deliberate and rational reasoning. The second framework tends to produce sustainable results in terms of permanent attitude correction. P. Kowalski and A. K. Taylor (2009) demonstrated the effectiveness of the second process framework, where a controlled and careful dissection of an incorrect idea facilitated the acquisition of correct information. Refuting false information was more successful in changing the attitude and belief than not refuting the same incorrect information. Likewise, messages which were relevant to the audience's goal had higher receptivity. Careful and deliberate processing of information and correction may assist individuals in dealing with inconsistencies and misinformation, and finally in accepting corrections.

The ***Fuzzy-Trace Theory***, a dual-trace conceptualisation of reasoning, further explains the persistence of past beliefs and attitudes. According to this model, people tend to process gist information faster. Fuzzy representations are often activated automatically and faster than messages that supply detailed information. When both gist and detailed information are associated with a belief and compete for memory retrieval, gist information succeeds because it is faster. Past beliefs persist because details are not retrieved strategically, but the gist being interesting and memorable is promptly retrieved. Recent studies of attitude and belief have shown that emotional content and tone of information affects change. Negative images tend to be associated with a greater susceptibility to false memories for a major misleading detail at subsequent sessions. Therefore, negative emotions make attitude change tougher, despite multiple attempts at correction.

Social Influence

Every individual is part of a group that provides support in various ways. Individual growth is highly influenced by the group he or she belongs to. Groups can be smaller at the micro level, like office colleagues or college friends, or larger at the macro level, like society, people of the same caste, language, ethnicity or country. A group may be understood as a system of individuals who mutually interact, remaining interdependent, pursuing common objectives and following common norms that regulate their behaviour. Such groups build a social environment. Individuals are compelled to join a group or a social environment for serving various self-interests like personal and family security, maintaining status, finding self-esteem and recognition, and achieving goals. Social environments fulfill the psychological, cognitive, emotive and other needs of individuals. In turn, social influence becomes the principal cause or motivation behind the regulation of the attitudes of members of social groups. These groups are formed due to various factors like a common neighbourhood, uniformity in status, profession, similar likes or dislikes, common objectives, etc.

Here, we are interested in examining the social influence on an individual who is already a member or intends to be a member of a given society. Social psychologists observe that social influence motivates individuals to perform better in areas where they excel, provided that individual performance is evaluated and rewarded. But when the overall performance of a social group is evaluated, members are less motivated to perform beyond their average ability, and some may not perform as expected. This phenomenon of underperformance is known as social loafing.

Social loafing is characterised by a reduced contribution of individual members while working as a team because the credit for performance goes to the whole team rather than to individuals. In government offices and administration, social loafing is a common problem because there is no transparent and foolproof mechanism to recognise and credit individual performance. The reasons behind lower performance when working as a group are as follows:

1. Group members often overlook individual responsibilities and accountability and shift them to the entire group, which is perceived as faceless and illusive.
2. Fewer opportunities for recognition and reward of individual efforts results in lower motivation levels for work.
3. Absence of other groups for comparing performance leads to lack of competitiveness.
4. Inadequate coordination and synchronisation among group members.
5. Members may lack a sense of belonging to the group, viewing it as a mere agglomeration of unconnected individuals.

Social influence also gives rise to the *polarisation effect*, where an individual's opinion is aligned with the group's opinion. The group's opinions and decisions are seen as being final and supreme in any matter, and individual members are influenced by the overall tendency of the group as a whole. Members who share similar opinions are seen as the in-group and are easily recognisable as a subgroup within the larger group.

Belonging to a group influences an individual in various ways, and other members of that group individually exert their influence, compelling him/her to conform to their views. This is known as social influence: a process in which the attitude and behaviour of an individual within a social group is influenced by the apparent or actual presence of others. Sometimes, social influence can become so powerful that we may start behaving in ways contrary to our real nature. Conversely, if we resist social influence, then we may be able to exert our influence on the group. In this way, social influence gives rise to conformity, compliance and obedience.

Conformity: Individuals tend to adhere to social norms and align with the group even if they realise that blindly following group norms may not be in their best interest. Defying these norms might result in negative consequences, yet conforming is often perceived as a natural and unquestionable behaviour. As discussed earlier, individuals seek social environments for various purposes, and conformity contributes to the smooth functioning of society. Defying group norms can lead to psychological discomfort and a sense of incongruence within society. It may result in social exclusion or disapproval, constituting a form of personal affliction. The fear of 'what will people say about me?' is a powerful motivator to conform. Adhering to norms is viewed as the simplest way to avoid disapproval from peers. Norms are often accepted as the collective will of the majority and the right course of action without much contemplation. Human beings, being cognitive misers, tend to act in accordance with the perceived majority opinion. The degree of conformity is influenced by factors such as the group size, nature of the task, whether the behaviour is displayed publicly or privately, personality types, and so on.

Compliance: Compliance involves responding to requests from others even in the absence of a specific norm. It often leads to actions contrary to the individual's own attitudes or beliefs, driven by the natural inclination to avoid unpleasant situations or conflict. Compliance can be achieved through various psychological techniques, such as the 'foot-in-the-door technique'. In this approach, a small request is initially presented, which is hard to refuse. Once this initial request is complied with, a larger request is made. The individual, having already entertained a request, may feel compelled to comply with the subsequent one to avoid discomfort associated with refusal. Another technique for ensuring compliance is the 'deadline technique', where limited time is provided for consideration, creating a sense of urgency to accept an offer contingent on compliance. The 'door-in-the-face technique' involves making a larger request initially. When this request is not accepted, a smaller, more reasonable request is presented, which was the actual target. This technique often results in greater compliance with the second, more moderate request.

Obedience: Obedience refers to behaviour in response to the directives of higher authority or a respected individual. The key factor driving obedience is the fear of punishment, distinguishing it from compliance. Individuals believe that the authority possesses effective means to enforce orders, leading them to obey without necessarily considering the consequences, as the burden of responsibility lies with the commanding authority.

People enter social environments for multiple reasons, giving rise to mutual interactions that foster both competition and cooperation. When members of a social group align themselves to achieve a common goal, a sense of cooperation emerges. Conversely, to enhance individual influence and realise self-interest, competition arises. A cooperative group exerts social influence promoting notions of fraternity and collectiveness but lacking individual identity. In contrast, a competitive group exerts social influence encouraging competition and self-identity. While a competitive group may attract animosity, conflict and disharmony, it also has the potential for substantial rewards. The acceptability of a particular type of social influence for an individual depends on the reward mechanism, interpersonal communication and quid pro quo.

REFERENCES

Ajzen, Icek, and Martin Fishbein. (1977). 'Attitude–behavior relations: A theoretical analysis and review of empirical research'. *Psychological Bulletin 84*(5): 888–918.

———. (2005). 'The influence of attitudes on behavior'. In *The Handbook of Attitudes*, eds. D. Albarracin, B. T. Johnson and M. P. Zanna, 173–221. New York: Lawrence Erlbaum Associates.

Ajzen, Icek, C. Timko and J. B. White. (1982). 'Self-monitoring and the attitude–behavior relation'. *Journal of Personality and Social Psychology* 42(3): 426–435.

Bakunin, Mikhail. (1873). *Statism and Anarchy*. Cambridge University Press.

Bornstein, R. F. (1989). 'Exposure and affect: Overview and meta-analysis of research, 1968–1987'. *Psychological Bulletin* 106(2): 265–289.

Converse, Philip E. (1964). 'The nature of belief systems in mass publics'. In *Ideology and Discontent*, ed. D. E. Apter, 206–261. New York: The Free Press.

Corlett, Philip R., and Natasza Marrouch. (2018). 'Social cognitive neuroscience of attitude and beliefs'. In *The Handbook of Attitudes, Volume 1: Basic Principles*, 480–519. New York: Taylor & Francis.

Critchley, Hugo D. (2005). 'Neural mechanisms of autonomic, affective, and cognitive integration'. *JCN: The Journal of Comparative Neurology* 493(1): 154–166.

Cunningham, W. A., M. K. Johnson, J. C. Gatenby, J. C. Gore and M. R. Banaji. (2003). 'Neural components of social evaluation'. *Journal of Personality and Social Psychology* 85(4): 639–649.

Cunningham, W. A., C. L. Raye and M. K. Johnson. (2004). 'Implicit and explicit evaluation: FMRI correlates of valence, emotional intensity, and control in the processing of attitudes'. *Journal of Cognitive Neuroscience* 16(10):1717–1729.

Cunningham, W. A., D. J. Packer, A. Kesek and J. Van Bavel. (2009). 'Implicit measurement of attitudes: A physiological approach'. In *Attitudes: Insights from the New Implicit Measures*, eds. R. E. Petty, R. H. Fazio and P. Brinol, 485–512. New York: Psychology Press.

Eagly, Alice H., and S. Chaiken. (1993). *The Psychology of Attitudes*. Jovanovich College: Harcourt Brace.

Epley, N., and T. Gilovich. (2006). 'The anchoring-and-adjustment heuristic: Why the adjustments are insufficient'. *Psychological Science* 17(4): 311–318.

Fishbein, Martin, and Icek Ajzen. (1975). *Belief, Attitude, Intention, and Behaviour: An Introduction to Theory and Research*. MA: Addison-Wesley.

Griffith, David A., and Qimei Chen. (2004). 'The influence of virtual direct experience (VDE) on on-line ad message effectiveness'. *Journal of Advertising* 33(1): 55–68.

Kowalski, P., and A. K. Taylor. (2009). 'The effect of refuting misconceptions in the introductory psychology class'. *Teaching of Psychology* 36(3): 153–159.

Kunda, Ziva. (1990). 'The case for motivated reasoning'. *Psychological Bulletin* 108(3): 480–498.

Kunst-Wilson, William Raft and R. B Zajonc. (1980). 'Affective discrimination of stimuli that cannot be recognized'. *Science* 207(4430): 557–558.

Montoya, R. Matthew, R. Horton, J. L. Vevea, M. Citkowicz and E. A. Lauber. (2017). 'A re-examination of the mere exposure effect: The influence of repeated exposure on recognition, familiarity, and liking'. *Psychological Bulletin* 143(5): 459–498.

Regan, D. T., and R. Fazio. (1977). 'On the consistency between attitudes and behavior: Look to the method of attitude formation'. *Journal of Experimental Social Psychology* 13(1): 28–45.

Rholes, William S., and Su Bailey. (1983). 'The effects of level of moral reasoning on consistency between moral attitudes and related behaviors'. *Social Cognition* 2(1): 32–48.

Schattschneider, E. E. (1942). *Party Government*. New York: Farrar & Rinehart.

Schumpeter, Joseph A. (1943). *Capitalism, Socialism and Democracy*. London: George Allen & Unwin.

Snyder, M., and D. Kendzierski. (1982). 'Acting on one's attitudes: Procedures for linking attitude and behavior'. *Journal of Experimental Social Psychology* 18(2): 165–183.

Snyder, M., and W. B. Swann. (1976). 'When actions reflect attitudes: The politics of impression management'. *Journal of Personality and Social Psychology* 34(5): 1034–1042.

Telch, M. J., A. R. Cobb and C. L. Lancaster. (2013). 'Exposure therapy for anxiety disorders: Procedural variations, clinical efficacy, and change mechanisms'. In *International Handbook for Anxiety Disorders*, Vol. 2, eds. P. Emmelkamp and T. Ehring. Aimes, IA: Wiley-Blackwell.

Topolinski, S., and F. Strack. (2009). 'The architecture of intuition: Fluency and affect determine intuitive judgments of semantic and visual coherence and judgments of grammaticality in artificial grammar learning'. *Journal of Experimental Psychology: General* 138(1): 39–63.

Tversky, Amos, and D. Kahneman. (1974). 'Judgment under uncertainty: Heuristics and biases'. *Science* 185(4157): 1124–1131.

Zajonc, R. B. (1968). 'Attitudinal effects of mere exposure'. *Journal of Personality and Social Psychology* 9(2, Part 2): 1–27.

Zanna, M. P., J. M. Olson and R. H. Fazio. (1980). 'Attitude–behavior consistency: An individual difference perspective'. *Journal of Personality and Social Psychology* 38(3): 432–440.

QUESTIONS

1. What factors affect the formation of a person's attitude towards social problems? In our society, contrasting attitudes are prevalent about many social problems. What contrasting attitudes do you notice about the caste system in our society? How do you explain the existence of these contrasting attitudes? (UPSC 2014)
2. 'Integrity without knowledge is weak and useless, but knowledge without integrity is dangerous and dreadful.' What do you understand by this statement? Explain your stand with illustrations from the modern context. (UPSC 2014)
3. How could social influence and persuasion contribute to the success of the Swachh Bharat Abhiyan? (UPSC 2016)
4. Young people with ethical values and conduct are not willing to come forward to join active politics. Suggest steps to motivate them to come forward. (UPSC 2017)
5. Explain the structure of attitude giving an example in the context of bureaucratic attitude.
6. How does attitude guide behaviour? Explain with the help of examples.
7. What do you understand by persuasion? How does persuasion become a useful tool in development administration? Explain.
8. What is bureaucratic attitude? Explain the various causes behind this administrative evil.

7

APTITUDE

> **KEY CONCEPTS**
> Introduction; Aptitude for the Civil Services; Intelligence; Role of Personality in Learning; Aptitude versus Attitude

INTRODUCTION

The word aptitude derives from the Latin word *aptus*, meaning the quality of being apt, fit, or possessing a natural tendency, inclination, ability, talent or quickness to learn and understand. Aptitude is distinct from knowledge or learned skills as it refers to an inherent capacity to acquire and develop certain skills and competencies. Each professional domain necessitates specific traits in one's personality to excel and meet the expectations inherent to that particular service, whether within the private sector or public service. In this context, we aim to explore the aptitude required in civil services—an amalgamation of essential personality traits necessary to align with the principles of democratic governance, the spirit of the Constitution of India, internationally acclaimed practices in public administration and the ultimate establishment of a welfare-oriented government.

Civil services serve as the backbone of administration in India. Civil servants are responsible to the public at large and to their political and administrative bosses in particular. The role of a civil servant is multi-dimensional and dynamic, involving both decision-making and delivery of services. While daily tasks often adhere to deontological principles of duty, civil servants must assume a wider, more comprehensive role where rules and regulations give way to discretion and judgment. Aptitude is crucial in both scenarios—swiftly executing tasks based on established procedures and guidelines, and making quick decisions in discretionary matters. The complexity of the role requires a significant aptitude to navigate within the boundaries of the rule of law. Unfortunately, our bureaucracy is notorious for its sluggish, negligent, corrupt and irresponsible work culture. This discussion aims to explore the role of aptitude in administration, identifying attitudes and methods to cultivate the desired aptitude among young Indian civil servants.

There are different categories of civil services in India: the All India Civil Services, Central Civil Services, Indian Defense Services, State Civil Services, and other public services of the Central and state governments. Each category encompasses different kind of services. For instance, the All India Services (AIS) comprises three services: the Indian Administrative Service (IAS), the Indian Police Service (IPS) and the Indian Forest Service (IFS). Additionally, there are central services of Group A, such as the Indian Revenue Service

(Income Tax), Indian Revenue Service (Customs and GST), Indian Audit and Account Service, Indian Railway Traffic Service, etc.

APTITUDE FOR THE CIVIL SERVICES

Each civil service has distinct functions, but they all require certain specific common traits in terms of administrative ability, judgment and values. This commonality is crucial and can be assessed through a common test. While some services demand specific essential traits—for example, colour-blindness is not permissible in the Indian Police Service or the Indian Railway Traffic Service, or the requirement of adequate physical stamina in the Indian Forest Service and Indian Police Service—here we want to understand the most common features required in a candidate aspiring to enter the civil services of India and the states. These common features are defined as aptitude for civil services. Common aptitudes required for the civil services include:

1. Reading comprehension
2. Quantitative ability
3. Reasoning ability
4. Data interpretation and analysis
5. Writing skills
6. Scientific temperament (basic knowledge of science and technology)
7. Sound knowledge of geography, political science, history, social science, philosophy and other humanities subjects
8. Ethics or moral philosophy
9. Physical fitness

The abovementioned aptitudes are tested through a rigorous examination procedure that scrutinises and evaluates all the aspects as mentioned above. The question that arises is whether aptitude is innate (by birth) or can it be developed through practice. While many psychologists consider aptitude to be a genetic ability, others reject this uni-dimensional view. Aptitude signifies the possession of particular traits which can be cultivated and honed as needed with the help of appropriate training. Through substantial and sustained effort, one can achieve a level of excellence which may be effortless for someone possessing the relevant inborn aptitude. Aptitude is distinct from skill; skill refers to things learnt in the past whereas aptitude pertains to things that facilitate easier learning. Ability can be understood as what a person can do at present. We will now discuss the different aptitudes one by one.

1. *Reading comprehension* is the most important aptitude for civil servants. They are required to read, understand and respond to a multitude of letters, circulars, files, rules and guidelines from various government departments, ministries as well as the judiciary. The ability to not only read but also comprehend the underlying spirit of the content and to act accordingly is essential. Poor reading and comprehension skills can seriously hamper functioning and overall performance. For instance, when a civil servant is assigned multi-departmental tasks, receiving and responding to letters and circulars from all relevant departments in a district is routine. Proficiency in reading can significantly enhance decision-making.

2. A *quantitative aptitude* is equally essential for civil servants, irrespective of their service or department. Routine administrative tasks involve various mathematical exercises. Evaluating the performance of subordinates, distributing tasks and targets, and assessing progress in relation to estimates require a strong quantitative ability. Since mathematical knowledge is deductive, this aptitude is crucial for measuring targets, evaluating performance, and analysing various attributes of subordinates.

3. *Reasoning ability* is characterised by the capability to make sound judgments and construct rational arguments. In the realm of a civil servant's duties, which often involve subjectivity in decision-making,

reasoning ability is crucial for reaching sound decisions. Matters pertaining to departmental inquiries, verbal instructions from superiors, political considerations, and the mechanisms of public service delivery require extensive reasoning exercises. Additionally, reasoning plays a vital role in controlling one's behaviour when wielding significant power and discretion. As Plato eloquently stated, 'The unexamined life is not worth living', a civil servant's conduct in office can be examined through the lens of their reasoning ability.

4. The *ability to interpret, analyse and represent data* accurately is a fundamental method of supervision and review of the progress of government initiatives. Data representation is essential for presenting progress in various government schemes. It involves illustrating subsidiary factors that influence progress, both negatively and positively, as well as projecting costs and duration of the gestation period. Data encapsulates various performance aspects across different indicators. Today, every government department maintains online portals and websites that generate reports from real-time data, entered based on the progress of projects and activities. These reports, facilitated by efficient monitoring systems, encompass different verification mechanisms. For instance, the MNREGS portal generates diverse reports detailing the creation of man-days, initiation of new projects in various categories, progress of works with geo-tagged photographs at different stages, and the percentage of completed and ongoing projects in different categories. Developing software with an efficient monitoring system requires a strong understanding of data interpretation and logical reasoning. Regular reviews of scheme implementation on a monthly and quarterly basis form the bedrock of good governance. This robust review system is entirely dependent on the aptitude for data analysis.

5. *Writing skills* are a primary and vital tool for bureaucrats in their everyday work and functions, but it is a harsh reality that it is often criticised as red tape. However, our focus here is not on the kind of writing that causes endless delays in work or misguides superiors and political bosses. Instead, we emphasise writing that is lucid, clear, enables a multi-dimensional presentation of subjects, and is an objective portrayal of ground realities within the framework of regulations.

6. A *scientific temperament* is the need of the hour for adopting efficient methods of task completion and understanding the manifold challenges and obstructions in the way of developmental work, as well as maintenance of law and order. This aligns with our fundamental duties as enshrined in the Constitution of India.

7. A *sound knowledge of geography, history, political science and other humanities subjects* with reference to our vast and diverse country is essential in order to be able to administer well, formulate beneficial and relevant public policies and implement them efficiently.

8. Training in *ethics and morality* is crucial for civil servants as it helps them make decisions that are fair, just and morally sound. Adhering to ethical principles helps build and maintain public trust as citizens expect those in power to act with integrity and moral responsibility. Civil servants are accountable for their actions, and ethical standards help define acceptable behaviour. Accountability is essential for maintaining transparency and ensuring that public servants serve the public interest. Ethical training guides civil servants to act impartially, without bias or

self-interest. It also equips them with the skills to navigate conflicts of interest and resolve ethical dilemmas. Ethical conduct often aligns with legal standards but goes beyond mere compliance. Civil servants must understand the moral implications of their actions even in situations where the law might not explicitly dictate a particular course of action. Civil servants serve as role models; by embodying ethical behaviour, they set examples for others and contribute to fostering a culture of integrity and moral responsibility. We have discussed the role of ethics in earlier chapters and will explore some aspects in subsequent chapters as well.

9. *Physical fitness* is paramount in civil services, particularly in police and defense services. A proficient administrator undertakes regular tours, physically inspecting work on-site, interacting with people and soliciting their feedback. Frequent and extended field tours empower a civil servant to gain a deeper understanding of ground realities. This understanding proves invaluable in formulating robust and beneficial public policies later in career.

INTELLIGENCE

One of the most hotly debated topics in psychology, intelligence eludes precise definition. It encompasses the ability to learn from direct and indirect experiences, identify problems and solve them. Psychologist Robert Sternberg defines intelligence as 'mental activity advanced to adapt, select, and shape the real world purposefully for one's life'. It is true that we are born with a certain level of intelligence and also that we may never achieve intellectual abilities akin to those with a different genetic makeup. Equally, a person in a poor social environment with limited opportunities for intellectual growth may never realise the full potential of their genes.

Intelligence has different meanings for different cultures, age groups and skill sets. Rather than fixating on a definition, it is more beneficial to focus on understanding what all influences and shapes intelligence. In applying the concept of intelligence, several questions arise: does it represent a singular general ability of the human mind or does it encompass a range of abilities and aptitudes? Are there other types of intelligence such as emotional intelligence? Is genius innate and inborn, or is it socially developed and can be cultivated? There are many possible answers to each of these questions.

It is widely acknowledged that intelligence is a hereditary trait passed down through generations. Numerous studies have explored the link between intelligence quotient (IQ) and an individual's genes. Certain characteristics are known to be primarily genetic, such as facial features, height, colour of eyes; while others, like depression in men, have low heritability suggesting that the environment has a crucial role to play. A common method to assess the influence of genes and the environment is to compare the IQ levels of identical twins raised separately in very different environments. These studies have demonstrated that IQ has relatively higher heritability, with the majority of IQ differences between adults being genetically explained, but not all.

Studies suggest that there are specific genes that influence an individual's attitude towards learning, development, and the construction of mental abilities throughout life. Genetics is believed to be responsible for 75 per cent of adult intelligence, while the environment accounts for the remaining 25 per cent. However, it must be noted that research has identified only a limited number of specific genes that can be said to substantially impact IQ. Intelligence is better understood as a result of the complex and continuous interplay between multiple genes and diverse environmental stimuli, rather than being determined by any singular gene or genes. A significant group of scientists believes that up to 40 per cent of all genes may in fact contribute to overall intelligence.

Measuring Intelligence

Unlike height or weight, obtaining an exact measure of an individual's intelligence is challenging. Francis Galton was the first who attempted to standardise people based on intelligence, but his work was theoretical and lacked practical application. Influenced by Charles Darwin, Galton theorised that intelligence had a biological basis and suggested that selective breeding of intelligent individuals could produce increasingly intelligent offspring—Galton called this eugenics. During this time, the French government mandated that all children be sent to school for education. Alfred Binet and his associate Theodore Simon devised the Binet-Simon Test, for grouping children with similar abilities together so that they could be taught more effectively according to their potential. Unlike Galton, Binet did not believe in inborn intelligence; instead he saw it as a trait which could be developed and improved by practice. He intended his test to help identify children who needed more attention and a different way of learning. Unfortunately, Binet's test was misused for segregation and the results were used to label children as underperformers, hindering their opportunities. William Stern later incorporated aspects of the Binet-Simon Test and used them to create the famous Intelligence Quotient (IQ) test.

$$IQ = (mental\ age/chronological\ age) \times 100$$

These tests proved useful when applied to children who had successfully cleared developmental milestones, but were not useful where the age difference between adults was small. For example, there isn't much difference between a mental age of 30 and 31. Nevertheless, Lewis Terman, who was working at Stanford University at the time, encouraged the United States government to begin mass intelligence testing of adult American citizens and immigrants. These test scores were used for practical purposes, such as assigning jobs to military personnel during World War I. Unfortunately, they were also used for not practical and ethically problematic purposes, such as the mass sterilisation of young uneducated women. This approach to measuring human intelligence completely disregarded individual differences in learning, and clearly had catastrophic consequences.

In the early twentieth century, the fact that individuals differ with respect to intelligence, aptitudes and abilities gained wider acceptability. English psychologist Charles Spearman proposed that while people may possess varying individual aptitudes, these aptitudes were all correlated to what he called the G-Factor of intelligence. Building upon the ideas of Francis Galton, Spearman developed a statistical procedure known as 'Factor Analysis' to explain how one aptitude or ability could correlate with others to form clusters of abilities that collectively fall under the umbrella of the G-Factor. This G-Factor is a general intelligence factor that describes a person's overall intelligence; for example, someone with a higher G-factor is called a fast learner. However, placing a single numeric label on a person's intelligence was, and still is very problematic, and Spearman's theory has been extensively challenged. American psychologist Louis L. Thurstone administered 56 intelligence tests to participants and identified a range of 7 mental abilities, concluding that a high score in one did not predict a high score in others, thus disproving Spearman's G-Factor theory. However, when Thurstone's studies were replicated, it was found that a high score in one aspect of an intelligence test tended to predict a similar score in others, essentially supporting the notion of some kind of G-Factor.

Nevertheless, Spearman's theory fails to account for individual differences in learners and their intelligence. Instances such as a gifted artist with little aptitude for mathematics or a musician with mediocre language skills raise questions like: Can we determine a person's intelligence based on some aptitudes but not others? Do certain aptitudes carry more significance than others? Additionally, do individual differences outside of intelligence impact the ability to learn? Is it problematic to reduce a person's intelligence expression to a single test score? These questions become particularly pertinent when dealing with diverse learners, such as gifted and talented individuals or students with learning disabilities.

A highly talented student with exceptional mathematical ability might only exhibit an average ability in other subjects like languages or art. Moreover, some students excelling in one area may face challenges in another, such as a talented musician coping with dyslexia or attention deficit hyperactivity disorder (ADHD). These individuals, known as *twice-exceptional*, are often overlooked due to difficulties in assessment (such as an inability to attend to a test or insufficient language skills to read or answer test questions) or because of insufficient support for their learning disability due to a general belief that high ability in one area corresponds with high ability in others. It was recognising and identifying such learners that led Howard Gardner to theorise and assert that there are multiple intelligences beyond Spearman's G-Factor. These multiple intelligences include not only aspects of 'traditional' intelligence but also interpersonal intelligence, essential for effective leadership, and bodily kinaesthetic intelligence, crucial for skilled athletes or dancers. Modern intelligence theories now acknowledge the existence of various types of intelligence, enabling teachers to recognise and appreciate the diverse talents of learners in their classes.

Impact of Social Environment on IQ

Although genetics plays a pivotal role in determining IQ, the social environment also has a significant and substantial impact. Research shows that, in addition to genes and formal education, early family environments play a crucial role. Evidence suggests that a child's IQ is not fully formed at birth but evolves gradually, and is greatly influenced by parents and immediate environment, particularly until primary schooling, after which parental influence diminishes. Parents can enhance their children's IQ by improving their own education, habits, lifestyle and spending quality time with the child. Stimulating the child's mind through stories, books and exposing them to narratives about the world outside the home contributes enormously to cognitive development. Certain activities like language learning and musical training have been associated with enhanced brain function. Music is believed to improve the brain's capacity to visualise and manipulate objects in space and time and improve mathematical abilities.

The concept of *brain plasticity* suggests that the brain remains adaptable and keeps evolving and renewing itself throughout life, with a substantial capacity for transformation. This means that the environment directly impacts our brain. Studies have shown that a stimulating environment increases the brain's thickness, the number of neurons, and new connections between these neurons even in the elderly. Conversely, a stagnant environment can lead to a decline in responses by as much as 60% within a week. All of this supports the advice to continually engage and stimulate the brain throughout life, incorporating a broad range of interests, activities and skills, including mental, physical, aesthetic, social and emotional aspects.

ROLE OF PERSONALITY IN LEARNING

Unsurprisingly, personality plays a significant role in learning, as revealed in research studies on the Big Five personality traits: extraversion, agreeableness, neuroticism, openness and conscientiousness. T. Chamorro-Premuzic and A. Furnham (2003a and 2003b) conducted studies with university students, assessing academic performance in exams and end-of-year projects while isolating personality from other influencing factors. *Conscientiousness* was the most influential factor, their findings revealed, highlighting the importance of a hardworking, organised and ambitious personality for excelling in the learning process. *Neuroticism* emerged as the second most influential dimension, impacting mental stability and affecting other performance measures. Neuroticism was sometimes seen as a factor that induces anxiety, jeopardising performance during examination-like situations of stress.

Openness demonstrated an impact on performance, representing a personality trait characterised by imagination and curiosity about the external world. Psychology students generally exhibited high levels of openness. Individuals with high openness tend to be more adventurous and creative, while those with lower levels are more traditional and inclined toward conventional thinking. In the Chamorro-Premuzic and Furnham 2003 studies, the authors also considered academic behaviour such as absenteeism and teacher predictions, but none of these factors showed influential power comparable to personality traits—a finding that might be encouraging for many students. However, since personality traits often intersect with and relate to other influencers in complex ways, careful consideration is essential before drawing any definitive conclusions.

Intelligence has long been recognised as a key determinant of learning ability, and while traditionally considered more important than other factors, several studies have indicated that its role in learning should not be overestimated. According to some studies, intelligence has a direct bearing on conscientiousness (Busato et al. 2000) and openness (Blickle 1996). The relationship between personality and conscientiousness is self-explanatory, and the results obtained regarding openness are explained by the correlation of lexical intelligence with the aesthetic and idea scales within this personality factor. In-depth investigations and research have now revealed that the assumed inherent link between intelligence and learning was exaggerated. Vittorio Busato et al. (2000) found only a trivial contribution of intelligence, which was far outweighed by personality. Although we cannot deny the role of intelligence in learning, when considering a learned population with not much difference in individual intelligence levels, personality plays a major role. Therefore, due caution must be exercised when interpreting such relationships and drawing conclusions.

Motivation is another influential factor impacting higher learning and one of the key determinants of performance and achievement (Green et al. 2006). There is ample evidence to suggest that motivation is inherently linked to personality traits (Clark and Schroth 2010), depending on the kind of motivation an individual learner possesses. Most motivation theories generally treat motivation as a unitary concept, varying from very little to very high motivation. However, some theories argue that it is not a unitary concept but rather, based on orientation and types. Motivation asks why something needs to be done, and in answering this question, the type and degree of motivation come into play. The *self-determination theory* posits that the orientation of motivation involves the different reasons and goals that constitute an action, answering why an action is performed. For example, a civil servant may be highly motivated to run a government programme out of personal interest or because they want to gain popularity among colleagues and superiors. Here, the quantum of motivation may not vary significantly, given that it is their duty, but the orientation of motivation may vary, impacting the quality of the job done.

There are two different types of motivation: intrinsic and extrinsic motivation (Deci and Ryan 1985). *Intrinsic motivation* is defined according to the self-determination theory, and is regulated by the inherent craving for competence and self-determination. Intrinsic motivation arises when individuals seek self-satisfaction and pleasure. A civil servant who is intrinsically motivated to perform his duties does so voluntarily, enjoys activities related to positive feelings while doing their job, and views acquiring new skills as a healthy challenge to their present competencies.

Thus, interest in the activity or subject is important, and so is a sense of making progress (ibid.). Bureaucrats who desire to continue learning for the sake of learning and enhance their education level through higher studies related to their field are more intrinsically motivated. On the other hand, bureaucrats who are *extrinsically motivated* view higher studies as a means to other ends, such as enhancing career prospects, securing a better posting, promotions, or improving their profile. They may also be motivated by rewards and punishments, which depend on success or failure in a job. Extrinsic motivation is neither driven by nor dependent on interest or enjoyment.

It was initially believed that extrinsic motivation is devoid of the desire for self-determination. However, more recently it has been argued that there are three levels of extrinsic motivation in the context of learning and self-determination.

1. *External regulation*: The motivating factor and behaviour is external to the individual, for example, taking a specific course for the sole purpose of acquiring a degree to enhance one's personal profile for future career growth.
2. *Introjected regulation*: Motivation is driven by external pressure to impress others with one's skills, given the high-profile image of civil servants as select talents of the country. Learning takes place when a bureaucrat feels the need for self-aggrandisement, or the need to alleviate a sense of inadequacy or guilt about not being proficient enough in their tasks.
3. *Identified regulation*: A civil servant performs a particular behaviour because they think it is important to them personally. For example, if they have experienced the value of higher studies in their career and view it positively, their learning is sustained as long as they find it valuable.

It has been argued that intrinsic and extrinsic motivations are incompatible. As one of William Perry's students at Harvard University once said,

'I can't afford to get interested in this course because I have to get a good grade' (Lin, McKeachie and Kim 2001). Thus, being interested in a subject and learning for life (intrinsic motivation), which is one of the goals of higher studies, may not be the best approach for obtaining a good profile and career advancement. On the contrary, higher intrinsic motivation has been linked to higher academic performance (Harter and Connell 1984). M. V. Covington (1999) agrees with S. Harter and J. P. Connell (1984) and argues that working for a good profile and career advancement is not separate from valuing learning. In fact, a combination of intrinsic and extrinsic motivation seems to be the most effective approach for acquiring a good profile while also encouraging civil servants to study subjects that they find genuinely enjoyable and interesting, to learn for a broader understanding, and to gain life experience beyond acquiring degrees and qualifications.

APTITUDE VERSUS ATTITUDE

Aptitude is the ability to learn something, and it varies to different degrees in individuals. Aptitude, to a large extent, remains fixed and cannot be significantly modified. However, with the right attitude, it can be properly harnessed and utilised to acquire learning and skills. The transformation of aptitude into a skill is greatly influenced by the individual's attitude. Aptitude alone cannot yield remarkable results without the right attitude. Individual attitude, motivation and personality create an environment conducive for utilising aptitude optimally. Unutilised aptitude serves no purpose. Aptitude is primarily a quantitative concept, while attitude is qualitative and plays a significant role in exploiting aptitude. Aptitude may require formal and informal tests for assessment, whereas attitude is apparent and self-evident. The crucial distinction lies in the fact that individuals can be trained to overcome weaknesses in aptitude, but weaknesses in attitude are far more challenging to identify and address through training. In other words, behavioural problems

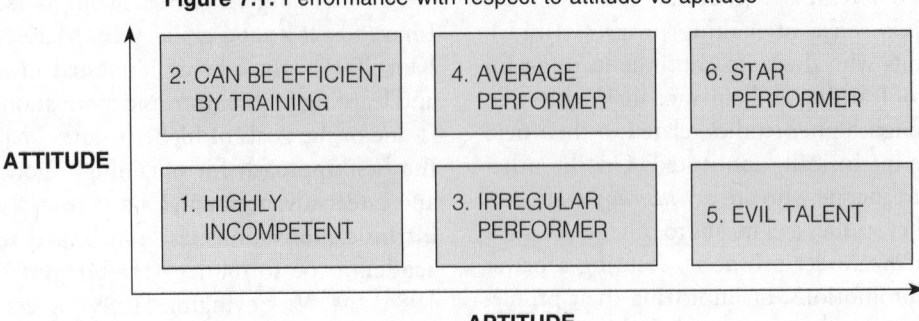

Figure 7.1: Performance with respect to attitude vs aptitude

Source: Created by authors.

rooted in attitude cannot be easily changed and require considerable and sustained effort. Attitude is intrinsic to the individual, and the motivation for change must come from within; external efforts to motivate someone to change their attitude are often futile.

In government, a significant proportion of civil servants display both a low aptitude and a poor attitude towards their work. Those responsible for implementing public policies and schemes are often highly incompetent and corrupt (category 1 in Figure 7.1). This is attributed to nepotism, corruption, flaws in appointment procedures and inadequate or virtually nonexistent on-the-job training. However, individuals with low aptitude but a strong positive attitude can be transformed into an efficient and productive workforce (category 2 in Figure 7.1). Political executives harnessing such a workforce often witness unexpected positive outcomes.

Within government, many professionals fall into the category of moderate aptitude and low attitude, leading to irregular performance (category 3 in Figure 7.1). They receive occasional appreciation for their work but are equally criticised for apathy and inconsistent performance. In India, a significant portion of middle-line managers occupies this category.

Individuals with moderate aptitude and a positive attitude hold crucial positions in government. They are average performers, consistently delivering results, but their work rarely leads to revolutionary change (category 4 in Figure 7.1). These bureaucrats are often favoured by political executives for achieving tangible outcomes. Some administrators with high aptitude but poor attitude are known for their performance through exertion of power over subordinates and the use of punishment, delivering quick but short-lived results, often based on manipulation (category 5 in Figure 7.1).

The need of the hour is for star performers with high aptitude and a positive attitude, with honesty, integrity and accountability (category 6 in Figure 7.1). They prioritise systematic reforms over hasty delivery of mere quantitative output. Such individuals can bring positive, sustainable change, create history and leave a lasting impact.

REFERENCES

Blickle, G. (1996). 'Personality traits, learning strategies, and performance'. *European Journal of Personality* 10(5): 337–352.

Busato, Vittorio V., F. J. Prins, J. J. Elshout and C. Hamaker. (2000). 'Intellectual ability, learning style, personality, achievement motivation and academic success of psychology students in higher education'. *Personality and Individual Differences* 29(6): 1057–1068.

Chamorro-Premuzic, T., and A. Furnham. (2003a). 'Personality traits and academic examination performance'. *European Journal of Personality* 17(3): 237–250.

———. (2003b). 'Personality predicts academic performance: Evidence from two longitudinal university samples'. *Journal of Research in Personality* *37*(4): 319–338.

Clark, M. H., and C. A. Schroth. (2010). 'Examining relationships between academic motivation and personality among college students'. *Learning and Individual Differences* *20*(1): 19–24.

Covington, M. V. (1999). 'Caring about learning: The nature and nurturing of subject-matter appreciation'. *Educational Psychologist* *34*(2): 127–136.

Deci, E. L., and R. M. Ryan. (1985). *Intrinsic Motivation and Self-determination in Human Behavior*. New York: Plenum.

Green, J., G. Nelson, A. J. Martin and H. Marsh. (2006). 'The causal ordering of self-concept and academic motivation and its effect on academic achievement'. *International Education Journal* *7*: 534-546.

Harter, S., and J. P. Connell. (1984). 'A model of children's achievement and related self-perceptions of competence, control, and motivational orientation'. *Advances in Motivation and Achievement* *3*: 219-250.

Lin, Y. G., W. J. McKeachie and Y. C. Kim. (2001). 'College student intrinsic and/or extrinsic motivation and learning'. *Learning and Individual Differences* *13*(3): 251–258.

QUESTIONS

1. What do you understand by 'values' and 'ethics'? In what way is it important to be ethical along with being professionally competent? (UPSC 2013)
2. How does interplay between aptitude and attitude determine the performance of a professional? Explain with examples.
3. What do you understand by aptitude? What are the factors which determine a person's aptitude?
4. How far does social influence determine the exploitation of aptitude by oneself? Explain with the help of an example.
5. What are the five important traits of personality? Explain.
6. Give an account of the aptitudes indispensable for a civil servant with the help of examples.

8

EMOTIONAL INTELLIGENCE

> **KEY CONCEPTS**
> Introduction; Why is Emotional Intelligence Important?; Classifying Emotional Intelligence; How to Achieve Emotional Intelligence; Working with Emotional Intelligence; Models of Emotional Intelligence

INTRODUCTION

We have many examples of great leaders, distinguished administrators and successful public servants who did not hold degrees from prestigious business schools or renowned educational institutions. Conversely, there are numerous instances where individuals with academic excellence from such institutions, often attributed to their high intelligence quotient, did not achieve any remarkable success in their lives. The key to success lies not solely in academic knowledge, technical expertise, or years of experience: what distinguishes star performers from the mediocre is emotional intelligence.

Emotional intelligence (EI) refers to the ability to recognise, understand, manage and effectively use our own emotions and those of others. It is a set of skills and competencies that enable us to navigate our social environment, build positive relationships and make informed decisions based on emotional cues. The word emotion is derived from the Latin word *emovare*, signifying continuous change and movement. Emotions are believed to have evolved through natural selection, aiding humans in adapting to their environment and meeting life's challenges.

The term 'emotional intelligence' was first used by Wayne Payne in 1986 in his doctoral thesis, 'A Study of Emotion: Developing Emotional Intelligence, Self-integration, Relating to Fear, Pain, and Desire'. Payne's work emphasised that emotional ignorance is a root cause of many societal problems. Peter Salovey and John D. Mayer (1990) further developed Payne's work, defining the term emotional intelligence as a form of social intelligence that involves an individual's ability to monitor their own and others' emotions, differentiate between them, and derive meaningful insights to guide their thoughts and actions. Salovey and Mayer concluded that individuals must know and be able to regulate their own emotions, as well as others', in order to achieve better results in every aspect of life.

American psychologist Daniel Goleman popularised emotional intelligence in 1995 with his book *Emotional Intelligence: Why It Can Matter More than IQ*. Goleman presented emotional intelligence broadly, identifying it, explaining its significance, and illustrating how it can be fostered. Emotional intelligence is not measured by IQ tests, says Goleman. As a person rises in an organisation, greater emotional intelligence is required to handle responsibilities effectively, he asserts. While Goleman's fascinating study on cognitive and emotional development may not convincingly establish EI as a clearly recognisable and well-defined aptitude, his report is nonetheless a compelling and practical guide to emotional mastery.

WHY IS EMOTIONAL INTELLIGENCE IMPORTANT?

Our emotions play a central role in our thoughts, actions and decisions. Emotional intelligence is a key factor in personal and professional success, contributing to effective communication, conflict resolution and leadership. EI is often contrasted with cognitive intelligence (IQ) as it focuses on the emotional and social aspects of intelligence rather than purely cognitive abilities. Research shows that individuals with high EI tend to excel in various areas of life, including leadership, teamwork and overall wellbeing.

Emotional intelligence serves as a tool for understanding the trajectory of one's career, identifying the causes behind setbacks in family life and work life, and negotiating social environments. It is imperative for successful leadership and a critical factor in reaching and maintaining the pinnacle in any field, even in highly technical careers that are conventionally considered mechanical in nature. Organisations that learn to operate in an emotionally intelligent manner are the ones that will thrive in today's competitive market and the foreseeable future.

Emotional intelligence manifests in the workplace when bosses provide subordinates with constructive feedback regarding their performance. It draws on a range of evidence, from brain function to social dynamics, to reveal how we distort our most intimate relationships, our everyday lives, and our shared reality by burying painful insights, knowledge and memories. This self-deception is a vital means of our psychic self-preservation, a means of survival in which we all collude as a society. However, while some self-deceptions can be benign, they can also be dangerous, destructive and life-diminishing.

The Utility and Relevance of EI

The relevance of EI today extends beyond the private sector, gaining increasing importance in the day-to-day operations of government. As the rules governing government work evolve rapidly, public servants are now assessed not only for their intelligence, training, efficiency and expertise but also for their ability to handle themselves and others effectively. This criterion is increasingly applied when selecting individuals for special tasks, deciding who stays and who goes, determining promotions, and predicting who is likely to excel and rise or be passed over and demoted.

Regardless of the field of work, the expertise and quality of work crucial for important positions are now measured by these new standards that have little to do with traditional school and college education, as purely academic abilities become less relevant. These new standards assume one's intellectual ability and technical know-how for the job and instead emphasise on personal qualities like initiative, empathy, adaptability and persuasiveness—qualities essential for effective leadership. This heralds a paradigm shift, recognising that emotional competence is absolutely essential to fully harness the potential of talent and IQ.

The reason we fail to tap into people's full potential is the deficiency in our emotional competence as well as theirs. The competencies required for effective leadership and tasks beyond routine work are often lacking due to a significant gap in cognitive and emotional skills. Some competencies are purely cognitive, rooted in knowledge, such as analytical reasoning or technical expertise. Others are linked to the integration of thoughts and feelings, constituting emotional competence. This capability, grounded in emotional intelligence, leads to outstanding performance in the workplace.

The Mind–Body Connection

Can the mind heal the body? The Buddhist tradition says yes, and now many Western scientists are beginning to agree. In the book *Healing Emotions*, there is a record of an extraordinary series of encounters between the Dalai Lama and prominent Western psychologists, physicians and meditation teachers that shed new light on the mind–body connection. It provides insights into various aspects of emotional intelligence, such as compassion as medicine, the nature of consciousness, self-esteem, and the intersections of mind, body and spirit. Can the realms of science and philosophy collaborate to identify destructive emotions like hatred, fear, insecurity, a sense of superiority, self-righteousness and religious fundamentalism? If so, can they transform these emotions for the betterment of humanity? As the Dalai Lama suggests, 'With the ever-growing impact of science on our lives, religion and spirituality have a greater role to play in reminding us of our humanity.'

CLASSIFYING EMOTIONAL INTELLIGENCE

Emotional intelligence gauges an individual's intelligence within the emotional realm, known as emotional competencies. These emotional competencies are further classified into two categories: personal and social emotional intelligence.

Personal Emotional Intelligence

Personal emotional intelligence, as personal competencies, encompasses self-awareness, self-regulation and motivation, which together determine how we manage ourselves.

1. **Self-awareness**: Acknowledging, identifying and understanding our emotions, our strengths and weaknesses, values and motivations, our state of mind, our preferences and choices, and the resources available to us. The inherent ability to discern subjective currents has deep roots in evolution, with the brain area responsible for gut feelings and intuition developing earlier than the centre for rational thought (the neo-cortex). Intuition and gut feelings enable us to access information from our internal reservoir of emotional memory, which serves as our own repository of wisdom and judgment. This ability is pivotal to self-awareness, which serves as the foundational skill for three key emotional competencies: emotional awareness, accurate self-assessment and self-confidence.

    Emotional awareness: Acknowledging our emotions, understanding what triggers them, how they impact and determine our performance, and utilising our values, beliefs and preferences in decision-making.

    Accurate self-assessment: Knowledge of our personal capacities and limits, a clear sense of our strengths and weaknesses, recognition of areas that need improvement and change, and the ability to learn from experience.

    Self-confidence: The courage and self-belief that reassures individuals about their personal strengths, their inherent value, their tested capabilities and their beliefs and goals.

2. **Self-regulation**: The ability to control our internal mental states, propensities, impulses, and the available resource pool. It encompasses elements such as self-control, righteousness, conscientiousness, compatibility and openness to new ideas. Under stressful conditions, the brain operates in ways where emotions can hinder its functions. For instance, when giving a speech before a critical audience, or at a job interview, anxiety or nervousness or overconfidence may undermine one's performance.

Our working memory plays a crucial role in understanding, reasoning, perspective planning and learning. It functions optimally when the mind remains calm and composed. However, in emergency situations, the brain switches into a self-protective mode and operates within the frequently functioning modules, bypassing complex thought processes typical of working memory. These neural mechanisms and brain circuitry have evolved in the course of human evolution. That is why in emergencies or crises, individuals often encounter troublesome emotions like anxiety, fear, frustration and anger.

3. **Motivation:** The driving force or internal and external factors that stimulate an individual's desire and energy to be continually interested and committed to achieving a particular goal, completing a task, or engaging in a specific behaviour. It involves the emotional and psychological processes that initiate, guide and maintain goal-oriented actions. Motivation can be influenced by a variety of factors, including personal goals, values, social norms, internal satisfaction, and external rewards like desire for achievements and recognition. Understanding motivation is essential across fields such as psychology, education, management and sports as it plays a crucial role in determining both individual and collective behaviour.

Social Emotional Intelligence

Social emotional intelligence includes competencies like empathy and social skills, which determine how we handle others, contribute to building positive relationships, foster collaboration and navigate social complexities.

Empathy: The capacity to understand and share the feelings of others, show compassion and connect with them emotionally. It is about understanding how others think and reason in a given situation and why, and their expectations from us. Empathy includes awareness of the situation, social environment, respect for diversity, being attuned to social dynamics, cultural norms, political beliefs, understanding the perspectives of different individuals and groups, and consideration for others.

Social skills: The proficiency of inducing desirable responses in others. Social skills include using one's aura to influence others, persuasive and effective communication, active listening, conflict management, cooperation, coordination, team work and leadership. It also includes the ability to build lasting relationships and initiate change.

HOW TO ACHIEVE EMOTIONAL INTELLIGENCE

As discussed previously, possessing a high intelligence quotient alone cannot work wonders in an individual's life—especially in the career of a civil servant or one aspiring to be one. Unfortunately, our education system completely ignores the importance of emotional intelligence. Unlike general intelligence, emotional intelligence has the advantage that it can be developed at any age, and is not predetermined by genetics. Emotional intelligence can be acquired by anyone and it can be inculcated and enhanced through self-reflection, practice and learning from experience. We will now look at the systematic steps to acquire emotional intelligence.

1. *Recognise emotions*: Develop the ability to identify and acknowledge your own emotions as well as the emotions of others.
2. *Distinguish and examine emotions*: Differentiate between various emotions and objectively analyse their origins and triggers.
3. *Welcome and cherish emotions*: Embrace and appreciate the range of human emotions, understanding that each emotion serves a purpose.

4. *Contemplate on your emotions and their genesis*: Reflect on your emotions, delve into their roots and try and understand the underlying causes.
5. *Regulate your emotions*: Cultivate the skill of managing and controlling your own emotions effectively.
6. *Regulate others' emotions*: Develop the ability to influence and guide the emotions of others, fostering a positive and collaborative environment based on trust.

The first and crucial step is to acknowledge emotions. This requires being alert, empathetic, a good listener and a keen observer. The subsequent step involves discerning whether the expressed emotions are genuine or fabricated—a distinctive skill of a competent civil servant. This discernment sharpens with experience, demanding a keen insight to differentiate between authentic sentiments and feigned expressions. Mistakes at this stage can haunt civil servants throughout their careers, leading to decision paralysis from the fear of error. Some have erred by succumbing to political emotions, even with bona fide intentions. In the face of diverse emotions, it is essential to delve into their causes, minutely diagnosing their origins. Understanding the roots equips civil servants to anticipate their evolution and control them more effectively in the future.

The next, and often challenging, step involves regulating emotions. Since we have greater control over ourselves than others, it is advisable to focus on regulating personal emotions first. Identifying the origin of specific emotions facilitates better control over their supply. Extracurricular activities such as sports, meditation and group engagement serve as effective tools for regulating both personal and others' emotions. After achieving self-regulation, the focus shifts to controlling the emotions of others. This is the toughest and most demanding task which involves various psychological methods, including attitude change and persuasion. However, an established and seasoned leader of proven integrity can accomplish this challenging task.

WORKING WITH EMOTIONAL INTELLIGENCE

The practical application of emotional intelligence in governance has become inevitable in today's new public management approach to public administration. How does emotional intelligence as a competency go beyond individual efforts to become a pivotal factor for the efficiency and success of an entire organisation? Founders of the Consortium for Research on Emotional Intelligence in Organizations, Daniel Goleman and Cary Cherniss, examines the conceptual and strategic issues involved in defining, measuring and promoting EI in organisations in their book *The Emotionally Intelligent Workplace*.

Leaders and exemplary bureaucrats are distinguished not just by their IQs or their job skills, but by their emotional intelligence that determines how they interact, communicate, handle crises and lead. Pattern recognition and big-picture thinking are traits that allow leaders to discern meaningful trends from the information around them. Intellectual and technical superiority ultimately play little role in successful leadership. At the top executive levels, everyone needs competent cognitive skills, but being better at them does not make an exemplary leader; it is emotional competence that creates the crucial difference between ordinary leaders and trailblazers. Analyses conducted across 500 corporations, government agencies and non-profit organisations worldwide reaffirm that EI is the barometer of excellence in any job. Personal competencies grounded in self-mastery (such as accurate self-assessment, self-control, initiative and optimism) and essential relationship skills (such as service orientation, developing others, conflict management and building bonds) are crucial in this regard.

Applying Emotional Intelligence for Better Governance

Governance, a complex and multidimensional endeavour, frequently entails grappling with public problems that may be inherently more emotional than mechanical, and often shaped by highly situational factors. Executives, faced with these challenges, lack readymade solutions to navigate such intricate situations. The complexity of these problems is further heightened by the diverse expectations of the public, varying levels of understanding, moral considerations, cultural nuances, the political aspirations of public representatives and bureaucratic attitude. Present-day governance—which is centred around citizen satisfaction, the efficacy of various tools of good governance such as citizen charters, government outreach initiatives, the transformation of relationships from a master–slave dynamic to a service provider–client/customer model, transparency, and diagonal accountability—is intricately linked to EI. The success of these initiatives depends upon the adeptness of executives in employing emotional intelligence to comprehend and navigate the intricate web of emotions underlying public issues.

Government departments commonly grapple with problems of resource scarcity in terms of both manpower and funds. Addressing these effectively necessitates the use of emotional intelligence. Administrators endowed with emotional intelligence can adeptly allocate resources based on their competencies and self-confidence. Additionally, a nuanced understanding of the emotions of colleagues and subordinates, and their underlying causes is crucial. For instance, personal preferences misaligned with job responsibilities signifies a potential issue that EI can help recognise and address.

Curbing Corruption and Fostering Efficiency

Emotional intelligence plays a pivotal role in curbing the misuse of public funds and fostering administrative self-awareness, contributing to enhanced efficiency. It equips administrators with insights into motivational, ethical and political values, administrative expertise, experience, and levels of mental and physical fitness. Armed with this self-awareness, individuals can fulfill their roles justly, undertaking tasks that drive innovations for societal welfare. Moreover, emotional intelligence enables administrators to discern negative emotions such as fear, impulsiveness, anger, desire for monetary gain, pursuit of status and undue career advancement. By fostering self-awareness and mitigating potentially corrupt behaviour, emotional intelligence becomes an indispensable tool for bureaucrats, empowering them to navigate challenging situations with integrity and prudence.

Merely recognising emotions is insufficient for a civil servant; they must also be comprehended through the lenses of duty and morality. Bureaucrats need to be able to regulate these emotions, signifying the attenuation of negative emotions and the augmentation of positive ones. This entails maintaining utmost integrity and balance in behaviour, steering clear of both overconfidence and excessive compassion in any situation. An emotionally charged but inadequately regulated public servant may veer off course, jeopardising meticulously planned government initiatives.

A bureaucrat should eschew seeking public acclaim and popularity, refraining from appropriating credit for the success of government schemes. Misusing public funds to advance personal agendas without proper legislative sanction is a breach of duty. Government work conditions are challenging; civil servants may be posted in remote areas with harsh living conditions. In such circumstances, it is only their motivation and sense of duty that encourage them to persist and lead to success. For instance, implementing government programmes in regions characterised by geographical and social hardships demands an immense amount of drive, determination and motivation. Consistently monitoring various programmes to combat corruption and enhance efficiency also requires a high level of motivation to work tirelessly. Emotional regulation, therefore, becomes a linchpin for bureaucratic success, ensuring that public servants navigate challenges with resilience, ethical responsibility and steadfastness.

Collaborative Governance

A civil servant cannot execute all tasks single-handedly. Delegation, coordination and collaboration with subordinates are essential. Mobilising the public to leverage government welfare schemes is a crucial aspect of the job. When overseeing law and order or acting as a judicial or quasi-judicial authority, a civil servant must intelligently gauge and regulate emotions. Success in these roles hinges on the adept management of both personal and others' emotions—subordinates, politicians, local pressure groups, community advocates and citizens at large.

Empathy is a cornerstone trait for a public servant. The ability to comprehend people's needs, emotions and reasoning is vital, guiding the effective implementation of government schemes to minimise public grievances. Empathy fosters service orientation, instilling concern for the plight of the weaker and vulnerable segments of society. Emotional intelligence, particularly in the form of empathy, equips a civil servant to navigate the complex landscape of responsible governance, ensuring a more empathetic, responsive and inclusive administration.

Improving Policy Implementation

There are several government schemes that require the active involvement and participation of the common people for their success. Managerial skills alone would not suffice in such initiatives; a unique style of leadership and proficiency in social skills is required to mobilise and engage the public. It is more about teamwork rather than a one-man show. For example, schemes like MNREGS, Swachh Bharat Mission and Pradhan Mantri Awas Yojana (Rural) demand greater public awareness and cooperation. The successful implementation of such programmes hinges on the adept assessment and regulation of emotions among stakeholders and direct beneficiaries.

Often the problems of rural–urban migration, development of urban ghettos, open defecation, lack of basic health and primary education are not crises rooted in policy making as such but are rather related to ineffective, thoughtless and poor implementation of policy that lacks emotional intelligence-based social skills in the middle managerial level as well as in the operating core-level executives. Addressing these challenges mandates a comprehensive approach that integrates social skills and emotional intelligence into policy implementation strategies, fostering a more responsive and impactful governance framework.

Management versus Leadership

Bureaucrats at times mistakenly perceive administrative tasks through the lens of managerial skills alone. This misconception leads to a fundamental error in interpreting the role of civil servants in a country like India, where competencies for the job must extend beyond traditional managerial capabilities and duties. A public servant frequently finds themselves in a position of leadership, guiding, motivating and inspiring their team rather than solely managing its affairs and delegating. It is crucial to recognise that leadership and management are not mutually exclusive but complementary aspects of a public servant's profile. Achieving organisational strength requires a delicate balance between strong leadership focused on vision and inspiration, and robust management, ensuring resolution of conflicts, efficient execution and resource optimisation.

Leaders and managers both play distinctive, often overlapping, roles that are essential for the smooth functioning and success of any organisation (as seen in Table 8.1). Generally,

Table 8.1: Differences between a manager and a leader

MANAGER	LEADER
1. *Objective*: Managers concentrate on achieving specific objectives and tasks. Their primary concern is efficient execution and meeting short-term goals.	1. Leaders focus on creating and communicating a compelling vision. They inspire and motivate others by outlining a shared purpose and long-term goals.
2. *Approach to people*: Managers are task-oriented, emphasising completion of specific assignments and adherence to established procedures for achieving predefined goals.	2. Leaders build relationships, inspire trust and empower their team. They are more people-oriented, fostering a positive and collaborative work environment.
3. *Working style*: Managers rely on their formal authority to direct and control. Their influence is positional and involves overseeing day-to-day operations.	3. Leaders influence through inspiration, motivation, charisma and setting examples. They often lead by influence rather than by authority.
4. *Risk-taking*: Managers tend to be risk-averse, prioritising order, stability and consistency. They focus on minimising potential disruptions to ensure smooth operations, productivity and efficiency.	4. Leaders are more inclined to take calculated risks in pursuit of innovation, progress and excellence. They embrace challenges and encourage their team to do the same.
5. *Perspective*: Managers have a short-to-medium-term perspective, concentrating on achieving specific, measurable results within a set timeframe.	5. Leaders have a long-term perspective and focus on future possibilities and goals. They are less concerned with immediate results if it aligns with the broader vision.
6. *Delegation*: Managers delegate tasks based on specific roles and responsibilities, aiming for efficiency and timely completion of tasks as per set guidelines.	6. Leaders delegate authority and empower their team members to take ownership of tasks. They trust and encourage others to contribute to the shared vision.
7. *Response to change*: Managers may resist change if it disrupts established processes. Their focus is on maintaining stability, maximising productivity and quality control.	7. Leaders embrace change and act as change agents. They encourage creativity and adaptability to navigate new technology and emerging practices.
8. *Innovation*: Managers implement existing processes and structures efficiently. They ensure that tasks are carried out according to established protocols.	8. Leaders foster innovation by encouraging creativity and thinking outside the box. They inspire a culture of continuous improvement.

Source: Created by authors.

leadership is often lacking in the government system, and then a leader emerges who gains popularity through charisma. It should be understood that leadership is not dependent on a powerful and charismatic persona. Exemplary leaders do not operate in mystical or mysterious ways; they are ordinary individuals with some extraordinary acumen and abilities to overcome challenges.

MODELS OF EMOTIONAL INTELLIGENCE

There are three important models of EI, namely: Salovey-Mayer's Model, Goleman's Model and the Bar-On Model.

1. ***Salovey-Mayer's Model:*** Peter Salovey and John D. Mayer define emotional intelligence as an individual's ability to reason about emotions and to use emotions for enhanced

and constructive thinking. It comprises the ability to perceive emotions, recognise and evolve emotions in support of cognition, and regulate one's emotions to promote emotional cognition based on intellectual development. They suggested a model of EI with four major components:

a) Perception of emotions
b) Assimilation of emotions
c) Understanding emotions
d) Regulating emotions

2. **Goleman's Model**: Daniel Goleman asserts that emotional intelligence is more powerful than cognitive intelligence. He describes EI as a set of abilities and skills that can be inculcated by anyone and that can lead to better outcomes in all walks of life, both personal and professional. His model suggests that measuring IQ does not yield reliable results since it is often exaggerated. He stresses on the situation, 'when smart is dumb'. Goleman's model characterises two distinctive components of EI: personal emotional intelligence (self-awareness, self-regulation and motivation), and social emotional intelligence (empathy and social skills).

3. **Bar-On Model**: This model, developed by Reuven Bar-On, associates emotions or intelligence with specific personality traits that can contribute to professional success and everyday interactions with people. The Bar-On Model defines EI as an array of non-cognitive capabilities, competencies and skills that impact an individual's ability to achieve success by adjusting to the aspirations and compulsions of the related environment. It aims to assess the likelihood of one individual's success as compared to that of others. This model identifies five categories of relevant personality characteristics.

   a) *Intrapersonal skills*: These skills are related to an individual's emotional spectrum and how they handle the associated causes and effects of their emotional experiences. These are shaped by self-regard, awareness of one's emotions, assertiveness, self-realisation and independence.

   b) *Interpersonal skills*: These pertain to how one interfaces with society and adheres to social norms. These skills include empathy, social awareness and interpersonal transactions of behaviour.

   c) *Adaptability*: The ability to generate solutions to problems and manage conflicts associated with social interactions. It includes being flexible, open to others, taking ownership of social problems and successfully navigating diverse social environments and challenges.

   d) *Stress management*: Controlling impulsiveness, anxiety and mental stress while handling one's own emotions and the emotions of others.

   e) *General mood*: A broadly optimistic view of life that encompasses a general feeling of satisfaction, overall happiness and contentment.

The Bar-On model has evolved an Emotional Quotient Inventory (EQ-I) to measure emotional-social intelligence. It consists of a questionnaire of 133 phrases with five different answers each on a scale from Very seldom, Not true for me, Very often true for me, True for me, and Very frequent. Based on the individual's responses to this set of questions, the test can calculate EQ-I and infer which competencies and skills that individual possesses.

REFERENCES

Bar-On, R. (2006). 'The Bar-On Model of Emotional Social Intelligence (ESI)'. *Psicothema 18*(1): 13–25.

Salovey, Peter, and John D. Mayer. (1990). 'Emotional Intelligence'. *Imagination, Cognition and Personality* 9(3): 185–211.

QUESTIONS

1. What is 'emotional intelligence' and how can it be developed in people? How does it help an individual in taking ethical decisions? (UPSC 2013)
2. Anger is a harmful negative emotion. It is injurious to both personal life and work life.
   (a) Discuss how anger leads to negative emotions and undesirable behaviours.
   (b) How can anger be managed and controlled? (UPSC 2016)
3. How will you apply emotional intelligence in administrative practices? (UPSC 2017)
4. 'Emotional Intelligence is the ability to make your emotion work for you instead of against you.' Do you agree with this view? Discuss. (UPSC 2019)
5. It is not the crisis of IQ; rather it is the crisis of EQ in governance. Elaborate with the help of examples.

9
FOUNDATIONAL VALUES FOR CIVIL SERVANTS

> **KEY CONCEPTS**
>
> Introduction; Integrity; Objectivity; Impartiality and Non-Partisanship; Empathy; Dedication to Public Service; Tolerance; Compassion towards Weaker Sections; Courage of Conviction; Perseverance

INTRODUCTION

Civil servants play a key role in the governance of any country. They are the key people who contribute to realising the ideas and vision of the government and serve as the driving force behind both policy formulation and policy implementation at various stages. While different nations may adopt different approaches to the selection and recruitment of civil servants, the core values pertaining to civil services remain more or less universal, with few exceptions. Civil servants are vested with immense authority and discretionary powers to help them navigate the multifarious challenges in administration and in delivering public services. It is imperative to establish checks, both positive and negative, to ensure accountability in their roles. Civil servants are accountable for their conduct, their performance and decisions, and must embody and demonstrate a character grounded in fundamental values essential for fostering good governance, ethical administrative practices, and efficient public service delivery.

In India, civil servants are recruited on a merit basis through fair and open competition and examinations. Indian Civil Services, in the form of Central Civil Services, All India Civil Services, and State/Federal Civil Services form the backbone of Indian administration, where officers are recruited to serve as career bureaucrats. There are certain foundational or core values that all civil servants must possess: these include integrity, honesty, objectivity, impartiality and non-partisanship. These core values are essential for carrying out their work with dedication and commitment, ensuring higher standards across different fields of administration. These, in turn, determine the faith, trust and respect of political executives or ministers, the Parliament and common citizens. As Sardar Vallabhbhai Patel had pertinently advised civil servants, 'Above all, I would advise you to maintain the utmost impartiality and incorruptibility of administration. A civil servant can't afford to and must not take part in politics. Nor must he involve himself in communal wrangles.'

Civil servants are accountable to ministers, their superiors and the public under different dimensions of accountability, and ministers in turn are accountable to the Parliament. Core values such as integrity, honesty, objectivity and impartiality are essential for carrying out functions in the capacity of civil servants. Integrity puts duties and obligations of public service above personal interests; honesty is about being truthful and open; objectivity involves basing actions and decisions on a rigorous analysis of evidence; and impartiality pertains to acting solely according to the merits of the case and serving equally and impartially governments of different political persuasions. The code sets out standards of behaviour expected from a civil servant based on core values which are set out by legislation. Individual government departments may also have their own separate mission and value statements, including standards of conduct expected from a civil servant.

INTEGRITY

Integrity has the following sets of meanings: the state of being whole, complete or undivided; soundness or the quality of being unimpaired; uncompromising adherence to moral principles and an ethical code; honesty. Integrity is about being consistent in one's words, thoughts and actions. One is said to be a person of integrity if what one thinks, says and does are in harmony with each other.

For a civil servant, integrity involves thinking and acting in conformity with the vision and will of the present-day government and working as per its stipulated rules and regulations. His actions, decisions and communications with subordinates, superiors and the media must comply with the directions of the government as per its written orders and official communications. A civil servant must execute orders as per his/her understanding of them without manipulating facts. Integrity, understood as honesty and incorruptibility, is the most sensitive core value of the civil services. This is why there is provision for an integrity report in the Annual Performance Appraisal Report (APAR) of each civil servant, which must be submitted by the reporting officer as beyond doubt in each case. Given below is a partial list of dos and don'ts pertaining to the integrity required of a civil servant.

1. S/he must perform his/her duties and obligations responsibly.
2. S/he must conduct himself/herself professionally at work and earn the trust of superiors, ministers, the legislature, and the public at large.
3. S/he should utilise public funds and resources carefully and carry out fiduciary obligations judiciously.
4. S/he should speak to the media after receiving due authorisation and briefing from the government or the concerned minister or ministry.
5. S/he should present facts pertaining to relevant matters truthfully in front of higher authorities.
6. S/he should not misuse any information obtained in an official capacity in his/her own interest or in another's interest.
7. S/he should not disclose classified information and official secrets while in service.
8. S/he should not accept any gifts, favours or any kind of benefits from anyone which might compromise the fair and honest discharge of his/her functions in public interest.
9. S/he should not deliberately misguide his/her superiors, minister or the legislature.
10. S/he should not be pressured or influenced by any type of fear, coercion or temptation.

OBJECTIVITY

Objectivity is the quality of being fair, impartial and unbiased. In various contexts, especially in decision-making, administration, research, journalism, or evaluations, objectivity refers to the ability to approach situations, issues, or information without personal bias, emotions or preconceived notions. An objective viewpoint is based on facts, evidence and rational analysis rather than influenced by feelings or opinions. In essence, objectivity seeks a neutral and impartial perspective to ensure fairness and accuracy in assessments and judgments.

Objectivity is described as singularity in decision-making, characterised by the absence of subjectivity and bias, where personal opinions do not prevail over the most common opinions on any issue. Objectivity also entails the absence of personal opinions driven by vested interests. Civil servants should approach their work and work-related situations neutrally, without prejudice. Their professional opinions should be grounded in facts and rationality, reflecting a commonality of thought shared by other civil servants facing similar situations. For a civil servant, objectivity may be delineated as follows:

1. A civil servant must honestly, objectively and fearlessly advise their political master or minister based on a considered and rational analysis of the available facts and evidence.
2. S/he must take decisions well-grounded in evidence and facts, in the light of prescribed guidelines. S/he must see that his/her decisions do not vary on a case-by-case basis under similar circumstances, and must ensure consistency in decision-making.
3. S/he must take into consideration expert advice and precedents to avoid subjectivity and bias.
4. S/he must not ignore constraints and inconvenient facts that may arise during the process of decision-making.
5. S/he must not discourage, obstruct or cause needless delays in the implementation and execution of government decisions and policies once they have been finalised.

IMPARTIALITY AND NON-PARTISANSHIP

Impartiality is the quality or state of being fair, unbiased and free from favouritism or discrimination. Impartiality implies the objective and equitable treatment of all individuals or parties without showing preference or prejudice. It involves making decisions or judgments based on merit, evidence and established principles, rather than being influenced by personal opinions, affiliations or external pressures. Impartiality is a fundamental aspect of justice, ethical conduct, and fair governance.

Impartiality and non-partisanship may seem similar, but in the context of civil service they have different meanings. Impartiality pertains to the non-discriminatory attitude of a civil servant, while non-partisanship is associated with being politically unbiased. Impartiality includes not discriminating on the basis of religion, caste, creed, region, or belonging to a particular group when making decisions or advising a minister. It is closely linked with objectivity as someone adhering to objectivity would inherently remain impartial. Impartiality also aligns with the principles of equality and respect for diversity. Civil servants must not act in any way that unjustifiably favours or discriminates against particular individuals or group interests.

Non-partisanship, on the other hand, relates to political impartiality. A civil servant should not discriminate against public representatives based on their political affiliations. This means giving equal respect and attention to MLAs, MPs and other elected politicians regardless of whether they belong to the ruling party, opposition party or are independent. A civil servant should interact with all public representatives on par in a manner that avoids creating complications in the future, especially if another party comes to power.

In roles such as personal secretary, OSD (Officer in Special Duty), or secretary to a ministry, a civil servant must refrain from involving themselves in providing assistance related to the political agenda of a minister. Their focus should be solely on public welfare, and they should not allow official resources to be used for political purposes. Sardar Patel rightly emphasised that civil servants should not engage in politics. Furthermore, a civil servant should not express their political views in public. While they have the right to cast their vote as a personal choice, their vote must remain confidential.

EMPATHY

Empathy is described as the ability to sense, feel and understand the emotions and thoughts of others vicariously, without becoming overly involved, and to predict behaviour that may result from such mental states in the near future. It involves imaginatively projecting oneself into the mindset of others, essentially listening to their thoughts, feeling their pain or pleasure, and understanding their interests by placing oneself in their position. Often, these thoughts, feelings and interests are not explicitly communicated, requiring the application of emotional intelligence to extract them vicariously. A civil servant with the right attitude can effectively leverage the capacity of empathy. Attitude plays a crucial role in filtering out relevant and meaningful information during the interplay of affective, behavioural and knowledge components. Empathy serves as a powerful tool for making quick decisions in real-life problems. It aids in identifying shortcomings in government schemes, potential misuse and public grievances. Moreover, empathy contributes to the formulation of new schemes or programmes for public welfare by understanding the people's expectations from the government. Empathy is also useful for government machinery involved in maintaining law and order, and peace in the state.

A civil servant is endowed with considerable authority and power to implement government schemes. Many individuals attempt to illegitimately benefit from government officials by exerting influence through various means, and they are identified as touts who have connections with key government departments and ministries. A civil servant with a keen empathetic ability can easily discern and eliminate these unwanted and hazardous middlemen. Empathy is also crucial for maintaining a balance between personal and professional life. A civil servant should remain immune to emotional pressures from close family and relatives. Empathy plays a critical role in navigating situations where ethical constraints may hinder providing help. An individual's attitude must allow for the percolation of information that is crucial for being empathetic. Empathy serves as a powerful tool for understanding the impact of one's approach to professional duties and personal behaviour. It helps a person adjust their behaviour during performance while being aware of the impact and expectations of others. Empathy is valuable for comprehending the emotions of others and making judgments about the needs and intentions, good and bad, of other people. Generally, people tend to be self-centric and preoccupied with their own agendas, often disregarding others' feelings. Acquiring empathy requires time, and one needs to take a deep pause to mentally put themselves in place of others. Mere experience of emotion is insufficient if a person lacks adequate past experience of such feelings, their causes and meaning. Being empathetic does not mean being emotionally driven or vulnerable; rather, it is useful for preempting and avoiding corrupt actions and utilising information to improve professionalism and efficiency in public services.

DEDICATION TO PUBLIC SERVICE

Dedication is wholehearted commitment and devotion for achieving something, giving one's single-minded attention and making all possible efforts for a particular objective. Public servants are entrusted with the responsibility to serve the public, which is a colossal, multidimensional and challenging task that demands high levels of commitment and dedication. A public servant is expected to fully devote their knowledge, skills and expertise to meeting professional expectations and be engaged in their work round the clock. Dedication to public service is one of the essential core values for a civil servant; it requires quality time, enthusiasm, motivation and tireless effort in working for public welfare. The commitment to ensure prompt service delivery and prompt redressal of public grievances is absolutely vital. In India, dedication to public service is necessary to uplift the status of the downtrodden and weaker sections of society. A dedicated public servant is motivated intrinsically as well as extrinsically. Intrinsic motivation plays a crucial role when perseverance and persistent efforts are required to achieve social objectives. A sense of duty alone does not suffice—proactive and prompt action towards meeting objectives is necessary.

Limited government resources and the multiple constraints in utilising these resources means that civil servants often find themselves in situations where considerable individual efforts must be exerted to bring about significant positive change in policy-making and implementation. There are numerous examples where civil servants have undertaken innovative projects with community participation without spending government money. This approach represents true dedication to public service and welfare. However, civil servants should also be cautious about showcasing such dedication only for gaining popularity and seeking the limelight. The civil services are not a means to earn money, power and prestige. It is a way of achieving fulfilment by contributing to society while leading an average and satisfactory life as a career bureaucrat. It is a profession where money and status are not ends in themselves but serving the country and its people is the primary objective.

TOLERANCE

Tolerance can be termed as the capacity to accept and respect opinions, beliefs and practices that are incompatible with one's own and individuals who differ from us. It involves showing patience, understanding and forbearance in the face of varying perspectives, behaviours or customs, even if they conflict with our personal views or values. Tolerance promotes an inclusive and harmonious coexistence in a society marked by diversity, acknowledging that people may hold different ideologies, engage in distinct religious practices, or adhere to unique social and cultural norms. It is characterised by an open-minded and non-judgmental approach towards differences, fostering a spirit of acceptance, inclusivity and mutual understanding.

In a phenomenally diverse and multicultural country like India, tolerance becomes an absolutely essential core value for a civil servant. The Indian Constitution gives primary importance to respecting the cultural diversity of the nation, making tolerance a constitutional value. If there are erroneous practices or beliefs prevailing in a section of society, a public servant must not despise them or judge them but try to bring about change in attitude through awareness, education and reform. A civil servant must realise that if a section of society remains backward in terms of education, mindset, living standards and practices, it is equally the failure of the government of the day and the failure of the government machinery, and it must be considered a public duty to address this failure through available constitutional means.

With great power comes greater responsibility. Misuse of power influenced by bias, arrogance, sense of superiority, or a narrow intolerant mindset would divert the objectives of civil services. If someone lacks judgment or practices unacceptable social customs, it is also the result of unequal distribution of resources and economic deprivation. If there are backward or regressive beliefs and customs prevailing in a section of society, a public servant should do his duty by trying to change attitudes through education and by counselling people. A civil servant must take this as a challenge and show a positive attitude towards every section of society; their views regarding religion, belief, caste and creed, region and political ideas should not influence a bureaucrat's neutrality. Regardless of whether the government is rightist, leftist, or any other, the ultimate and only aim of civil servants should be the welfare and wellbeing of the people and the progress of the nation.

COMPASSION TOWARDS WEAKER SECTIONS

In India, systematic discrimination based on caste and religion has led to the emergence of a large population of economically and socially deprived individuals, and these vulnerabilities are invariably passed down through generations. Since independence, different governments have initiated efforts to bridge gaps and improve the situation of these people; it is the duty of civil servants to oversee proper and timely implementation of these programmes. Civil servants must assess the impact of government initiatives and constantly recommend improvements, including necessary policy amendments to address glaring socio-economic disparities in the populace. It is well-known that a large segment of society faces distress due to unsettled dues in exchange for their services. These outstanding dues contribute to the deplorable situation of weaker sections of society that deserve special administrative care and should be treated with empathy.

Civil servants are responsible for ensuring that funds allocated for welfare programmes for weaker sections are not misused by powerful individuals with a feudal mindset. It is a common phenomenon in India for politically and financially influential groups to benefit from government programmes, while the actual beneficiaries suffer. Public servants must remain empathetic and considerate towards weaker sections of society and proactively initiate and implement inclusive government programmes targeted to empower marginal communities and bridge socio-economic disparity. They should always bear in mind that their services are needed as long as they are willing to serve society. This compassionate approach is an essential trait for every civil servant in India.

It is an area where comments on a civil servant's attitude towards people from socio-economically deprived communities are sought in the annual appraisal report.

COURAGE OF CONVICTION

Courage of conviction is what encourages us to act according to our beliefs or ideologies despite opposition, criticism or persecution. Civil servants are entrusted with diverse duties, some of which have clear-cut and standardised guidelines for execution, while others rely on individual discretion and judgment. In some cases, civil servants may not find any related precedents or guidelines, and even seniors and colleagues may not be able to provide useful suggestions. For instance, an enforcement officer may have information related to unlawful activities involving a powerful politician and some officers. The officer wants to expose the racket but lacks sufficient evidence, and there is a risk of facing the wrath of the culprits who are influential people with political clout. In such situations, conviction is crucial; the officer should possess the ability to reach a clear and conclusive decision on the matter. Intuition often plays a role in determining the righteousness of the decision, followed by the courage and determination to proceed in support of that conviction. In the given example, taking steps against unlawful activities of the powerful based on information is conviction of principle. Courage of conviction involves acting without fear, pressure or concern about consequences with respect to oneself.

People may possess rationality, but only a few have the courage to act upon their beliefs, especially when doing so may also potentially harm them. In the civil services, factors such as the allure of good postings, a desire for status quo, and an unwillingness to accept failure or face unpleasant situations can obstruct the courage of conviction. A civil servant should have the confidence to express their views to seniors and political bosses without hesitation, relying on their ability, experience, and based on the evidence of hard facts. Inadequate or shallow knowledge of the ground realities of a situation is often a significant cause behind the lack of courage of conviction among civil servants. They should undertake regular tours of their area of jurisdiction, meet people, take feedback and conduct camps in problematic regions to understand the ground situation better. Building trust with stakeholders of government schemes, establishing cordial relationships and addressing grievances on the spot are crucial for civil servants.

A civil servant must have the courage to say 'No' to seniors and political bosses, both in writing and personally, especially when it comes to undoable, questionable or inadvisable tasks. As Sardar Patel famously said, 'Today my secretary can write a note opposed to my views. I have given that freedom to all my secretaries. I have told them that if you don't give your honest opinion for fear that it will displease your minister, please then you better go. I will bring another secretary.'

PERSEVERANCE

Perseverance can be understood as the act of striving single-mindedly despite facing any number of hindrances and difficulties in achieving a goal. According to Lorimer and Lechner, 'It is a value that refers to the measure of how strongly something is desired for its physical or moral beauty, usefulness, rarity etc., especially, expressed in terms of the efforts, money etc., that one is willing to expend in acquiring, retaining, or preserving it.' As one of the core values in civil services, perseverance is about achieving public interest or the delivery of public goods. Public servants must be aware of and constantly grapple with the many obstacles in the way of service delivery, including stringent rules and regulations, political interferences, low morale in government machinery, and the continuous struggle for the betterment of society. Public servants in higher echelons go through various tests and possess adequate virtues to produce desired results; however, very few can fulfill the job as per public expectations. The difference is often due to the lack of perseverance. Some key factors impacting low levels of perseverance include:

1. *Discouragement*: Hard work or enthusiastic efforts made to initiate change can fail or not achieve the desired results at the beginning of a civil servant's career due to limited experience. Many public servants become discouraged at this, fearing criticism for their failures or lack of acknowledgement and appreciation for their work.
2. *Procrastination*: It is the enemy of perseverance. In the field of administration various issues and problems arise daily, and important matters often suffer due to misinterpretation of their priorities. Sometimes crucial tasks suffer due to procrastination and entirely avoidable delays by officers, which leads to serious failures at work.
3. *Laziness*: Civil services demand energetic and agile officers. Physically fit and mentally tough officers are the ones who write success stories. Lazy and slow officers degrade the quality of governance because they lack the necessary energy, resilience and zeal for persevering.
4. *Lack of motivation*: There is little or no scope for out-of-turn pay hikes and promotions in the government. Public servants receive standard benefits at regular intervals irrespective of their continuous outstanding performance and perseverance against extreme odds. In other words, in government service, extrinsic motivational factors are few. The motivation has to be intrinsic and come from within.

Every civil servant should develop and follow their own individual code of perseverance to overcome the above-mentioned negative factors.

1. Never give up as long as you are convinced that you are right.

2. Be optimistic about creating a conducive environment once you have decided to keep struggling against the odds.
3. Be courageous and remain positive and undismayed in the face of challenges.
4. Don't get intimidated by people who try to discourage you or stop you.
5. Overcome all physical limitations and setbacks.
6. Be persistent and determined in trying to complete the job.
7. Always remember that the bigger breakthrough comes after defeating adversity.

QUESTIONS

1. (a) What do you understand by the following terms in the context of public service?
    (i) Integrity
    (ii) Perseverance
    (iii) Spirit of service
    (iv) Commitment
    (v) Courage of conviction
   (b) Indicate two more attributes which you consider important for public service. Justify your answer. (UPSC 2013)
2. Mere compliance with law is not enough; a public servant must also have a well-developed ethical sensibility for effective discharge of duties. Do you agree? Explain with the help of two examples, where (i) an act is ethically right but not legally; and (ii) an act is legally right, but not ethically. (UPSC 2015)
3. How are the virtues of trustworthiness and fortitude manifested in public service? Explain with examples. (UPSC 2015)
4. Why should impartiality and non-partisanship be considered as foundational values in public services, especially in the present day socio-political context? Illustrate your answer with examples. (UPSC 2016)
5. One of the tests of integrity for a civil servant is the complete refusal to be compromised. Explain with reference to a real-life example. (UPSC 2017)
6. Examine the relevance of each of the following in the context of civil service:
    (a) Transparency
    (b) Accountability
    (c) Fairness and justice
    (d) Courage of conviction
    (e) Spirit of service (UPSC 2017)
7. 'In doing a good thing, everything is permitted which is not prohibited expressly or by clear implication.' Examine the statement with suitable examples in the context of a public servant discharging his/her duties. (UPSC 2018)
8. State the three basic values, universal in nature, in the context of civil services and bring out their importance. (UPSC 2018)

10
CONTRIBUTIONS OF MORAL PHILOSOPHERS AND THINKERS FROM INDIA AND THE WORLD

> **KEY CONCEPTS**
> Indian Philosophers; Ethics in Religion; Western Philosophers; Chinese Philosophers; Social Contract Theory; Contemporary Critique of Social Contract Theory

INDIAN PHILOSOPHERS

Indian moral philosophy boasts an incredibly rich tapestry of thinkers who have profoundly influenced ethical discourse through the ages. Spanning diverse religious and philosophical traditions, these luminaries have contributed unique perspectives on morality, virtue, and the human quest for a good and righteous life. These include Kautilya's influential treatise on political ethics and statecraft, *Arthashastra*; Gautam Buddha, whose ethical teachings rooted in compassion and right understanding guide followers on the Eightfold Path towards ethical living; Mahavira, the 24th Tirthankara of Jainism who laid down ethical principles centred around non-violence, truth and asceticism; Adi Sankaracharya, the theologian who consolidated the doctrine of Advaita Vedanta; the *Bhagavad Gita*, an epic poem and philosophical masterpiece that explores moral dilemmas and the nature of dharma or duty; Dharmakirti, a Buddhist logician whose discussions on ethics within the framework of Buddhist philosophy explore issues related to perception, inference and the nature of reality; Basava, a influential figure in the Bhakti movement whose ethical teachings within the Lingayat tradition emphasise devotion, equality and the rejection of caste-based discrimination, just to name a few. These ancient philosophers, among numerous others, have left an indelible mark on Indian moral philosophy, offering diverse ethical frameworks that continue to inspire seekers on their quest for a virtuous and meaningful life. Modern Indian thinkers and philosophers who have engaged with questions of ethics include Sarvepalli Radhakrishnan, M. K. Gandhi, Sri Aurobindo, B. K. Matilal, J. L. Mehta and Arindam Chakrabarti, to name just a few.

Kautilya

Kautilya, also known as Chanakya, ancient Indian philosopher, teacher, economist and political strategist, delves into political ethics, statecraft and governance in his seminal work *Arthashastra*, urging rulers to consider the welfare of their subjects. The *Arthashastra* raises a multitude of ethical issues pertaining to the Indian political environment which are as relevant today as they were in his times. Kautilya regards *artha* (wealth, money) as an important *purushartha* (object of human pursuit), and poverty as one of the crucial factors leading to the fallen state of human beings, and their deviation from ethical conduct. For Kautilya, economics and ethics are intrinsically interwoven, and this differentiates his *Arthashastra* from Adam Smith's *Wealth of Nations*.

Kautilya clearly stipulates common duties for all individuals: these include *ahimsa* (non-violence), *satyam* (truthfulness), cleanliness, compassion and tolerance. For the king, the primary duty is to ensure the happiness of his subjects, with his wellbeing tied to theirs. According to Kautilya, the king's personal interests should align with public interest and morality, and he must function as a public servant under a well-defined contract. Kautilya strongly advocates for a corruption-free and responsive state administrative system, based on various combinations of moral and immoral actions, public interest, actions against public interest, the king's interests, and actions against the king's interests. Kautilya posits that actions that are moral and in the public interest should prevail, regardless of whether they fulfil the king's interests. Moving beyond conventional moral obligations, he even emphasises that actions deemed immoral but serving both the public and the king's interests should also prevail. Kautilya highlights virtues such as austerity, leadership and moderation as indispensable for a king. A king must possess wisdom akin to a sage (*rajarishi*) and exercise control over his senses and desires to resist temptation and harmful influences, he asserts. Further, a government must operate strictly according to the rule of law.

Kautilya further advises that a king should not completely give up a worldly lifestyle, but should practise moderation by avoiding excessive indulgence in pleasures and refraining from extreme austerity. A good king should be a role model for his ministers and subjects, and should earn their respect through leadership and example rather than mere authority and power. For, as Kautilya rightly observed, 'If the king is energetic, his subjects will be energetic too. If he is lazy in performing his duties, the subjects will follow suit and eat into his wealth. Besides, a lazy king risks falling into the hands of his enemies.'

According to Kautilya, a king garners public support through virtuous deeds and fair administration of justice. Public support is crucial for maintaining a powerful and invincible empire as well as for ensuring its economic wellbeing. The king must allocate state resources to care for children, the old, the destitute, famine victims, childless women and others. Kautilya further recommends that if a government servant dies on duty, his wife and children should be entitled to receive his salary and food allowance. Kautilya believes that a just and well-structured punishment system encourages subjects to adhere moderately to *dharma* (righteousness), *artha* (wealth) and *kama* (pleasure). Conversely, a tyrannical king is despised, risking the wrath and rebellion of his subjects.

According to Kautilya, unethical behaviour cannot be controlled solely through rules, regulations and punishment. It requires shaping character and imparting values that are both ethical and practical, including good judgment, perceptivity, openheartedness, fairness, prudence, and an understanding of one's situation and relative position with respect to people and surroundings. Kautilya believes greed is the enemy of intellectual traits. A greedy person not only harms public interest but also jeopardises his own interests. While a sound knowledge of laws is necessary in developing rules, regulations and common prescriptions to guide human behaviour, morality, rationality and a sense of fairness are equally essential for character building and to foresee the negative consequences of wrongful actions.

Considering the king as a paid public servant, Kautilya contends that if a king neglects the welfare of his subjects, he must bear the sins of his people. Kautilya raises various questions on the right conduct of life and attempts to provide answers. He asserts that every person is obliged to support their family and dependents, and advocates penalties for those who fail to fulfil this duty. He prohibits individuals from abandoning their familial responsibilities even while pursuing the path of asceticism. Further, he states that parents who do not provide education to their children are acting against their children's wellbeing.

Kautilya adopts a pragmatic approach regarding the influence of corruption on public servants. He wisely observes, 'Whether an individual desires it or not, honey or poison placed on the tongue will eventually be tasted. Similarly, corruption or embezzlement of public funds by a government official starts from a small amount and escalates.' Sources of malpractice among government officials include lack of knowledge and skills, lethargy, gluttony, over-indulgence, lust, anger, fear and misuse of authority. Government servants must exercise control over these, he asserts.

Sarvepalli Radhakrishnan

Sarvepalli Radhakrishnan views morality as a subjective concept, distancing himself from traditional moral principles. He considers moral living as a necessary condition for attaining wisdom and fully endorses the idea that spirituality can only be realised through the pursuit of morality, as emphasised in various Indian religious texts. According to him, we exist in a world marked by selfishness, where people think rationally and are primarily motivated by economic principles to pursue self-interest, comfort and fulfil their animalistic desires. An ethical life is the only means to achieve the ultimate purpose in life. Radhakrishnan identifies the highest ethical ideal as *moksha* or spiritual realisation.

He rejects the Greek notion that 'man is the measure of all things', viewing it as an ignorance of other values in the pursuit of establishing pragmatic and communistic humanism. Radhakrishnan believes that practising spirituality in actions and intuitively realising it can establish universal brotherhood. Therefore, material progress and spiritual development should progress simultaneously in a person's life. He does not endorse morality in a rigid form that merely assigns righteousness to socially respectable conduct and correct behaviour; instead, he considers morality as a progressive idea aimed at discovering true moral goodness. The moral heroism exemplified by figures like Socrates, Martin Luther King, Gandhi and Jesus Christ does not define the scope of morality for Radhakrishnan as not everyone possesses such extraordinary moral insight, courage and self-discipline.

He further says, virtue is heaven, and vice is hell. Good and bad carry their own fruits in terms of rewards and punishments, respectively. Virtue leads to the ultimate social goal in a broader sense whereas vice leads to personal satisfaction. For Radhakrishnan, *dharma* is a combination of ethics and religion. Religion is not a cult or persuasion, but pertains to the laws of living a correct life, aiming to achieve the compound goal of mundane happiness and salvation. Thus, dharma is both dynamic and progressive but eternal in nature. Dharma comprises those ideals, institutions and objectives that shapes individual character and guides individual actions so that they fit into society while pursuing personal happiness and maintaining a complete balance in the routine activities of life.

He further describes *satya* (truthfulness) and *ahimsa* (compassion) as the two major tenets of spiritual life. One who is compassionate gradually becomes able to inculcate a moral attitude. This compassion should be expressed in words, thoughts and actions. Even our enemies deserve our compassion and love, which has the power to resolve the greatest of conflicts. Radhakrishnan considers truth as the highest virtue, achievable by transcending parochial selfishness and egocentricity. Truth can be realised through the ethical process of releasing ourselves from the prison of individualism and renouncing the ego and self-interest. According to him, divinity resides in the idea of a shared common humanity, a oneness which guides us to become devotional and compassionate. Ahimsa is also reverence for this human oneness.

Radhakrishnan believes that good and bad do not exist in reality as such, but are human constructs. Good pertains to actions that are beneficial for oneself and others, while bad is regarded as an obstruction in the path of such benefit. He accepts the law of *karma* and the freedom of will in connection with human life and the human condition. He believes that an individual's past deeds are responsible for their present condition, and that their present karma will decide their future; good produces good and bad produces bad, and it is never too late to prevent bad deeds to mend the future.

Sri Aurobindo

Sri Aurobindo envisions human potential as being sufficient for achieving higher goals in life through the process of evolving into a great soul. For him, ethics is a means of understanding the role of the highest authority or God in human life, and its objective is to bring about harmony in life through love, purity and human stamina. Ethics introduces the law of good, which is implied in the law of God, transcending all earthly laws. Ethics, as understood by Sri Aurobindo, pertains to the soul actively participating in such moral affairs, encompassing actions beyond mere knowledge and reason. Ethics prescribes dos and don'ts, permeating characteristics in conduct such as love, sacrifice, truthfulness, devotion and charity.

Sri Aurobindo challenges traditional ethical theories based on the law of abstraction. He argues that ethical motivation originates from the subconscious in the form of duty which is later understood in terms of law. In other words, laws are initially followed unquestioningly due to their perceived moral legitimacy, but the human rational faculty begins to question the reasonability and morality of laws. Once these questions are satisfactorily answered, laws take the form of ethical ideas. The entire process involves liberating prejudices and resolving conflicting moralities, ultimately streamlining the system of ethical conduct. Ethical awareness and advancement culminates in a human being attaining a divine character. At this stage it is the internal nature of man rather than his actions that determines morality. Actions may be confusing, but they are considered moral because they belong to a moral entity. Thus, Sri Aurobindo argues, man need not exert deliberate or special effort to be moral and virtuous, but becomes so naturally and effortlessly. Here, Sri Aurobindo aligns himself as a supporter of virtue ethics.

Sri Aurobindo asserts that for a man to attain an ethical nature, a spiritual transformation is necessary. The foundation of divine life lies in the human spirit which surpasses rationality, willpower and intuition, existing at the very core of human nature. The sprout of divinity originates from the seed of ethical spirit. This process of divine culmination should begin with individuals, Aurobindo contends, and such individuals should subsequently transfer these qualities to the community at large. In his view, no political instruments, in any form, can fully achieve the objectives of liberty, equality and fraternity. He believes it is the need of the time that gives rise to a true religion grounded in humanism and service to mankind. As a humanist, Aurobindo identifies God in human beings as a fundamental truth and a motivator for evolution towards becoming a 'supramental' being.

In contrast to Kant's theory of 'duty for duty's sake', Sri Aurobindo emphasises 'duty for God's sake'. He underscores the importance of indifferent, motiveless and unbiased work undertaken for the sake of God and the Greater Self or Universal Will. Aurobindo introduces the idea of the evolution of the common man through the intermediary stages of the 'overman' to the 'supramental being'. According to him, the supramental being, a divine entity dedicated to the service of humanity, transcends all traditional moralities, embodying consciousness, motivelessness and detachment. To ascend towards achieving a supramental status, Aurobindo prescribes four principal conducts to be followed:

1. Preference or desire of an individual
2. Laws, acceptable good and societal customs
3. An ideal morality
4. The highest transcendental law of nature

He further explains that personal desires in the form of physical and moral cravings should be satisfied and the pursuit of such satisfaction must be the principal rule of conduct. The scope and purview of personal satisfaction must be guided by the laws of the collectivity or society. The existence of an ideal morality, which transcends the idea of both personal satisfaction as well as societal laws, controls individuals and society in the interest of an ideal order of spirituality. Finally, above all social laws and individual values there is a divine law that represents the final objective of human progress from natural law to universal law. This universal law determines the conduct of collective spiritual life.

The idea of good and evil is central to Aurobindo's philosophy. He describes good as helpful in realising divine fullness whereas evil obstructs this progress. Evil and falsehood are products of ignorance or wrong knowledge. This ignorance is dispelled with the dawn of spiritual knowledge or truth. Aurobindo further explains the anomaly of labeling evil as good and good as evil on the basis of varying space and time. This happens due to the operation of cosmic forces in human life and the emergence of specific conditions in human mentality. These anomalous notions of good and evil arise due to disharmony in life.

According to Aurobindo, the gradual transformation of an individual from the objective of self to all, in other words, progression with the idea of self-sacrifice towards selfless divinity gives rise to ethical growth. Morality does not depend upon outcome, intention or objective; it depends on the development of conscience in terms of self-expression. Aurobindo does not consider reward and punishment as moral motivations, and he also refutes the law of karma in its popular sense. He considers that the soul uses this law as one of the instruments, and this law of karma does not solely decide the destiny of the soul. Finally, according to Aurobindo, the ultimate objective of all human beings is to develop themselves as supramental beings and then help others achieve this goal. All political and social organisation should endeavour to evolve such supramental consciousness, he asserts.

Thiruvalluvar

Thiruvalluvar was a Tamil poet and philosopher of the 4th century BC. His literary marvel *Tirukkural* is a collection of couplets on ethics, economics and human nature. The *Tirukkural* (or *Kural*) explicitly mentions morality to be the highest ideal. According to Thiruvalluvar, happiness is the right of every individual, but it must be attained through moral actions. He emphasises that morality is above happiness. Human life is meant for a greater cause and should not be confined within a small circle—it should transcend its boundaries and endeavour to achieve a moral social order. Thiruvalluvar asserts that morality arises when the human mind is free from guilt and impurities. A clean mind gives birth to pure thoughts that are reflected in an individual's words and actions. A person is immoral when their thoughts do not align with their words and actions.

He further states that one must consistently act morally whenever possible to the best of one's capabilities. Thiruvalluvar considers morality as essential and important in family life, asserting that individuals can practice morality within the family. He also warns against killing animals for religious practices and food. Thiruvalluvar identifies three important virtues of life: spirituality, charity and love. Spirituality is continuous remembrance of divine intelligence. Charity refines human life and human nature, for 'Accumulating a lot of wealth and eating alone without sharing is worse than the act of asking for alms.' He also underscores the importance of love in family life.

Numerous couplets in the *Tirukkural* pertain to good business ethics. Thiruvalluvar holds that ethical conduct is crucial for acquiring wealth with a good reputation; therefore, ethics in business practice is inevitable. He emphasises the importance of transparency and truthfulness in business transactions, and states that a business leader should be well educated and exhibit good behaviour.

In *Tirukkural*, righteousness is described by the term *aram*, and Thiruvalluvar explains that righteousness can be cultivated by refraining from four evils: envy, anger, desire and harsh words. *Aram* is considered one of the noblest values in Tamil classical literature, alongside others like *porul* (wealth), *inbam* (happiness), etc. Thiruvalluvar firmly believes in righteousness, asserting that people should take it seriously because righteousness itself has the power to thwart those who intend to harm others. *Aram* serves as a link between the individual and society, and acts as the guardian of society, thus contributing to social prosperity.

ETHICS IN RELIGION

Ethics is not derived from religious prophecies, nor is it based solely on the teachings of specific religious texts, or the dictates of higher religious authorities. Rather, religion provides a foundation for ethics to be understood and followed by the masses. All religions contain certain moral instructions that can be subjected to rational scrutiny to some extent. We discuss below some of the major religions and their ethical teachings.

Buddhist Ethics

Gautam Buddha holds a prominent place among the ethical scholars of India. Buddhism emphasises purity of mind and the compassion to cultivate love in human society. Buddhism urges individuals to investigate the causes of suffering (*dukha*) and find a balanced approach known as the middle path (or *madhyam marg*), avoiding extremes. Achieving this middle path demands considerable discipline and a high degree of spiritual development. While Buddhism does not explicitly use the term 'ethics', the concept of *sila* closely aligns with it. In Buddhism, moral disciplines are encompassed by 10 virtuous actions (*Dasa-Kusala-Kamma-Patha*) or 10 virtues that involve refraining from 10 negative actions: killing, stealing, adultery, lying, divisive speech, harsh speech, inactive conversation, greed for wealth, malice, and wrong view. The Mahayana sect of Buddhism outlines six perfections to be achieved in life which are as follows:

1. Generosity or charity (*dana*)
2. Moral discipline (*sila*)
3. Patience (*shanti*)
4. Perseverance (*virya*)
5. Meditation (*dhyana*)
6. Wisdom (*pragya*)

These perfections have different meanings and are used under different contexts. Generosity is related to charity for the deprived and poor. Patience may be described as calmness and peace of mind, being non-reactive and refraining from passions like fear, anger and retaliation. Perseverance is the skill of channelising efforts into constructive works that benefit the greater cause. Meditative stability is crucial to overcome rashness or impulsive decision-making and deviation from the right path. Wisdom is the knowledge of right and wrong, as discussed in Buddhist texts. For instance, to illustrate recognition of right bodily action, Buddha describes it as actions which do not cause one to harm the self or others.

While Buddhism does not provide a normative theory of ethics, it may be inferred from various texts that it follows a theoretical reconstruction based more on motivation and intention than consequences. Some Buddhist texts suggest that any action performed with good intention is good, while actions with bad intentions are deemed bad. Even actions motivated by a higher degree of vice are considered worse than those motivated by a lower degree of vice as the former cause more karmic damage than the latter.

Buddhist ethics can be viewed as ethics of virtues, with the Buddhist concept of *nirvana* resembling the Greek concept of *eudaimonia* or happiness or the good of different schools of ethics. Mahayana texts suggest that one's actions should lead to the wellbeing of all in a broader perspective, which is similar to a form of character consequentialism that evaluates the moral character of an individual based on the consequences of their actions. Theoretical structures within Buddhism vary, and different approaches to ethics remain a matter of debate among Buddhist scholars.

Jaina Ethics

According to Jaina ethics, the consequences of virtues include blessings in the form of rebirth as a great sage or a God-like suprahuman, while vices lead to painful rebirth among fallen people and in misery. The ultimate goal of life in Jaina ethics is to eliminate every form of passion. Individuals are therefore encouraged to transcend even virtuous actions that can lead to bondage, although this may be challenging for those engaged in worldly affairs. Jainas advise that auspicious actions that are governed by self-sacrifice and the rejection of passions should be performed throughout life, while divisive activities for self-interest should be shunned.

Jainas advocate following the path of three jewels: right faith, right knowledge and right conduct. Right faith (*samyak-darsana*) is defined as contentment of mind. Jainas believe perfect knowledge is attained with the help of right conduct. They emphasise that knowledge without right conduct is useless, and conduct without right knowledge is blind. Jainas highlight the importance of five vows (*panchanuvrata*): non-violence (*ahimsa*), truth (*satya*), non-stealing (*asteya*), celibacy (*brahmacharya*) and renunciation of wealth (*aparigraha*). They believe that an individual can subdue passions while walking on the path shown by these five vows on their spiritual journey.

According to Jainas violence is completely disastrous, first and foremost for the individual who is motivated by this passion to create sufferings for others. Jainas stress on liberation from all worldly things, and its extreme manifestation is seen in the idea of *Sallekhana*, a ritual in which a Jaina monk gradually renounces food and other essentials of life in stages, and concentrates fully on spiritual advancement. Through this process Jainas aim to rid themselves of the vicious effects of karma and the cycle of rebirth, undergoing a complete process of purification to overcome all passions and emotions.

Some scholars denounce the concept of Sallekhana, viewing it as a crime. However, it is misleading to consider it suicide. Suicide is generally a consequence of self-inflicted actions by an individual undertaken in a fit of emotion. A victim of suicide is also often a mentally weak individual, whereas a monk undergoing the process of Sallekhana is a mentally calm and spiritually sound person, free from all passions, worldly cravings, sadness and suffering. The practice of Sallekhana is not meant for common people because it requires possession of the right knowledge that can be achieved only through rigorous discipline and purity of mind.

Non-violence is a central and fundamental tenet of Jaina ethics. Jainas assert that lying, stealing, taking undue share, excessive pursuit of sensual pleasures and possessiveness are all aspects of violence. They classify false statements or lies into four categories:

1. Speech that denies the existence of a thing in its nature, in space and time.
2. Speech that misleads the existence of a thing in other space and time, and of a different nature.
3. Speech that explains or elucidates an object or event as being other than what it really is.
4. Condemnable, sinful and disagreeable speech that causes fear, pain, animosity, sorrow and an unrestful mind.

According to Jainas, untruth (*asatya*) leads to social disrespect, social blame and downfall. A virtuous person must therefore not utter a lie even by mistake or unknowingly because it will undermine their moral achievements.

Hindu Ethics

The study of ethics in Hindu religion has not been conducted in the systematic and structured manner in which it has been undertaken in Greece and Europe. Ethics in Hinduism, known as *dharma*—variously understood as duties, virtues, righteous conduct, laws, and 'the right way of living'—is considered the foundation of human life and is perceived in terms of moral orders and guidelines, with texts like the *Atharva Veda* prescribing and encouraging ethical and virtuous conduct in day-to-day life. For example, hymns in the *Atharva Veda* emphasises a son's submission to his father and like-mindedness with his mother, advocates for wives to speak sweet and beneficial words, discourages hatred among brothers, and encourages harmony among sisters. The *Atharva Veda* also labels certain behaviours as sinful, including unfulfilled promises, offences at dice, adultery and failure to clear debts. Principles of Hindu dharma can be traced across Hindu scriptures such as the *Veda*s, *Upanishad*s, *Bhagavad Gita*, and in other texts like the *Ramayana*, *Mahabharata*, *Nitishataka* of Bhartrihari, *Tirukkural* of Thiruvalluvar, *Manusmriti*, *Panchatantra* and *Hitopadesha*. However, barring a handful of works, these have not undergone systematic rational, philosophical or scientific study and inquiry with a focus on ethics.

Bhartrihari in his *Nitishataka* asserts that the noblest person relinquishes all self-interest to do good for others. Common individuals act for the sake of others when it is also consistent with self-interest. Those who harm others for their self-interest are seen as demons among humans, but there is no clear categorisation for those who harm others without any apparent reason.

In Hindu ethics, serious philosophical inquiries such as the nature of truth and the necessity of being truthful have not been extensively explored. Hindu ethics, except perhaps in the philosophy of Sankaracharya, is not absolute and universal but relative within the domain of Hinduism itself. Sankaracharya is one of the rare few Indian philosophers who made no formal distinction between theory and practice. The *Ramayana* and *Mahabharata* present numerous instances of ethical dilemmas and propose pragmatic solutions based on the given contexts. The *Veda*s glorify truthfulness (*satya*) in many instances, where individuals are consistently urged to 'speak truthfully and act truthfully'. The *Taittiriya Upanishad* highlights the importance of speaking the truth and practising virtue, advising against deviating from truth and virtue. The *Chandogya Upanishad* emphasises austerity, charity, and righteousness with *ahimsa*.

The *Bhagavad Gita* contributes significantly to the discussion of key ethical questions and dilemmas, and consistently emphasises the importance of virtue and doing one's duty. It delineates virtues that elevate an individual to a divine-like state; these include: fearlessness, truthfulness, purity of soul, commitment to knowledge, charity, austerity, non-violence, compassion, self-abstinence, calmness, abstinence from anger and hatred, among others. In Hindu ethics, the four principal goals of mankind are dharma, artha, kama and moksha. The *Gita* provides a framework for reconciling these goals by achieving wealth (artha), kama (desire) and moksha (liberation) in accordance with dharma (righteousness). Here, dharma is the foundational basis that sustains the social order and the existence of humanity. In the Karnaparva of the *Mahabharata*, dharma is delineated in terms of its practicality as that which sustains society, maintains the social order, determines the welfare and growth of humanity and also ensures the personal prosperity of individuals. The *Manusmriti* defines dharma as encompassing non-violence, truthfulness, sanctity, avoiding unfair means of accumulating wealth and controlling one's desires.

WESTERN PHILOSOPHERS

We discussed in Chapter 1 that ethics was systematically developed in ancient Greece by philosophers like Socrates, Plato and Aristotle, among others, whose contribution to the study of ethics in all its dimensions, particularly in the field of virtue ethics and teleology, have been foundational and immense. Besides the Greeks, Christian philosophers like Thomas Aquinas and St. Augustine also contributed substantially in laying the foundations of theological ethics, placing a strong emphasis on deontology and developing ethics from the perspective of law.

The Ancient Greeks

The ancient Greek philosophers were largely teleological in approach and focused on the concept of 'final good', considering it as the chief cause and motivator of happiness. Greek teleology was not divine but intrinsic, and introduced the idea of happiness as the ultimate and final goal, and delineated virtues of various kinds as a means to achieve such happiness.

The Sophists

The Sophists were educators engaged as paid tutors for young and affluent Greeks, focusing on instilling aristocratic virtues to prepare them for warfare and statecraft. The virtues imparted by the Sophists, known as *arete*, were initially associated with courage and physical prowess. As political consciousness grew in Greece, *arete* evolved from physical strength and prowess to the power of words and language, emphasising the use of rhetoric and debate to seek the attention of citizens and garner popularity amongst the masses.

The Sophists recognised the persistent conflicts between the inherent natural tendencies of human beings and social regulatory mechanisms, between the fundamental nature of worldly objects (both living and non-living) and the rules and regulations established to control and regulate human behaviour. They distinguished these conflicting ideas as *physis* (nature of things) and *nomos* (conventions or traditions). Physis was defined as a tendency to grow or an inclination towards internal change to achieve various forms of growth. Nomos, on the other hand, encompassed customs, rules, regulations, norms and conventions meant to control physis.

Heraclitus introduced the concept of nomos under two distinctions: human nomos and divine nomos. Human nomos referred to man-made norms, while divine nomos represented supernatural or divine norms. Heraclitus explained nomos as a fundamental control over the natural tendencies of living and non-living things, laying the groundwork for the debate on the scope and nature of nomos, particularly human nomos, leading to the evolution of ethics. Consequently, ethics emerged in the form of societal rules and norms designed to regulate human actions for the wellbeing of a harmonious society.

Antiphon, explaining the dichotomy between physis and nomos, argued that ideas based on nomos which are considered just are not entirely just because they are always in a state of conflict with physis. Further, rules and regulations created by human beings aim to control the natural tendencies of individuals seeking pleasure due to their basic instincts. Protagoras' famous statement,

'Man is the measure of all things' highlights the relativism in Sophist philosophy. It categorically asserts that the ultimate source of value is not God or moral laws but a human being—the individual is the standard for determining all values based on circumstances. This relativism, as explained by **Protagoras**, emphasises the subjectivity of ethics.

Significantly, the Sophists also recognised the power of speech, especially in the evolving democratic polity of ancient Greece. They considered the power of speech, or *logos*, a key virtue (*arete*) and believed that speech had a potent influence capable of controlling human emotions like pain, distress, delight and fear. Logos represented the logic behind an argument, employing reasoning and evidence to persuade an audience, and served as a method of persuasion in writing and rhetoric in ancient Greece. The Sophists taught the art of persuasion using the power of speech.

Socrates (470–399 BC)

A renowned philosopher, Socrates is celebrated for his teachings on ethics and his distinctive instructional approach. Greek scholars preceding Socrates had delved deep into metaphysics, exploring the fundamental nature of reality, the interrelationship between the mind and the existence of matter. Profoundly affected by the suffering caused by the Peloponnesian War, and having lived through its terrible aftermath, Socrates studied in depth the repercussions of wars and societal animosities. He sought to determine the best way to live life, weighing the merits of morality against immorality, despite the inherent short-term losses associated with a moral way of life. He endeavoured to draw conclusions about whether happiness resulted from the satisfaction of desires or if it lay in virtuous behaviour, forsaking immediate physical pleasures. According to Socrates, happiness is the ultimate goal of life, a desire that ultimately lies within an individual's control, and he believed each one of us can attain happiness through our own efforts. Socrates' concept of happiness transcends physical pleasure: it is a divine feeling or a spiritual state of inner peace unaffected by worldly affairs. This state can be achieved by controlling bodily desires and harmonising the different aspects of the soul.

Socrates was driven by the determination to elucidate two fundamental points:

1. The ultimate goal for all individuals is unconditional happiness or good (*eudaimonia*).
2. Happiness, as the ultimate desire, is not contingent on external objects in the world; instead, it depends on how these objects are used to attain that ultimate goal or employed in ways that lead to its attainment. These external objects encompass various qualities, physical appearances, bodily power, money, or any other desirable attributes. For instance, a wise person will use money judiciously to enhance their happiness, while a foolish and ignorant person may misuse it, ultimately leading to a worse state. Similarly, physical beauty and intelligence can be misused for manipulation and misdeeds.

Socrates devoted himself to the pursuit of true knowledge and eradication of ignorance. His method of questioning, aimed at revealing ignorance and acquiring right knowledge, earned him the reputation of being the wisest man of his time. This questioning method fosters self-knowledge, dispelling prejudices, hearsay and flawed reasoning that can potentially give rise to vanity, conceit and erroneous beliefs, all of which contribute to preserving self-identity and ego.

Socrates believed that wisdom is the key to happiness, describing virtue as synonymous with wisdom or self-knowledge. Virtue and happiness are inseparable, and the pleasure derived from pursuing virtue and true knowledge surpasses pleasure derived from satisfying merely animalistic desires. Contrary to the common belief that pleasure is an end in itself, Socrates asserted that it is an integral part of a virtuous life, and that acting virtuously provides deep satisfaction and inner peace.

Socrates famously said that, 'An unexamined life is not worth living.' This principle is central to his method of philosophical questioning, rooted in the acknowledgment that he knows nothing. The dictum comes from Plato's *Apology*, a compilation of the speeches Socrates gave during his trial. Faced with the choice between death, being exiled from Athens, or a vow of silence, Socrates chose death. Socrates' extraordinary life and death inspire and encourage us to embrace our humanity fully and to use our highly developed faculty of thought and reasoning to raise our existence above the merely animalistic. Socrates believed that a life lived mechanically, following an unthinking mindless routine and rules dictated by others, without ever examining whether or not one truly wants to live by those rules is essentially not worth living.

Plato

Plato, Socrates' most famous disciple, developed an ethical framework centred around an ideal city-state. Plato's philosophical enquiries aimed to identify the underlying relations that give rise to the formation of a city-state. He argues that the existence of a city is necessitated by our lack of complete self-sufficiency. Human beings have diverse needs, compelling them to seek assistance from each other. People work together as partners and helpers, initially driven by physical and economic needs such as obtaining food, clothing, shelter and essential tools. This cooperative effort, rooted in fulfilling basic human needs, gives rise to a 'minimal city'.

Plato goes on to elaborate on how, driven by higher demands, a 'maximal state' comes into existence. He illustrates this idea by referencing his self-subsistent 'minimal city', which comprises farmers, craftsmen and other classes of inhabitants. Here, Plato seeks to allocate different tasks to various segments of society based on their expertise and preferences, or the 'one person-one job' rule, aiming for economic efficiency aligned with demand and supply. In the 'maximal state', Plato categorises city inhabitants into three main classes:

1. A class of philosopher kings and queens
2. A professional army
3. Fellow citizens or the polity

For the internal and external security of a prosperous and peaceful city, Plato advocates the need for a well-trained professional army, guided and overseen by a philosopher king or queen. Recognising that individuals are born with diverse abilities, Plato introduces the rule of 'one person-one job'. This rule signifying division of labour is integral to Plato's vision of a just and well-ordered society where justice is also ensured by 'doing your own thing'; that is, each citizen must perform their designated duties and tasks without interfering in those of others.

Plato's entire framework for social order and the establishment of political institutions is built on his psychological principle. To maintain internal harmony and external security, he emphasises the importance of incorporating a holistic education including moral psychology into the training of the army. In Plato's ideal republic, kings and members of the army are regarded as guardians. They must be friendly and compassionate towards citizens while displaying fierceness towards enemies, under the guidance of a philosopher king or queen. Plato underscores the necessity for a ruler to also be a philosopher. It is the philosopher ruler's duty to design the curriculum for the army's training, which should encompass the right forms of inspiration and aesthetic sense, including poetry, music and other fine arts, combined with physical training, to instil the right attitudes in the soldiers.

The responsibility and supervision of education is entrusted to the ruling class, which must be selected from among the soldiers based on several tests of wisdom and character. Rulers should possess unwavering conviction that their wellbeing is intricately linked to the wellbeing of their fellow citizens. Plato establishes stringent codes of conduct for both the ruling and military classes concerning their approach to civic duties. Notably, members of these classes are required to lead a communal life, devoid of private homes, families and personal property. Plato prioritises the establishment of a political order that ensures the overall happiness of the entire city, even if it means sacrificing the happiness of a particular class and individuals. This aligns Plato's views more closely with utilitarian perspectives.

To elucidate virtue, Plato delineates four cardinal virtues:

1. Wisdom (*Sophia*): Wisdom, being the sole purely intellectual virtue, is exclusively possessed by the ruling class. Plato contends that a ruler must possess wisdom, and that a philosopher is the most suitable individual to govern society.
2. Courage (*Andreia*): Courage is a virtue specific to the military class. A courageous soldier can safeguard the state, while a timid one may pose a threat.
3. Moderation (*Sophrosune*): Moderation encompasses the virtues of self-control, prudence and temperance. It combines belief with a certain disposition that upholds order and a shared conviction in selecting a ruler who can exercise control over citizens. Plato's notion of self-mastery is central to his ethical theory and is more than mere abstention from physical pleasure; Plato equates it with practical wisdom (*phronesis*).
4. Justice (*Dikaiosune*): Justice is determined by the perfect balance among the other three virtues. It is exemplified by 'doing your own thing', representing a proactive state of mind that ensures no citizen encroaches upon what belongs to another or is deprived of what is rightfully theirs. Given the significant potential for the two classes to disrupt this balance of justice, the right kind of education can regulate their appetitive part, preventing them from exceeding their assigned roles and tasks.

Plato aligns the threefold division of the city with that of the human soul. The soul, like the city, is also classified into three parts:

1. Rational part
2. Spirited part
3. Appetitive part

The rational part of soul corresponds to the ruler class, the spirited part is associated with the military class, and the appetitive part pertains to the rest of the people whose defining motivation is material gain. According to Plato, justice is achieved when all three components or aspects of the soul are proportionally represented in the citizens. If any one of these components predominates, the state of justice is compromised.

Aristotle

Aristotle asserts, in his *Nicomachean Ethics*, that ethics is not merely about knowing or understanding what is good but cultivating habits to attain it. Knowledge alone is insufficient to produce goodness: the habit of consistently acting virtuously is essential to achieve it. Uninterested in compiling a list of inherently good things, Aristotle instead grapples with the challenge of resolving ethical conflicts and dilemmas, and assigning priority to one desirable good over others. In the process of determining the highest good, he arrives at the concept of *eudaimonia* or happiness, which possesses three characteristics:

1. It is desirable for itself.
2. It is not desirable for the sake of some other good.
3. All other goods are desirable for its sake.

Since as humans we possess a rational soul, we must seek a good that aligns with our humanity, setting us apart from other species. The capacity for reason empowers individuals to lead better lives, guiding them to develop virtuous habits and act ethically. However, virtues alone are insufficient if other goods are lacking, says Aristotle. One must have sufficient required goods to be fortunate enough to consistently and habitually act virtuously. Aristotle places great emphasis on the role of fortune in achieving the highest good in life, stating that an unfortunate person cannot be virtuous by habit. Here, fortune includes the presence of loving parents, good friends, a caring life partner and good fellow citizens.

Aristotle further defines virtue as a golden mean between two vices, representing a state where two extreme ideas find equilibrium. For example, courage is a virtue situated between the two extremes of cowardice and rashness. Aristotle introduces a twofold classification of virtue:

1. Intellectual virtue
2. Ethical virtue or virtue of character

Intellectual virtue pertains to the part of the soul involved in reasoning, while ethical virtue concerns the part of the soul incapable of reasoning but capable of following reason. Intellectual virtues are further categorised into theoretical wisdom and practical wisdom. All free individuals possess the potential to develop ethical virtue and practical wisdom from birth. They must inculcate good habits of ethical virtue in childhood, and as their reasoning faculties mature, they should acquire intellectual virtue. Aristotle does not advocate for an ascetic lifestyle because human desires can neither be entirely eliminated nor unduly suppressed. Instead, he advises that as rational intelligent beings, we must self-regulate our desires and maintain a virtuous mean between them.

Stoic Ethics

For the Stoics, *eudaimonia* or happiness, which is the ultimate goal of human life, involves living in harmony with nature, in accordance with both cosmic nature and the nature of living and non-living things. Cosmic nature refers to events unfolding in a rationally organised universe, guided by the will of God (Zeus), making the Stoics teleologists in their understanding of nature. The nature of living and non-living things reveals a certain order and organisation within the universe, illustrated through mechanisms such as the food chain, natural urges, attraction towards the opposite sex, and reproduction.

Theory of appropriation: According to the Stoics, all living organisms in their early stages possess an innate impulse towards self-love rather than pleasure. This initial relationship is directed inward. As organisms, particularly humans, mature, they begin to form social connections. Endowed with reason, humans can ascertain their own true good. The Stoics assert that virtue is the sole real good, both necessary and sufficient for attaining happiness, in contrast to Aristotle, who posits that fortune plays no role in happiness.

A virtuous life, according to Stoics, is devoid of all human passions, which can negatively impact the soul. It involves appropriate emotional responses shaped by rationality and a desire to fulfil personal, social, professional and civic responsibilities. Reasoning abilities develop gradually, reaching a stage of perfection. Once a person has developed reason, their actions become appropriate, guided by reasonable justification. For instance, a health-conscious person goes for morning walks as an appropriate act. However, perfect acts, deemed necessary and sufficient conditions for virtue, only emerge when reasoning reaches perfection. Thus, virtuous actions signify the appropriate acts of a human being, but the reverse is not necessarily true. Virtuous actions indicate perfect acts, and perfect acts signify virtuous actions.

In Stoic philosophy the concepts of good, bad and indifferent are carefully defined. Good is what is complete and perfect according to nature for a rational being. For a rational being the perfect nature is the perfection of reason, and this perfection is virtue. Conversely, when reason is corrupted, leading to misery, bad or evil arises, and this state is associated with vice.

Thus, virtue creates good, and vice creates evil. Things which are neither good nor evil are considered indifferent. Indifferent outcomes result from unreasoned actions, even when a person possesses perfect reason. An individual's disposition may also deviate from reason due to psychological disturbances, which the Stoics refer to as passions.

The Stoics recognise four passions: pleasure, appetite, distress and fear. These passions introduce deformities in reasoned actions. The soul of a virtuous being exhibits three positive states or affective responses: joy, caution and wish. The virtuous person is not emotionless like dead wood, and experiences passion, but mindfully discerns between virtue and vice. Here, the Stoics follow Aristotle in pursuing the concept of the golden mean.

Epicurus (341–270 BC)

Epicurus, a prominent philosopher of the Hellenistic period, embraced materialism and empiricism as the foundations of his philosophy. His ethical framework is grounded in hedonism, emphasising the pursuit of pleasure. As a materialist seeking the fundamental material particle, Epicurus identified atoms as the smallest building blocks, explaining all natural phenomena through his atomic theory. His mechanistic view, replacing a teleological approach based on God, led him to adopt atheism and reject the fear of God. He criticised Aristotle's intrinsic teleology, exemplified by the notion that teeth are perfectly designed for chewing.

Epicurean ethics revolves around egoistic hedonism, positing that intrinsic value lies in actions that bring about one's own pleasure. Other things are deemed valuable solely because they serve as instruments to secure personal pleasure. Despite his hedonistic stance, Epicurean ethics is nuanced and subtle, advocating for a virtuous and moderately ascetic life as the optimal path to pleasure. Epicurus categorised pleasure into two types: moving pleasure, experienced during the satisfaction of a desire (e.g., the pleasure of tasting delicious food), and static pleasure, arising from the fulfilment of a desire.

Epicurus defined happiness based on three essential components: good companionship (meaningful friendships), freedom (self-sufficiency and independence from everyday concerns and politics) and an examined life (having the time and space to reflect and contemplate).

Epicurus contributed to a well-developed contractarian theory of justice and viewed it as a mutual association entered into a contract for the collective benefit of all involved. According to him, justice is an agreement 'neither to harm nor be harmed'.

Epicurus places immense value on friendship, considering it the most precious aspect of life. 'Friendship dances around the world,' he said, asserting that only a wise person knows the true value of friendship, and is willing to make sacrifices, even to the extent of giving one's life for a friend. Epicurus highlights the importance of friendship as the foremost means to achieve pleasure.

Christian Philosophers

Christian philosophers like St. Augustine and Thomas Aquinas centred their philosophical enquiries around God's commandments, virtue, justice, faith and love in their discourses concerning morality. St. Augustine said that God granted Man perfect freedom to choose between good and evil. Citing the example of Adam, he says when Adam chose evil, he was justly punished, and the consequences of his sin were inherited by each subsequent generation of the human race in the form of an inherent corruption in human nature. This corruption results in an inherent inability to make the right choices, thus necessarily making all human beings sinners. However, St. Augustine emphasises that God, in His infinite mercy, also provided a solution by sending His Son, the second in the Trinity, by way of a redeeming sacrifice in order to satisfy divine justice.

The Seven Cardinal Sins

The Seven Cardinal sins, also known as seven capital vices or seven deadly sins, are fundamental vices representing potent passions that adversely impact the rational mental faculty of human beings. The concept of vices was introduced by Aristotle in his golden mean principle where he attempted to associate two vices with a virtue. The seven cardinal sins originated from the initial list of eight evil thoughts in Greek, as proposed by the fourth-century monk Evagrius Ponticus. This list was later revised by Pope Gregory I into a compilation of seven sins. St. Thomas Aquinas incorporated this list into his *Summa Theologica* and referred to them as capital sins. These were consolidated into a single list within Christian tradition after extensive contemplation by various Christian scholars. The Seven Cardinal Sins are lust, gluttony, greed, sloth, wrath, envy and pride. While each sin has a broad interpretation, our focus here is on understanding their significance in the context of civil services.

1. *Lust*: Lust refers to an intense desire for materialistic and sensual pleasure. Dante characterises lust as a disordered irrational affection or longing for an object or individual, akin to a restless storm symbolising a loss of control over the propensity to enjoy material and sensual pleasure. In the context of civil services, it is essential for civil servants to maintain neutrality about their place of posting and avoid becoming overly attached. The provision of periodic transfers for civil servants is intended to overcome undue attachment to place or office of posting. Instances abound where officers, due to excessive emotional attachment, repeatedly seek accommodation in a particular post, leading to serious consequences such as conflicts of interest and a degradation of public service values.

2. *Gluttony*: Understood as excessive consumption of anything, gluttony literally refers to the overconsumption of food. In a broader context, it emphasises self-interest over and above the interests of others. Civil servants, despite working on a reasonable salary, may experience insecurity about future financial requirements. Public service is not just a job like any other but a high commitment for the wellbeing of the public and the nation. The fear of scarcity may compromise the rational acknowledgment of adequate emoluments for services rendered to the government. This fear may lead to corruption and the misappropriation of public funds, eroding the public servant's integrity. It is crucial for public servants to limit their needs and avoid overindulgence in an expensive lifestyle.

3. *Greed*: Synonymous with avarice, cupidity or covetousness, greed involves a longing and pursuit of acquiring material possessions. Unlike lust, which involves indulgence and continuous enjoyment, greed is related to mere accumulation without considering the consequences, and is characterised by hoarding, stealing and plundering, especially by wielding power. Civil servants must distance themselves from this vice as greed can lead to the abuse of authority, coercion of subordinates, and exploitation of common citizens. It is a major contributor to corruption in public life, eroding institutional values within civil services and posing significant dangers to society and the nation.

4. *Sloth*: Sloth refers to a habitual laziness or disinterest in any kind of exertion. Sloth is a serious misconduct that involves neglecting one's responsibilities and showing a total lack of concern for others: the world, people, and oneself. It impedes individuals in all their undertakings and can become a potential cause for a total lack of empathy. From a religious standpoint, sloth pertains to a neglect of duties and obligations

to God such as attending prayers and helping others. For civil servants, sloth is a significant challenge as officers may become inactive and lazy due to the lack of external motivation at work. Many officers tend to misuse the immunity they are provided under constitutional safeguards, because of which dismissing a civil servant from service is often considered more challenging than recruiting one. If such behaviour is adopted early in their career, it seriously hampers learning and growth and no experience is gained from the job since a lazy officer is reluctant to work, leave alone work well. This weakens the entire system, breeds inefficiency and corruption, and brings all development and progress to a grinding halt.

5. *Wrath*: Wrath refers to the extreme uncontrolled emotions of anger and hatred, often leading to the desire for vengeance to correct a perceived or supposed grievous wrong or injustice. It is characterised by irrational rage, with potential for violence. For instance, if a loved one or object is harmed or threatened by harm, individuals may feel the need to exact revenge on those they hold responsible for the perceived harm. Dorothy L. Sayers, in her translation of Dante's *The Divine Comedy II: Purgatory*, describes wrath as 'love of justice perverted to revenge and spite'. Civil servants wield a wide range of authorities and powers, and it is crucial for them to exercise this power judiciously and fairly under all circumstances, no matter the provocation. Instances exist where superiors have imposed disproportionate punishment on subordinates for minor mistakes. Disciplinary action must never be driven by anger or spite but by reason. Civil servants must at all times maintain a calm, rational and alert mind free of all types of extreme emotions.

6. *Envy*: Envy is feeling resentful, covetous and jealous of another's attributes, possessions, status, capabilities or happiness, accompanied by a strong desire to possess them, and deriving pleasure from witnessing others brought low. Dante describes envy as a longing to dispossess another of what is his. According to St. Thomas Aquinas, envy has three stages: the first involves diminishing another's status, wellbeing or happiness; the second entails finding joy in another's misfortune, or feeling sad or angry at their fortune or happiness; and the last stage is developing hatred for that person. Envy is a profoundly disruptive force in anyone's life. Civil servants should not harbour envy for their colleagues' advancing careers or promotions. It has become a common practice to undermine the careers of emerging fellow officers by plotting vigilance inquiries or fabricating false complaints against them. This erodes professional camaraderie and solidarity, and tarnishes the image of civil services.

7. *Pride*: Pride is an irrational belief in being inherently superior, more important and valuable than others. Pride poses a significant challenge in the lives of civil servants as it hinders self-scrutiny of their conduct and performance and makes individuals less receptive to criticism. An officer who nurtures excessive and undue pride in their authority and capabilities may become biased in their thinking, decisions and actions. They may consider others, both subordinates and superiors, as inferior, disregard the advice of colleagues and deny others credit where it is due. This mindset hampers teamwork, collaboration, cooperation, organisational growth and innovation. As Alexander Pope aptly wrote:

> Of all the causes which conspire to blind
> Man's erring judgment, and misguide the mind,

What the weak head with strongest bias rules,
Is pride, the never-failing vice of fools.

Thomas Aquinas (1225–1274 AD)

St. Thomas Aquinas was a prominent Italian priest, theologian and jurist whose philosophy has profoundly impacted Western thought. The ethical framework of St. Thomas Aquinas blends two apparently disparate traditions: Aristotelian eudaimonism and Christian theology. On the one hand, like Aristotle, Aquinas posits that an act is good or bad depending upon whether it aids or obstructs attainment of the proper human end—the *telos* or final goal towards which all human actions strive. The telos is eudaimonia, or happiness, for which the cultivation of intellectual and moral virtues is necessary. On the other hand, Aquinas believes that virtue alone cannot help achieve complete or final happiness in this life or union with God. Achieving this ultimate end requires divine grace as human efforts alone are insufficient. God's influence is crucial for humans to attain perfection and earn divine beatitude. Aquinas, a devout Christian, acknowledges the concept of original sin inherited from Adam, which taints the human race, inclining them towards corrupt actions. Given the human propensity to misuse free will against the divine will, he emphasises the need for God's grace to uphold the good and overcome evil.

Meta-ethics: As elucidated in his *Summa Theologica*, Aquinas' meta-ethics revolves around two powers of reason. The *cognitive* power, embodied in the intellect, enables us to comprehend and understand things, including their inherent goodness or badness. The *appetitive* power, or the will, is the aspect of reasoning associated with desire. Aquinas defines will as a person's inclination towards the good as discerned by their cognitive power. In essence, the will responds to the intellect's judgment of what is good or worthy of choice. Every act of the will is contingent upon preceding acts of the intellect, with the intellect supplying the will with the object to which it inclines. This object, identified as the good, serves as the final cause, moving the will towards it as an end.

In Aquinas' framework, human actions are those within the realm of voluntary control, distinguishing them from the actions of non-rational animals. Individuals make choices based on reasoned considerations of what they perceive as good (and bad). Aquinas emphasises that these human actions are not solely products of free will (*liberum arbitrium*) but involve the interplay of both intellect and will. Consequently, human actions are guided by reasoned judgments about what is good, with the identified good serving as an ultimate end.

Aquinas offers several definitions of virtue, stating that a virtue is a habit that prompts and motivates an agent to perform its proper operation. As reason is deemed the proper operation of human beings, a virtue is a habit that predisposes us to reason well. Aquinas enumerates the following four virtues:

1. *Prudence*: It is the knowledge required to determine the right reason with respect to an action in order to make sound moral judgments. Prudence encompasses two types of knowledge: i) general moral principles guiding actions; and ii) specific circumstances in which a decision is required.
2. *Temperance*: This virtue has a dual meaning. Firstly, it denotes a form of moderation applicable to every moral virtue in its narrower sense, focusing on moderating physical pleasures related to eating, drinking and sex. It addresses the common inclination to temporarily sacrifice one's wellbeing for obtaining transient goods, restraining the 'concupiscible' passion, or the appetite for what is pleasurable, and avoidance of harm. Secondly, temperance refers to a restrained desire for physical gratification, recognising that desire for bodily pleasure cannot be eliminated.

Subsidiary virtues under temperance include chastity, sobriety, abstinence, etc.

3. *Courage*: Aquinas defines courage in the context of the 'irascible appetite', representing the desire for what is challenging to attain. Courage is the virtue that modifies the irascible appetite with the help of its subsidiary virtues. Difficulty in achieving or avoiding certain objects may arise, inducing fear to some extent and discouraging adherence to reason. Fear is not inherently contrary to reason; there are things that we should rightly fear, such as untimely death or a bad reputation. Fear becomes detrimental to reason only when it prevents individuals from facing what they ought to endure. In such situations, we need a virtue that moderates those appetites that prevent us from undertaking more daunting tasks. According to Aquinas, courage is that virtue. We need courage to overcome our fears and endure harrowing circumstances. However, courage does not only diminish fear; it also fights the irrational zeal to recklessly confront challenges. Thus we need courage to maintain a balance between excessive fear and unreasonable daring.

4. *Justice*: This is the virtue that governs our relationships with others, signifying a consistent and principled desire to treat each person according to their merit. Aquinas, in his *Summa Theologica*, classifies justice into legal (or general) and particular justice; and further classifies particular justice into commutative and distributive justice.

Legal justice aims to regulate our actions in accordance with the common good, emphasising the welfare of the community over individual benefits. As each community member contributes to the whole, laws are enacted to govern interactions for the benefit of everyone. This falls under the realm of legal or general justice, governing interactions between citizens. In contrast, *particular justice* directs attention to the wellbeing of individuals, such as neighbours, colleagues and loved ones. Aquinas emphasises that the proximate concern of particular justice is not the common good but the good of individuals and individual needs.

Following Aristotle, Aquinas recognises two types of particular justice: commutative and distributive justice. Both seek to preserve equality by giving to each person their dues. *Commutative justice* concerns the mutual dealings between individual citizens, ensuring fairness in buying and selling transactions. It seeks to maintain equality, where each person pays back in proportion to what they have gained from others. *Distributive justice* addresses the fair apportionment of collective goods and responsibilities among members of a social community, and ensures that resources and duties are distributed equitably. In distributive justice, dues are not quantified by magnitude but by 'due proportion'. Here, 'due' is contingent upon the deserving needs an individual should have fulfilled, based on moral obligations to support those in need, taking into account their efforts and life circumstances. The implementation of reservations in public employment falls under the purview of distributive justice.

Table 10.1: Justice according to different philosophers

Philosopher	Justice
Plato	Perfect balance between wisdom, courage and moderation.
Thomas Aquinas	Legal and particular, commutative and distributive
Epicurus	'Neither harm another nor be harmed.'
John Rawls	Justice as fairness

Source: Created by authors.

Table 10.2: Virtue defined by various philosophers

Philosopher	Virtue
Sophists	*Arete* or excellence pertaining to bodily courage or prowess; intellect and knowledge, later encompassing *logos* or power of speech.
Socrates	Wisdom
Plato	Four cardinal virtues: wisdom, courage, moderation, justice
Aristotle	Golden mean
Stoics	Perfect actions are dictated by reason, and are free from all passions.
Thomas Aquinas	Cardinal virtues: prudence, temperance, courage, justice

Source: Created by authors.

Natural law: Aquinas was a natural law theorist. According to him, every law is ultimately derived from eternal law that refers to God's providential ordering of all created things to their proper ends. Aquinas defines law as a rule or measure of human acts that either induces individuals to act or restrains them from acting. A law serves as a guide and measure of human action; it determines whether an action is good or bad depending upon its conformity to the relevant law and reason. In other words, reason is the measure by which we evaluate human acts, and law, according to Aquinas, governs all human actions and is itself the expression of reason.

Aquinas posits that as rational beings we participate in God's eternal law and divine order as God creates in us both the desire for and the ability to discern what is good. He calls this ability the 'light of natural reason' and this participation in the eternal law by rational creatures is what he calls the 'natural law'. Thus for Aquinas, natural law is but an extension of the eternal law, wherein God ordains us to final happiness by implanting in us both a knowledge of and inclination towards goodness.

Note here that natural law, as per Aquinas, is not an external source of authority, nor is it a general deontic norm from which more specific precepts are inferred. Instead, natural law is a fundamental principle woven into and inherent to the fabric of human nature which illuminates and instils in us a desire for goods that facilitate the kind of flourishing that is proper to human beings.

John Locke

Locke writes that 'all the requisites of law are found in natural law'. In order to establish a legalistic framework for morality he considers what constitutes law:

1. Law must be founded on the will of a superior.
2. Law must perform the function of establishing rules of behaviour.
3. Law must be binding on humans since there is a duty of compliance owed to the superior authority that institutes laws.

Natural law is rightly called law because the above three conditions hold good in the case of natural law. Locke asserts that morality is universal and something that can be clearly understood by human reason. Morality based on natural law can be rationally discovered; it is deductive knowledge like the knowledge of mathematics. Human beings do not need to collect different empirical experiences in order to build moral principles. Natural law can be discovered by applying a rigorous set of logical principles to a set of clear and well-defined ideas about human nature, God and society.

Regarding the establishment of law, Locke introduces the idea of moral motivations, and discusses two types of moral motivations:

1. *Reward and punishment*: A law must instil the fear of punishment for its violation. This view is based on Locke's hedonistic theory of human motivation, where pleasure and pain are the primary motivating factors for all human thought and action. According

to Locke, good and evil are determined by what causes pleasure or pain. A good action produces pleasure and diminishes pain, while an evil action produces pain and diminishes pleasure. Reward is the consequence associated with the decrees of a rightful legislator. The practical force of moral law arises when we compare our actions against these laws, determine the degree to which they conform or do not conform to the law, and consider the pleasure or pain we will personally experience. For Locke, the rightful legislative power over another is predicated on the ability of the former being to effectively impose sanctions on the latter. God, according to Locke, is just such a rightful superior who has the power to direct our actions by rewards and punishments of infinite magnitude and duration, in this life as well as other lives.

2. *The righteousness of morality*: The other moral motivation is righteousness of morality. Locke suggests that obedience to the law of a superior authority can be of two types, based on two kinds of obligation:
   i) Rightful or legitimate authority provides the first ground for obedience.
   ii) Obeying the law for the sake of conscience versus obeying out of fear provides the second ground for obedience.

Thomas Hobbes

Thomas Hobbes witnessed the many transitions in the West from the medieval to the modern between the sixteenth and seventeenth centuries. The discovery of the New World, advancements in commerce and industry, the Reformation, the growth of rationalism and a scientific temperament, the rise of secularism, coupled with the decline in Christianity, collectively transformed Western civilisation. During this period, the theory of natural law as eternal divine law came under intense scrutiny, and major philosophers such as Descartes, Spinoza, Locke and Leibnitz, attempted to reconcile the emerging secular order with traditional Christian morality.

Hobbes, a revolutionary secular philosopher, challenged the notion that ethical norms were rooted in God's cosmic plan (teleology), asserting instead that they originated from social and political consensus. Greatly disturbed by the English Civil War, and having personally witnessed the beheading of Charles I, Hobbes' moral and political thinking was motivated by a desire to prevent wars and conflict.

State of Nature: Hobbes began by contemplating what the world would be like without morality, which he termed the 'state of nature'—a place he envisioned as ruled by chaos, fear and the constant threat of violent death, where 'human life would be solitary, nasty, poor, brutish, and short'. Hobbes argued that in the absence of morality, there would be no room for commerce, industry, art, literature or culture. He justified these dire circumstances based on the principles of supply and demand for essential resources. With resources being scarce, and individuals relatively equal in power, fierce battles would erupt to secure these limited resources and for survival, leading to a state of nature that is essentially a state of perpetual war.

Social Contract: Expanding his theory, Hobbes argued that while it is in our interest to agree to peace, it is not rational to comply with agreements unless there is a coercive power to enforce them. To prevent deception and ensure compliance, a coercive power is necessary. The agreement between individuals to establish laws for peaceful coexistence based on mutual self-interest and survival, and an agency to enforce those laws is termed the 'social contract'. Additionally, he proposed the 'laws of nature' as a second idea to explain how individuals, without *a-priori* moral laws in the state of nature, could devise rules for peaceful living. These laws of nature, distinct from the medieval concept of natural law, constitute the set of rules that make harmonious coexistence possible.

Theory of Morality: Morality, in Hobbes' framework, is thus constituted by mutually agreed-upon rules and advantageous conventions, justified by self-interest. These rules do not exist before human social contracts and are created through agreements within the constraints dictated by self-preservation and self-interest. Hobbes contends that morality is not discovered but is formed by human agreements, with no antecedent moral truth prior to the social contract. Actions are neither moral nor immoral before the contract is signed, and society disallows, allows, or remains indifferent to certain conducts. Hobbes' political theory emerged from his concept of a coercive agency ensuring compliance with the social contract.

Nietzsche

German philosopher Friedrich Wilhelm Nietzsche contends that contemporary morality promotes mediocrity and hinders the evolution of stronger and morally superior individuals. He rejects Christian morality and criticises Christian ethics for suppressing the development of a more advanced moral compass in favour of increasing the average moral population. Nietzsche argues that the foundation of higher ideals and human excellence cannot be established on the traditional morality upheld by present-day values.

Nietzsche challenges prevailing moral values, asserting that people often accept something as moral merely because it is recommended by tradition or dictated by authority, without questioning its true value, rationale or acceptability. He critiques the deontology-based morality that prescribes rules and norms for greater happiness in life, hindering human advancement and creating a specific type of individual. Notably, Nietzsche identifies himself as an 'immoralist', not in the literal sense of being immoral, but in outright rejecting the morality based on traditions and customs, advocating for a 'noble aristocratic morality' that allows individuals to overcome mediocrity.

In his hugely influential polemical work *The Genealogy of Morals* (1887), Nietzsche argues that traditional morality finds its source not in any divine or transcendental authority but in man. Through genealogy, a critical process explaining the evolution of human customs and traditions, Nietzsche demonstrates that all values and ideals result from specific historical circumstances. He distinguishes between master and slave morality, where values like courage and dominance emerge within the ruling class (masters), while the weaker class (slaves) develops a different set of values. Nietzsche contends that traditional morality is centred on a herd morality, characterised by rules and regulations preached by religions or prophets, which he strongly critiques and condemns. Herd morality leads people into mediocrity and promotes egalitarianism, restricting the pursuit of higher ideals.

Nietzsche's morality is described as autocratic, advocating strong moral values such as courage, revenge, dominance and self-exposition while rejecting values like kindness, compassion and humility that are foundational in Christianity. He criticises the Christian glorification of pity, arguing that it undermines human greatness and obstructs the path of natural selection, preventing the strong and the capable from thriving. Nietzsche opposes deontology based on fixed moral values and criticises Kant's Categorical Imperative, seeing it as a continuation of Christian morality that subjugates innate human inner strength, intelligence and ability.

CHINESE PHILOSOPHERS

Chinese moral philosophy has a rich and diverse history, spanning centuries and shaping the intellectual and cultural traditions of East Asia. Some key schools within Chinese moral philosophy include: Confucianism that emphasises ethical and moral values, social harmony and the cultivation of virtue; Daoism that emphasises naturalness, simplicity, spontaneity and living a virtuous life by aligning oneself with the natural order of the Dao; Mohism (a utilitarian tradition promulgated by Mozi in China around 300 BC) that promotes universal love and impartial concern for all people; and Neo-Confucianism that sought to integrate Confucian principles with Buddhist and Daoist ideas. Chinese moral philosophy continues to influence contemporary thought, both within China and globally.

Confucius (551–479 BC)

China's most renowned philosopher, teacher, reformer and political theorist, Confucius is considered the paragon of Chinese sages whose ideas have profoundly influenced East Asian thought and living, shaping the moral framework for interpersonal relationships, governance and education in Chinese culture and society. In imperial China he held the esteemed position of a moral instructor, scholar and trainer for the aristocracy, and stressed the significance of ritual and proper conduct for rulers, promoting ethical governance. The *Analects* and *Thicket of Sayings* contain passages that articulate the ideal conduct expected of a virtuous individual, often referred to as a 'gentleman', underscoring moral principles that foster ethical behaviour and moral character. Reminiscent of the concept of virtue in Greece, these principles revolve around five pivotal conducts, as listed in the *Analects*: benevolence (*ren*), righteousness (*yi*), ritual propriety (*li*), wisdom (*zhi*) and trustworthiness (*xin*).

1. *Benevolence*: Often described in the *Analects* as 'caring for others', benevolence encompasses conduct that shows consideration towards others and is genuinely good for them. The *Analects* provides specific situations illustrating benevolent actions, like treating people on the street as honoured guests attending a sacrifice, being reticent and humble in describing yourself, not speaking in a cunning or deceptive manner, showing respect to others at the workplace, and remaining loyal in relationships. These acts are considered the greatest of virtues, and a gentleman would rather embrace death than compromise on these virtues. Scholars like Mencius, who came after Confucius, further elucidated benevolence as a virtue that arises from cultivating an emotional disposition of compassion upon recognising another's distress. The *Analects* show that benevolence is nurtured and inculcated within the family and through ritual activities.

2. *Righteousness*: In the *Analects*, righteousness is described relative to circumstances involving public responsibility. Here, integrity and fairness play a crucial role. Confucius suggests that a virtuous person should consider righteousness when faced with opportunities for profit and advantage, refraining from attaining such things against righteous principles. Thus, righteousness involves selflessness and is grounded in steadfastness in the face of temptation. For Confucius, the essence of righteousness lies in inculcating a value system that remains unwavering, unaffected by convenience or lure of personal gain.

Sometimes benevolence and righteousness may seem to represent contradictory ideas. The *Records of Ritual* differentiates these two virtues, stating that 'in conducting one's household, pity overshadows righteousness. Outside the house, righteousness overrules pity'. This implies that while family matters may at times prioritise compassion over righteousness, in external or public matters, righteousness takes precedence over compassion. The reverence that compels us to serve our father in the house is similar to that which compels us to serve our lord outside. The text emphasises that 'Treating nobility in a noble manner and the honourable in an honourable manner is the summit of righteousness.'

3. *Ritual propriety*: Confucius defines ritual propriety as being sensitive and attentive to social customs and showing willingness to fulfil responsibilities related to rituals. He places emphasis on adhering to past traditions and customs, advocating for actions in accordance with rites. He stresses the importance of understanding the reasoning and the emotional significance behind rituals.
4. *Wisdom*: Confucius describes wisdom as the virtue that enables a gentleman to discern between crooked and straight behaviour in others, and segregate people into those who can be reformed and those who cannot. Wisdom is also the ability to know and understand things as they are and, as Confucius explains to his disciple Zi Lu, 'Wisdom identifies understanding a thing as understanding it, and ignorance of a thing as ignorance of it'. Further, he asserts, a wise person is never confused.
5. *Trustworthiness*: This virtue enables an individual to serve as an adviser to rulers and chiefs. In the *Analects*, Confucius describes trustworthiness succinctly as, 'If one is trustworthy, people will give one responsibilities.' Trustworthiness is not only an expression of true friendship between equals and those of similar status but is also important in relationships with those of contrasting status. Emphasising its key role in relationships between superiors and subordinates, and in matters of governance, Confucius states that trustworthiness is mightier than power, the art of flattery, or eloquence, and asserts that 'If people find their ruler untrustworthy, the state will not survive.'

In addition to these five virtues, Confucius also mentions others such as loyalty (*zhong*) and courage (*yong*).

Principle of reflexivity: In the *Records of Ritual* Confucius observes that the virtuous must 'only seek things [i.e., qualities or virtues] in others that he or she personally possesses, and only condemn things in others that he or she personally lacks.' This principle underscores the importance of self-awareness, self-improvement and personal integrity. Confucius encourages individuals, especially rulers and those in positions of power, to be introspective and recognise their own virtues and flaws before passing judgment on others and expecting subjects to adhere to certain values. By embodying the virtues they seek in their subjects and others, rulers contribute to creating a more harmonious and morally upright society.

Daoism or Taoism

Daoism or Taoism, along with Confucianism, is one of the two main most important philosophical systems in China. The foundations of Daoism are said to lie in the philosophy of Zhuangzi (4 BCE), who is often regarded as the Plato of Daoism, while Laozi is considered as its Socrates. The term *dao* holds diverse meanings, such as way, path or norms. Daoism, particularly through its naturalistic theory, emphasises complete passivity concerning natural events. According to Daoist principles, a person should refrain from initiating changes against their surroundings and instead learn to adapt to them. Daoism presents the notion that 'The highest virtue is not virtuous, therefore it has virtue.' This perspective revolves around not conforming to conventional moral expectations. Laozi underscores the relativity of knowledge and values, stating that such opposing extremes gain meaning and relevance only in relation to each other; otherwise, such contrasts are meaningless.

A philosophical tradition encompassing both metaphysical and ethical aspects, Daoism emphasises inculcating naturalness, simplicity and spontaneity as virtues, and offers insights into living a virtuous life by aligning oneself with the natural order of the Dao or the 'Way'. There are three primary components of Dao:

1. *Human (Social) Dao*: This relates to normative space-time structure, representing ways in which individuals interact within societal contexts.
2. *Tian (Natural) Dao*: Also known as Heavenly Dao, this is associated with the constants of science, describing the consistent patterns in the ways things have occurred and will continue to occur in the natural world.
3. *Great Dao*: This suggests the overarching consistency in the unfolding of the universe, encapsulating the historical development of everything. Unlike Human Dao, Tian Dao and Great Dao are considered constant.

SOCIAL CONTRACT THEORY

Nearly as old as philosophy itself, the theory of social contract posits that the moral, social and/or political obligations of individuals are contingent upon a contract or agreement among them. It argues that people live together in society in accordance with an agreement that establishes rules of conduct for mutual benefit. Philosopher Stuart Rachels suggests that morality is a set of rules governing behaviour that rational people accept on the condition that others accept them too.

Social contracts can be explicit, such as laws, rules and regulations, or implicit, such as raising funds for disaster relief, helping the poor and needy, etc. Each country and government sets down certain principles that describe the social contract governing its citizens. Every member who is a part of the contract is bound to follow it. Regardless of whether social contracts are explicit or implicit, they provide a necessary framework for preserving harmony in society.

Socrates uses something quite like a social contract argument to explain to Crito why he must remain in prison and accept the death penalty. However, modern social contract theory as we know it was given its first full exposition and defence by Thomas Hobbes. Thinkers like John Locke and Jean-Jacques Rousseau have subsequently made major contributions to this influential theory. In the twentieth century, John Rawls propounded his social contract theory based on Kantian Categorical Imperatives, which was further developed by David Gauthier and others. In recent times, social contract theories have been critiqued for their shortcomings from various points of view, including feminism and race-consciousness.

Socrates' View of Justice and the 'Social Contract'

Socrates argues that he must accept the death penalty and not try to escape prison because he is bound to a social contract that has existed between him and Athens since his birth. He owes his legitimate existence as an Athenian citizen to the customs of this city, like his parents' marriage, his birth, his education and upbringing. He has lived by the laws of Athens and his thoughts, words and actions obey Athenian laws. Importantly, this relationship between the city and its citizens based on a contract is not coercive. Once they are adults and have experienced how the city regulates itself, citizens are free to leave the city, or stay. Staying shows an agreement to abide by the city's laws and traditions and to accept the punishments it metes out. And, having made an agreement that is itself just, Socrates asserts that he must now abide by this agreement and obey the law, in this case, by staying and accepting the death penalty.

In answering the question 'what is justice?' in the light of a social contract, Plato's brother Glaucon, in the *Republic* (Book II), says: 'A man would desire to be able to commit injustices against others without fear of reprisal, and to avoid unjust treatments by others without being able to do injustice in return.' Justice then is 'the conventional result of the laws and covenants that men make to avoid these extremes'. Being unable to commit injustice with impunity and fearing reprisals, men decide that it is in their best interests to submit themselves to norms of justice.

But Socrates does not accept this view, arguing that justice is desirable for its own sake and that the just man is the happiest man. From Socrates' point of view, justice has an enormously higher value than the prudential value suggested by Glaucon. Socrates elucidates two contrasting views in the *Crito* and the *Republic*, respectively. In the *Crito*, he uses the argument based on social contract to show why it is just for him to remain in prison, whereas in the *Republic*, he rejects the social contract as the source of justice. Socrates holds the state as the highest entity, morally and politically, and hence worthy of a man's highest allegiance and respect. A just man knows this and acts accordingly, recognising his obligation to the state by obeying its laws. However, justice is much more than simply obeying laws in exchange for others also obeying them, for personal security and gain. Justice, Socrates asserts, is the state of a well-regulated soul, and so the just man will necessarily also be the happiest man. Justice is more than simple reciprocal obedience to law; it includes obedience to the state and the laws that sustain it. Thus, Plato becomes the first philosopher to suggest a representation of the argument in the light of social contract theory. And Socrates comprehensively rejects the idea of social contract as the original source of justice.

Social Contract Theory of Hobbes

Thomas Hobbes lived during the English Civil War (1642–1648), the most crucial period of early modern England's history. The war saw a clash between the king and his supporters on one side, the Monarchists, who preferred a monarch's traditional authority, and on the other side, the Parliamentarians, notably led by Oliver Cromwell, who demanded more power for the quasi-democratic institution of the Parliament. Hobbes represented a compromise between these two factions.

Hobbes rejected the theory of the divine right of kings, propounded by Robert Filmer in his *Patriarcha, or the Natural Power of Kings*. Filmer argued that a king's authority was vested in him by God, and such authority was absolute; and therefore the basis of political duty lay in our religious duty to abide by God's order in the form of a king. According to this view, political obligation is subsumed under religious obligation. Hobbes also rejected the early democratic view of the Parliamentarians that power ought to be shared between parliament and the king.

Having rejecting both these views, Hobbes occupied a ground that was both radical and conservative. He said political authority and obligation are based on the individual self-interests of members of society, who are all understood to be equal, and no single individual is invested with any essential or special authority to rule over the rest. At the same time, Hobbes also maintained the conservative position that the monarch, whom he called the sovereign, must be ceded absolute authority if society is to survive. This authority should be established according to a social contract.

Hobbes' political theory comprises the theory of human motivation and the theory of social contract. The former is based on psychological egoism, and the latter is based on the hypothetical 'State of Nature'. In *Leviathan* (1651), he presents the idea of morality and politics based on the theory of human nature, which is considered parallel to the sciences of non-living bodies in the universe. His psychological theory is based on the mechanism of the evolution of the universe from matter in motion. According to Hobbes, a similar mechanism is involved in forming human macro behaviour out of the effects of certain kinds of micro behaviour which are sometimes visible in us. Thus, behaviour such as body movements are produced by other actions inside us, which are in turn caused by mutual interactions with living and non-living things, finally giving rise to human behaviour. The terms 'good' and 'bad' have no meanings other than unfolding our appetites and aversions. Thus, moral terms do not represent any objective state of affairs but are representations of individual likes and dislikes.

In addition to subjectivism, Hobbes also asserts that humans are necessarily and exclusively driven by self-interests. Everyone seeks to achieve what is best for them and responds mechanistically in terms of obtaining what is desired and avoiding what is not. This is a universal claim that covers all human actions whether related to particular human desires or are more generalised, or concern friends or strangers. According to Hobbes, even the nurturing of children is based on self-interest. Hobbes further argues that human beings also have the rational capacity to pursue their desires through the best means available, regardless of the results they may yield, by employing addition and subtraction, and comparing sums to achieve their ends.

From these premises of human nature, Hobbes constructs a provocative and compelling argument for the submission of people to political authority. He imagines a situation before the establishment of society that he calls the 'State of Nature'. This is the natural condition of mankind, characterised by a perpetual 'state of war of all against all' in which everybody seeks to destroy others to gain power incessantly, and life remains 'nasty, brutish and short'. According to Hobbes, humans are naturally self-interested, but also rational. In order to live in a civil society that nurtures their own interests, they will choose to submit to a sovereign authority, and figure out ways to overcome the 'State of Nature' and construct a civil society. The first and foremost law of nature says that 'each man will be willing to pursue peace when others are willing to do the same, all the while retaining the right to continue to pursue war when others do not pursue peace. Men can be expected to construct a social contract that will afford them a life better than the one they had in the 'State of Nature'.

The social contract comprises two fundamental tenets. First, there must be consensus to abandon the rights individuals possessed against each other in the 'State of Nature'. Second, they must confer authority and power upon any one person, entity or group of persons to enforce the initial contract. In other words, a common law and an enforcement mechanism are needed to overcome the 'State of Nature'. The sovereign is conferred with the authority and power to impose punishments for the violation of the contract. In the 'State of Nature' there was no entity powerful enough to control and overawe all the people, but in the social contract an artificially created legitimate superior can compel people to cooperate. Living conditions under the authority of a sovereign may often be harsh, but it is always better than living in the 'State of Nature'. Whatever the standard of execution of affairs managed by a sovereign may be, people cannot justify opposition to his power because it is the only thing which stands between them and what they most desire to avert in the 'State of Nature'.

According to Hobbes, society, morality, political ideas and other related things are all conveniences that are conventional in nature. Before the social contract, nothing was unethical and unlawful. Once the contract is established, society becomes possible, and people can be expected to keep their promises, cooperations and traditions. The social contract is the most fundamental source of all goods pertaining to a better life.

Social Contract Theory of John Locke

Hobbes' theory of the State of Nature was used by all social contract theorists directly or indirectly. John Locke also uses it, but he defines the subject–sovereign relationship differently. Locke's most impressive political writings are contained in his *Two Treatises of Government*. The first treatise rejects Robert Filmer's influential theory of Divine Right of Kings. The second treatise, titled 'An Essay Concerning the True Original Extent and End of Civil Government', details Locke's own views about civil government, its objectives and justifications. For Locke, the 'State of Nature' is the state of absolute liberty to conduct life as one thinks best, free from any interference of others, and is thus the most natural condition of humanity, but it does not grant a license to transgress morality. Unlike Hobbes' idea, the State of Nature for Locke has no authority or sovereign to enforce laws, but it is not a state devoid of morality. The State of Nature is pre-political, but not pre-moral. Here morality is discovered through the law of nature, which according to Locke, is the fundamental basis of all morality, endowed to us by God. This law commands that 'people not harm others with respect to their life, health, liberty, or possessions'. Since all individuals belong equally to God, this divine command restrains actions that could harm others and prohibits immoral behaviour, while pursuing one's interests free from interference. This type of restriction is comparatively more peaceful than that discussed by Hobbes in his social contract theory.

In Locke's Social Contract Theory, the 'State of Nature' is not a 'State of War' but it can devolve into a state of war over disputes of property. The 'State of Nature' facilitates complete liberty where people understand the law of nature and do not harm each other. 'State of War' begins as soon as one individual declares war on another by stealing from them or trying to enslave others. Since there is no powerful authority to control the situation, the 'State of Nature' endows others with the propensity to defend themselves against the culprit. Once the war begins, it goes on. This situation compels people to renounce the 'State of Nature' and come together to form a civil government.

The notion of private property is central to Locke's arguments for the formation of civil government and the social contract that enacts this. According to Locke, private property comes into existence when human labour combines with raw materials of nature. For example, a farmer can claim ownership over farmland because he transforms a piece of land in nature into a productive resource through his physical efforts. This led Locke to conclude that Americans own the land of America, although they are not natives to it. Thus, one who utilises the basic materials of nature is the legitimate owner of that material. But there are limits to how much property one person can acquire because one is not permitted to take more from nature than one can utilise properly, thereby leaving others devoid of sufficient resources for themselves. Nature is given to all of mankind by God for common subsistence, and one should take only their fair share. The need for civil government arises to provide protection for individual property.

According to Locke, the 'State of Nature' is not a condition of isolated individuals, as in Hobbes' social contract theory, but maintained by mothers and fathers with children or by families in the form of conjugal societies. These conjugal societies are formed on the basis of voluntary agreements to care for children together, and grounded in morality rather than any political ideology. The transition to a political society occurs when individual men, representing their families, unite in the 'State of Nature' and contract to relinquish power to punish those who violate the law of nature on their own. This power is surrendered to a civil government, and upon doing so, they become subject to the will of the majority. In other words, they voluntarily submit themselves to the authority of a superior body, entering into a contract to abandon the 'State of Nature' in favour of forming a society as 'one body politic under one government'. With the establishment of a political society and civil government, individuals acquire three elements that were absent in the 'State of Nature': laws, judges to adjudicate these laws, and executives to enforce these laws. Finally, men are united into a commonwealth for the sake of preserving their properties, lives, liberty and wellbeing.

Locke also predicts the circumstances in which the compact with the government is annihilated, and men are justified to defend the authority of a civil government. In other words, when executives misuse their power, or act as tyrants by destroying the democracy, annihilating the legislature and restricting people from making popular laws for themselves, it results in a reversal into the 'State of Nature', and specifically into a 'State of War' with the contractees. This reversal automatically awards the right to self-defence to the contractees as they possessed before making the contract. Thus, when the government becomes tyrannical and acts against the interests of the people, people have the right to overthrow the government and create a political society afresh.

Social Contract Theory of Rousseau

Jean-Jacques Rousseau (1712–1778) lived and worked through one of the most turbulent periods in French history that marked the renaissance of modern France. His contributions played a significant role in the intellectual movement of the time, as evident in his articles and discussions. Rousseau gained prominence with two well-known essays, the First Discourse and the Second Discourse, written in response to an essay competition sponsored by the Academy of Dijon. The Second Discourse provides a comprehensive description of the chronological development through which humanity transitioned from the 'State of Nature' to the formation of civil society. According to Rousseau, the 'State of Nature' was a peaceful and utopian period where people lived solitary but uncomplicated lives, with limited needs easily fulfilled by nature's abundance. The small population meant little or no competition and individuals seldom viewed each other as competitors; hence there was no conflict or fear. People were simple, pure-hearted and had no intention to harm one another. As time passed and population increased, nature faced biotic pressure, leading to resource deficit. This prompted people to come together in families and small communities, introducing division of labour. New discoveries and inventions brought comfort to life, providing individuals with leisure time. Leisure also led to comparisons, fostering feelings of shame, envy, pride and contempt.

According to Rousseau, the introduction of private property played a crucial role in transforming the State of Nature into a state characterised by greed, competition, jealousy, vanity, inequality and vice, and thus marked humanity's fall from grace out of the idyllic State of Nature.

According to Rousseau, the emergence of the concept of property accentuated inequality, as only a limited number of individuals possessed property, while others were compelled to work for them. This gave rise to social classes. Those with property sought to safeguard their possessions from those without, who might forcibly dispossess them. They established government through a disguised social contract, ostensibly to promote equality, wellbeing and protection for all, but its true purpose was to maintain the existing state of inequality and protect property. For instance, personal property, like a home and personal belongings, is linked to basic liberty, but an absolute liberty to accumulate unlimited private property is unjust as it violates the fundamental rights and liberties of others.

Social Contract Theory of John Rawls

John Rawls (1921–2002) was profoundly influenced by the ideas of Immanuel Kant, who declared that 'individuals are the kingdoms of ends and means'. For Rawls justice is neither divine nor natural, but purely the result of individual rational human choice. The 'self' is prior to its ends and thus, any relevant theory of justice must be based on human rationality emerging from human understanding, he asserted. Rawls visualised society as a fair and just system of cooperation between free and equal citizens, and formulated his understanding of justice as a theory of social contract in which all are equal stakeholders and all have equal status.

Rawls' predecessors Hobbes, Locke and Rousseau expounded on the concept of the social contract within the framework of natural law, examining the justification of political authority and individual rights, particularly concerning property. Central to their discussions was the idea of the 'state of nature', a hypothetical scenario devoid of law and order, necessitating the establishment of governance to ensure equality under the social contract. Events like the American and the French Revolutions exemplify the application of these ideals, advocating for principles such as 'life, liberty and the pursuit of happiness' and 'liberty, equality and fraternity' respectively. Similar notions of justice are enshrined in documents like the Indian Constitution. However, the dominance of the social contract tradition gradually waned, to be supplanted by utilitarianism and intuitionism for much of the following century.

Rawls' Theory of Justice

The Theory of Justice by John Rawls in 1971 is a seminal and profoundly influential work in political philosophy. Rawls further refined his theory in subsequent works, including *The Basic Liberties and Their Priority* (1982), *Justice as Fairness: Political not Metaphysical* (1985), and *Justice as Fairness: A Restatement* (2001). Rawls challenged the intuitionist perspective of justice, asserting that while intuition may offer valuable insights into justice, it lacks the capacity to construct a coherent political philosophy. Instead, he strongly advocated for the incorporation of fair procedures in establishing societal justice, emphasising their sustainability and ability to engender acceptance among all parties, even those who may be disadvantaged by the outcomes. By prioritising fair procedures, societies can evolve systems of economic and political distribution over time, fostering a more equitable and just social order, he argued.

In *Justice as Fairness: A Restatement*, Rawls articulates two foundational principles of justice that form his theoretical framework. The *first principle* guarantees to all individuals the basic equal rights and freedoms needed to secure the fundamental interests of free and equal citizens and to pursue a broad range of what is considered 'good'. The first principle states that all individuals must possess equal rights to the most exhaustive array of basic liberties, provided such liberties are also compatible with the same liberties for all.

The *second principle* pertains to the distribution of goods and opportunities, enabling fair competition and securing the means and resources needed to preserve their self-respect as equal and free individuals. Recognising that not everything can be equally distributed, Rawls stipulated that inequalities must be justified by conditions of fair equality of opportunity and are permissible only if they maximise the welfare of the most vulnerable. The second principle thus outlines acceptable forms of social and economic inequalities, stipulating that they must adhere to two conditions: the *equality* principle and the *difference* principle.

1. The *equality principle* states that positions of power and opportunity must be accessible to everyone under fair and equal conditions. It emphasises the fair and equal distribution of basic liberties, rights, goods and opportunities among all members of society, including political rights and liberties, freedom of speech and assembly, as well as the right to own property and hold personal savings. It asserts that social and economic opportunities should be equally accessible to everyone, irrespective of socio-economic status, race, gender, religion or other characteristics. Rawls argued that a just society must ensure that all individuals have a fair starting point and an equal chance to pursue their life goals.
2. The *difference principle* stipulates that socio-economic inequalities must be such that they benefit the least advantaged members of society to the greatest extent possible, following the principle of fair distribution. It holds that social and economic inequalities are acceptable only if they are structured in a way that maximise the wellbeing of the least privileged and the most vulnerable. One cannot be denied greater advantages in terms of inequalities if it improves

conditions of the least advantaged members of society, provided they are better off than they would be under all possible alternative arrangements. This principle recognises that some level of inequality may be necessary to incentivise productivity and innovation but mandates that such inequalities must contribute to the overall improvement of society, especially for those least advantaged.

These two principles operate independently in an orderly manner. The equal distribution of social and economic goods is impossible without the just distribution of civil liberties. In other words, the application of the second principle relies on the application of the first principle, and civil liberties cannot be sacrificed at the expense of greater social and economic goods.

Justice as Fairness

In his final essay, Rawls posits that 'justice as fairness' serves as the moral and philosophical bedrock for democratic institutions, aiming to reconcile citizens' claims to liberty and equality within a societal framework. This concept necessitates a careful examination of public political culture, including the formation and foundational laws that underpin familiar political ideas, such as constitutional rights and liberties. Rawls identifies certain fundamental ideas as central to shaping the notion of 'justice as fairness' that closely align the idea of justice with common-sense understandings in daily life:

Social cooperation: The notion of citizens as free and equal individuals engaged in cooperation. He contends that social cooperation must embody three essential features: i) adherence to publicly accepted rules and procedures; ii) incorporation of fair terms of cooperation that are reasonable and widely publicly acknowledged; and iii) a focus on promoting rational advantage or common good for all parties involved.

A well-ordered society: A society governed and regulated by widely-accepted and shared principles of justice. Rawls identifies three dimensions of a well-ordered political society: i) mutual recognition among citizens that all will adhere to the same principles of political justice; ii) the effective regulation of political and social institutions within a coherent system of cooperation; and iii) the centrality of the basic structure of society as the cornerstone of justice as fairness.

Social Contract Theory of David Gauthier

David Gauthier (1932–2023) presented a modified social contract theory that builds upon the social contract tradition and Hobbesian moral and political philosophy, but Gauthier introduces a distinctive perspective rooted in rational choice theory and contractarian ethics. In his book *Morals by Agreement* (1986), Gauthier concurs with Hobbes on the necessity of an agreement among exclusively self-interested but rational individuals. However, he diverges on the need for an external sovereign for enforcing the compact, asserting that rationality alone can ensure mutual cooperation and the preservation of the agreement.

Gauthier illustrates his point using the 'Prisoner's Dilemma' as an example. He draws a crucial lesson from this scenario, emphasising that in interactions where others' actions impact one's interests and vice versa, rational individuals fare better when they act cooperatively. By favouring others' interests, a person simultaneously serves their own.

To uphold rationality within ourselves, Gauthier proposes self-constraint during mutual interactions. He advocates for individuals to become '*constrained maximisers*' rather than '*straightforward maximisers*', as they would be in the 'state of nature'. Both types of maximisers consider the strategies of others during interactions, but straightforward maximisers neglect the benefits of cooperation. Gauthier contends that in situations like the Prisoner's Dilemma, where the actions of others affect oneself and vice versa, rationality dictates that one's own interest is better pursued through cooperation. People, driven by rationality, constrain the maximisation of their utility by internalising fundamental morality. Here, there is no need for an external sovereign to enforce the compact; instead, the internalised enforcement arises from a morality grounded in rationality. Consequently, 'Morals by Agreement' emerge from the rational decisions of exclusively self-interested individuals in the absence of a sovereign regulator.

CONTEMPORARY CRITIQUE OF SOCIAL CONTRACT THEORY

The social contract theory has long been considered one of the most appealing and important socio-political theories. However, it has consistently faced criticism from various contemporary philosophers, particularly feminist and race-conscious thinkers who have raised substantial and valid objections.

Feminist Critique

Feminist criticism that scrutinises the impact of prevailing theories and traditions on women's lives have expressed serious concerns about the social contract theory, which encompasses all segments of society. In her book *The Sexual Contract* (1988), feminist and political philosopher Carole Pateman argues that the theories of Hobbes, Locke and Rousseau, though ostensibly aimed at defining the relationship between men and women through an idealised contract, serve to perpetuate male dominance. Pateman suggests that while the social contract rejects the patriarchal ideas advocated by Robert Filmer, the original pact merely becomes an instrument for the control and domination of women.

According to Pateman, the social contract theory reinforces patriarchal control over women through three primary contracts: the marriage contract, the prostitution contract and the surrogate motherhood contract. These contracts, she contends, facilitate male control over women, perpetuating one man's domination over a specific woman. Rather than promoting freedom and equality, these contracts are centred around male sexual access and control over women's reproductive capacities. They ensure equal access to women by men in various aspects, replacing one form of classical patriarchy with another form of modern patriarchy, now distributed among multiple men rather than concentrated in a single individual.

In social contract theory, the contractors are portrayed as liberal and rational individuals, embodying figures such as the Hobbesian man, Locke's proprietor, Rousseau's Noble Savage, Rawls' person in the 'original position', and Gauthier's Robinson Crusoe. This liberal individual is depicted as a universal, raceless, sexless and classless representative of humanity at large. However, as many philosophers have argued, this so-called liberal individual does not represent an abstract universal humanity but is instead a specific, historically centred individual.

For instance, the Hobbesian man is specifically a bourgeois man of early modern Europe during the emergence of capitalism. Several feminists contend that Hobbes' concept of the liberal individual is an essentially masculine one. The social contract theory is implicitly driven by the idea of an 'economic man' who seeks to maximise his interests and enters into contracts for this purpose. However, this economic man does not encompass every section of society, and particularly overlooks the roles of children and women. The social contract neglects the welfare of children and women.

Further, the growing influence of the *ethics of care* has led to severe criticism of the social contract theory for its inadequate consideration of individuals' moral and political duties. The theory is seen as a mere mechanical pact that determines rights and obligations without addressing meaningful relationships based on moral considerations, ethics and human psychology. It fails to account for relationships grounded in love, care, affection, responsibility and dependence, such as the mother–child relationship.

The 'Racial Contract': Charles W. Mills' Critique

According to Charles W. Mills, the social contract is not a genuine agreement at all; it is nothing but a disguised 'racial contract'. In his book, *The Racial Contract* (1997), Mills exposes the inherent flaws of the social contract theory, and argues that the contract establishes criteria for determining who will be recognised as a legitimate moral and political person eligible to enter into the contract. In the Western world, only certain individuals—essentially, white men—were empowered to meet these criteria and enjoyed elevated social status. Others were denied even basic human rights and relegated to the status of mere objects within the contractual framework.

Mills emphasises that 'race' is not just a social construct but, more importantly, a political construct. He cites Locke's assertion that 'Native Americans did not own the land they lived on because they did not farm it' as an example of a racial contract justifying the enslavement of millions of Africans, the slaughter of Native Americans and the enslavement of the Aboriginals of Australia by the white settlers. Throughout history, certain classes have exploited people, land and resources by virtue of their illegitimate superiority justified through the racial contract.

QUESTIONS

1. 'Falsehood takes the place of truth when it results in unblemished common good.' —*Tirukkural*. Analyse and discuss with examples. (UPSC 2018)
2. Analyse John Rawls's concept of social justice in the Indian context. (UPSC 2016)
3. 'An unexamined life is not worth living.' —Socrates. Discuss. (UPSC 2019)
4. 'Accumulating a lot of wealth and eating alone without sharing is worse than the act of asking for alms.' Explain.
5. A good man must not lie even by mistake because it destroys his good achievements. Elaborate with the help of examples.
6. Virtue and happiness are inseparable. Explain.
7. Justice entails doing your own thing, without interfering in the work of others. Explain this in the context of public administration.
8. Explain the idea of justice with the help of the views of different philosophers.
9. Explain the statement: 'What the weak head with strong bias rules, is pride, the never-failing vice of fools.' —Alexander Pope
10. Explain the notion of virtue with the help of examples.
11. Rewards and punishment serve as important moral motivations. Explain with the help of examples.

11

ETHICS IN PUBLIC ADMINISTRATION

> **KEY CONCEPTS**
>
> Status and Problem; The Politics-Administration Dichotomy; The Principles of Administration; Public Administration as Political Science; Public Administration as an Independent Discipline; Ethical Concerns in Government; Low Road Approach; High Road Approach; Public Service Ethos; Ethical Minimum and Ethical Maximum; Ethical Dilemma in Government; Ethical Dilemma in Private Institutions

STATUS AND PROBLEM

In a democracy, every public servant is eventually accountable to the public. Public functionaries serve as trustees of the people, and are entrusted with the responsibility of caring for people's needs through an exercise of their authority. There are various instruments that define such accountability under the statutes.

It is ethics that provides the basis for framing laws, rules and regulations. The role of ethics in public administration has many dimensions, some of which are given below:

1. Codifying (that is, arranging according to a system or plan) ethical norms and practices.
2. Determining a framework that can overcome any conflict of interest.
3. Formulating a mechanism for imposing pertinent codes.
4. Framing rules concerning the qualification and disqualification of a public servant from public office.

Public Administration was introduced as a subject of study in 1887 through the efforts of Thomas Woodrow Wilson (1856–1924), who served as the President of the United States from 1913–1921. Since then, this subject has evolved and undergone several changes under different paradigms. American businessman Nicholas Henry, in his book *Public Administration and Public Affairs* (1975), detailed the evolution of Public Administration under five successive paradigms:

1. The Politics-Administration Dichotomy (1887–1926)
2. The Principles of Administration (1927–1937)
3. Public Administration as Political Science (1950–1970)
4. Public Administration as Management (1956–1970)
5. Public Administration as Public Administration (1970s onwards)

THE POLITICS-ADMINISTRATION DICHOTOMY

In 1887, Woodrow Wilson first emphasised the study of Public Administration as a separate discipline in his essay, 'The Study of Administration'. He made a distinction between politics and administration, which came to be known as the politics-administration dichotomy.

Wilson's view was taken forward by Frank J. Goodnow (1859–1939), who stated, 'Politics has to do with policies or expressions of state will. Administration has to do with the execution of those policies' (Goodnow 1900). American historian Leonard D. White (1891–1958) emphasised, 'Politics should not intrude on administration' (White 1926). German sociologist and political economist Max Weber (1864–1920) proposed the idea of bureaucratic management. Weber's bureaucratic model had the following characteristics:

1. The provision of defined services. Competencies are determined by laws, rules and regulations, on the basis of which functions are determined and provided with decision-making powers.
2. The provision of career bureaucrats, who are not allowed to engage in secondary professions.
3. A hierarchical organisation, comprising management positions and subordinate services.
4. Recruitment of bureaucrats through open competitive examinations.
5. Fixed salaries and the provision of retirement after a certain age.
6. Well-structured mechanism of disciplinary action, to be levied by superiors to control subordinates.
7. Provision of promotion on the basis of objective criteria.
8. The separation of functions and individuals who perform such functions.

THE PRINCIPLES OF ADMINISTRATION

In this period, it was also believed that there existed certain principles that ordered the field of Public Administration, akin to those that existed in the sciences, which could be enunciated systematically. An administrator should master these principles and apply them to the field of administration. Significant work in this phase was undertaken by M. P. Follet, Henry Fayol, Luther Gulick and Lyndall Urwick. These scholars were in favour of the inductive method of theory building from cases derived from the study of human organisations, and the theories thus deduced should be capable of governing any human organisation.

American mechanical engineer F. W. Taylor (1856–1915), known for his methods to improve industrial efficiency, over-generalised the human factor and offered a principle of Scientific Management, which stated that productivity could increase if jobs were made simpler and by optimising them. Taylor believed that it was the role and responsibility of manufacturing plant managers to determine the best way for a worker to do a job, and to provide the proper tools and training.

PUBLIC ADMINISTRATION AS POLITICAL SCIENCE

In the year 1938, American business executive Chester I. Bernard (1886–1961) put forward two ideas:

1. He rejected the dichotomy in public administration.
2. He exposed the shortcomings of scientific validity in public administration.

It was argued that public administration cannot be separated from politics because administration relates not just to the implementation of policy framed by politicians; rather, it plays a crucial role in framing the policy, too. After 1950, Public Administration as a discipline was developed through two methods: an excessive use of case studies and through the study of development administration.

PUBLIC ADMINISTRATION AS AN INDEPENDENT DISCIPLINE

During this period, Public Administration also developed as an interdisciplinary subject with the confluence of Politics, Economics and Organisational Theory. We also see the emergence of New Public Administration (NPA), which emphasised more on values rather than on efficiency and effectiveness, and aimed at making administration more public, prescriptive and client-oriented. Later, in the late 1980s, New Public Management Theory (NPM) became popular, and David Osborne and Ted Gaebler wrote their bestselling *Reinventing Government: How the Entrepreneurial Spirit is Transforming the Public Sector* (1992), in which they advocated treating the public as customers or clients. The NPM is widely accepted at all levels in the government of every country, and was later remodelled as a digital-era government by Janet and Robert Denhardt (2003) to exploit the potential of Information Technology in the field of administration.

> **New Public Administration**
>
> New Public Administration is a movement that emerged in the 1970s to address the challenges and demands of the public sector. It aims to define how government organisations should work to formulate and implement public policies, and does so through its principles and features, such as democratic citizenship and citizen empowerment.

ETHICAL CONCERNS IN GOVERNMENT

The public and private life of a civil servant is not as simple as it appears to be. Although there are adequate rules and regulations, guidelines and office traditions governing the taking of administrative decisions, civil servants are often ill-equipped to handle several incidents that occur frequently, and which demand a certain amount of discretion. Faced with such problems, recourse is usually taken to earlier precedents and conventions; however, what happens when personal intuition and rationality run counter to such past actions? All too often, the tried and tested practices of office work are set aside, and newer methods of decision-making are resorted to by innovative, smart and upright officers for the sake of good governance. Even judicial perspectives can be seen to change from time to time. What these situations call for forms the subject of study, propelled largely by ethics as the principal factor.

Ethical issues are regarded as circumstances imbued with questions of law, duty and morality, in which, despite the presence of proper guidelines, rules and precedents, a civil servant finds themselves unable to take a decision. On the one hand, these decisions are put through rigorous ethical scrutiny, and on the other hand, factors such as an absence of conviction, fidelity, incentives, respect and pity, and the presence of fear serve to influence the final outcome of the concerned issue. These situations are faced at all levels, from lower-level bureaucrats to middle-line managers to those at the apex of the hierarchy. We can understand these situations with the help of a few examples.

> **Case Study 1**
>
> A is a young RR (regular recruit) IAS officer, posted as Collector of a district. His boss, the Divisional Commissioner, is a promotee IAS officer.* A is respectful to all seniors, regardless of whether they are RR or promotee IAS officers. A's Commissioner is a mysterious person, and he intends to take undue advantage of A. However, each time A refuses politely. A has now fallen into the habit of not listening to his boss carefully, and sometimes misses out on vital instructions. The Commissioner has taken a

tough stance against A, and has begun complaining to other higher officers, stating that A discriminates against him on the basis of the distinction between RR and promotee.

* Note: *Provincial Civil Services officers (SDMs), who were recruited through the State Civil Services Examination), when promoted to posts manned by IAS officers (DM or an equivalent post, or above) are called promotee IAS officers. Regular recruits are IAS officers who cleared the UPSC CSE to become the DM or occupy the above posts.*

Case Study 2

Mr A, a young officer of the State Civil Service, is BDO of Block B, a post he has joined recently. The Swachh Bharat Mission is on full swing across the state. The highly motivated Mr A is determined to transform his Block into an open defecation-free zone before the prescribed deadline. To this end, he organises night camps (*Ratri Choupal*) every night in one of the villages of his Block. One night, during a visit to the village, he learns that the Gram Panchayat-level officer, Mr D, never visits the village, as he lives in a city located 100 km away. The administrative lethargy of his subordinates both infuriates and dismays Mr A, who asks why he had not been informed about the careless conduct of Mr D. He comes to know that Mr D has not been coming to his duty since the day of his appointment to the post; moreover, Mr D works privately as a personal security guard of a politician and muscle man of that district, which provides him protection from all the superior officers. Mr A is also advised to not take any action against him, as no one will be bold enough to support him.

In spite of the clear-cut guidelines and sufficient power vested in Mr A, who can write to his superiors asking for the termination of Mr D's services, Mr A doubts whether the appropriate authority (in this case, the District Collector) will act on the report against Mr D. He also introspects to assure himself that his actions are not solely intended to satisfy his own ego and demonstrate his authority. Finally, Mr A concludes that he does not seek to destroy the conceit of Mr D or establish his authority; rather, his actions are motivated by his duty. Mr D has been drawing a salary without performing his job, and as his conduct is unlawful, he must be punished. Mr A sends a text message to the District Collector and solicits his advice. The District Collector replies, 'I will act according to the law and immediately remove Mr D from the service. However, I also warn you to be ready to face the wrath of Mr D's *de facto* boss. If that happens, I will not be helping you out.'

A lot of questions and ethical concerns emerge from Mr A's dilemma:

1. Should Mr A take action against the delinquent government employee?
2. Will his actions be supported by the higher authorities?
3. Will his actions lead to his facing the fury of the culprit?
4. Are his actions motivated by a need to satisfy his ego and display his authority, or purely to take corrective action against Mr D?

Most people mistake the above considerations for ethical dilemmas. However, these are the consequences of fear, confusion and the absence of courage of one's conviction. We will now look at a few more examples.

Case Study 3

Mr A is a Sub-divisional Magistrate. The previous incumbents had a tradition of according respect to the representatives of MLAs and MPs, who were even allowed to attend the official meetings. Mr A's strong faith in democratic ideals leads him to distinguish clearly between the democratic representatives of the public and those working for different politicians. He does not invite non-governmental people like the representatives of MPs and MLAs and other political party workers to the official meetings. This behaviour is severely criticised by the local politicians. Mr A knows that in the present era of participatory administration, the support of the common people is required to implement government programmes, but he does not consider political workers as legitimate representatives of the people and refuses to involve them in the official meetings. There are guidelines stating that representatives of MLAs and MPs can attend meetings to which those MLAs and MPs have been officially invited, but are unable to attend because they are attending sessions of the Legislative Assembly or Parliament, respectively.

Case Study 4

Mr A is MLA of a constituency and an honest politician. His political worker compels him to speak to the District Collector, in an attempt to garner unfair support in a matter involving the former. While Mr A understands that this action goes against his ideals, the political worker in question is very dear to him.

All the above case studies show how conflict and confusion can be created in the mind of a public servant. Ethical concerns in government can be defined in terms of matters related to the official duty of a civil servant, in the light of rules concerning conduct, regulations and administrative procedure on the one hand, and her/his own conscience, compassion and humanism on the other. We can classify these into different categories that emerge from the interactions between different organs of the government. The clashes may occur between political authorities and permanent public servants; bureaucrats over the role and supremacy of their services (such as IAS versus IPS); between the executive and the judiciary; between RR and promotee officers; misuse of authority in terms of coercion and exploitation of junior officers, etc.

A public servant must always act according to the rules and regulations (deontology). There are different ways to locate the most ethical answer to a dilemma. However, there are certain situations in which laws are silent and discretion is the need of the hour. These discretionary powers must be exercised with due care and responsibility. These ethical concerns demand different approaches of ethical studies, such as deontology, teleology, virtue ethics, etc (see Chapter 2). The irony of ethical studies in administration lies in the fact that it revolves around the bigger administrators rather than field-level executives or lower-level bureaucrats. It is widely accepted that crises stem not from policymaking but from policy implementation, and a large chunk of the bureaucracy that implements schemes and programmes at the field level belong to the state civil services or comprise very young officers of the All India Civil Services and Central Civil Services. As we all know, India lives in its villages, and real development can be recognised when it takes place in rural areas.

The bedrock of rural development is the Panchayati Raj system, or decentralised local self-government. Problems at the grassroots are faced by Sub-divisional Officers, BDOs, Tehsildars and other officers at the block or sub-division level. The overall development is based upon the performance of these lower-level bureaucrats. Although their jurisdiction, in terms of area and budget, is not very extensive, their responsibilities are much larger in magnitude. The real political and administrative obstructions are felt at this level, and unless we remove ethical ignorance at the ground level, we cannot achieve the desired progress.

Our federal civil services have been unable to attract talented people or inculcate quality training to the officers. Service conditions are very poor: for instance, salaries are low, and there are very few amenities and opportunities for promotion. There is no proper scientific training system; a complete ignorance of the officers' mission, vision and values; severe exploitation by the higher officials and politicians; and discrimination faced by officers of the All India Civil Services. Transfers and postings, the struggle for excellent service records that can aid promotion, and a performance based on the maintenance of the status quo have undermined the lower-level bureaucracy. This is why our federal civil service is not motivated enough to shore up the local economy of India. The basic problem is well-identified: the bureaucracy is weak, inefficient, unmotivated and irresponsible, and works only through fear and undue incentives. The question is: How can this negative attitude, inferior aptitude and weak public service values be overcome? No one seems to be concerned with these issues as they are considered absurd. The bureaucracy as a whole chases quantitative targets and regards changes in its core values as impractical and naive. Most highly acclaimed and high-performing officers are those who bring about progress through fear, firm actions, and by defaming their subordinates publicly. This fear-based functioning of the government machinery is arguably the principal cause behind the poor bureaucratic efficiency in India.

According to American statesman and diplomat John Adams (1735–1826), 'A constitution is a standard, a pillar, and a bond when it is understood, approved and beloved. But without this intelligence and attachment, it might as well be a kite or balloon flying in the air.' This statement lays emphasis on inculcating constitutional values. The 'New Public Administration' provided the theoretical basis to figure out a methodology that could integrate morality and public service. When it comes to administrative discretion, decisions should reflect moral values. Ethical approaches in public administration can be classified under two parts: the 'low road' approach that emphasises a formal adherence to laws, rules and regulations, and the 'high road' approach that emphasises social equity.

LOW ROAD APPROACH

This approach deals with ethical issues in public administration that are related to rules and regulations. It is about setting minimum standards beyond which a public servant's conduct should not fall; it provides a framework for the ethical conduct of a public servant. In the Indian context, the rules of conduct governing central civil services and the Central Civil Services (Classification, Control and Appeal) or CCS (CCA) rules are examples of the instruments devised under the low road approach. Rules pertaining to the utilisation of government resources (for official work only and not for personal use) are also detailed in the manuals and rule books. This approach reduces ethical behaviour of a public servant to merely staying out of trouble; rather than shaping a public servant into a moral agent, it reinforces the under-confident, under-resourced, powerless, 'office boy' image of the public servant that erodes their self-respect.

Figure 11.1: Low road approach

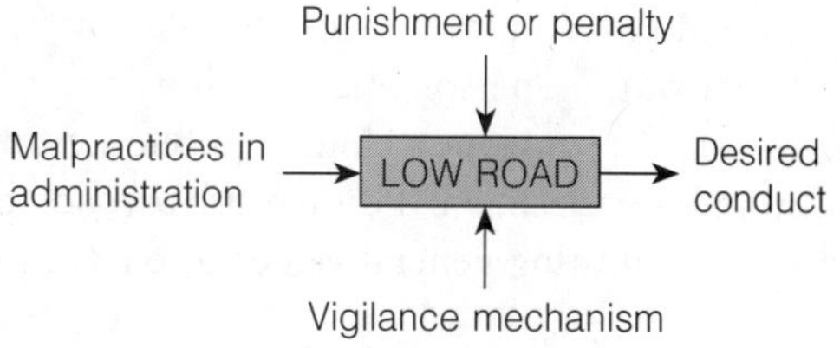

Malpractices in administration → LOW ROAD → Desired conduct
(Punishment or penalty ↓ ; Vigilance mechanism ↑)

This approach lacks any shared values and is intended to probe possible corruption which retards the pace of development and eventually affect the public interest. This is a compliance approach which relies on external control, in terms of laws, rules and regulations, and a minimum level of ethics. Its focus is to restrict malpractices in public administration. These strict rules fortify a false image of the career civil servant because it trains them to emphasise small, everyday issues and overlook the ethically significant dimensions of public service in the quest to adhere to written rules.

HIGH ROAD APPROACH

Under the high road approach of ethics, two dimensions are emphasised: one is based on 'social equity' and the other is related to the subject of 'new public administration'. Social values should be added to efficiency, effectiveness and economy (the 3Es) for assessing the performance of public servants. In other words, an ethical administration should be actively involved in ameliorating the status of the downtrodden through political and economic welfare, which has often been overlooked in traditional democratic regimes. This approach is based on normative political theory and humanistic psychology (which believes that humans, as individuals, are unique beings and should be recognised and treated as such).

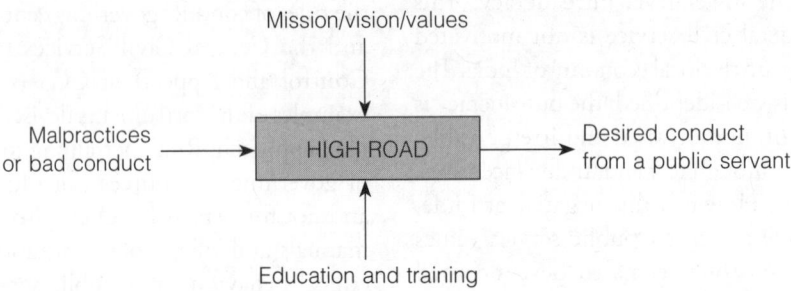

Figure 11.2: High road approach

The high road approach emphasises internal control by developing moral judgement, which results in the creation of a squad of public servants-cum-moral agents. This approach has its roots in New Public Administration and the idea of social equity. All morality is personal because an individual is morally accountable for her/his behaviour. A person plays various roles in life—a parent, someone's child, a public servant, a customer, a citizen, etc. Humanistic psychology helps in inculcating general values to enable the successful and ethical conduct of all such affairs. The government should also inculcate a similar multidimensional morality in civil servants, rather than circumscribing their ethical understanding.

At times, a high road approach can create the evil of hyperbolism or exaggeration, which is even more dangerous than immoralism and can lead to moral cynicism. The low road and high road approaches fall on two opposite extremes. A desired position would be a fusion of these two extremes.

Table 11.1: Comparison of different approaches of ethics in public administration

	Low Road	High Road	Fusion
Focus	Compliance	Integrity	Both
Trait	Legal	Normative	Both
Result	Lawful conduct	Ethical conduct	Both
Tools	Laws, rules and regulations	Mission, vision and values/morality	Both
Training	Pedagogical	Andragogical	Both

These theoretical models provide the basic guidelines that can bring about efficient administration in India. However, implementing these models at the ground level is a complex task. We will try to find the best possible method to do so in our further discussions. It is not possible to continue motivating the bureaucracy through repetitive training in order to sustain these values as long as the values themselves are not fully accepted and transformed into habit; as Aristotle rightly pointed out, virtue is both knowledge and a habit. Its answer lies in the quest for leadership, and this responsibility has to be shared by all the officers of the All India Civil Services and Central Civil Services. In states, this leadership must be based on hierarchy and lessons should trickle down continuously during official meetings and seminars. Every review meeting must start with helping the team recognise the mission, vision and values of the organisation, and they should then be motivated to achieve progress not only in quantitative terms, but also qualitatively. This practice can change the attitude of our bureaucracy.

We have provided a detailed discussion of the methods to recognise the aptitude of our low-level bureaucracy. Besides the bureaucracy, we also have to talk about the inculcation of such attributes on the part of our politicians. As politicians are both the *de jure* and *de facto* drivers of our government, they formulate legislations and decide the direction our country takes. And yet, nobody seems to be concerned about their training. The education and training necessary for their day-to-day business in the area of governance is not imparted. If such training is given, it is in name only, and imparts no knowledge of the philosophy of governance. We have an ethics committee in the Rajya Sabha and the Lok Sabha, but in the State Legislative Assemblies and Councils, these are either not formed or are not functional. These committees ought to conduct an academic training in ethics for our elected representatives.

PUBLIC SERVICE ETHOS

'Ethos' is an ancient Greek word that means 'character'. It has come to mean the distinguishing character, sentiment, moral nature or guiding beliefs of a person, group or institution. In the context of public service, it means an ideology as well as a value or cluster of values expressed through public service. According to Gerald E. Caiden, public service ethos is a linchpin, the backbone of values, and the basis of integrity in public service and ethical values. Robert Denhardt stated, 'Ethos represents the fundamental character or disposition of a group by delineating the ideals that inform the beliefs and practices of the group's members.' As an ideology, public service ethos is described as the idea of performing in the public interest rather than in one's personal interest, and showing a willingness to work altruistically for the common good of the public at large. It is about working continuously with a team spirit and involves integrity in dealing with public affairs. The bureaucratic ethos pertains to classical public administration theories, while the democratic ethos pertains to the New Public Administration and New Public Service doctrines.

ETHICAL MINIMUM AND ETHICAL MAXIMUM

> The division into high road approach and low road approach is the basis for assessing the ethics minimum and ethics maximum divisions in the light of justice, ethos and transparency. The ethical minimum–ethical maximum or low road–high road continuum determines the equilibrium in regulations and values by evolving an ideal blend of these to form a public service framework. Both low road and high road approaches are two opposite extremes. (Mantysalo 2016)

Both have their pros and cons. Researchers advocate for a middle road that can be achieved through a fusion approach that integrates these two extreme approaches. A useful model derived thus from this fusion is the compliance-integrity continuum, based on rules and regulations that exert an external check and where integrity is based on values and morality. Four different ethics management aspects are generated along this continuum in public administration, which are: ethical minimum, ethics management, ethical management and ethical maximum.

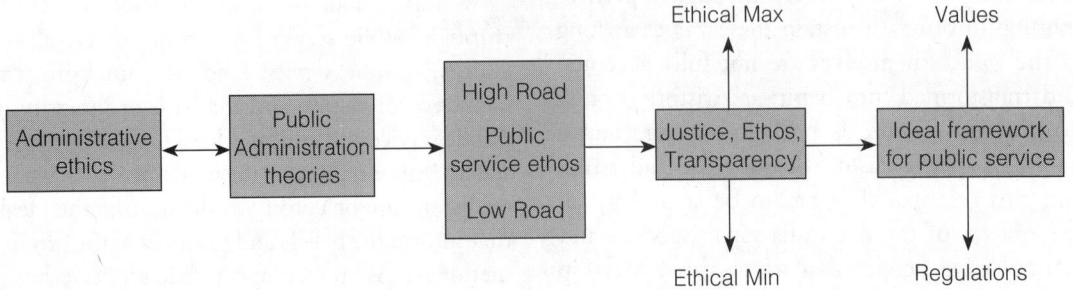

Figure 11.2: Ethical Minimum-Maximum Continuum

Ethical Minimum is a model based on low compliance and low integrity, and stems from a lack of external checks. The performance is geared towards the achievement of the desired results.

Ethics Management is dependent on external checks, but ethics is not internally inculcated by the public servants. Greater focus is placed on higher compliance with the help of stringent rules and regulations. If something is legally correct, then it is considered acceptable behaviour, regardless of any moral compromise that might have taken place.

Ethical Management is the refined version of ethics management with an increased role given to values and integrity. Some members of an organisation follow a strong ethical framework, and commitment to value-based leadership and ethical decision-making become the hallmark of administration. But this is difficult to achieve in the absence of well-defined ethical codes. If it is left in the hands of agents who should (ideally) be committed to ethical values in their conduct, then the ideal situation often does not come about because of various weaknesses in their all to human natures.

Ethical Maximum is the perfect blend of strong compliance and high integrity. Here, institutional arrangements for the ethical conduct of agents are complemented by the inculcation of strong ethical values in the agents themselves. In ethical maximum, leaders are committed to proactively promoting ethical values such as transparency and accountability. Similar to the fusion road approach, ethical maximum is about doing the right thing in the right manner.

ETHICAL DILEMMA IN GOVERNMENT

An ethical dilemma arises when a person has to choose between two or more available options, all of which may be morally correct but may conflict with each other. Ethics and morality are inseparable since they both deal with questions of right and wrong. What constitutes ethical behaviour is determined by societal or cultural norms, while what constitutes moral behaviour is determined by an individual's decision, based on her/his own sense of right and wrong. Ethical dilemmas can be very complex and lead to extremely difficult choices. For instance, a physician might have to decide whether to continue the treatment of a terminally ill patient at the request of family members, or deny such treatment. Continuing the treatment could prolong suffering and also incur additional expenditure. On the other hand, withholding treatment might free the patient of the pain by letting destiny take its course. Respecting the wishes of the family and doing what's best for the patient are both professionally acceptable and ethically correct; however, the choice of which could be considered the best course of action is very personal and pertains to individual morality.

Some incidents demand a level of personal responsibility, and a closer look at the actions and decisions taken under ethical guidelines through a moral lens. Socially responsible behaviour on the part of individuals might even affect the society at large. Littering is a simple example of social ethics: by throwing trash on the roadside, an individual adversely affects the environmental balance and also ignores her/his societal responsibility to keep their surroundings clean.

Ethical skills include the following components:

1. The ability to identify and formulate moral problems.
2. The ability to reason about moral issues.
3. The ability to clarify one's own moral aspirations.

To achieve these goals, we can use two types of training approaches, *first*, the theoretical-normative approach which aims to provide knowledge about ethical theories, principles and norms, and teach participants how to apply these norms. The *second* approach attempts to influence behaviour by teaching participants how to think logically and critically about ethical issues while resolving ethical dilemmas. A combination of these approaches should be used in ethics training programmes, in accordance with the needs of trainee groups. Teaching through case studies based on ethical dilemmas is the most effective methodology.

With the help of logical reasoning, we can understand how to resolve a dilemma pertaining to prioritisation of duties when we are faced with multiple duties to perform. A person may stand in any number of distinct relations with others, and each relation provides the ground for considerations that dictate our performance in any given situation. Consequentialists oversimplify these relations and state that we all belong to each other in terms of both collective and personal actions, or, in other words, each person around an individual is a potential beneficiary of that individual's action. All human beings stand in relation to one another, such as that 'of promisee to promiser, of creditor to debtor, of wife to husband, of child to parents, of friend to friend, of fellow countryman to fellow countryman and the like,' as W. D. Ross stated.

Each of the above relations lays the ground for a duty that is seen *prima facie*. Moral decision-making then comes into play, involving the meticulous comparing and weighing of all relevant *prima facie* duties against one another to decide which would emerge as the most important. The *prima facie* duty tries to deviate from the actual duty, nudging us towards taking it up prior to the other duties. However, we often find that the *prima facie* duty is only seemingly more significant, while not being so in reality. *Prima facie* duties are illusory in nature and camouflage the moral urgency; this confusion dissipates with careful contemplation.

On the other hand, in order to identify our actual duty, we have to settle for a well-considered opinion. This opinion is the result of a careful scrutiny of the circumstances, appealing to common sense, past precedent, and so on. Once an individual learns to recognise her/his duty, the chances of an ethical dilemma are reduced to a significant extent.

As we know, public services are dynamic in nature. A civil servant may find themselves at a juncture where they have more than one option. If s/he follows purely administrative procedure without being empathetic and emotionally intelligent, the end objective will never be achieved. On the other hand, if s/he follows the voice of their inner morality, official guidelines might be violated. Generally, an ethical dilemma in administration takes place in the absence of clear-cut guidelines or law, which brings a high amount of discretion into the picture. This dilemma is nothing but the presence of more than one compelling solution to a problem in day-to-day administration. The best way to rid oneself of dilemma is to have a very sound understanding of rules, regulations, official procedures, and one's own official duty and authority. No civil servant should take up matters outside their own jurisdiction.

The dilemma also emerges from the multiple chains of command, especially where there is no conformity among them. We can understand this from the example of a District Collector who serves as the representative of the government in a district. Part of the IAS, he is the sole authority in the district and functions to implement the will of the government. He is also the coordinator for all departments of the state government, receiving directions as well as advice from the people's representatives and his superiors. During the process of executing any decision, he has to consider every view. The more the instructions, the greater the possibility of conflict and dilemma. Some civil servants may even launch their own innovative ideas in the districts, which can at times clash with the programmes of the government; at other times, they may even deploy all available resources of the district administration for that purpose. Such a situation creates a paucity of time for the government employees in which to run the legitimate programmes and schemes. A civil servant must understand the importance of efficient performance in the execution of legitimately sanctioned government programmes, and steer clear of self-made programmes whose only purpose is to establish one's identity and advance one's own career.

In the absence of proper departmental guidelines, self-imposed programmes can create a dilemma for the subordinate officers. A civil servant should rather introduce innovations in government programmes to augment their quality and efficiency, rather than working according to a personal agenda. For example, running a programme in a drought-prone district to improve the underground water table and conserve the water in rivers should not involve the unauthorised utilisation of funds, nor should the BDOs be asked to compel the Gram Panchayats to carry out the task on their own. In a situation such as this, the BDOs face an ethical dilemma: Should they obey the District Collector's oral orders or the written directions of the government with respect to the utilisation of funds? To resolve this conflict, it is advisable to follow the written orders. Besides this, a dilemma also emerges when a public representative seeks to implement a particular programme without proper sanction. While public representatives are motivated to serve their constituencies and view problems from their specific points of view, the government has its own concerns while implementing programmes. A civil servant has limited scope to bend the schemes in a manner that could serve both interests. When the viewpoint of the public representative is carefully considered as well as moral, and yet the civil servant's hands are tied because of government rules, s/he will try to resolve the dilemma in a way that could accommodate both public opinion and government orders.

ETHICAL DILEMMA IN PRIVATE INSTITUTIONS

Today, the private sector has emerged as almost equal to the government in terms of furnishing services and commodities to the people. The private sector is mostly based on the philosophy of economist Adam Smith, who advocated a 'free market mechanism' that sees capitalism as the most suitable mode of economy. However, the government has some civic responsibilities that are based on the ideals of socialism. By itself, the government cannot fulfil all the diverse needs of the people, nor can it ensure a greater serving capacity. This is why it has to employ the services of private organisations to serve certain needs of the community, and these private organisations do so in exchange for a fee. Being profit-driven, the private sector has no constitutional or legal obligation to serve the people; yet they must be brought into the purview of morality because of the following reasons:

1. They carry out their activities with the help of public money.
2. Public limited companies utilise the public fund through issuing initial public offers (IPOs) and other debt instruments (Indian Depository Receipt [IDR], Global Depository Receipt [GDR], etc.).
3. The free market mechanism is based on the laws of demand and supply. Demands are solely created by the public, and supply is in turn based on public behaviour.
4. The resources of a country belong to the community, and the people of that region are the real owners of those resources. These resources are utilised by the private sector in their production process. Thus, the private sector owes the people and becomes morally accountable to the community.

Their ethical concerns are similar to those of the government sector. The satisfaction of the people who are the direct or indirect customers of private institutions ought to be taken into consideration. There must be a robust customer care service that can function as a grievance redressal mechanism. The utilisation of public money must be audited and the activities and business practices of the private sector must be supervised. Their conduct must be scrutinised in the light of laws, rules and regulations. This philosophy gave birth to the concept of corporate governance.

Social science scholars have long suggested that trust in market dynamics and governments are indispensable to successful governance. According to multiple recent public polls, given the current economic crisis and recent corporate and political shortfall, citizens' trust in the government has dropped to an all-time low. In his 2011 book, *The Price of Civilization: Reawakening American Virtue and Prosperity*, Jeffrey Sachs exposed the rapid decline in social responsibility and the glorification of morality as a tradition. The reluctance to make morality the pivot of all activities is the cause behind the current political and economic turmoil. According to scholars such as Sachs, it is not possible to resolve the current economic, political and global setbacks without restoring faith in governance and public administration. However, this theory has certain limitations and such action might arguably be unfeasible without accentuating ethics in the private sector and putting into place an ethics-based *laissez faire*. Several reasons have compelled us to ponder over this contradiction between trust in government and the ethics of private-sector activities.

Professor of Public Administration Camilla Stivers, in *Gender Images in Public Administration: Legitimacy and the Administrative State* (1993), argued the presence of a dichotomy between public and personal lives, where morality is confined to public life. She applied a gender lens to the field of public administration, through which she studied issues of status, power, leadership, legitimacy and change. Similarly, Dwight Waldo's article 'Development of Theory of Democratic Administration' (1952), published in *American Political Science Review*, emphasised that modern governance sought to address any potential chaos resulting from the escalated demand and pressure of the private sector through a standardisation of the regulatory mechanism based on impartiality and non-interference. The inability of governments to deal with the system shocks of the 1970s and the global meltdown caused by the overwhelming influence of *laissez faire* might have compelled the introduction of morality in the private sector.

Globalisation and the increasing presence of market-driven values in public life and the consequent shock suffered by morality within personal spaces have led to a decline in social responsibility. The quest for individual freedom and rights has led us to overlook ideals such as duty and prioritising the community. Egoism and materialism have dismantled the idea of mutual cooperation. This danger had been identified in the past as well, and exposed from time to time by various scholars. For example, Wilhelm Ropke, in *A Humane Economy* (1960), emphasised the need for a strong insulation of moral values to cope with the adverse impact of *laissez faire*.

Finally, the incongruence between market-based ideals and those of morality and social duty pose a dilemma. The values defined in free-market narratives are at odds with the social responsibility defined by the government. The cause behind this incompatibility lies in people's impatience: morality and social responsibility demand a long-term investment in the free market mechanism, and people are unwilling to be patient for such a long time.

In the end, one cannot deny that citizens have lost trust in the government and in public administration. The introduction of a governance shaped by the values of the market, the assaults on the capability and credibility of administration, and the limits placed on morality and social responsibility in personal life have led to a deterioration of the 'moral retrieval capacity' of both the government and society.

Hence, any ethical renaissance or moral transformation will depend on the spirit motivating the private sector. Governance has become 'too private' and the private sector has become 'too egocentric' in matters of administration to regain citizens' trust. Michael Sandel, in *Justice: What's the Right Thing to Do?* (2009), suggested that if someone chooses ethical behaviour because it is beneficial for business, that person has probably either misconstrued what it means to be ethical, or does not intend to be ethical at all. Ethics, when directed towards the purpose of achieving a target, is no longer ethical. It is dangerous to use ethics as an instrument to gain profit, as such a trend will set a new tradition of cynicism. The invasion of market-driven values in our personal lives and the marketing of governance are contradictory mechanisms when it comes to developing trust in the government. Corporate ethical frameworks such as the United Nations Global Compact and the Caux Principles seek to provide an appropriate foundation, but are clearly not sufficient.

The ethical dilemma in private institutions is slightly different from that in the government. The major ethical concern here is more related to morality than to following the rules and regulations. Private institutions are an important part of development in the present era of liberalisation, privatisation and globalisation, and occupy a parallel space beside government institutions. As crucial commodity and service suppliers, it is necessary for them to abide by ethical guidelines in order to maximise the happiness of and minimise any inconvenience of the customers. While private institutions also confront ethical or moral dilemmas, such situations here are more deliberate and less dependent on deontology, and relate more to the consequentialism of moral philosophy. Private institutions are profit-driven and motivated to increase the number of customers, whose satisfaction is directly related to increased sales. These institutions are the sole owners of the commodities and services they provide. The government does attempt to regulate the unethical practices followed by these institutions: irrational price increases in order to increase their profits, deliberate interference in the mechanism of demand and supply through hoarding, and trade monopoly. The private sector also tries to influence government authorities and take undue advantages to enhance their profits. Crony capitalism is undermining fair business practices and misappropriation of the natural resources that belong to the society and the local population is proving harmful. To combat this, the government has put in place significant rules and regulations, such as the Essential Commodities Act, the Competition Commission of India, Companies Act, and regulators like the Securities and Exchange Board of India (SEBI), Reserve Bank of India (RBI), Insurance Regulatory and Development Authority of India (IRDAI), etc.

Here, we do not aim to determine deontology for private institutions; rather, our aim is to investigate situations which create ethical dilemmas for these institutions and their officers. We can explain them with the help of some examples.

Case Studies

Example 1: Let us suppose a talented student of a private school has lost his parents in an accident. Now he cannot continue his studies because he cannot pay the school fees. The Principal of his school wants to help him, but should he allow the student to continue the education gratis? On the one hand, he has to consider the financial concerns of his organisation and on the other hand, morality states that he offer sympathetic consideration to the case of this student.

Example 2: Suppose you are the owner of a pharmaceutical company and you come to know that your company can invent a drug that can alleviate the pain of a deadly disease spreading in a tribal community. However, the limited demand and low purchasing power of the community in question means that this enterprise is unlikely to be profitable. You can always choose to research a different drug aimed at a disease that is not as dangerous, but which will garner greater profits because of high demand. Most of the time, the second aspect involved in the dilemma pertains to profit, loss, or the question of your organisation's continued existence.

REFERENCES

Cooper, Terry L. (1998 [1982]). *The Responsible Administrator: An Approach to Ethics for the Administrative Role*. San Francisco, CA: Jossey-Bass, 4th edition.

Denhardt, Janet V., and Robert B. Denhardt. (2003). *The New Public Service: Serving, Not Steering*. Armonk, NY: M.E. Sharpe.

Goodnow, Frank Johnson. (1900). *Politics and Administration: A Study in Government*. New York: Macmillan.

Mantysalo, Venla. (2016). *Ethical Minimum or Ethical Maximum?* Vaasan Yliopisto, University of Vaasa, Helsinki. Available at https://www.uwasa.fi/materiaali/pdf/isbn_978-952-476-657-9.pdf (accessed February 2024).

Osborne, David, and Ted Gaebler. (1992). *Reinventing Government: How the Entrepreneurial Spirit is Transforming the Public Sector*. Reading, MA: Addison-Wesley.

Rohr, John A. (1989 [1978]). *Ethics for Bureaucrats: An Essay on Law and Values*. Public Administration and Public Policy, 2nd edition.

Sheeran, Patrick J. (2006 [1993]). *Ethics in Public Administration: A Philosophical Approach*. Jaipur: Rawat.

Wakefield, Susan. (1976). 'Ethics and the Public Service: A Case for Individual Responsibility'. *Public Administration Review* 36(6): 661–666.

White, Leonard D. (1926). *Introduction to the Study of Public Administration*. New York: The Macmillan Company.

QUESTIONS

1. There is a heavy ethical responsibility on the public servants because they occupy positions of power, handle huge amounts of public funds, and their decisions have a wide-ranging impact on society and environment. What steps have you taken to improve your ethical competence to handle such responsibility? (UPSC 2014)

2. Two different kinds of attitudes exhibited by public servants towards their work have been identified as the bureaucratic attitude and the democratic attitude.

(a) Distinguish between these two terms and write their merits and demerits.
(b) Is it possible to balance the two to create a better administration for the faster development of our country? (UPSC 2015)
3. Explain the process of resolving ethical dilemmas in Public Administration. (UPSC 2018)
4. What is meant by the term 'constitutional morality'? How does one uphold constitutional morality? (UPSC 2019)
5. Most of the time, perceived ethical dilemma in public administration is no dilemma. Critically evaluate with the help of examples.

12

SOURCE OF ETHICAL GUIDANCE

> **KEY CONCEPTS**
>
> Laws, Rules and Regulations as Sources of Ethical Guidance;
> Conscience as the Source of Ethical Guidance

LAWS, RULES AND REGULATIONS AS SOURCES OF ETHICAL GUIDANCE

When faced with ethical dilemmas, whether pertaining to a government or a private organisation, a person needs to have a clear understanding of the right course of action. This understanding depends in turn upon the wisdom and rational power of that person. Here, wisdom refers to cognitive power, that is, knowledge of the available rules and regulations defining the legitimacy of a course of action, and rationality pertains to the ability to choose the most appropriate course of action. In such an situation, s/he should consult with others and, after learning the correct rules and regulations, act accordingly. The question is: When should one obey deontology (the rules already in place) which appears to conflict with rational action? The response is: these rules and regulations were put in place after much contemplation over a long period of time. The cognitive ability of an individual cannot transcend the collective consideration of a community or a legislative body. An individual's knowledge is always incomplete and partial, and so it is better to follow the set rules and regulations. Adherence to such rules also means an escape from guilt, should the consequences turn out to be negative.

In ancient times, there was no significant distinction between law and morality. In Hinduism, the fundamental sources of law were religious texts such as the Vedas and the *Manusmriti*. Later, certain obligations were laid down in Mimamsa Philosophy. Similarly in the West, the Greeks developed the doctrine of the 'natural right', and in the name of 'natural law', the Romans laid the foundation of law. Christian theology was the linchpin in the idea of natural law. In post-Reformation Europe, after the yoke of the Church had been thrown off, law and morals were viewed as separate ideas, with law perceived as being inherited from the state, while morals emerged from the domain of religion or one's conscience. With the advent of natural law theories during the seventeenth and eighteenth centuries, law was again seen as connected with morals.

Further, in the nineteenth century, English legal theorist John Austin (1790–1859) promulgated that law is wholly separate from morals. According to him, law is 'A rule laid down for the guidance of an intelligent being by an intelligent being having power over him' and 'the command of the sovereign'. He believed that moral matters are not a subject of study for jurisprudence. Austin's idea of law was based on the coercive sovereign will of the state, which ushered in the process of legal reforms in cessation. Legal scholars of France and Germany then sought a legal philosophy that could overcome the stagnation of law as a subject. This resulted in the evolution of the ethical/moral or philosophical school of jurisprudence.

Ethics studies the difference between right and wrong. Law, on the other hand, is intended to maintain social order through the imposition of certain restrictions and to deliver justice. As such, law was not related to the old conventions and traditions of society; rather, it had taken the shape of an independent subject based on the principle of what 'ought to be'. Law and justice are interrelated, and the principal characteristic of ethical jurisprudence is the idea of justice related to philosophical or ethical scrutiny. Law is the means to achieve the ends of justice.

Hugo Grotius, Immanuel Kant, Johann Gottlieb Fichte, Georg Wilhelm Friedrich Hegel, Friedrich Wilhelm Joseph Schelling and Wolfgang Kohler were the important exponents of ethical jurisprudence. Grotius stated that natural law emerges from the social nature of man, and natural law and morality are both based on the idea of righteousness. The rules pertaining to human conduct emerge from correct reasoning, which leads to their acceptance in society. It is the approval of the community, rather than the approval of the state, which enables these rules to survive. Kant believed that morality and law are not similar because morality relates to the intrinsic propensity of people to act in a particular way, while law relates to those acts to which people can be coerced. In other words, morality deals with the inner life while law deals with external conduct. According to Kant, the concept of right is 'the sum of the conditions under which the choice of one can be united with the choice of another in accordance with a universal law of freedom'.

One of Kant's categorical imperatives suggests that moral laws are universal. One should 'act only in accordance with that maxim through which you can at the same time will that it become a universal law', that is, if you do an action, then everyone else should be able to do it as well. His famous proposition is 'duty for duty's sake' or, in other words, that duty is always obligatory. His definition of law states: 'Law is the aggregate of the conditions under which the arbitrary will of an individual may be combined with that of another under a general inclusive law of freedom.' His idea of law, which compels obedience from individuals in any given situation, gives it the shape of moral duty. Moral judgement or law are '*a priori*' statements; they are related to what ought to be.

Fichte's legal theory bases itself on the conscience of a reasonable man. He said that it is the moral duty of every individual to respect the liberty of others. According to him, the state should ensure the protection of only those rights that are necessary for personal existence, and that an individual becomes a member of a state through the fulfilment of civic duties. Legal philosopher Herbert Lionel Adolphus Hart (1907–92) described the system of law as a union of primary and secondary rules. His theory posits the view that laws are rules made by humans and that there is no inherent or necessary connection between law and morality. However, he also emphasised the various instances where morality and law coexist.

According to German jurist Ludwig Arndts von Arnesberg (1803–78), there are various ways in which law differs from morality.

1. Law considers an individual to be a person who acts according to free will, while morality encourages us to act in a manner that can lead to good.
2. In law, individuals are considered as part of the community they live in, while morality guides them to act in the right manner even when alone.
3. Law pertains to external conduct while morality pertains to internal determination and intentions.

4. Law regulates conduct through external coercion, while morality seeks a free self-determination towards the good.

According to H. J. Paton, morals or ethics is the study of the supreme good. Law tells us what is convenient in that space and time, while ethics focuses on the individual rather than the community. Law is concerned with the relationship of an individual with others in a society rather than with the personal excellence of their character and is not concerned with motives, while ethics considers motive all important. But merely saying that ethics deals only with the individual and his internal character while law deals with external conduct is providing too narrow a definition. Moreover, the ethical responsibility of an individual cannot be considered without also considering their obligation to others in the community.

John S. Mackenzie synthesises these viewpoints and explains how law acts as a source of ethical guidelines. According to him, ethics is related to the study of what is right or good in human conduct, and emphasises conformity to those laws, rules and regulations in accordance to which an individual ought to behave. As per the principle that states that all law establishes moral standards, morality becomes dependent on the law. A conduct is said to be right or wrong according to the judgment of law. External laws are divided into four parts: law of the community, the group or tribe; law of society; law of the state; and the law of God.

Some scholars consider morality a part of law despite the distinction between them. It is believed that the law in action is not a mere system of rules and regulations or of certain principles, such as the principle of good or the principle of equitability. Through the involvement of such principles in the legal process, moral content is attached to the law, but a lack of moral content can never be a ground to reject a law. According to British judge and legal philosopher Patrick Arthur Devlin (1905–92), public morality is the binding force of any community and the key function of law, particularly criminal law, must be to maintain this morality. Any human conduct that incites reprobation, intolerance and abomination must be suppressed by legal force in the interest of societal integrity. As he said, 'The suppression of vice is as much the business of law as the suppression of subversive activities.'

CONSCIENCE AS THE SOURCE OF ETHICAL GUIDANCE

The word 'conscience' is derived from the Latin word *conscientia*, which means 'knowledge within oneself. Its meaning refers to the moral knowledge that is shared with one's self by oneself only. Here, self signifies that the source of morality lies not outside the self; rather, it resides within. This internal source ranges from God (in the religious point of view, such as in Christianity), one's cultural realm and upbringing in a secular environment, and the 'super-ego' as propounded by psychologist Sigmund Freud's structural model of the psyche. From a psychological point of view, conscience involves a process of self-evaluation, introspection, and awareness of one's behaviour, three aspects that, while appearing to be the same, possess psychologically different meanings.

Introducing morality within oneself has several dimensions. For instance, moral knowledge can be shared with oneself to ensure that one's behaviour remains congruent with one's own morality, or it might refer to the introduction of a morality that is unacceptable to one's rational faculties. Here, even the meaning of 'self' has wider connotations: it may be taken as one's inner soul, or an external, even imaginary, spectator, or a transcendental entity such as God. Conscience might refer to a congruence between one's conduct and the adopted moral standards, and might be defined as the acknowledgement of the moral standard itself.

Generally, an appeal to one's conscience is made over an issue that suffers from a lack of moral clarity. Conscience supplies an awareness of deeply inculcated moral principles; we are motivated to act according to their dictates, and we weigh our actions with respect to these principles. As a moral idea, conscience originated in the works of Greek playwrights in the fifth century BC, after the downfall of the city-states. The absence of a political authority demanded that the self conduct itself under the guidance of its own conscience. We can say that despite the existence of external regulators in society, the notion of conscience was chosen to ensure self-discipline. During the Quit India Movement, for example, Gandhi had appealed to citizens to follow their own conscience in the fight for freedom from colonial rule. Formally, the word 'conscience' began to be used in seventeenth-century England during the crisis of religious authority, when philosophical and political discourses were appealing for the freedom of conscience as well as immunity from religious forces. The notion of a conscience does not pertain to a specific moral belief, but aims at the assessment of one's behaviour as per the voice of one's inner soul. It is not associated with any one psychological or moral belief but is a cluster of beliefs, and exposes its incongruence with personal thoughts. It is subjective because it does not revolve around specific principles.

The idea of conscience is ethically neutral because the appeal to conscience is not scrutinised through the lens of ethics. Instead, it is viewed through one's inner beliefs and personal morality. An action does not become morally good or bad, acceptable or unacceptable simply by passing the test of conscience. For example, the morality or immorality of euthanasia cannot be decided on the basis of the conscientious opposition or conscientious support of the people. We can declare that conscience is related to the subjective dimension of morality; however, there will always be ethical principles that can be considered objective. Conscience only refers to what an individual believes, independently of any external, objective ethics. Individual awareness of one's own conscience accompanies the awareness that other people may hold different beliefs, even on the same issue. For example, one's conscience might not allow them to accept a bribe, but s/he cannot tell others to not do so. Conscience is devised strictly for personal guidance.

Our conscience acts as a judge rather than a mute spectator. According to Adam Smith, conscience, or what he calls 'the supposed impartial spectator', is akin to a philosopher who judges one's conduct. It is not a neutral spectator, but generates the sentiments of approval or disapproval of oneself. In the Catholic view, conscience serves to witness God's law in our heart; as Pope John Paul II had said, 'Conscience passes a moral judgement of acquittal or condemnation about man and his conduct.' Similarly, Kant viewed conscience as an inner court, defining it as the practical reason that holds the duty of human beings for the acquittal or condemnation of their conduct in every case which comes under law. The self-awareness brought about by our conscience brings our conduct under moral scrutiny, to be judged by the standards of our practical reason. In its role as judge, the conscience never punishes, but encourages deep cogitation about the issue at hand. Since our everyday behaviour follows certain moral standards, any negative emotion signals the incorrectness of an action. The super-ego, in Sigmund Freud's definition, is the ethical component of the personality and provides the moral standards by which the ego operates.

> It is the part of our personality that attends prohibitions, inhibitions and moral constraints, and takes the form of conscience to execute its control over one's impulses and instincts by producing negative evaluative feelings towards an individual, such as aggressiveness towards the ego and guilt (Freud 1930).

Conscience also plays an epistemic role in terms of providing knowledge pertaining to divine laws, social customs and rituals. Such knowledge is neither empirical nor rational, but is a mediated knowledge. Knowledge is retrieved from within the individual without involving the conscience. Conscience can never generate new moral principles but only provides us access to moral knowledge. Akin to intuition, conscience does not involve any external or transcendental authority like God; rather, it encourages one to look inward into oneself. Joseph Ratzinger, or Pope Benedict XVI (1927–2022), believed that we carry a memory of what is good or true, and the conscience has the potential to recall this internal echo. The secular explanation of conscience emphasises one's own culture and upbringing instead of an external divine source, in contrast to a religious explanation. Conscience is the faculty that evokes social norms, and exerts their influence on moral psychology. This interpretation involves cultural dynamics over which we have limited control, and culture or educators can, at times, be highly immoral. In this sense, conscience is a relative notion, changing with social, cultural and familial situations.

Philosopher Jean-Jacques Rousseau (1712–78) believed that a good education could eradicate all corrupt influences. The objective of education is to inculcate a critical assessment of practices and, if necessary, substitute them with better practices that our conscience approves of. He further stated that conscience is the innate morality, the essence that remains after childish errors and biases are removed. It provides a foundation for ideas of justice and virtue inside our hearts, through which the behaviour of both ourselves and others can be critically assessed. According to Rousseau, while reason may mislead people, conscience never does. A true mentor, conscience serves the same function for the soul as instinct does for the body. A person who follows her/his conscience is in fact following the correct laws of nature. Obeying the call of nature, if we conform to the voice of our conscience, we will experience ecstasy. The epistemological study of conscience proclaims it as cognitive, emotive and intuitive moral knowledge, rather than purely rational. Scottish philosopher and historian David Hume (1711–76) said, 'Reason is entirely inactive, and it can never produce so active a thing like conscience.' To quote Paul Thagard and Tracy Finn, 'Conscience is a kind of moral intuition that is both cognitive and emotional.'

Conscience also upholds a sense of duty and encourages us to act according to our morality and moral beliefs. In other words, it emphasises internal motivations rather than any external authority.

The Kantian notion of conscience relates to a feeling of contentment or displeasure after either complying with or ignoring moral principles, which motivates a certain manner of behaviour. In other words, conscience is not only an inner court but also the source of a sense of duty. He further said that every human being, given that s/he is considered to be a moral entity, always carries a conscience within her/himself. Human beings possess four natural predispositions: moral feeling, love for neighbours, respect for oneself and conscience.

The exercise of self-assessment undertaken by our conscience often gives rise to positive and negative emotions, which in turn create mental traumas of different degrees, sometimes leading to self-punishment. Humans are geared to act morally so as to avoid the self-punishment produced by negative emotions such as remorse, guilt, shame, fear, etc. As our conscience is an important source of moral motivation, its freedom is a fundamental requirement for the creation of a moral environment. Powerful political or religious regimes often jeopardise this freedom of our conscience. Some fundamental notions support the defence of conscience, major ideas regarding which surfaced in the sixteenth and seventeenth centuries. We will discuss two major arguments in this regard.

The **first argument** relates to the defence of the freedom of conscience, from compelling others to either believe or not believe in something, or change their views. The state has the power to impose certain practices in order to maintain the social order, even when citizens claim that such laws breach the freedom of their conscience.

Conscience is a matter of private belief rather than action, and comes under reasonable restrictions in the interests of maintaining social order. The **second argument** relates to situations when someone is not sure about the correctness of the impulses of one's conscience, or when conscience runs contrary to moral principles. Given our own struggles with our conscience, we should never impose the dictates of our conscience on others, or compel anyone to follow a course of action that might prove to be morally wrong. This argument is related to the opinion of English philosopher John Stuart Mill (1806–73), who defended the freedom of conscience, stating that conscience should allow the free expression of any opinion, specifically contrary opinions. This notion is similar to the dialectical method propounded by Hegel. Here, two opposing ideas interact and subsequently give way to a clearer moral idea. Mill suggests that the freedom we have to contradict and disprove our own opinions is the very condition which justifies following the truth for the sake of action.

> **Hegel's Dialectic Method**
>
> Hegel's dialectic method focuses on ideas and thoughts. He proposed that the solution to problems concerning material things lay in reanalysing these things, thereby arriving at a synthesised new idea of the particular thing's essence.

The right to our freedom of conscience is supported by the United Nations' Universal Declaration of Human Rights. Article 18 states, 'everyone has the right to freedom of thought, conscience and religion'. This Article has wider connotations related to the freedom of action in conformity with one's conscience. Some examples related to this notion are: rejection of military service at the time of conscription, opposition to immoral medical practices such as sex-selective abortions, etc.

REFERENCES

Scheller Jr., Arthur. (1952–53). 'Law and Morality'. *Marquette Law Review* 36(12).

Fuller, Lon L. (1964). *The Morality of Law*. New Haven and London: Yale University Press.

Freud, S. (1930). 'Civilization and its Discontents'. In *The Standard Edition of the Complete Psychological Works of Sigmund Freud*. Vintage Classics.

Lloyd, Dennis. (1985). *Introduction to Jurisprudence*. Lloyd Lord of Hampstead and Freeman M. D. A., Stevens, 5th edition.

Mitchell, Basal. (1980 [1967]). *Law, Morality and Religion in a Secular Society*. Oxford Paperbacks, Vol. 18. New York: Oxford University Press.

QUESTIONS

1. What do you understand by the term 'voice of conscience'? How do you prepare yourself to heed the voice of conscience? (UPSC 2013)
2. What is meant by 'crisis of conscience'? Narrate one incident in your life when you were faced with such a crisis and how you resolved the same. (UPSC 2013)
3. How does 'crisis of conscience' manifest itself in the public domain? (UPSC 2019)
4. Law and ethics are considered the two tools for controlling human conduct so as to make it conducive to a civilised social existence.
    (a) Discuss how they achieve this objective.
    (b) Giving examples, show how the two differ in their approaches. (UPSC 2016)
5. How does law differ from morality? Explain with the help of some examples.
6. Conscience is a kind of moral intuition that is both cognitive and emotional. Explain.
7. Reason is entirely inactive, and it can never produce so active a thing as conscience. Explain.

13

ACCOUNTABILITY

> **KEY CONCEPTS**
> Accountability and Ethical Governance; Types of Accountability;
> Accountability and New Public Management

ACCOUNTABILITY AND ETHICAL GOVERNANCE

The advent of the concept of 'State' led to a contract between the State and its citizens. In exchange for a promise to look after their welfare, the State acquired control over its citizens. To prevent the abuse of power by different organs of the State, the concept of accountability came into existence. Both the State and society confined themselves within the limits decided by the Constitution, laws, rules and regulations. Various organisations of the State and society were allotted different statuses, and made answerable to different institutions in an attempt to create a system of checks and balances. Today, the scientific management system has become the linchpin in the introduction of private administration practices in public administration to establish the concept of accountability.

The term 'accountable' originates from the Latin *computare*, 'to count'. 'Accountability' refers to the acceptance of responsibility for honest and ethical conduct towards others. It works on the principal-agent relation—the principal oversees, directs and enforces the agents through formal or informal means. The concept of accountability comprises of answerability and enforcement. The principal can hold agents to account for their conduct, and keep a check on their performance. Moreover, the principal may even compel the agents to act according to formal rules of conduct. The key to good governance, accountability is a formal tool to ensure the effectiveness of the government machinery.

The term 'accountability' relates to the term 'responsibility'. Responsibility has wider connotations as it is used vis-à-vis judicial, political and economic relations. There is a rich literature in the field of 'theory of law', and especially in terms of penal laws with respect to responsibility. In the context of public administration, responsibility is used to mean capacity, accountability, virtue and liability. Here, capacity refers to the power of a civil servant to function as an authority, while responsibility relates to a set of rules, laws and regulations to be exercised as duty. Liability is about a civil servant accepting the consequence of their own actions, or the actions of others in their position, while functioning as an office-bearer. In terms of accountability, responsibility refers to the fact that a public servant has to be answerable to her/his immediate superior, as well as to external authorities who monitor her/his functioning.

We will now discuss accountability in terms of its three dimensions: vertical, horizontal and diagonal. **Vertical accountability** is fixed in a hierarchical manner, from the lower to the higher levels. Authorities at the higher level play a direct role in holding the lower-level functionaries to account for their performance in the chain of command. This can be seen in the top-down or principal-agent relationships. For instance, public officers are answerable to their superiors and ministers. The official mechanisms of the Annual Performance Appraisal Report (APAR), disciplinary action and compulsory retirement in public interest are some of the formal institutional tools that implement vertical accountability.

Parliament also plays a key role in fixing vertical accountability. Here, Parliament functions as the principal while public servants are agents, and the principal-agent relationship is determined through various parliamentary committees and the mechanism of parliamentary questions. Through vertical accountability, Parliament can oversee the implementation of laws, policies and programmes. In another sense, Parliament is also an agent of the citizens. On behalf of the electorate (the principal), legislators oversee the performance of public servants. The electorate holds legislators to account at the time of elections, and underperforming legislators are recalled and replaced. Yet another informal process exerts vertical accountability: when people form associations for lobbying both the government and private sectors through the use of processions, protests, burning of effigies and negative publicity.

Horizontal accountability relates to the checks-and-balances mechanism put in place between parallel authorities. The top-down principal-agent relationship is absent here, and a simple example is the relation between Parliament and the judiciary. The constitutional power of the judiciary to review the decisions and oversee the performance of the legislature fixes horizontal accountability, for example, the Comptroller and Auditor General (CAG), and vigilance and other auditing agencies. The continuous assessment of government officials is another example of horizontal accountability. In this dimension, while formal mechanisms are present to ensure answerability, its effectiveness is decided on moral grounds.

> Social accountability, which is becoming rapidly popular, is also referred to as society-driven horizontal accountability. Here, 'society' represents civil societies, community advocates and pressure groups, who are the key actors in this dimension.

The next dimension of accountability is **diagonal accountability**. Contradictory views abound with respect to the involvement of vertical accountability and horizontal accountability actors. Generally speaking, diagonal accountability determines an enhanced social accountability in government departments. Its major components are:

1. Participation of community advocates in horizontal accountability mechanisms.
2. Well-informed community advocates.
3. Effective mechanisms to ensure accountability.
4. Effective enforcement mechanisms.

Social audit committees, quasi-legal forums and civil committees appointed by the government are examples of the diagonal dimension of accountability. Therefore, we can say that diagonal accountability is a specific approach to achieve effective social responsibility. It can sometimes create obstacles in the path of administrative functionaries and retard the pace of development, and community advocates can at times have the upper hand over government officials and take up a large proportion of their official time. They may also demand undue advantages, an aspect that is fast becoming a cause for concern in public administration. The World Bank has also emphasised that social accountability can solely perform the function of diagonal accountability.

TYPES OF ACCOUNTABILITY

Accountability can be classified into the following types:
1. Political Accountability
2. Administrative Accountability
3. Professional Accountability
4. Democratic Accountability

Political Accountability

Political accountability has two dimensions: vertical and horizontal. The former relates to the relationship between the office bearer at the apex of the public administrative structure, who is both appointed and removed on the basis of political confidence. This includes the Prime Minister, the President, ministers, and top-level bureaucrats. In the horizontal dimension, legal and constitutional provisions govern the link between the government and Parliament. In the presidential form of political system, a horizontal relationship is missing; this form is solely driven by vertical accountability. On the other hand, the Parliamentary form of political system is driven by horizontal accountability. The mechanisms of censure, impeachment, no-confidence motion and removal of higher authorities are examples of horizontal accountability.

The main features of political accountability are:
1. Autonomy or discretion of the agents involved.
2. Evaluation is done mainly with the overall results in mind, generated by the organisation they head and for their conduct.
3. Different methods are used according to the legal and constitutional systems of different countries.
4. Superior officers at the top of the hierarchy are the agents of control (in legal and political terms) in the vertical dimension.
5. Parliament is the agent of control in the horizontal dimension, and citizens—the electorate—have the final control over evaluation.

Administrative Accountability

Like political accountability, administrative accountability too has two dimensions: vertical and horizontal. The former relates to the link between superiors and subordinates in government offices. On the other hand, the horizontal dimension links an individual office bearer of a public office to the citizens, and to other external agencies of monitoring and control such as the CAG, Lokpal, Lokayukta, etc. It is better defined and has greater homogeneity than political accountability. Administrative accountability revolves around legality and obligations, and has greater objectivity. In the vertical dimension, duties and obligations are regulated by a well-defined deontology aimed at strict compliance with administrative duties, which determines efficient governance.

Public servants are answerable to their superiors for their conduct and the quality of their performance. The superior (the disciplinary authority) is invested with powers to penalise subordinates for their wrongdoings. (In the Indian Civil Services classification, Control and Appeal Rules provide for a vast array of disciplinary action to control the functioning of public servants with the help of the appropriate authority.) The provision of the Annual Performance Appraisal Report effectively strengthens the vertical administrative accountability.

The main features of the classical concept of administrative accountability are:
1. The complete subjection of public officials and administrative units to a wide set of laws, rules and regulations.
2. Based on a strict hierarchical relationship.
3. The establishment of various external agencies aimed at keeping a check on the conduct of office bearers through the use of horizontal accountability.

Professional Accountability

The credit for developing the notion of professional accountability goes to Barbara Romzek and Melvin Dubnick. This relates to the development of public administration as a mature profession. As this field is considered an attractive profession for highly educated and talented people, the enlargement of public administration and adoption of technical specifications in the field of governance involves demanding a level of professional accountability which in turn depends on regulating the behaviour and conduct of career bureaucrats. Professionalism in the public services involves implementing ethical practices while exercising discretion in the utilisation of public resources. This type of accountability determines the personal criteria and the limit to which technical knowledge can be utilised in the field of public administration, under legal purview.

A certain professionalism can be introduced by individual public servants by creating their own criteria based on general guiding principles, which are therefore not fixed, but dynamic in nature. For instance, the former Chief Election Commissioner T. N. Seshan completely reformed the functioning of the Election Commission of India (ECI). He made it clear that the office of the ECI is not a part of the Government of India; instead, it is an independent body which functions under the Indian Constitution. He set aside the convention of writing 'Government of India' along with 'ECI', and introduced a certain professionalism and a fair and clean election process to strengthen democracy in India. He strictly implemented a moral code of conduct during elections, which was an ideal document of merely academic interest and not enforced in letter or spirit before his era.

Democratic Accountability

Democratic accountability pertains to the accountability of public servants to citizens in a society. Administrative actions demand social acceptance, and its legitimacy depends on the democratic will of the society. Public administration ought to involve citizens in the process of governance as it works in the latter's interest. To an extent, democratic accountability entails civic participation in decision-making and policy formation. This involves diagonal accountability: for example, whenever the government intends to implement any major scheme, it seeks public opinion, as well as ideas and suggestions. Democratic accountability also involves the social and diagonal dimensions of accountability.

Democratic accountability establishes a check on the absolute autonomy of public office bearers. It supports a relative autonomy instead, in terms of soliciting public support and the cooperation of social groups (although their opinions are not binding). It enhances the performance of public administration and establishes good governance in the country.

ACCOUNTABILITY AND NEW PUBLIC MANAGEMENT

The recent administrative theory (mentioned earlier) known as 'reinventing government' or 'new public management' (NPM) was largely adopted across the world, albeit with different levels of intensity. While it was adopted in India as well, it was unable to take proper shape on the ground. The NPM has the following characteristics:

1. A change in focus from compliance to established rules and procedures to the outcomes of administrative affairs.
2. Reduction in the number of unnecessary rules and procedures, thereby making administrative work simple, swift and citizen-friendly.
3. Decentralisation of power and responsibilities.
4. Public servants are equipped with sufficient autonomy to pursue the goals and targets of government programmes, formulate internal guidelines to achieve these goals, and have a certain measure of accountability vis-à-vis their achievements.

5. Trimming administrative units and making them economical in the interest of financial prudence, which results in a decrease in expenditure.
6. Introducing private-sector management practices, privatisation of public-sector undertakings (PSUs), and competing with the private sector in service delivery without interfering with free-market mechanisms.
7. Seeking greater public participation in government programmes geared towards social development, so that society could be the decision-maker while the government monitors and facilitates.

Table 13.1: Characteristics of different forms of accountability

	POLITICAL	ADMINISTRATIVE	PROFESSIONAL	DEMOCRATIC
BASIS	Working as per the political and schematic provisions provided by the government	Working as per legal rules and regulations	Working as per the technical rules and practices of the profession	Working as per the aspirations of the public at large
INTERNALLY ACCOUNTABLE TO	Superior political authority	Higher political executive, e.g., Minister, Mayor, Chairperson Administrative superior	Technical and administrative heads of the organisation,	
EXTERNALLY ACCOUNTABLE TO	Parliament	External supervisory authority, e.g., Vigilance, Audit Citizens Court of justice	External supervisory authority	Community advocates Social groups
OUTPUT	Political scrutiny Resignation/dismissal	Revision of past administrative action Compensation for citizens Sanction or recognition of the official involved	Sanction or recognition of the official involved	Taking an administrative decision Revision of administrative decisions Democratic approval of administrative decisions

The NPM introduces fewer regulations in the administrative framework in terms of the rules and procedures that control the actions of public servants. The increased autonomy empowers them to achieve better results. This relaxation from stringent norms is accompanied by a code of conduct and ethics that are not coercive; rather, they help to overcome various problems related to the officials' conduct.

Accountability has to be fixed in such a manner that problems arising due to the involvement of the private sector can be addressed and a swift resolution found. The solution lies in clear-cut legal and political guidelines for the ministries and departments, issued from time to time by the government. This is not intended to replace the classical mechanism of control, but rather to revamp it as per the new code of management.

The model of accountability in the market-based NPM is not supposed to blur either the objectives enshrined in the Constitution or the principles of objectivity, neutrality, fairness and other values of public service. Vertical accountability is to be reduced and the diagonal and horizontal dimensions of accountability are to be strengthened on a large scale. It needs to be remembered that the practices of private-sector management cannot always be applied without modification in the government, as an unthinking adoption of private-sector practices can jeopardise the public framework of the government.

REFERENCES

Cendon, Antonio Bar. (2000). 'Accountability and Public Administration: Concepts, Dimensions, Developments'. In *Openness and Transparency in Governance: Challenges and Opportunities*, ed. M. Kelle, 22–61. Network of Institutes and Schools of Public Administration in Central and Eastern Europe.

Brereton, M., and M. Temple. (1999). 'The New Public Service Ethos: An Ethical Environment for Governance'. *Public Administration* 77(3): 455–74.

Bovens, Mark. (1998). *The Quest for Responsibility: Accountability and Citizenship in Complex Organisation*. Cambridge, UK: Cambridge University Press.

Jabbra, Joseph G., and O. P. Dwivedi. (1988). *Public Service Accountability: A Competitive Perspective*. West Hartford: Kumarian Press.

QUESTIONS

1. What does 'accountability' mean in the context of public service? What measures can be adopted to ensure individual and collective accountability of public servants? (UPSC 2014)
2. How are accountability mechanisms fixed in the new public management? Explain by giving the example of a government organisation.
3. Explain the different types of accountability, including all its dimensions.
4. Explain the role of accountability in New Public Administration.
5. What are the different components of diagonal accountability? Explain.
6. How far is accountability useful in determining ethical governance?

14

STRENGTHENING OF ETHICAL AND MORAL VALUES IN GOVERNANCE

> **KEY CONCEPTS**
>
> Introduction; Ethics Training for Public Servants; Steps taken by India in Ethics Training

INTRODUCTION

After a lot of discussion over the ethical actions prescribed for humans, we have learnt that values are the key determinants that will help us avoid corrupt action and establish justice in society. A training in ethics for our public servants becomes inevitable in order to strengthen moral values and inculcate a sense of duty in them. We will now throw light on the efforts of different national and international organisations to design ethical standards as well as the mode of training imparted to all public servants at different levels in the hierarchy.

The term 'public servant' comprises the entire government machinery, including legislatures as well as the judiciary, which benefits from the public exchequer. India has a very poor track record when it comes to training in ethics or moral philosophy for its public servants. It is only recently that the Union Public Service Commission (UPSC) and a few State Public Service Commissions (SPSCs) have included ethics as one of the papers in the Civil Services entrance examination. What is worrying is that a large percentage of public servants, including older civil servants, are unfamiliar with the details of ethics. We will discuss possible ways to impart ethical values to public servants, keeping in mind the different practices in the field of training in ethics in different countries of the world. Countries beset by overwhelming corruption usually confront a number of challenges that result in the introduction of strong and holistic reforms. They also struggle to find the resources necessary for imparting ethics training. The citizens of such countries, on the other hand, exasperated with the constant corruption, insist on reforms, in the form of criminal trials, arrests, disciplinary action, removal from service, etc., of the corrupt public servants. Since ethics training and restoration is time-consuming and does not yield results in a short period of time, these countries need to rely on anti-corruption and preventive measures. Unfortunately, ethics training is not a priority for these countries, and the allocation of funds for such training in a corrupt environment is also considered risky.

The crucial reason for the sluggish development in this regard is the lack of political will. While political leaders of various countries show their commitment to building an ethical environment by their support for ethics and anti-corruption training, they themselves do not attend such training programmes. Exhorting public officials to be honest and yet not demonstrating such commitment themselves sends out a wrong message, and discourages public servants from following an ideal course of conduct. The absence of leadership at the summit level along with an environment of corruption culturally ingrained as part of the 'normal' business of life are the prime causes behind the lack of seriousness where ethics training is considered.

Nevertheless, the importance of integrity training in order to put in place lasting measures to combat corruption is increasingly being recognised. Many international organisations like the Organization for Economic Cooperation and Development (OECD), Asian Development Bank (ADB) and the United Nations (UN) recommend that countries boost their efforts to educate their public officials in ethics. International funding agencies like the International Monetary Fund (IMF), World Bank and ADB also emphasise such training in recipient countries. A lot of support is required from both political bodies and society to impart such training programmes. For instance, the European Union (EU) played an important role in encouraging ethics training in EU member countries.

'Ethics Training for Public Officials', a study prepared by the OECD Anti-Corruption Network for Eastern Europe and Central Asia (ACN) and SIGMA, in cooperation with the OECD Public Sector Integrity Network states that more efforts are needed to increase political and social support for ethics training programmes. 'Many experts agree that new and advanced approaches to ethics training should be promoted, and that the quality of such training should be improved, especially in countries with serious problems of integrity in the public administration, including many SIGMA and ACN countries.'

SIGMA, or Support for Improvement in Governance and Management, is a joint initiative of the EU and the OECD, and is mainly financed by the EU. SIGMA carefully monitors the governance systems and important government institutions, as well as a country's legal structures and action plans related to reforms in public administration. It prescribes tools and scientific methodologies based on psychological research to improve the quality of the legal and administrative reforms being carried out by various countries.

The OECD network for public-sector integrity works for government reforms, focusing on measures to safeguard integrity and prevent malpractices such as corruption and bribery in public offices. It monitors the trends and methodologies followed by corrupt practices, develops mechanisms to safeguard against and prevent corruption, prepares statistics and disseminates them globally. It provides valuable feedback and suggestions for the OECD to enable the framing of a robust strategy to fight corruption. It helps to address issues related to the redefining of core values such as integrity, transparency and accountability, and re-establishes trust in the government. It also reviews sensitive issues related to the private-public interface such as procurement, lobbying and conflicts of interest. Ethics training for public officials is important to inculcate integrity in its true sense. The OECD council recommended that member countries strive to bring about changes in the functioning of government organisations by promoting ethical conduct in public service. Following OECD recommendations, all member countries showed their commitment to improving ethical conduct by adopting these in their systems of governance.

The OECD recommendations were as follows:

1. The development and occasional review of official practices, policies, programmes, procedures and organisations related to the ethical conduct of public servants.

2. Putting in place high standards of conduct in government functioning as well as anti-corruption mechanisms.
3. Including an ethical perspective in management frameworks so as to imbue public service with the correct values.
4. Incorporating integrity in the compliance-based approach to developing a model of ethics management.
5. Analysing the impact of public administration reforms on the ethical conduct of public servants.
6. Using a fusion approach in public service to ensure high standards of ethical conduct.

The recommendations also included 12 principles for managing ethics in public administration:

1. Ethical standards for public service should be unambiguous.
2. The legal framework should also incorporate these ethical standards.
3. Public servants should be well-versed in ethical guidelines.
4. Public servants should be well-versed in their rights and related obligations to expose malpractices in public office.
5. Political will to create an ethical work culture should complement the ethical conduct of public servants.
6. The decision-making process should be transparent and subject to public scrutiny.
7. There should be clear-cut guidelines related to the interaction between the public and private sectors so as to avoid any conflict of interest.
8. Public servants should exhibit and popularise ethical conduct in public service.
9. All policies, procedures and administrative practices should incorporate ethical practices.
10. Public-service conditions and human resource management should follow stringent ethical norms.
11. There should be a robust accountability framework in public service.
12. Provision for disciplinary actions with clear-cut procedures to tackle instances of corruption.

ETHICS TRAINING FOR PUBLIC SERVANTS

Ethics training for public officials is important to inculcate a notion of integrity in its truest sense. The UN Convention Against Corruption (UNCAC) has asked countries to promote training programmes and educational workshops for capacity building with respect to the proper and dignified functioning of public offices. These workshops focus on specialised training to enhance an awareness of the risks and consequences of corruption.

Training in ethics and integrity with a focus on anti-corruption is a part of the curriculum of government officers in many countries. Designing and delivering effective training on ethics is a mammoth and complex task, especially when it targets thousands of public servants. It also involves a significant risk of failure because classroom training alone is incapable of dealing with all the programme objectives.

The idea of a study on ethics training for public servants was presented by the OECD Anti-Corruption Network, and the project was developed by the OECD–EU SIGMA programme, together with ACN and in cooperation with the OECD Public Integrity Network. The project involves the following steps:

1. Data collection about the existing ethics training programmes in the participating countries.
2. Assessing the policies and prescribing required amendments.
3. Designing case studies to explain and teach the necessary tools.
4. Preparing a checklist of items required for effective training.

The effective implementation of ethics training depends on several factors, which are political, social as well as economical.

- Ethics training ought to be integrated with all anti-corruption and pro-integrity policies and programmes.
- It will produce observable results only in the long term.
- Ethics training should not exclude political support, as this support provides it with a strong leadership. Lack of such leadership from above undermines the motivation of public servants.
- The ethical training of political executives is also required for holistic reforms.

Ethics training must be integrated with the comprehensive public policy on anti-corruption, and should conspicuously reflect in the programme documents of all major schemes of the government. It should have a legal basis in public administration, and one particular agency should be set up to take care of the overall framework, and centralise the planning, coordination, module development and evaluation of outcomes. The most important thing in ethics training is to choose the targeted trainees carefully, because of the budgetary constraints. Initially, master trainers should be raised from among the employees based on their interests, previous service record, public image and communication skills. These master trainers should be treated as human capital, who can start a chain reaction in ethics training.

The targeting of specific groups should be prioritised, as it then becomes easier to chalk out the practical requirements of different and specific groups based on their needs and the nature of their work. These groups can be categorised according to their work profiles and areas of risk. It is also advisable to develop ethics training modules for elected public representatives. Finally, ethics officers in ministries, departments and at the district level should be appointed after proper training, and they should then be given the role of master trainers so that ethics training can reach the grassroots-level public officers.

An assessment of ethics risk in working areas and designing a training programme to cater to the needs of specific organisations will help to make ethics training practical, rather than remaining a merely formal exercise. A specialised survey related to ethics could be a useful tool for such an assessment. Training programmes should not be lengthy, and the time allotted for the training should be utilised optimally. The programmes can include a combination of philosophical theory and case studies, tailor-made to suit the needs of a particular organisation. The use of evaluation methods to assess both the knowledge received by the participants and identify areas in the training programme that require further improvement is also recommended.

Training in ethics should incorporate legislations and ethical codes put in place for public servants. Often, government functionaries remain ignorant of such codes, and sometimes overlook these vital regulations. It is important that they understand the philosophy behind the necessity of such anti-corruption reforms. It is also imperative to provide practical guidance on ethical behaviour in situations where rules and regulations contradict traditions, or where they are unable to provide a clear resolution to problems. There are various grey areas where appropriate guidelines are not readily available, and the training on ethics should address these risk situations.

Many countries have evolved strategies, programmes and policy documents incorporating ethics training as an essential component. Recognising the problem that threats to integrity and values can pose in public administration, ethics training is often required in the context of anti-corruption and integrity strategies. The inclusion of ethics training in strategy documents in order to abolish corruption and establish good governance is a positive indicator in the field of public administration. This strategy will be successful when all activities related to this programme should have a strict timeline, legal boundaries and adequate budgetary provisions. Ethics training can be more effective if provisioned as a legal requirement, for at least those categories of office-bearers who pose a high integrity risk. In many countries, public officials have a legal right to avail ethics training and attend such training programmes at regular intervals. This right is established by public service legislation itself. For instance, in the USA, executives are required to enrol in ethics training, and in Turkey, ethics training is mandatory for all public officials.

In addition to legal provisions on ethics training, some countries appoint 'Ethics Commissioners' to carry out business pertaining to ethics in each department. In India, the vigilance wings of individual departments can be given this responsibility. In this context, provisions to ensure that such training is imparted to political leaders can also prove effective. In Australia, a special training on integrity is imparted to the political advisors of ministers. In many other countries, local administrations have their own training programmes. Internal human resource departments can play an important role in the delivery of such training programmes, especially in departments that have no specialised training institutions.

Ethics training is a mammoth task and demands adequate financial provisions. This is why an assessment of need in specific areas is important to achieve the optimum results. A need assessment can prioritise the training areas and improve the cost-effectiveness of the programme. Many countries conduct surveys and studies to analyse the level of integrity of public servants, the trust that citizens place in public offices, the prevalence of corruption, etc., to assess the necessity of training. These surveys are carried out by the government as well as by non-governmental organisations (NGOs), and different agencies have the responsibility for different types of surveys. However, while these surveys can identify the general issues, they are not sufficient to assess specific ethics training needs. Rather, surveys that focus on different aspects of ethics in public administration on a regular basis can carry out a more accurate profile of the needs of ethics training; examples can be surveys focusing on 'values in civil service', 'competence of civil service', 'trust deficit in citizen-public office relation', 'crony capitalism', etc.

The training programme should involve a number of case studies to enable competency in dealing with situations related to ethical dilemmas. A value-based approach cannot work everywhere and every time, as ethical dilemmas are often defined by contextual nuances, even in similar situations. The objective of training should be to equip officials to recognise an issue, analyse it systematically, and figure out the best way to overcome such instances, rather than looking for an objectively correct solution. There is no one correct answer to complex situations, even though the guiding values and principles offer helpful indications. In the long run, practising the values on a daily basis and encouraging others to do so is the most effective way to nurture an ethical work culture. Integrity management and ethics training both demand constant effort and a sense of ownership.

The institutionalisation of ethics commissions is the need of the hour. Decentralising activities pertaining to ethics training would be a strategic step towards integrity management in government functioning.

STEPS TAKEN BY INDIA IN ETHICS TRAINING

Ethics training in India, particularly in the government, was planned on the basis of the recommendations of the Second Administrative Reforms Commission (Department of Administrative Reforms and Public Grievances, Government of India [DARPG-GOI]) on 'Ethics in Governance' for Group A and Group B officers. The DARPG is the nodal agency of the Government of India for administrative reforms pertaining to both Central and state governments. This department strives to ensure good governance with the help of knowledge sharing related to administrative excellence and international best practices. According to the fourth report of the Second Administrative Reforms Commission, 'Ethics in Governance', good governance can be brought on surface with the help of strong ethical values enshrined in our constitution as well as preached in the religious texts.

On the recommendations of a directive issued by the GOI, Administrative Training Institute (ATI) Mysore constituted a sub-committee to train master trainers. The objective of this training is to enable participants to inculcate the spirit of the Second Administrative Reforms Commission, that is, to bring about good governance based on a strong foundation of ethics. This training will enable participants to recognise ethical components of their everyday dealings with the public and of governance; understand the principles behind ethical values in public service and the role of public servants. It equips government officials with the tools and methods necessary to adopt transparency in public service in the fight against corruption.

The methodology used in this programme comprises visual, auditory and kinaesthetic components. The IC Centre for Governance is a nodal agency in the planning and execution of the sessions at the Initiative for Change (IC), Asia Plateau, Panchgani. Retired bureaucrats and private experts are the principal partners of this programme, financial assistance for which is provided by the United Nations Development Programme. Trainers are grouped into teams, which then provide training at the state-level Administrative Training Centres. The need of the hour is to ensure that such training is disseminated to all, both vertically and horizontally. Some of the trainers have been designing similar modules for children, the general public and private-sector employees.

REFERENCES

Administrative Training Institute, Mysore. (2013). *Training Module on Ethics in Governance*. Available at http://darpg.gov.in/sites/default/files/Ethics_in_Governance_2nd_ARC.pdf (accessed June 2024).

Organisation for Economic Co-operation and Development (OECD). (2013). *Ethics Training for Public Officials. A Study Prepared by the OECD Anti-Corruption Network for Eastern Europe and Central Asia (ACN), and SIGMA, a joint EU-OECD initiative, principally financed by the EU, in co-operation with the OECD Public Sector Integrity Network*. Available at http://www.oecd.org/corruption/acn/resources/EthicsTrainingforPublicOfficialsBrochureEN.pdf (accessed June 2024).

QUESTIONS

1. How can ethical and moral values be strengthened in public administration?
2. Give a brief account of the initiatives taken by Government of India in imparting moral values in administrators.
3. Morality in administration can be brought about by teaching it, rather than through the use of punishments. Explain.
4. Suggest some measures for strengthening moral values in governance.
5. Ethics training is emphasised in Indian public administration. Do you agree? Give reasons to support your view.

15

ETHICAL DILEMMA

> **KEY CONCEPTS**
> Introduction; Trolley Problem; How to Handle Ethical Dilemma

INTRODUCTION

According to Belgian-American novelist Mary Sarton (1912–95), 'The moral dilemma is to make peace with the unacceptable.' Often, a person confronts a situation where two or more courses of action are possible, and surprisingly, all the possible options appear to be correct. There is no dilemma when the most correct answer is available for a situation, and other answers are far removed from the criteria of assessment. This cannot be termed an ethical dilemma, as ethical dilemmas occur in symmetrical situations and refer to a situation where one has to choose a course of action out of two or more available moral imperatives, either of which seems acceptable. The problem arises when one course of action is given priority, which inevitably defeats the moral imperatives of other available courses of action.

An ethical dilemma also arises when two or more available courses of action are equally immoral, unacceptable or undesirable. In such cases, one has to choose the most ethical solution; however, there may also arise a situation where one has to choose the least unethical option.

One must remember that there is no single correct answer to any ethical problem; the endeavour should be to figure out the answer with the greatest potential to produce an optimal outcome. Some ethical issues being currently debated are that of abortion, graded absolutism, the Samaritan's dilemma, euthanasia, and the right to suicide, and the dilemmas these issues cause revolve around conflicts between ethical principles. This is also termed as a conflict between deontology and teleology, or, in simple words, between 'right' and 'good', respectively.

When we study the history of ethical dilemmas, the first example we find is cited in the Bible; similarly, the *Mahabharata* and *Ramayana* also provide various examples of moral dilemmas. For instance, Abraham was confronted with a classic ethical dilemma when he was commanded by God to sacrifice his son Isaac: the dilemma was between sacrificing his son and disobeying God. Other examples relate to the decisions taken by Ram in the *Ramayana* to abandon his throne on the orders of his father, King Dasrath, and later to renounce his wife Sita after public censure. In the *Mahabharata*, the great warrior Arjun was confronted with an ethical dilemma during the Kurukshetra war, as explained in the *Bhagavad Gita*. These examples highlight the conflict between teleology and deontology.

In the Western philosophical world, the Greek philosopher Socrates demonstrated an ethical dilemma through the principle of repaying one's debts. He argued that if one borrows a weapon from a friend who might misuse it unmindfully and violently, it will be wrong to return the borrowed weapon. The second popular example of an ethical dilemma is related to French philosopher Jean Paul Sartre's (1905–80) existentialism.[1] Citing the example of a young man who lived with his mother and whose brother had been killed while protecting his country in a war, he asks: Should the young man go to war to stop the invasion of his country, or should he remain at home to care for his mother? Since World War II, we have been facing several ethical dilemmas concerning the waging of war, euthanasia, the Hippocratic oath, etc., which we have discussed in detail in earlier chapters.

> **Existentialism** is a form of philosophical inquiry that studies human existence. It is the philosophical belief that we are each responsible for creating purpose or meaning in our own lives. Existentialist philosophers explore questions related to the meaning, purpose and value of human existence.

An individual faces a moral dilemma when s/he confronts two or more available choices for action; however, all the available options are contradictory yet moral in all respects, and s/he can choose only one path. Issues of applied ethics such as the legality of euthanasia, the issue of capital punishment, and priority allocation pose moral dilemmas; in India, for example, under Section 302 of the Indian Penal Code (IPC), whoever commits murder shall be punished with death or imprisonment for life, and shall also be liable to be fined—here, the degree of punishment that ought to be awarded poses a dilemma.

Kant provides a logical argument against the occurrence of ethical dilemmas. He emphasises that duties are categorical imperatives and thus unquestionable, because the rules undergirding them are compulsory leave no room for digression. However, Kant is not completely correct as his logic would fail when confronting the example cited earlier of Section 302 of the IPC. He further recognised the conflicting 'grounds of obligation' and stated that intensive reasoning and application of mind will expose the insufficiency of most grounds, and the final ground will emerge as the most effective. In Kant's explanation, ethical dilemma do not contain conflicting obligations; rather, there are conflicting grounds of one obligation. An effort should be made to dispel such confusion. Actions which do not fall under the category of 'morally necessary' or 'morally impossible' are morally permissible, because they are morally neutral. In this way, all actions can fall under one of three categories: the necessary, the impossible and the permissible. Duty comes under two groups: perfect duties and imperfect duties. The former duties are not contradictory as all related actions are necessary here. On the other hand, imperfect duties do not consider any action necessary, which increases the scope of conflicts and subjectivity in decision-making.

An utilitarian approach rejects the possibilities of an ethical dilemma (see Chapter 2 for more details on utilitarianism). As utilitarians consider utility the final source of moral obligation, this utility is what filters out incompatible courses of action. While other systems have no standard by which to weigh conflicting actions, utility performs this role in the utilitarian approach. In utilitarianism, the maximisation of utility—in terms of pleasure, happiness, satisfaction, etc.—is the sole criterion determining what is right. When resolving dilemmas, utilitarianism has two options: succumb to unreasonable reduction in the final outcome, resulting from an establishment of homogeneity of utility (an average distribution of utility) or accept the heterogeneity of utility where it may sacrifice the advantage in resolving conflict by choosing between the different available means to achieve the desired end.

R. M. Hare emphasises intuitionism to resolve moral dilemmas (see Chapter 2 for more details on intuitionism). He divides moral conflicts into two levels: an intuitive level and a critical level. At the intuitive level, dilemmas are irresolvable, but at the critical level, they need to be resolved. At the critical level, particular actions are considered right or wrong on the basis of utility, after which they are incorporated to form an 'epistemological prior' (a general rule independent of experience). A readymade set of rules is used as a *prima facie* principle to inculcate moral understanding and generate guidelines for general, everyday situations. These principles form the basis of our intuitive judgements, and in turn help us to come to an unambiguously 'right' decision.

Philosopher Francis Herbert Bradley supports Hegel's charge against Kant's theory of 'duty for duty sake'. This theory is a formal instrument that fails to address conflict in duties, which is a very common occurrence in daily life. The theory emphasises the sanctity and unbreachable status of law; however, instances abound in real life where breaking these laws becomes inevitable. For instance, Kant's claim that a lie can never be considered the right conduct fails to address situations that prioritise duty over the truth. Bradley highlights Hegel's belief that self-realisation serves as the final good for human beings, and says that moral conflicts are inevitable in the course of self-realisation. These can take place under three situations:

1. 'My station (anchoring position) and related duties.'
2. 'Beyond what the world expects.'
3. 'The morality of one time is not the same as that of another time.'

An individual is a member of a community, and hence the realisation of oneself is also a realisation of community interests in the form of social duties. Although it is true that 'the morality of one time is not the same as that of another time', there are limitations to adhering to 'my station and its duty' if it corrupts the community.

The modern intuitionist view of W. D. Ross, which states that we can know moral truths through intuition, resolves ethical conflicts by differentiating between two types of duty. The first is *prima facie* (at first sight) duty and the second is duty *san phrase* (without exceptions). Only *prima facie* duties are conflicting in nature, as they are neither actual duties nor the illusion of one; rather, this duty is just an objective fact about an act, particularly attitudes and virtues like fidelity, reparation, gratitude, justice, beneficence, self-improvement and non-maleficence. An act is a *prima facie* duty (a 'parti-resultant attribute') when it has at least one right-making feature. On the other hand, actual duty is a 'toti-resultant attribute', that is, it is related to an act due to its complete nature. There are three categories of arguments related to genuine ethical dilemmas:

1. Arguments pertaining to moral sentiments.
2. Arguments pertaining to the plurality of values.
3. Arguments pertaining to single-value conflicts.

Arguments pertaining to moral sentiments are based on an exposition of emotions like regret, remorse or guilt, which arise as a consequence of the resolution of a moral dilemma. Moral dilemmas resemble conflicts of desire rather than conflicts of factual belief. When confronting conflicting desires, those that are rejected surface in our memory as regrets, and are termed irrational and immoral by English philosopher Bernard Williams (1929–2003). Regret is the aftermath even when both available courses of action are seen to produce undesirable results. According to Ruth Barcan Marcus, if a genuine moral dilemma can be said to exist, the statement of guilt will be a befitting response to its resolution. He further stated that the function of guilt is to motivate individuals to avoid such dilemmas in the future.

In the context of the plurality of values, there is a plurality of genuine moral values as well, which is an essential factor. Philosopher E. J. Lemmon emphasises plurality thus: 'There may be several means to reach the point of what ought to do, and what ought not to do. Another statement is derived from the previous status, commitment, and personal ethics of an individual.' American philosopher Thomas Nagel claims, while developing a pluralist argument, that there are contradictory and irreconcilable values based on obligations in relationships, aims, instrumentality, rights, the desire for flawlessness and personal commitments. These five values fall under two groups—agent-centred (personal) values and outcome-centred (impersonal) values.

The last argument vis-à-vis the emergence of moral dilemmas pertains to the notion that under some situations, a single moral value comes into conflict with itself. Marcus developed this argument and explained it with the help of an example: an individual can make two promises and then realise that both cannot be kept at the same time. He explains this further by taking the example of saving innocent lives. There might be an instance where only one life can be saved, and in such a case, a single moral value will confront conflicting actions. The trolley problem can be viewed as a hypothetical problem belonging to this category.

TROLLEY PROBLEM

The trolley problem is an experiment related to ethical dilemma that creates a hypothetical situation. A typical conundrum, it represents a clash between utilitarianism and deontology. The trolley problem has evolved during different phases and poses a myriad hypothetical scenarios pertaining to an ethical dilemma. It tries to bring into focus the probable ethical courses of action that people should follow in different situations. The original riddle was framed by contemporary British philosopher Philippa Foot in 1967. A trolley is running over a railway track. This main track bifurcates after a distance. You are standing near the lever that can switch either of the two paths towards the direction of the trolley. You notice that in one of the approaching tracks, five people are tied up, unable to move. On the other track is one single person. You are left with two options:

1. Do not interfere at all and let five persons be killed on the approaching track.
2. Pull the lever and divert the trolley to the other track, where one person will be run over.

What will be the more appropriate ethical action in this situation? This original problem was further elaborated by J. J. Thomson (1967), Michael J. Costa (1987) and Peter Unger (1992). These variations pose different ethical problems and compel us to seek ethical solutions in such real-life situations.

The next variation of the trolley problem was presented by Thomson in 1967. The trolley is moving on the track, but an obstruction caused by a heavy object can stop it from approaching the five people tied on the track. You are standing with a fat man near the track. The only way to stop the trolley is to push the fat man on the tracks in front of it. You can save five lives in lieu of one. Should you proceed with this option? Another variation of this option states that if the fat man is himself responsible for tying up the five people, intending to kill them, then should you push him in front of the running trolley to save the five innocent lives?

Michael J. Costa put forward the loop variant of the trolley problem in 1987. In his set-up, the fat man is on a side track which joins the main track on which the five people are tied up. You can switch the track to divert the trolley on to the side track where the fat man can obstruct it, thereby saving the lives of the five people. Will you flip the switch?

Unger modified some of the conditions of the trolley problem. In his vision, a trolley is moving on a track towards five people who are unable to move. A diversion is possible by engineering an accident with the help of another trolley; however, this will cause a derailment and lead to both trolleys falling down a hill and into a yard where a man is sleeping. The sleeping man would be killed in the collision. Will you cause such a situation?

All versions of this thought experiment can be answered in consonance with the logic that killing a person is less desirable than letting a person die, because the former becomes 'active killing' while the latter can be termed 'passive killing'. In the original trolley problem, pulling the lever will save five lives while taking another as an indirect consequence. In the second scenario featuring the fat man, direct killing comes under culpable homicide amounting to murder, with a clear intention to kill. This is explained as the principle of double effect, which clarifies that indirect harm is permissible in the interests of achieving the greater good, although direct harm is not permissible, despite any good it might produce.

Psychological studies reveal that the moral intuitions of an individual evolve through being a virtuous member of a society. The practice of virtue helps people to refrain from actions that involve violence through personal contact (for instance, grabbing the fat man and pushing him onto the track). The trolley problem seems analytically unrealistic, but in the present-day context, the use of drones, self-driving cars, euthanasia, etc., are cases of genuine problems that require moral scrutiny.

HOW TO HANDLE ETHICAL DILEMMA

How an ethical dilemma should be handled depends on the situation you find yourself in, in relation to it. There are some steps to follow when an individual is confronted with an ethical dilemma:

1. Develop a knowledge of the ethical problem and achieve competency regarding the same.
2. Figure out all alternative strategies to address the issue.
3. Choose the best available strategy that would lead to an optimal realisation of the desired goal.
4. Implement the selected strategy with moral courage.

A rational decision does not always ensure moral consequences because reason alone cannot assure the pursuit of justice. From a managerial point of view, an individual needs to learn the systematic way to tackle ethical problems:

1. Do not make a judgement in haste; give yourself the proper time to ponder upon the issues in a holistic manner.
2. Discuss the situation with your colleagues or seniors who can provide positive inputs.
3. Process the problem through ethical principles. Start with deontological principles, then with the teleological, and you will finally find the answer that will correspond to your virtue, which in turn will come with experience and a commitment to values.
4. Be emotionally intelligent while taking inputs, collecting facts and delivering judgements.
5. Under deontological scrutiny, codes of conduct and rule-books should be interpreted without any bias.
6. Under teleological scrutiny, try to interpret the general code of ethics, which may serve the desired outcomes.
7. Make your decision and be firm about it. Share your resolve with related persons.
8. Keep an eye on the consequences of the decision and give it more thought to understand whether it can be handled differently.

REFERENCES

Cathcart, Thomas. (2013). *The Trolley Problem, or Would you Throw the Fat Guy Off the Bridge?* New York: Workman Publishing Company.

Gowans, Christopher W. (1987). *Moral Dilemmas.* New York, Oxford: Oxford University Press.

QUESTIONS

1. Explain the process of resolving ethical dilemmas in public administration. (UPSC 2018)
2. Most of the time, an ethical dilemma is actually no dilemma. Critically evaluate.
3. Explain, with the help of real-life examples, the potential dilemmas that occur in the day-to-day work of a public servant.
4. The moral dilemma is to make peace with the unacceptable. Explain.

16

ETHICS IN INTERNATIONAL RELATIONS

> **KEY CONCEPTS**
>
> Introduction; Ethical Theories of International Relations; Different Ideologies of International Relations; Ethics of International Funding

INTRODUCTION

As it evolves, every country constructs its own ethics and moral traditions, which find reflection in the behaviour of its citizens. Customs, laws, rules and regulations result from moral contemplation and their successful implementation in society. While at its core morality remains the same throughout the globe, attributes and methods differ from one country to another. We will attempt to unpack the fundamentals of the ethical conduct of different countries in order to understand them better. Ethical guidelines have been framed in all civilisations since time immemorial. Aristotle's ideas in Greece, Marshall McLuhan's concept of a global village (which posits that people throughout the world are interconnected through the use of new media technologies), and similar ideas focused on the ethics of interaction among different nation-states. Ethical questions related to war and peace, trade regulations, migration, religious activities, etc., are key concerns in the study of international relations. In traditional theories of international relations, ethics had a limited role. After World War II, ethics was viewed as ineffective, and the laws and institutions that sought to revamp international relations were termed 'misplaced moralism'. Later, a realist paradigm that did not consider ethics useful emphasised the need for a value-free social scientific approach in the transaction of international affairs, particularly in the USA.

Returning to history, ethical questions concerning international relations emerged during the period of imperial expansion. Here, St. Augustine's advocacy of the 'just war theory' is important: this theory postulates the belief that war, while terrible, is less so with the right conduct, and cannot always be considered the worst option.

> For St. Augustine, a war needed to comply with three ideals in order to be considered just:
>
> 1. It had to have a just cause.
> 2. It had to be declared just by a recognised official authority.
> 3. It could only be waged with the rightful intention, that is, to ultimately preserve civil order and bring about lasting peace.

The ethics underlying relationships between nations during times of war are complex. Unethical war practices are sometimes criticised by the citizens of even those nations who have initiated the war. The killing of civilians, even those who resort to armed protest, plundering cities and villages in war time, and torturing imprisoned soldiers are some ethical concerns that are taken into consideration in the light of just war principles. The classical doctrine of a just war is based on a justification of war (*jus ad bellum*) and the way wars should be fought (*jus in bello*).

The theory of just war has a long history, dating back to St. Augustine and St. Thomas Aquinas. The rules of *jus ad bellum* pertain to the circumstances under which states can acceptably wage war, while the rules of *jus in bello* serve as guidelines for fighting fairly once war has begun. According to *jus ad bellum*, a just cause of war should be declared by a legitimate authority, and the intentions of that authority should be equally just. War must be the last option, resorted to only after exhausting all other peaceful alternatives to resolve a conflict. *Jus in bello* specifies the conduct during war, which follows the principles of discrimination and proportionality. According to the former, the combatants must be distinguished from non-combatants such as civilians and prisoners. The principle of proportionality declares that the means used in war must not lead to devastation, and annihilation must not be the objective of a war. Although the doctrine of just war draws on ethics, realists contend that war has nothing to do with ethics. Ethics was created for ordinary individuals in everyday situations. In their capacity as statesmen, leaders are freed from the constraints of the law in their handling of extraordinary circumstances.

Consequentialism emphasises the ends: if the ends are just, the means to achieve them can be overlooked. This theory justifies war on the grounds of its consequence. Yet another strand states that when one nation-state wages war against another, it is the moral obligation of other nation-states to come together to protect the victimised state.

Since the end of the Cold War, human rights have become the central theme for the international community. Liberal political theorists, feminists, and radicalists criticised the idea of Realism and a value-free social science, instead advocating issues related to ethics in international relations. Ethics, as a subject of systematic study, finally found a place in the field of international relations in the 1980s, with the culmination of feminist approach in the international arena. The dilemmas related to international relations are:

1. Pluralism
2. Rights and Fairness
3. Just War
4. Intervention
5. Nuclear Ethics
6. Human Rights and Citizenship
7. Ethical Globalisation

> Feminist methodologies for International Relations paved a new way to enquire into feminist questions. The new development indicators like the Gender Development Index (GDI) of the United Nations Development Programme have facilitated feminist international relations scholars in their comparison of the efforts of nations to bring gender equality into all issues. Feminist scholars also emphasised the transnational activism of women and gender constructs during war and civil riots.

ETHICAL THEORIES OF INTERNATIONAL RELATIONS

We shall now discuss the theories pertaining to global justice in international affairs. First, we will summarise John Rawls' theory of international justice, which advocates a communitarian approach. Second, we will elaborate upon Peter Singer's cosmopolitan approach to global society.

John Rawls' Theory of International Justice

A Theory of Justice (1971) is a work of political philosophy and ethics by the philosopher John Rawls, where he provides a moral theory alternative to utilitarianism and addresses the problem of distributive justice. He wrote the 'Law of Peoples' that incorporated the fundamental beliefs underpinning the idea of a just international order. He constructed his theory on the following premises:

1. People, not states, are the key actors in international relations. The interests of states do not take primacy over the interests of the people.
2. Only well-ordered societies can establish a just international order. By 'Law of Peoples', Rawls meant 'a particular political conception of right and justice that applies to the principles and norms of international law and practice'. It is based on constitutionality and shoulder the burden of international responsibilities. 'Decent hierarchical peoples' also feature as parties to the Law of Peoples; the inclusion of 'decent hierarchical peoples' is demanded by the notion of toleration, a notion Rawls sees as integral to liberalism. This refers to non-violent people who respect human rights, but do not support democratic regimes. The remaining people belong to non-liberal societies: some are outlaws, some are unable to contribute to international peace and justice, and some states do not allow their people to participate in political-decision making, although they may provide protection to some human rights.

According to Rawls, liberal societies tend to coordinate with similar societies to determine 'fair terms of political and social co-operation'. They think rationally and reasonably in their governance of the international community, and collectively follow certain core moral principles to bring about a just international environment. Further, Rawls describes liberal societies under eight principles, which make up the Law of Peoples:

1. Peoples (as organised by their government) are free and independent, and their freedom and independence is to be respected by other peoples.
2. Peoples are equal and parties to their own agreements.
3. Peoples have the right of self-defence, but no right to war.
4. Peoples are to observe a duty of non-intervention.
5. Peoples are to observe treaties and undertakings.
6. Peoples are to honour human rights.
7. Peoples are to observe certain specified restrictions on the conduct of war (assumed to be in self-defence).
8. Peoples have a duty to assist other peoples living under unfavourable conditions that prevent their having a just or decent political and social regime.

Further, Rawls argues that there might be exceptional circumstances in which despotic, violent, inhuman and unstable societies violate these aforesaid principles. In conclusion, a communitarian approach emphasises orderly conduct and the creation of a moral environment. A just world can be achieved by powerful nation-states when they act according to the norms of international political morality.

Peter Singer's Theory of World Justice

Peter Singer, a prominent Australian cosmopolitan philosopher, emphasised the need for a global unity of economy, law and society. The increasing effects of globalisation have led to increasingly effective transactions among states, which is destroying the sovereign character of nation-states. The time has come to reorganise the world into a 'global village'. According to him, a new international ethics that can serve the interests of a global citizenry is the need of the hour. Criticising the sovereign character of states, Singer also questions their ethical significance.

Singer's cosmopolitan project does not call for an annihilation of the cultural and political diversity of nation-states; rather, it focuses on the universal cohesion of people, irrespective of their citizenship. While social and cultural diversity must be respected and protected, a successful universalism demands one culture and one society. A balance can be established with the help of effective global institutions. Taking the example of poverty, he further states that penury needs to be understood as the responsibility of the affluent section of society, who ought to contribute at least a part of their annual income to help in the alleviation of poverty. Singer's cosmopolitan perspective is based on the redistribution of wealth, and prioritises human welfare over state sovereignty.

DIFFERENT IDEOLOGIES OF INTERNATIONAL RELATIONS

Realism

Realism, the oldest ideology of international relations, has its roots in the political thoughts of the ancient Greek civilisation. Realists believe that sovereign states are the principal actors in the international system. International institutions, NGOs, multinational corporations, individuals, and other sub-state or trans-state actors are seen as having little independent influence. Thucydides, the author of *History of the Peloponnesian War*, is known as the father of realism. Socio-political thinkers like St. Augustine, Niccolo Machiavelli and Thomas Hobbes contributed significantly to the development of realism. Scholars such as Herbert Butterfield, Edward Hallet Carr, Robert Gilpin and George Kennan further enhanced the study of realism in the twentieth century. In spite of several shortcomings, realism maintains its place as a robust political ideology of internationalism. It includes the primacy of power in maintaining the world political order, the position of the state in world politics, the egocentricity of human nature, and the emphasis laid on consequentialism in ethical judgements.

Realists believe that human beings are self-centred and place their interests above those of others. This makes the world order difficult to sustain. Realists seek a solution to this situation according to the original human nature rather than an answer based on ethics. They believe a solution can be found in the balancing and counterbalancing of state power. Emphasising the centrality of power, they argue that politics, whether domestic or international, is essentially a quest for power. In the absence of a central authority in world politics, this power becomes more pronounced. Further, in their view, statesmen who do not acquire power risk being victimised by others who do.

As realism focuses on a state-centric approach, they consider the nation-state the principal actor in world politics. Sovereign states strive to enhance their economic and military power with respect to other nation-states in order to bring about a balance in power status among themselves. This global federalism based on nation-states determines the international political order. Realism presumes the absence of any global controlling authority recognised by the world community, which therefore functions in a decentralised and anarchic environment, or, in other words, runs as a self-reliant system. Finally, Realism proposes consequential ethics. Morality is compromised as greater importance is placed on national security, because power balancing is considered the principal instrument of foreign affairs. Although realism appears to be amoral, in reality it has a different kind of morality, which provides a contrast between political morality and individual morality. Decisions are taken in the light of the ideals of consequentialism.

Idealism

The roots of idealism can also be traced to ancient philosophy, although it has begun to be utilised only in recent world politics. Thomas Aquinas and Dante Alighieri were the two major early scholars of idealism. They both emphasised reason as a tool to tackle international problems and restore the world political order. Taking a position in between extreme realism and idealism, Aquinas' philosophy of Thomism is based on the belief that reason and faith are both necessary to achieve true knowledge. It means that Thomists acknowledge there is a natural order to things that can be known through reason; at the same time, revelation from God is required to know certain truths about God and morality. Dante accepted the idea of the development of an international government to determine peace and justice, although he advocated the role of a centralised political authority, in the form of a monarchy, for resolving inter-state conflicts.

The political idealism of contractarian theorists developed in the form of political liberalism (see Chapter 2 for details on contractarianism). They were in favour of having consent as the basis of all political processes under a constitutional government that would protect human rights. This theory is famously termed as 'liberalism' by international relation theorists. Kant supports a system of informal federalism of republics or nation-states, but argues that some form of centripetal force, in the form of a centralised global power, is necessary to regulate the individual states in the federation. Woodrow Wilson, too, advocated the creation of a global institution, and played a pivotal role in the formation of the League of Nations, the first worldwide intergovernmental organisation whose principal mission was to maintain world peace. Idealists have faith in the capacity of human beings to bring welfare and peace in the international environment.

Differences between idealism and realism:

1. While Realism strives for power in foreign affairs, often overlooking morality in the process, idealism depends on morality in even the evolution of international peace and justice.
2. Realism functions according to the beliefs of consequentialism, whereas idealism follows deontology.
3. Idealists seek to protect individual rights, liberty and human dignity, and reject autocratic and despotic regimes. They advocate the spread of constitutionalism and give priority to international law and transnational institutions.

Principled Realism

Principled realism is a middle path that combines the morality of idealism with the balance of power favoured by realism. It is also referred to as neoliberalism or realistic idealism. British historian and diplomat E. H. Carr (1892–1982) states that international politics demands a balanced approach that incorporates elements of both realism and idealism. On the one hand, principled realism emphasises moral values in international politics, and on the other, it advocates the responsible use of power by nation-states. Principled realists believe that democratic institutions like constitutionalism, the rule of law, human rights and social justice affect international politics as a whole. According to them, foreign policy should incorporate moral values while determining global welfare without compromising security, peace and public order.

ETHICS OF INTERNATIONAL FUNDING

The international community is a global society of many countries, some of which are developed, some underdeveloped, while yet others are poor. It is the moral obligation of developed countries to help the poor countries. Peter Singer says,

> How well we come through the era of globalization (perhaps whether we come through at all) will

depend on how we respond ethically to the idea that we live in one world. For the rich nations not to take a global ethical viewpoint has long been morally wrong. Now it is also, in the long term, a danger to their security.

International funding is categorised into funding related to development, and emergency relief funding on humanitarian grounds. Development funding is offered to those nations that are deprived of economic resources and lack technological advancement. Aid is provided on the basis of long-term assistance to alleviate poverty and foster economic growth. The growth of such nations is adversely affected by instances of civil war, social distrust, cultural backwardness and large-scale corruption. Emergency relief is given in the form of foreign aid during natural calamities such as earthquakes, droughts or epidemic outbreaks. For instance, when the tsunami of December 2005 caused great havoc in the coastal countries of the Indian Ocean, Western countries led by the USA responded promptly with all manner of assistance to the affected areas.

Development funding is generally provided as low-interest loans, grants, or bilateral and multilateral cooperation. These are known as official development assistance. The objective of such assistance is to ameliorate the poverty and underdevelopment of poor nations and thereby usher in global economic justice. Various economic studies have shown that the correlation of aid and economic growth offers no conclusive results. This means that mere foreign aid will not help if the political environment is not conducive to developmental activities. The misuse of foreign aid has also emerged as an area of concern. For example, Israel and Egypt received bilateral aid from the United States Agency for International Development (USAID), but this money was largely misused, as a result of which no significant reform took place. At times, funds entering a country in the name of development activities are swallowed up by corruption and terrorism. It is more effective for various countries to pool in funds and channelise it through international financial institutions, rather than depending on bilateral aid.

Sometimes, development aid and emergency aid cannot be segregated. In circumstances where there is widespread starvation and disease, international funds are utilised to combat both disasters. In a global society, there is no central authority that will control and manage global resources. Individual nations take possession of and responsibility for these resources within their territories. However, some public goods cannot be confined within these boundaries. For instance, the shared resources of the Earth, such as the oceans, rivers, land and the atmosphere, have to be maintained through the cooperation of all the nations. Developed countries can conserve the quality of such resources; for example, they can reduce industrial waste by using modern technology, which less developed economies do not have access to. Ultimately, it is the duty of developed nations to assist poor nations in this regard. Air and water pollution, which transcends boundaries, leads to the degradation of the Earth's environment and, in the long run, the economic growth of all nations.

REFERENCES

Amstutz, Mark R. (2000 [1999]). *International Ethics: Concepts, Theories, and Cases in Global Politics*. Lanham, MD: Rowman and Littlefield.

Cassidy, John. (2002). 'Helping Hands: How Foreign Aid Could Benefit Everybody'. *The New Yorker*, 18 March.

Hoffmann, Stanley. (1981). *Duties beyond Borders: On the Limits and Possibilities of Ethical International Politics*. Syracuse, NY: Syracuse University Press.

Singer, Peter Albert David. (2002). *One World: The Ethics of Globalization*. New Haven: Yale University Press.

Walzer, Michael. (1977). *Just and Unjust Wars: A Moral Argument with Historical Illustrations*. New York: Basic Books.

QUESTIONS

1. At the international level, bilateral relations between most nations are governed on the policy of promoting one's own national interest without any regard for the interest of other nations. This leads to conflicts and tensions between the nations. How can ethical considerations help resolve such tensions? Discuss with specific examples. (UPSC 2015)
2. Strength, peace and security are considered the pillars of international relations. Elucidate. (UPSC 2017)

17

CORPORATE GOVERNANCE

> **KEY CONCEPTS**
> Introduction; Ethics of Corporate Governance; Corporate Governance in India; Corporate Social Responsibility

INTRODUCTION

With the government taking on a greater role in the provision of goods and services to citizens and the increasing importance of the private sector, a need has arisen in the corporate section to establish a specific structure and relationships so as to determine its direction and performance, and apply mechanisms for their regulation. The corporate governance system is a mechanism set up to benefit all possible stakeholders. The management is the agent that runs the firm on behalf of the stakeholders, who are the principals. Corporate functioning involves steering, guiding and directing the organisation with the help of boards and regulators.

The Board of Directors is the pivotal arm of corporate governance. It deals with the stakeholders and primary contributors, as well as subsidiary contributors like the employees of the firm, suppliers and financiers. The modus operandi of corporate governance depends on various legal, regulatory and institutional frameworks already in place in the country. Regulators make their rules under the legal parameters provided. In other words, corporate governance is the regulation of management in the interests of the firm and the shareholders. It is the shareholders who elect the directors and auditors and vote for key positions and decisions at regular intervals. Investors are looking to reap profit, while managers are responsible for ethical practices aimed at checking corruption.

According to corporate finance specialist Marc Goergen (2012), corporate governance deals with the conflict of interest between investors and managers. Corporate governance comprises three groups:

1. The firm's shareholders, who invest money and approve major policies and business transactions.
2. The Board of Directors, which is elected by the shareholders to monitor the management.
3. The senior executives, who actually run the organisation and are responsible for its day-to-day business transactions.

The philosophy behind corporate governance pertains to the allocation of power among these three groups. An efficient corporate governance structure motivates companies to augment their worth through entrepreneurial skills and new ideas, and also creates accountability to regulate the risks involved.

ETHICS OF CORPORATE GOVERNANCE

With the advent of public shareholding in corporate firms, corporate governance has had to establish a legal mechanism to separate ownership from management. Since the twentieth century, large firms have become increasingly necessary and widespread. An important reason is that these firms require huge investments which the earlier family-owned firms found difficult to supply. This shift from 'private limited' to 'public limited' was generally implemented under a two-tier corporate hierarchy. The Board of Governors or Directors comprise the first tier; these are the elected shareholders of the company. The second tier comprises the apex body of the management; these are the employees hired by the Board of Directors/Governors.

Directors of the Board are elected by the shareholders. They are of two types: inside directors and outside or independent directors. The inside directors are chosen from within the company and can be salaried employees of the company as well. The independent outsiders are neutral and completely unrelated to the company. This second group of independent directors has been devised to establish public advocacy and in the public interest, or to establish ethical governance within the company. The Board of Directors elects a Chairperson of the Board, who functions as the leader of the corporation and is responsible for its smooth and effective functioning. S/he presides over board meetings and coordinates with the higher-level executives. S/he maintains corporate values and formulates a business strategy by representing the board as a whole.

The inside directors play a key role in collectively approving policy decisions related to finance, budgets and marketing. They approve any proposed extension of the company, new ventures, and prospective business relationships. Hailing from within the management team, they are known as the Executive Directors. The outside independent directors have the responsibility to determine the interests of stakeholders as well as of the society at large. They are expected to put forth unprejudiced and impartial views on all matters discussed at board meetings. In other words, they function as the ethical protectors of the company.

The principal objective of any company is to augment profits, grow and increase its ambit of influence. This objective can even be fulfilled through unethical practices. There are too many instances of the top management and board manipulating balance sheets, misappropriating government resources and failing to disclose hazardous activities. To check such malpractices, the state has put various legal provisions in place. Ethical aspects of corporate governance have been detailed under the Companies Act, which include corporate social responsibility and regulations among others.

CORPORATE GOVERNANCE IN INDIA

The growth of any company depends on its transparent and ethical functioning. High-profile scams in the Indian corporate sector adversely affected the economy and also led to a trust deficit vis-à-vis corporate affairs. The Ketan Parekh scam, the Satyam scam, and many others led to the realisation that a robust corporate governance mechanism was urgently required. The Indian Companies Act of 2013 promulgated some mechanisms to protect the interests of stakeholders. The scope of proxy advisory firms, which provide inputs to stakeholders, has been enlarged, and this has improved the governance.

A company with a robust corporate governance displays greater trustworthiness. The association of reputed independent directors with an ethical outlook also has a positive effect on the share prices of a company. Investors trust such people, and demonstrate their confidence by investing in the company. Foreign institutional investment is thereby influenced by better corporate governance. The Indian Companies Act, 2013 introduced internationally acclaimed practices of corporate governance for the sustainable growth of the

> **Notable Scams in India**
>
> **Ketan Parekh**, a former stockbroker from Mumbai, was convicted in 2008 for involvement in the Indian stock market manipulation scam that occurred from late 1998 to 2001. During this period, Parekh artificially rigged the prices of certain chosen securities, using large sums of money borrowed from banks including the Madhavpura Mercantile Co-operative Bank, of which he himself was a director.
>
> The **Satyam scam** refers to a huge corporate fraud committed in 2009 by Ramalinga Raju, the founder and chairman of Satyam Computer Services. He admitted to exaggerating sales, earnings, cash balances, and personnel numbers in the company's books. He also acknowledged utilising money from the firm for personal use.

corporate sector in India. These determine the greater participation of shareholders in decision-making and emphasises value-based business practices that eventually protect the interests of society at large.

India has a tradition of family-owned business houses in which family members hold the top management positions. These business houses list themselves on the stock exchange in an attempt to enhance their business with the help of public money; however, they often do not institute any corresponding administrative reforms in the company's affairs. Promoters who make large investments in the company in its formative years try to reap disproportionate benefits. They look for ways to fund their sister companies from the original company's assets through extended loans offered on liberal terms and conditions. The family members draw lucrative pay packages at the cost of the shareholders. The Companies Act, 1956 had sought to address these issues. It was mandatory to seek the permission of the Government of India while fixing the salaries to be paid, and other benefits, including loans to directors, were also capped at a certain limit. The approval of stakeholders was necessary before appointing the owners' relatives in the company.

In the last decade, we have witnessed several instances of corporate fraud and the failure of corporate governance. Most companies follow norms merely on paper, and not in the spirit in which they were intended. Nepotism is rampant in the appointment process. The Securities and Exchange Board of India (SEBI), India's capital market regulator, has been directed to evaluate the directors of the Board. The amended Companies Act, 2013 enhanced the role of independent directors by making them responsible for the interests of both employees and shareholders. The remuneration of Chief Executive Officers (CEOs) of Indian companies is arguably too much. A committee of board members, comprising a majority of independent directors, is usually organised to make policies in this regard. Such policies should be transparent and placed annually in the public domain.

In the Indian corporate sector, the founding members of a company involve themselves in all policy decisions, irrespective of their legal position. They influence all plans of succession to a great extent. Privacy policies and data protection frameworks are weak in Indian companies, making a strong IT infrastructure that can check the mishandling and misuse of data the need of the hour. Insider trading poses the biggest threat to Indian companies. India has witnessed a slew of structural and regulatory reforms, such as the Companies Act and SEBI's directions regarding listing and disclosure. Better coordination among all agents is imperative to achieve the desired ethical practices that can bring about good and effective governance.

A panel of 21 members under the chairmanship of Uday Kotak was formed by SEBI in June 2017, which submitted a report on corporate governance. Some of its important recommendations were as follows:

1. All companies with public holdings of more than 40 per cent will need to segregate the roles of Chairperson and CEO. Combining these roles results in a lack of oversight, which carries within itself the potential risk of abuse of high positions. A separate Chairperson can monitor deviations from the mandate and put reformative measures in place.
2. The minimum strength of the Board should be increased to six members, with at least one woman member as independent director.
3. At least half the members of the board should be independent directors of listed companies.
4. The Board should discuss succession planning and risk management at least once a year.
5. Directors should attend at least half of the total Board meetings held in a financial year. If they do not attend the stipulated number of meetings, their continued presence on the Board will be subject to the shareholders' approval.
6. Companies should publicly disclose the pertinent skills of the directors, and the age of non-executive directors should not exceed 75 years.
7. An independent director cannot serve more than eight listed companies, and a managing director can serve in the post of independent director in only three listed companies.
8. Board meetings should be convened at least five times in a year. Boards should meet every quarter to discuss the financial health of the company.
9. The minimum sitting fees of independent directors should be halved to Rs 50,000 per meeting from Rs 100,000, as mentioned in the Companies Act, 2013 for the top 100 companies by market capitalisation.
10. The SEBI should be empowered to act against auditors under the securities law.

CORPORATE SOCIAL RESPONSIBILITY

Every corporate activity utilises resources and impacts the society at large. As the resources belong to the society, the philosophy behind Corporate Social Responsibility (CSR) is to provide compensation for the effects of the business process. Moreover, as corporate firms are also legal citizens of the nation, they must possess certain ethical values based on philanthropic ideals. There is no single definition of CSR, and different organisations have their own versions of it. The European Council (EC) defines CSR as 'the responsibility of enterprises for their impact on society. Each firm ought to adopt a process to integrate social, ethical, humanitarian and environmental concerns into their business processes and core strategy.' It must be understood that CSR is neither charity nor sponsorship; it does not relate narrowly to a shareholder's wellbeing but is related to all aspects of a society.

In earlier phases, CSR in India was implemented as charity, and sometimes run on the whims of bureaucrats with narrow visions. Later, CSR activities were given a procedural form and sought to be implemented in a holistic manner. Governed by Clause 135 of the Companies Act, 2013, CSR covers companies with an annual turnover of Rs 1,000 crore and more, or with a net worth of Rs 500 crore and more. The Companies Act, 2013 has introduced the concept of CSR under Schedule VII, where it lists the activities related to community welfare under broad categories.

In India, the idea of CSR is related to the sustainable development of business. Every company ought to set up a CSR committee comprising three or more directors, including at least one independent director. The CSR committee formulates and recommends a CSR policy to the Board, incorporating the activities and the amount to be spent. It also monitors the implementation of the CSR policy from time to time. As per the guidelines of the Companies Act, 2013, the following activities come under the purview of CSR:

1. Eradicating extreme hunger and poverty.
2. Promoting education.
3. Promoting gender equality and empowering women.
4. Reducing child mortality and improving maternal health.
5. Combating the human immunodeficiency virus (HIV), acquired immunodeficiency syndrome (AIDS), malaria and other diseases.
6. Ensuring environmental sustainability.
7. Introducing vocational skills to enhance employment.
8. Social business projects.
9. Contributions to the Prime Minister's Relief Fund (PMRF) or any other fund set up by the Central or state governments for socio-economic development and relief, and for the welfare of Scheduled Castes and Tribes (SCs and STs), backward sections of society, minorities and women.

The 2013 Act mandates that companies spend at least two per cent of their net profits of the preceding three years on CSR activities. If they do not do so, they will need to furnish an explanation for this failure in the director's report. Since CSR activities involve expenditure from the company's profits, it is often considered undesirable and unsustainable with respect to the company's growth. CSR activities do not only provide social benefits, but are also directly beneficial to a company's business. The business environment is growing increasingly complex and competitive, and the expectations of stakeholders are no longer limited to their own interests. Now, other concerns, which include human resource practices, environmental issues, ethical business practices, etc., come within the ambit of corporate activities. A robust CSR programme brings greater repute and can even help companies accrue massive benefits. Some of these benefits are as follows:

1. CSR helps to obtain *de facto* as well as *de jure* approval of business activities from the community. There are many law and order concerns in setting up a business. Companies can operate on a particular piece of land only after the community's approval. At times, the local community protests against such establishments, due to various social, environmental and economic reasons. In other words, it is not just the government who provides the license to operate; the *de facto* approval of the community is also a key factor. An aggressive CSR programme can mend a trust deficit and smoothen the way to a hassle-free business operation.
2. Several studies reveal that a company with a robust CSR programme has a good reputation among job seekers as well as employees on ethical grounds, thereby helping it to attract talent.
3. Some CSR activities involve skill development programmes that can help create employability. Participants are prepared for future employment within the company itself. A company well-known for its employment generation under CSR is always welcomed by the local community.
4. CSR activities transform a company into a good corporate citizen. Such companies are also recognised by various global rating agencies.

REFERENCE

Goergen, Marc. (2012). *International Corporate Governance.* Harlow, UK: Pearson.

QUESTIONS

1. Corporate social responsibility makes companies more profitable and sustainable. Analyse. (UPSC 2017)
2. How do you see corporate responsibility for the community? Explain the steps taken in this regard by the Government of India.
3. Give some innovative suggestions to reduce corporate fraud in India.
4. Give an account of the activities which can be carried out under corporate social responsibility by corporate firms.
5. The private sector owes society for their survival. Elaborate this in terms of the social responsibility of corporate sectors.

18

PUBLIC SERVICE

> **KEY CONCEPTS**
> Introduction; Meaning of 'Public' in Public Service; Public Interest;
> Conflict of Interest; Public Service Values

INTRODUCTION

The theory of the 'divine right of kingship' characterised the sovereign as a divine entity. This idea gradually waned once the political intelligentsia of the time began their metaphysical inquiries into such divine institutions. They rejected the divine right of kingship in the interest of the common people. It was being said that the State was a juridical entity vested with public power. In their view, sovereignty was vested in the nation rather than in an individual, or even in a so-called divine authority like a king or a queen.

Disputes concerning the nature of the State have been persisting since the inception of the State, and remains an unsolved conundrum. The State undoubtedly possesses enormous power, and people have been striving to figure out the principles that could legally circumscribe the domain of State power. Today, the wielding of public power is related directly to the duties of the State with respect to its subjects. As St. Augustine said, in support of this notion, 'Those who command serve those whom they appear to command.' Similarly, in the context of World War I, Woodrow Wilson had declared, 'It is the war of emancipation. Not until it is won can men live anywhere free from constant fear or breathe freely while they go about their daily tasks and know that Governments are their servants, not their masters.' If the sovereignty of the State is absolute and the State is given the freedom to wield that power as per its own wishes, then the State would be placed beyond any regulatory mechanism.

There are various theories concerning the limitations of State power, such as Max Stirner's theory of anarchism, Jean-Jacques Rousseau and Maximilien Robespierre's theory of absolutism, Mahatma Gandhi's ideal non-violent state of enlightened anarchy, etc. German scholars

> **Max Stirner's Theory of Anarchism**
>
> German philosopher Max Stirner (1806–56) proposed that the most commonly accepted social institutions—including the notion of state, property as a right, natural rights in general, and the very notion of society—were mere illusions, 'spooks' or ghosts in the mind. He advocated egoism and a form of amoralism, and considered the world and everything in it, including other persons, available to one's taking or use without moral constraint. For him, rights did not exist in regard to objects and people at all.

> **Absolutism**
>
> Absolutism is a political system in which a single monarch, usually a king or queen, holds complete and unrestrained power over a country. The power of an absolutist government may not be challenged or limited.

proposed 'the doctrine of self-limitation of state' to reconcile two opposing thoughts. According to this theory, while the State possesses the power of self-determination, it may limit itself by the law which it enacts itself. Within the purview of its own law and contract, its powers are limited but the State's sovereignty is not breached because it is imposing these limits upon itself, by its own will. It is a voluntary subordination; in its true sense, a State is not limited by the law it has laid down, as it can change such a law at any time. The State is even above international law, which exists for the sake of nation-States, and not vice-versa. These limitations on State powers aim to ensure the protection of individual rights, promote peace and security, prevent abuses of authority, and foster cooperation among States. By upholding these limitations, States contribute to the development of a just and orderly international system.

It must be remembered that while the State is the creation of the human mind and possesses absolute power, the individuals who are vested with public power cannot be conflated with the State. Nor are they the organs of the State, although they appear to be part of the sovereign collective. These individuals, who wield power of their own, function in the name of the State under the rule of law.

Members of a society seek to fulfil their needs through a mutual exchange of goods and services under the division of functions suggested by Plato (see section on Plato in Chapter 10). A society cannot survive without such reciprocal exchange of different services offered by different members, and this imposes a duty upon every member to enhance their own activity and personal aptitude, and contribute to the society with their full potential. People are subordinated to social legislations. Persons who wield authority over others, whether they be called King, President, or Prime Minister, are no different from citizens, except in the fact that they wield greater authority. They have to act in accordance with the duty assigned to them with respect to their specific aptitudes for the realisation of social needs. Persons in authority therefore have a juridical duty to work for the collective interest of society.

Public service is the fundamental duty as every activity is carried out in the collective interest of society. The public authority has a duty to ensure that all social functions are discharged smoothly. This definition implies that persons in authority are duty-bound to ensure uninterrupted public service, and are authorised to use coercive power if the operation of public service is obstructed in any way. However, they cannot claim any ownership of power and sovereignty; they discharge their duty as per the rule of law, and the people are equally obliged to submit to the rule of law (and not to the authority conferred in the individual). This leads to the idea of the requirement of an institution that the public could turn to, should the public authority not fulfil their duties of service. The French public law known as *recour pour exces de pourvoir* ('rules on appeals for abuse of power by the authority') is the most appropriate example in this regard.

People demand security from the State, which provides them three services: the service of war to protect the national territory from invasions; service of the police for internal peace; and service of justice to maintain social order. With the passage of time, the purview of public service was broadened. The resultant increase in the number of services was due to economic changes in the national economy. The State had to ensure many public services, for instance, transportation, postal and telegraph, banking, electricity, etc., and the number of services is only increasing by the day. On the other hand, the social conscience also ascribes new duties to the people in authority, such as poverty alleviation, education and social justice. This increase in public services has diluted the sovereign authority of the State. Greater responsibility for public welfare shifted the focus on the central idea of law and order to the developmental administration, which was compelled to institute a decentralisation of authority and a sharing of power. Public law is no longer limited to maintaining law and order; it is now more inclined to ensuring that public services are undertaken efficiently.

The notion of State responsibility with regard to the provision of public services has entered the domain of public law. Here, we can quote the examples of the MGNREGA (Mahatma Gandhi National Rural Employment Guarantee Act, 2005), the Food Security Act, Right to Education Act, etc. The replacement of the concept of sovereignty by the concept of public service has increased the responsible character of the State. The State's obligation to cater to public service also enforces an obligation to redress any grievance created due to the unavailability of a public service, or malfunctioning of the organisation responsible for it. The provision of judicial recourse reinforces the idea of public service. Any grievance resulting from State inefficiency should be repaired with resources from the government treasury. Equally, if a few people are erroneously given exceptional benefits, they should be obliged to return it to the government treasury.

MEANING OF 'PUBLIC' IN PUBLIC SERVICE

The usage of the word 'public' in different circumstances is a matter for discussion. When the word 'service' is appended, such as services to the public, services supplying public goods, services from service, and so on, we are referring to public services, which the government is responsible for. With the increasing demand for public services and constraints of capacity on the part of the government, the private sector has begun to play a growing role. The question emerges: Should these services be categorised as public services? There are specific criteria used to describe the public nature of services, as devised by M. Shamshul Haque of the University of Singapore:

1. The extent to which it is not related to the private sector. Values like impartiality, openness, equality and representation differentiate these services from private services.
2. The perspective and type of beneficiaries. The more the number of beneficiaries and the broader range, the greater the chances of the service being termed 'public'. Shared public interest and universal acceptance enhances this.
3. The socio-economic implications of the services.
4. The magnitude of government accountability regarding the supply of services.
5. The level of public trust in the organisation responsible for the service.

This definition should be measured along a qualitative rather than a quantitative scale. It can be seen that the public nature of services is diminishing under the current structure of government. The modern State looks after four sectors:

1. Strategic core
2. Exclusive activities
3. Non-exclusive activities
4. Production of goods and services for the market.

The ownership of the first two sectors should lie in the hands of the State, while the rest should be catered to by private organisations. Non-exclusive activities comprise education, health, research and culture, and as these services pertain to basic human rights, they should be financed by the State. However, they do not demand the involvement of State power, with financing being the only major responsibility. In this situation, 'non-governmental' ownership is the way in which such services are catered to. These services are public because they serve public interests, are of and for everyone, and are not profit-driven.

The individuals responsible for dispensing public services are known as public servants, irrespective of the nature of their work. Public servants may be elected, selected, temporary, permanent, full time, or part time. Any individual who handles a certain amount of public money can be termed a public servant. Section 21 of the Indian Penal Code provides an exhaustive definition of a public servant in the Indian context; however, the philosophical definition is broader. We can see that a lot of public services provided by the State fail to have the desired impact. This is because State leadership under elected governments and public servants in most developing countries fail to broaden the criteria of what is 'public', as mentioned by Haque.

PUBLIC INTEREST

While the term 'public interest' is used frequently, no specific definition is provided for it. This term is similar to concepts such as 'common interest', used during the period of Aristotle in Greece, 'common good', as given by Thomas Aquinas and Rousseau, and the idea of 'public good' as propounded by John Locke. In the contemporary political and legal scenario, public interest is explained as the holistic sum of different types of interests related to people of a particular State. It should not be confused with public interest in general. The ambit and scope of public interest depends entirely on the context in which it has to be defined. In general, it refers to the good order and functioning of a society, and to government aid to ensure the wellbeing of the public at large; in other words, it relates to the proper and legitimate distribution of common goods as well as the approach of citizens towards these common goods. It also includes special interests under certain special circumstances.

In the modern definition, the ambit of public interest is enlarged, and it is described as the common interest of the community as a whole. It encompasses the collective goals and values of society based on a consensus, the sum of all private and special interests, and the final outcome of the self-interests pursued by individuals. Sometimes, disputes arise due to the conflict between the common public interest and the self-interest of individuals, whereupon the expression 'public interest' is described as a balance between public and private interests. Public interest can be explained with the help of its dimensions, outcomes, inputs, process and approach. Outcome is considered the substance of any decision made in the public interest. This decision should address broader public expectations rather than the narrow self-interests of a particular group. It should not curtail the supply of common goods and services to the community (in both quantity and quality), and refrain from diverting them towards private interests.

One first has to decide whether a matter belongs in the public interest. To do so, it should:

1. Fulfil all the legal requirements and pertain to a responsible exercise of power.
2. Comply with government policies and be free from all biases.
3. The process adopted should be impartial and free from any discrimination.
4. Public officials should act apolitically while taking decisions in public interest, or in other words, procedural features should be the key determinants behind the exercise of discretionary powers.
5. All decisions taken should include reasons with regard to cost and proportionality.
6. All decisions should abide by office procedures and include proper scrutiny and appropriate record-keeping, so that the information can be made accessible to the public.
7. There should be a balanced approach while addressing conflict.
8. Official duties should be carried out honestly and in good faith to avoid any perceived conflict.

CONFLICT OF INTEREST

Every individual or organisation has a variety of interests, which may be financial, non-financial, direct or indirect. Conflict arises when a particular interest proves detrimental to other interests. Here, we are concerned with such conflicts in the life of a public servant. A public servant is usually a career bureaucrat who enjoys security of employment in lieu of serving fearlessly in the public interest. It becomes difficult when her/his interest goes against that of the public. According to the values of public service, public servants should have no personal interest while carrying out their duties; their influence and authority arise from the public office they occupy. Their position or influence is meant for the welfare of the public and should not be used to serve personal interests.

Today, citizens of every country have increasing expectations from their governments with respect to standards of service delivery, and maintaining values such as integrity, transparency and dedication to service. Public servants have huge resources and authority conferred on them, which must be mindfully utilised to fulfil public interests. In the public sector, a conflict of interest arises when an official's personal needs or interests affect their performance of public duty. To combat these situations, a legal framework should be put in place to distinguish between 'actual', 'apparent', 'real' and 'potential' conflict situations.

With the increasing role of private organisations in the field of governance, the challenges have become more complicated. A public servant holding public office has enormous powers of decision-making and ability to take action for realising public interests, but at the same time, s/he is also a member of the public, a private citizen with similar rights and interests. The officials are trusted to not misuse their official positions in the pursuit of unreasonable private interests, or take advantage of their position. The scope of a breach of trust may arise in the situation of a conflict of interest. Figure 18.1 explains the dual role of a public servant.

Figure 18.1: Dual role of public servants

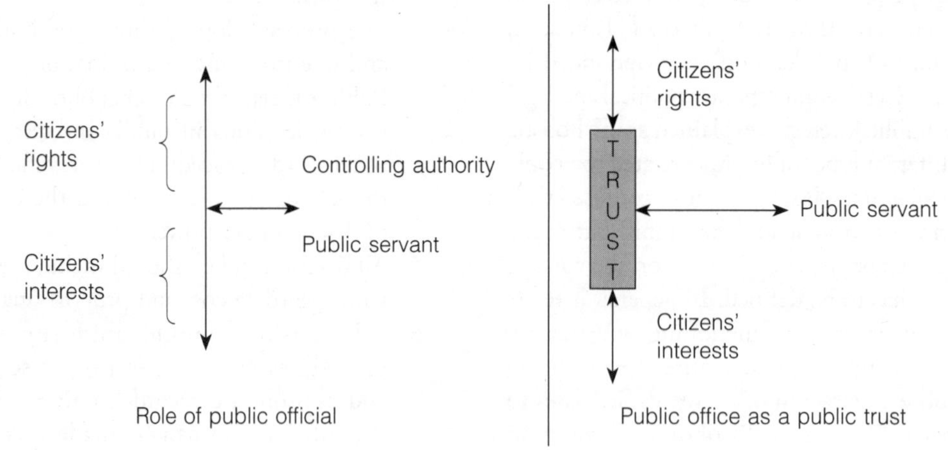

Source: Created by authors.

The public office is akin to a public trust wherein the public servant is entrusted to take decisions that influence the rights and interests of citizens. The trust placed in a public servant states our belief that s/he will always carry out their professional duties without any undue influence of personal or private interests. This trust should be maintained in order to keep public service values intact (see Figure 18.2).

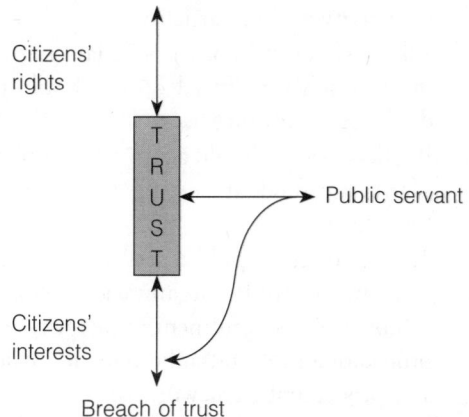

Figure 18.2: Conflict of interest

Source: Created by authors.

There is no other way to overcome such conflict and adhere to one's duty than maintaining integrity and other values of public service, as Figure 18.2 shows. The situation depicted in the figure is known as an 'actual' or 'real' conflict tof interest. When trust is breached and official powers and resources are utilised for personal gain, the conflict of interest takes the form of corruption. Such situations of conflict will persist if the private interest is not disposed of. Sometimes, situations may arise where organisational interest conflicts with public interests. This is known as an organisational conflict of interest.

With the emerging practices of new public management and greater partnership of private organisations with the public sector, such instances may increase. The lateral entry (for example, filling higher bureaucratic positions in any way other than the conventional system of hierarchical promotion of career bureaucrats) in the bureaucracy might create an organisational conflict of interest, if it is not addressed with due diligence. Posting a neutral, external administrator as the head of the organisation (department or secretariat) serves to maintains a check and balances organisational interests with the public interest. These interests may be myriad, such as devising the cadre strength, creating new posts at the apex level to accommodate a greater number of officers, cutting down certain posts, etc. Moreover, in legislative organisations, the power to increase salaries and other emoluments lies with members of the organisation, which serves as another example of an organisational conflict of interest.

This conflict of interest can be managed by defining and managing the private interests of the public servant with the help of stringent conduct rules and effective vigilance mechanisms.

Apparent Conflict of Interest

Certain conflicts have the potential to lead to actual, negative consequences, and can erode public confidence in the government as well as in the integrity of the public servants and/or the organisations they work in. Any apparent conflict of interest should be taken seriously and all suspicions should be addressed and investigated thoroughly. An apparent conflict of interest is also known as actual or real conflict of interest. To take an example, Mr A is a consultant in a state Department of Women and Child Development. His brother owns a business that makes packaged nutritional foods for children and pregnant women. The department is consulting with Mr A for their upcoming programme to create ready-made Take Home Ration (THR). Mr A's brother holds an important position in the market of such packaged food. Although Mr A is an honest person, this situation can lead to an apparent conflict of interest.

Potential Conflict of Interest

Potential conflict of interest is defined as a situation that may arise in the future when the personal interests of a public servant conflict with the public interest, even though the formal position of the concerned official has no bearing on her/his private interests. A potential conflict of interest is converted into an apparent conflict of interest in the absence of proper mechanisms that can address such instances. For instance, a businessman-cum-politician who owns an aviation company should not accept the portfolio of the Civil Aviation Ministry; similarly, a defence supplier should not accept the portfolio of the Defence Ministry. This is why civil services conduct rules are devised, with various provisions that prohibit and preempt potential conflict of interest, for example, provisions such as the cooling-off period and restrictions on reemployment for certain public office-holders.

Managing Conflict of Interest

Although a conflict of interest is not *ipso facto* corruption, it ought to be recognised as a potential threat to the image of public administration as well as the efficiency of public office. The following measures can be taken to manage conflict of interest in the public sector:

1. Public servants should be objective in their decision-making and while dispensing advice, and base their actions on the merit of the case rather than on personal gain or any prejudices related to religion, organisation, politics and preferences.
2. Public servants should keep in abeyance such private interests that can jeopardise their neutrality in official matters.
3. Public servants should not make use of any confidential information received during the performance of official duty.
4. Public servants should not seek or accept any undue advantages from others that may influence their performance while holding public office.
5. Public servants should not take the benefit of information obtained in the course of their official duties, especially when seeking employment after relinquishing public office.
6. Public servants and public organisations should conduct themselves in a way that will pass every public scrutiny, that is, in a lawful manner and also in congruence with public service values such as integrity, objectivity and impartiality.
7. All areas related to a potential conflict of interest with official duties should be disclosed in advance.
8. Public servants should act in an exemplary manner aimed at setting an example for others.
9. The conduct of public servants and the working of public organisations should exhibit their commitment to integrity and professionalism, and adhere to the policy and procedural framework.
10. The organisation should promote a healthy work culture and put in place an adequate management framework that can check such conflict of interests.
11. Training programmes must be devised for the staff to enable them to learn how to overcome such situations.

In India, a slew of measures have been taken to avoid any conflict of interest in the public lives of career bureaucrats as well as people's representatives. The code of ethics and code of conduct stipulate several checks on the actions of permanent executives. We will discuss them in detail in Chapter 19. Measures to address conflict of interest in the public lives of members of legislatures are also important. Some provisions have also been made for public representatives, although they are not very comprehensive in the case of civil servants. For members of the Rajya Sabha, the following provisions have been put in place under the code of conduct:

1. If members realise that there is a conflict between their private interests and the public trust held by them, such a conflict should be addressed in a manner that prioritises public trust over private interests.

2. The private interests of members and their families should not come into conflict with the public interest. In the event of such conflict, public interest should not be placed in jeopardy.
3. Members should never accept any benefits in lieu of their votes on the floor of the House.
4. Members should never accept any gift that may conflict with the honest discharge of public duties.

Similar provisions have been made for members of the Lok Sabha:

1. Members should leverage their position for the wellbeing of the public at large.
2. In any instance of conflict of interest, public interest should be held above private interests.
3. Members should adhere to high standards of morality, decency and public values.

Besides the above codes of conduct, in India, provisions have been made for the disclosure of the interests of members in both the Lok Sabha and the Rajya Sabha. For instance, the Chairperson of the Rajya Sabha may rule that before participating in the proceedings, a member should disclose all personal interests pertaining to the matter at hand. The Rules of Procedure and Conduct of Business in the Lok Sabha provide that the Speaker may investigate any conflict of interest that could influence the voting behaviour of a particular member. The Rules of Procedure and Conduct of Business in the Council of States, Rule 293, provides for the maintenance of a 'Register of Members' Interests' by the Committee on Ethics of the Rajya Sabha. This register comprises information pertaining to any remunerative directorship position, regular activities related to remuneration, shareholding of a controlling nature, paid consultancies and professional engagements of members.

The Constitution of India also provides for the disqualification of a member of the legislature if s/he holds any office for profit.

PUBLIC SERVICE VALUES

Public service values pertain to the standards that should be held by those in public office. A complex system of laws, rules and regulations have been set up to regulate the conduct of public servants; however, these are only effective in the case of public servants at the lower echelons, who do not enjoy authority or discretionary powers. It is not possible to completely regulate the conduct of public servants who occupy positions in the higher echelons, because of the provisions and compulsions that confer a substantial discretionary role to such office-bearers.

In such a situation, these officials are held to higher moral standards. Several committees have been constituted to work out these standards and carve out ideal values for public officials. One such well-known endeavour is the standardisation of public service values, known as the Nolan Committee recommendations. In the UK in 1995, the Committee on Standards in Public Life delineated seven values of public life:

1. **Selflessness**. Public servants holding public office should decide matters solely in the public interest. They should not be motivated by their self-interest. The decisions taken by public servants should not be aimed at gaining any material benefits for themselves, or for people close to them.
2. **Integrity**. Officials holding public office should not function under the influence of external individuals or organisations. Their actions should be free of any outside financial liabilities or obligations that can lower the standards of public service.
3. **Objectivity**. All decisions taken by public servants should be based on merit. A public servant carries out different functions while holding public office, such as: appointing suitable candidates for vacant positions, awarding contracts against invited tenders, offering recommendations for rewards and benefits. All such choices should be made objectively and in an unbiased manner.

4. **Accountability**. Officials holding public office should always be held accountable to the public for their decisions and conduct. They should cooperate in any public scrutiny of their organisation/department.
5. **Openness**. Decisions taken by public servants should be open and transparent. All decisions should be recorded and be accessible to the public, with the exception of specific cases. A public servant should always be able to provide a reason behind any decision.
6. **Honesty**. Public servants must be vigilant enough to foresee any situation that could give rise to a conflict of interest. They should immediately declare such a situation, and take measures to overcome it and protect the public interest.
7. **Leadership**. A public servant should strive to promote all these standards and set an example of leadership.

REFERENCES

Bailey, S. (1964). 'Ethics and the Public Service'. *Public Administration Review* 24(4): 234–243.

Bertok, Janos. (2003). *Managing Conflict of Interest in the Public Service: OECD Guidelines and Country Experiences*. Paris: Organisation for Economic Co-operation and Development (OECD).

Bozeman, B. (2007). *Public Values and Public Interest: Counterbalancing Economic Individualism*. Washington: Georgetown University Press.

Duguit, Leon. (1923). 'The Concept of Public Service'. *Yale Law Journal* 32(5): 425–35.

Second Administrative Reforms Commission. (2005). *Fourth Report: Ethics in Governance*. Government of India: Department of Administrative Reforms and Public Grievances. Available at https://darpg.gov.in/arc-reports (accessed April 2024).

QUESTIONS

1. What do you understand by the term 'public servant'? Reflect on the expected role of a public servant. (UPSC 2019)
2. 'The good of an individual is contained in the good of all.' What do you understand by this statement? How can this principle be implemented in public life? (UPSC 2013)
3. Public servants are likely to confront issues of 'conflict of interest'. What do you understand by the term 'conflict of interest' and how does it manifest in the decision-making of public servants? If faced with such a situation, how would you resolve it? Explain with the help of examples. (UPSC 2015)
4. Conflict of interest in the public sector arises when
   (a) official duties,
   (b) public interest, and
   (c) personal interest
   are taking priority one above the other. How can this conflict in administration be resolved? Describe with an example. (UPSC 2017)
5. What is meant by public interest? What are the principles and procedures to be followed by the civil servants in public interest? (UPSC 2018)
6. What is mean by conflict of interest? Illustrate with examples the difference between actual and potential conflicts of interest. (UPSC 2018)
7. How do you interpret the term 'public' in public service? Explain with the help of some examples.
8. The current public policy encourages an enhanced role of the private sector in public affairs. How do you understand private participation to realise public interest as a crucial part of public service?

19
PROBITY IN GOVERNANCE

> **KEY CONCEPTS**
>
> Philosophical Basis of Governance; Good Governance; Key Challenges in Governance; Social Capital: A Shared Destiny; Philosophical Basis of Probity; Code of Ethics and Code of Conduct; Citizen's Charter; Utilisation of Public Funds; Probity in Governance and Challenges of Corruption; Measures for Curbing Corruption and Ensuring Probity in Governance; Fourth Report of the Second Administrative Reforms Commission: Ethics in Governance; Causes of Corruption; Ethical Framework; Recommendations Related to Ethical Framework for Ministers; Ethical Framework for Legislatures; Code of Ethics for Civil Servants; Ethical Framework for the Judiciary; Legal Framework for Fighting Corruption; Protecting the Honest Civil Servants; Seventh Report of the Second Administrative Reforms Commission

PHILOSOPHICAL BASIS OF GOVERNANCE

Earlier in the book, we have discussed public services and the public interest. The concept of governance is closely related to the word 'public', and is a tool to implement and establish the notion of the public effectively. Doing so requires the exercise of legitimate authority in the concerned organisation or State. Governance is directly related to authority, which is used to regulate the behaviour of the people involved in public service. Max Weber provides a three-fold classification of authority:

1. Traditional authority, connected to history
2. Charismatic authority, embedded in the personality
3. Legal authority, based on neutral and unbiased rules.

In a democracy, politics is an integral part of governance. Politics is a way to represent the collective approval of the public which is to be governed. Governance also encompasses non-political actors like state institutions and civil societies; the former are the public and the latter the private actors of governance. Thus governance is the way through which power is exercised through the institutions of a country, and it can be defined as

> exercising the political, economic and administrative authority to manage a country's resources for development. It incorporates the voice of the society in terms of their interest, mode of exercising

rights by institutions of state and citizens, and a mechanism to reconcile the differences in pursuit of the collective good.

> **Definitions of Governance by Various Institutions**
>
> 'The exercise of economic, political and administrative authority to manage a country's affairs at all levels. It comprises mechanisms, processes, and institutions through which citizens and groups articulate their interests, exercise their legal rights, meet their obligations, and mediate their differences.'
> (United Nations Development Programme, 1997)
>
> 'Governance is the exercise of political, economic and administrative authority necessary to manage a nation's affairs. It is the process by which decisions are made and implemented (or not implemented) within Government. Governance is the process by which public institutions conduct public affairs and manage public resources.'
> (IMF, *Manual on Fiscal Transparency*, Glossary, 2007)
>
> 'Governance has been defined to refer to structures and processes that are designed to ensure accountability, transparency, responsiveness, rule of law, stability, equity and inclusiveness, empowerment, and broad-based participation. Governance also represents the norms, values and rules of the game through which public affairs are managed in a manner that is transparent, participatory, inclusive and responsive. Governance therefore can be subtle and may not be easily observable. In a broad sense, Governance is about the culture and institutional environment in which citizens and stakeholders interact among themselves and participate in public affairs. It is more than the organs of the government.'
> (UNESCO International Bureau of Education)

According to the United Nations Development Programme (UNDP), governance has three pillars: economic, political and administrative. Economic governance involves the economic affairs of a country, as well as its relationships with outside economies. It studies the economic indicators of a country and strives to enhance the quality of life. Political governance is related to the stability, reputation and credibility of the government, which reflects in its policy formulation. Administrative governance now enters the picture to ensure that these policies are implemented effectively. Governance, as we know, pertains to decision-making and the process involved in the implementation of the decision taken.

While in general parlance government and governance are used interchangeably, the two have different meanings. Government pertains to the wielding of authority, ruling of citizens and controlling the behaviour of the people. Governance, on the other hand, is about management, without any use of coercion. Government is based on law and the maintenance of law and order and upholding peace, whereas governance is not a rule-based mechanism of control. Governance is open to inputs in the form of suggestions and complaints. It calls for leadership to motivate society and fulfil all developmental goals. Research has concluded that governance is a multi-level phenomenon. The Commission on Global Governance defines governance as:

> The sum of the many ways individuals and institutions, public and private, manage their common affairs. It is a continuing process through which conflicting and diverse interests may be accommodated and cooperative action may be taken. It includes formal institutions and regimes empowered to enforce compliance, as well as informal arrangements that people and institutions either have agreed to or perceive to be in their interest.

We can thus state that governance is geared to solving common problems pertaining to the society, organisations, and national and global issues through different methods. R. A. W. Rhodes groups governance into seven broad categories:

1. Corporate Governance
2. Good Governance

3. New Public Management
4. New Political Economy (Marxist-influenced)
5. International Relations/Interdependence (including the European Union)
6. Socio-cybernetic Systems Theory
7. Network Governance

GOOD GOVERNANCE

Governance is the art of managing issues pertaining to public services. The decision-maker should have all the virtues required to be a good manager, and be free from any dominant, pre-existing attitude, hasty decision-making, malpractices, and reliance on personal whims. Plato cited four cardinal virtues central to bringing about good governance in society; prudence, courage, temperance and justice. Good governance has eight principal characteristics: participation, rule of law, responsiveness, transparency, orientation towards consensus, equity and inclusiveness, effectiveness and efficiency, and accountability.

To ensure good governance, all segments of the social and political spheres, and the public, private and civil societies should contribute seriously. Decentralisation of government is intended to achieve the greater participation of all. In India, the Constitution has provided for Panchayati Raj Institutions (PRI) to encourage such decentralisation. Every country needs to sustain law and order, and establish peace for better governance, which is possible by the rule of law. The basic philosophy behind governance is public consensus, that is, a collective approval to the wielding of authority under the rule of law. Rule of law is a famous doctrine given by British jurist A. V. Dicey in his book, *The Law and the Constitution* (1885), and is the principle that no one is above the law. Dicey describes rule of law under three fundamental concepts: supremacy of law, equality before law, and predominance of the legal spirit.

Rule of law is the legal principle that stipulates that a nation should be governed by law and not the arbitrary rules of individuals. It gives principal dominance to the law within society and all the organs of the state. Aristotle's statement, 'law should govern', supports this principle. Every citizen, including the lawmaker, comes under the purview of the law. The rule of law determines transparency, sustenance, accountability and the procedure established by law, and takes care of the timely delivery of justice. The Indian concept of rule of law is both formal and substantial and is an integral part of good governance.

Governance can be considered good if it is responsive and prompt for all citizens, with no unnecessary delay or arbitrary distinctions. Transparency in governance increases trust in authority and enables public order and

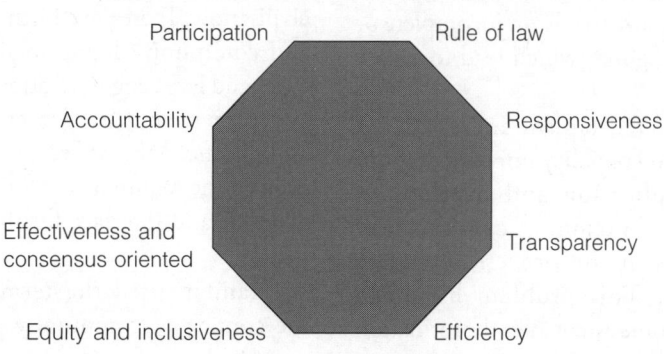

Figure 19.1: Characteristics of good governance

Source: UNDP 1997.

expectations. After the implementation of the Right to Information in India, transparency has increased substantially. Policymakers should involve the public in the making of policies and procedures. The consensus of minority groups should be taken into consideration to overcome any bias. Governance should include all men and women in the process of growth. All of society should feel a part of the development of the country. Resources might be limited; however, we can enhance their effectiveness by utilising them better. All decisions should be taken in the public interest. Accountability is a key component of good governance and should include all decisions taken by private institutions in the public interest.

KEY CHALLENGES IN GOVERNANCE

The key challenges in governance include:

1. Policymaking and its implementation. In India, states are the principal implementing agencies for most government policies. Sometimes, however, due to a difference of opinion with the Centre, states do not implement the policies.
2. With a change in government, old policies are often replaced, overlooking the impact they have had on the society.
3. At times, adequate resources in terms of budgetary allocations and human resources are not forthcoming.
4. In India, there is a lack of pertinent data, and field observations are often fudged. Policymakers have to rely on incomplete or manipulated figures, which lead to policy failure.
5. Bureaucratic red-tapism increases the gestation period of policy implementation. Besides, duplication and overlaps in bureaucratic functioning can also lead to deadlocks in the process of policy formulation. This problem has been overcome to some extent after the formation of the Niti Aayog.
6. Citizens' participation is an important part of governance. This, however, is always missing while moving from policymaking to its implementation.
7. Corruption is also a big challenge in governance.

SOCIAL CAPITAL: A SHARED DESTINY

The term 'social capital' was first used by L. J. Hanifan, a state supervisor for rural schools in Virginia in 1916, and extensively used later by Robert Putnam. Putnam defined social capital as:

> Whereas physical capital is related to physical objects and human capital is related to the human's characteristics, social capital is related to bonds among individuals which give birth to social networks, the norms of quid-pro-quo and mutual trust. In this way, social capital is closely related to civic virtues. The social capital differs from civil virtue in its use in a sense network of mutual relations. A society of many virtuous but isolated individuals is not necessarily rich in social capital. (Ninth Report, Second Administrative Reforms Committee)

According to the World Bank, 'Social capital is not just the collectivity of the institution which bases a society; rather it is a bond that holds them together.' As Mahatma Gandhi said, 'A government builds its prestige upon the apparently voluntary association of the governed.'

Collective efforts and cooperation have been the most important since the inception of civilisation. These gave birth to social coexistence and community living in the form of villages, cities and large agglomerations. In course of time, government and the larger society took shape and distanced themselves from individuals. Thus evolved the requirements for mutual networking, dialogue and interface for the resolving of social issues.

Hanifan used the term 'social capital' in the context of community participation in the successful running of schools. Social capital was recognised as a concept in social science literature in the 1980s, and soon became an important concept in economic and development theory as well. Social capital encompasses institutions, relationships and norms that help to make the social interface more productive. Social capital is based on trust, mutual understanding, shared values, and behaviour that knits members of a community together and provide opportunities for joint action. A sense of belonging and strong social networking can lead to greater benefits in a society.

Social capital is enriched by strong social cohesion and entrepreneurship, and is a crucial factor in social, economic and political growth. This process forms a specialised community and institutions known as social capital institutions or the third sector. Important third-sector organisations are civil societies, trusts/charitable institutions, NGOs, self-help groups (SHGs), cooperatives, etc.

The major roles of social capital institutions are:

1. **The Service Role**. This motivates people to solve public issues at their own level. Non-profit organisations serve as the first line of defence through flexible mechanisms. These institutions help the government in the distribution of public services, especially in remote areas, which are prone to being overlooked or inefficiently served. Non-profit organisations play a major role in planning hospitals, educational institutes, social service agencies and civil organisations.
2. **The Value Guardian Role**. These institutions help in inculcating social values among the people and work as 'value guardians' in society. They serve as vehicles of individual initiatives in furthering public services and public goods.
3. **The Advocacy/Social Valve Role**. Non-profit institutions mobilise public attention to social problems, and give public voice to societal concerns. These institutions act as a safety valve that helps to sustain democracy and public order.
4. **The Community Building Role**. Social capital organisations boost social cohesion by fostering bonds of trust and reciprocity.

Social capital can further good governance in several ways:

1. It can define government accountability and enrich policymaking by inducing innovation. It enhances the efficiency of public-service delivery through citizen involvement.
2. Social capital can bring different players onto a single forum on important issues.
3. It helps to provide inclusive development to the nation. Women's Self-Help Groups/Micro-Credit Institutions are examples of collective participation which lead to better execution of government schemes.

PHILOSOPHICAL BASIS OF PROBITY

The political meaning of probity has often been misinterpreted as honesty, and hence probity was considered a moral rather than a political virtue. Nietzsche considered *Redlichkeit* (probity) as embodied truth. Following Greek philosophers, especially Cynics, probity can be considered an expression of free speech or truth-telling. Probity is ranked above truth, and exists in the public realm. It lends itself to evaluation by others and has a shared character. The importance of truth lies in the public sphere. In his famous essay 'What is Enlightenment', Kant states that 'freedom of thought is possible only in [the] public and open space shared with others'. Nietzsche upholds *Redlichkeit* (probity) as the highest form of truth and said, 'Probity, truthfulness and love of wisdom belong to the genius of the heart.' Probity refers to the scientific attitude required in an honest pursuit of the truth. The highest virtue of all, it cannot be standardised, but reconciles virtue with happiness. Probity is becoming, it is everlasting and a form of purified consciousness of the self.

Probity plays a crucial role in governance because governance depends upon public satisfaction. Governance should be based on the truth and the expression of free speech. It should always be open to scrutiny in the public sphere. We will now discuss the different means by which probity can be assured in governance.

CODE OF ETHICS AND CODE OF CONDUCT

Although all citizens are subject to the law of the land, these laws should be more rigorous in the case of public servants. Any individual conferred with the authority to direct the destiny of citizens must be both ethical, and be seen to be ethical. To overcome any clashes between public action and private interest, a code of ethics and of conduct are required. A code of ethics would cover wider norms related to good behaviour and governance. On the other hand, a code of conduct would stipulate a more specific list of acceptable and unacceptable conduct. Together, a code of ethics and of conduct provide the ethical yardstick by which to measure the behaviour of professionals in an organisation.

For civil servants, the code of ethics takes the form of value statements and beliefs that impose certain restrictions on their conduct. These are general philosophical guidelines with their own mission, vision and value statements. The code of ethics emphasises the role of civil servants in society, and playing this role demands an adherence to ideals. Every citizen, and even outsiders, repose faith in government institutions. The conduct of civil servants should always be geared towards winning the trust of the people. The code of ethics comprises teleological statements that emphasise outcomes in terms of the general and everyday conduct of civil servants.

A precise code for professionals helps to create a positive and healthy work culture, and also deal with personal dilemmas and social pressure. At times, codes such as these appear to curtail fundamental rights to some extent; however a closer look shows how crucial they are in making the life of a civil servant hassle-free, comfortable and systematic. Some important advantages of the code of conduct and of ethics are as follows:

1. These codes help in everyday decision-making as well as in crucial planning. For example, if a political or religious group seeks undue favours, the code of conduct can be resorted to in order to refuse the favour and avoid an unpleasant situation. A civil servant can refuse to accept gifts that can influence decision-making in the future, on the strength of these codes.
2. These codes determine the ideal behaviour of civil servants, which enhances the reputation of the government. People still have faith in civil servants precisely because of these restrictions imposed by the rules of conduct. This trust plays an important role in upholding peace, and law and order in the society.
3. Subordinate staff display a greater commitment to civil servants because of the trust and respect built on the strength of this ideal code of conduct. This respect and loyalty is hard to find in private organisations.
4. Restrictions imposed by these codes help a civil servant to avoid all legal complexities or misconduct, which may retard the pace of official functioning. For example, trials in a court of law related to bribery may extend the relevant project by an indefinite period of time.

The behaviour enunciated in the various conduct rules comprises general norms and a code of ethics, such as 'maintaining integrity and absolute devotion to duty', and not indulging in 'conduct unbecoming of a civil servant'. However, these were not sufficient to direct a civil servant. There was no code of ethics or general philosophical guidelines in India in the early years, unlike many other countries. Later, there was a demand to frame norms in terms of a code of ethics. A draft Public Service Bill sought to lay down such rules. Later, the Central Civil Services (Conduct) (Third Amendment) Rules, 2014 and similar rules for the All India Services were provisioned, to cater to the demand for a code of ethics. A code of ethics was incorporated under rule 3, 'General', in the Central Civil Services (Conduct) Rules, 1964 and the All India Civil Services (Conduct) Rules, 1966. Similarly, other conduct rules were framed for members of the Railway Services and State Civil Services of various states, which describe the overall ethical attitude desired in the civil services. Some of them are:

(1) Every Government servant shall at all times—
   (i) maintain absolute integrity;
   (ii) maintain devotion to duty;
   (iii) do nothing which is unbecoming of a Government servant;
   (iv) commit herself/himself to and uphold the supremacy of the Constitution and democratic values;
   (v) defend and uphold the sovereignty and integrity of India, the security of the State, public order, decency and morality;
   (vi) maintain high ethical standards and honesty;
   (vii) maintain political neutrality;
   (viii) promote the principles of merit, fairness and impartiality in the discharge of duties;
   (ix) maintain accountability and transparency;
   (x) maintain responsiveness to the public, particularly to the weaker sections;
   (xi) maintain courtesy and good behaviour with the public;
   (xii) take decisions solely in public interest and use or cause to use public resources efficiently, effectively and economically;
   (xiii) declare any private interests relating to her/his public duties and take steps to resolve any conflicts in a way that protects the public interest;
   (xiv) not place herself/himself under any financial or other obligations to any individual or organisation which may influence her/him in the performance of her/his official duties;
   (xv) not misuse her/his position as civil servant and not take decisions in order to derive financial or material benefits for herself/himself, family or friends;
   (xvi) make choices, take decisions and make recommendations on merit alone;
   (xvii) act with fairness and impartiality and not discriminate against anyone, particularly the poor and the under-privileged sections of society;
   (xviii) refrain from doing anything which is or may be contrary to any law, rules, regulations and established practices;
   (xix) maintain discipline in the discharge of her/his duties and be liable to implement the lawful orders duly communicated to her/him;
   (xx) maintain confidentiality in the performance of her/his official duties as required by any laws for the time being in force, particularly with regard to information, disclosure of which may prejudicially affect the sovereignty and integrity of India, the security of the State, strategic, scientific or economic interests of the State, friendly relation with foreign countries or lead to incitement of an offence or illegal or unlawful gain to any person;

(xxi) perform and discharge her/his duties with the highest degree of professionalism and dedication to the best of her/his abilities.

The code of conduct for civil servants is a comprehensive document that comprises a set of rules pertaining to the conduct of members of an organisation. This rule book elaborates upon the code of ethics and includes every aspect of professional life, such as how to deal with the media, financial transactions, personal relationships, etc. It provides an extensive guide for civil servants regarding their source of income, transaction of gifts, utilisation of government resources, and conduct in public places. It imposes reasonable restrictions on the unlimited freedom of speech and writing in a public forum without due authorisation from the government. It also checks the political inclinations of civil servants to a great extent. In other words, the code of conduct comprises of deontological statements with strict dos and don'ts. Some of the rules are related to:

1. Employment of near relatives of Government servants in companies or firms
2. Taking part in politics and elections
3. Joining of associations by Government servants
4. Demonstrations and strikes
5. Connection with the press or other media
6. Criticism of Government
7. Gifts
8. Private trade or employment
9. Public demonstrations in honour of Government servants
10. Movable, immovable and valuable property
11. Consumption of intoxicating drinks and drugs

Although the code of ethics and code of conduct are meant to guide civil servants, their efficacy is still questionable. These codes are not morally enforceable, except under threat of disciplinary action initiated by a competent authority.

CITIZEN'S CHARTER

Good governance is the linchpin of the holistic development of any country. The three basic components of administration essential to good governance are transparency, accountability and responsiveness. Good governance revolves around the idea of efficient service provision to citizens. Citizens should have easy access to public services, which should be provided to them within a fixed time frame. A citizen's charter drives such efficient service provision on the part of the government to their citizens.

The notion behind the framing of a citizen's charter is the realisation of the mutual trust that exists between masters (citizens) and servants (public servants). The idea of a citizen's charter was first introduced in the UK by John Mayor in 1991. It aimed to empower citizens vis-à-vis public service delivery under six basic tenets: quality, choice, standards, value, accountability and transparency. Put simply, a citizen's charter is about enhancing the quality of public services provision, with predetermined standards as per the expectations of citizens with a foolproof grievance redressal mechanism in case the desired service standards are not met. The government spends public money on service delivery. Value for money is also a major element in a citizen's charter. The accountability of both public servants and organisations involved in the process of service delivery is fixed. Public service delivery is bound by rules and procedures, and schemes are launched with the help of information technology.

All countries have adopted a similar citizen's charter in different forms. India adopted it in 1997. In a conference attended by the chief ministers of various states and administrators of UTs, held on 24 May 1997 in New Delhi and presided over by the Prime Minister of India, an 'Action Plan for Effective and Responsive Government' at the Centre and states was adopted.

Citizen's charters were adopted for services in the larger public interest, such as railways, Public Distribution System, social justice, etc. These charters detailed the standards of service to be offered under prescribed time frames and a platform for grievance redressal in case of sub-standard service delivery or no service delivery.

The Department of Administrative Reforms and Public Grievances (DARPG) of the Government of India was the key department that developed the Citizen's Charter as a fully functional document. The detailed guidelines and prescriptions were communicated to the various government departments. Every department and agency had to constitute a task force comprising citizen users, senior officials and implementing staff. The charter has to comprise:

1. Vision and mission statements
2. Details of services provided by the department
3. Details of service users/clients
4. User group-wise service details, and the details of the grievance redressal mechanism
5. Expectations of service users/clients.

The Citizen's Charter was meant for the citizens, and the government was urged to frame it in very simple language so that all citizens could understand it easily. A help desk was provided to guide the uneducated users. The charter was intended to be realistic, helpful and free from the rigorous administrative process. It also aimed to provide a conducive environment for its implementation by training the staff, and bridging the gap between public servants and citizens. It was also important to ensure that only eligible citizens are allowed access to public services. The main focus was on defining the standards to determine the quality of service, provided within a given time frame. A robust grievance redressal mechanism was also to be created to ensure accountability in the service delivery system. The Citizen's Charter was to be displayed on the office walls, and advertisements were create to inform the people and disseminate the idea.

The general structure of the Citizen's Charter should comprise of a brief statement related to the services provided by a department. It should also address the interface between service providers and service users, in terms of a window, a desk, or other amenities. The Charter must include information on the relevant person who will deliver a particular service, as well as its provisions to ensure an informed citizenry. There is also provision for appeal to a higher authority in case of non-delivery of a service, with all the requisite information such as name, contact details and location of the authorised officer. The government should seek the help of citizens to improve the Charter further. Each ministry, department or public-sector undertaking proposes their Citizen's Charter, and a nodal officer is designated to take care of the overall functioning. The nodal officer should be selected only after careful assessment. S/he must be empathetic and emotionally intelligent.

A task force responsible for the formulation of a Citizen's Charter should include the valuable suggestions of stakeholders. The charter should be implemented along with an awareness campaign, spread through all possible means of communication. The success of any charter lies in the attitude of the public officers responsible for service delivery. A training programme should be organised to motivate the implementing officers, and bring about a change in their attitudes where necessary. The performance of the Citizen's Charter should be regularly monitored through a robust integrated mechanism. The performance analysis should be released in the public domain, in the form of a quarterly or an annual report. Regular performance evaluations should also be conducted within organisations by the higher authorities, and in this regard, self-evaluation by the implementing staff is a good practice. This can be done with the help of surveys and feedback. External evaluation, in terms of social auditing, is also an effective method; here, random samples of service users from different locations are surveyed.

A good Citizen's Charter must possess an effective complaint handling mechanism. User complaints are one of the most reliable indicators to identify and address shortcomings. It can be used through Total Quality Management (TQM) to enhance the quality of service delivery. Effective complaint handling should include the possibility of acknowledgement on an IT-enabled platform. The complaint should be recorded and distributed to the concerned officers for redressal. A clearly defined time frame should accompany each stage, and progress should be reported back to the complainant at every stage. Redressal options may include an apology or explanation, with immediate action. It can also include delay compensation to the beneficiary by the service provider for not ensuring service within the prescribed time frame. A grievance redressal mechanism cannot succeed without the cooperation of public servants. In this regard, Janelle Barlow and Claus Moller devised eight steps in a fundamental method, called the Gift Formula. This considers the complaint a gift, as it will help to understand consumer behaviour in response to the government programme. The Gift Formula has proven effective:

1. Say 'Thank you'.
2. Explain why you appreciate the feedback.
3. Apologise for the mistake.
4. Promise to do something about the problem immediately. Take responsibility.
5. Ask for necessary information.
6. Correct the mistake promptly.
7. Check customer satisfaction.
8. Prevent future mistakes.

Dos and Don'ts for Implementing the Charter

Do

1. Make haste, slowly.
2. List areas of interface (where citizens come to public offices to avail of the public services).
3. Phase out areas for the introduction of small steps (remove unnecessary formalities to bring in efficiency in the system with respect to timely and fast delivery of services).
4. Involve customers and staff in formulating and implementing them (feedback from service users and service givers should be incorporated while preparing a charter).
5. Prepare a Master Plan for formulation and implementation over five years and budget for the period. (A plan should be prepared according to the budgetary provision in the schemes related to service delivery. Availability of manpower and funds will determine how much and how fast services can be offered to eligible citizens).
6. Win consumer confidence with small, highly visible measures (take measures which are not very expensive but easy to incorporate, and which are effective in service delivery and bolster customers' trust).
7. Be responsive to the need for charters to be evolving in nature (the framework of service delivery should be flexible so that innovations can be easily incorporated. The Charter should be futuristic and free from rigidity, and it should be updated in response to the new requirements).
8. Inform the customers of the proposed commitments (the customer should be fully aware of the number of services and their quality in terms of the time limit given by the concerned public office).
9. Use simple language (The language of the Charter should be simple and in the language of the customers of the services, for instance, Hindi and regional languages).
10. Train the staff (staff involved in service delivery must be trained in their job and

training should be imparted to sensitise them).
11. Delegate power (power should be delegated to the lower echelons so that effective and time-bound service may be provided).
12. Set up systems for feedback and independent scrutiny (citizen feedback and third-party performance evaluation should be done periodically, and the feedback incorporated in the service delivery mechanism).

Do Not

1. Do not only make haste (quality of service delivery must not be compromised in pressure to ensure timely delivery).
2. Do not be unrealistic (the provisions related to the standard of service delivery must not be too high).
3. Do not take on more than you can commit (targets should be within budgetary allocations and availability of human resources).
4. Do not involve only senior officers in their formulation and implementation (the lower echelon, who will mostly be involved in service delivery, should be part of the Charter formulation, because their inputs are crucial).
5. Do not rush into an overall package for the whole Ministry/Department/Organisation (the Charter should be need-based. A general Charter for all offices of a Ministry/Department/Organisation will not work).
6. Do not promise more than you can deliver.
7. Do not look upon it as a one-time exercise, with a final outcome.
8. Do not inform customers unless you are sure of delivering the service.
9. Do not leave yourself out (every person involved in the formulation of the Charter should ensure her/his role in the service delivery mechanism under the implementing charter).
10. Do not centralise.
11. Do not continue blindly without periodic assessments of performance.

Citizens have great expectations from the government when it comes to service delivery. They seek the following characteristics in the public office with respect to the delivery of public services:

1. **Reliability**. The public office should consistently provide high-quality services that adhere to the desired standards. The performance of a public office should not be seen as declining or fluctuating when it comes to delivering results.
2. **Responsiveness**. Customers should always be responded to. If any customer raises a grievance, the public office should take note and act accordingly.
3. **Credibility**. The public office should be sensitive about the customer's interest. The customer should feel that the promised service will be delivered in a time-bound manner. In case of any technical error, the public office should proactively help to address the discrepancies.
4. **Empathy**. Attention needs to be paid to the customer's needs.
5. **Courtesy and care**. Public service officers should always demonstrate a willingness to serve, as per the promised charter.

There are six important principles of the Citizen's Charter:

1. Published standards
2. Openness and information
3. Choice and consultation
4. Courtesy and helpfulness
5. Redressal when things go wrong
6. Value for money

Figure 19.1: A sample format for a Citizen's Charter

1. The Aim/purpose of this charter is to work for better quality in public service
2. (Enumeration of services delivered by the department) We deliver the following services:-
   a)   b)   c)   d)
3. Our aim is to achieve the following service delivery/quality parameters

   Name of Service   Service Delivery Standard   Remarks
   Time limit (days/hours/minutes)
   a)
   b)
   c)
4. Availability of Information: Information on the following subjects can be obtained from our officers listed below:

   1. Information   2. Name of the   3. Designation   4. Located at   5. Telephone/
      relating to   officer   Fax/e-mail
   a.
   b.
   c.
5. For information outside Office hours, please contact

   Availability of prescribed forms

   Title of the Form   Fee to be paid   Whom to contact
   a)
   b)
   c)

   Forms are also available on the worldwide web .... (where applicable) and can be downloaded at..

6. Complaint redressal systems

   Courteous and helpful service will be extended by all the staff. If you have any complaints to make with respect to the delivery of the above standards you are welcome to register your complaints with the following officers

   Name   Designation   Located at   Telephone/Fax/e-mail
   a)
   b)
   c)

   We have also created a website for registering complaints at www .... You are welcome to use this facility.
7. A centralised customer care centre/grievance redressal centre has also been established at _____ where you can lodge your complaint.
8. All complaints will be acknowledged by us within _____ days and final reply on the action taken will be communicated within _____ days.

(Contd.)

Figure 19.1: (*Contd.*)

   9. Consultation with our users/stakeholders
      - We welcome suggestions from our users.
      - We conduct _____ polls.
      - We hold perodical _____ meetings with users/user representatives and if you wish to be associated with this please contact _____ at _____.
      - Please also enter your details at our website www......... indicating your willingness to be available for consultation, survey on the points enlisted in the Charter.
   10. We seek your co-operation on the following:

      Citizen's Charter is a joint effort between us and you to improve the quality of service provided by us and we request you to help us in the following way (give details relevant to the departments concerned)

      a)

      b)
   11. Guide Book/Hand Book/Consumer Helpline

      We have published a Handbook for the guidance of our customers. Please contact _____ Officer for more details.

      Our helpline number is _____

      Our customer information centre is located at _____ Phone No. _____

      Other information

      a)

      b)

      We are committed to constantly revise and improve the services being offered under the Charter.

      LET US JOIN HANDS IN MAKING THIS CHARTER A SUCCESS!

What Makes a Good Charter?

A good charter should contain the following elements:

1. Emphasis on customer needs
2. Simple language
3. Service standards
4. Effective remedial measures (Grievance Redressal)
5. Training of the staff
6. Delegation of power
7. Effective feedback mechanism
8. Close monitoring
9. Periodic review

UTILISATION OF PUBLIC FUNDS

Public funds belong to the citizens of the country. The prevailing idea is that public funds are the tax payers' money, which should come back to the citizens in the form of social welfare. In other words, the dues created in this process should be cleared in the form of public welfare. Public funds should be used exclusively in the public interest, directly or indirectly. The public servant must keep some principles in mind while utilising these funds. These principles are popularly known as 'canons of financial propriety', and every officer about to spend from public funds should follow, and teach others to follow, the strict economy.

The important principles or canons pertaining to the utilisation of public funds are:

1. Every officer should utilise public money prudently and carefully.
2. The expenditure should not disproportionately exceed the demands.
3. The officer should not use public funds to her/his advantage, either directly or indirectly.
4. The expenditure of public funds should not be targeted towards a particular group or an individual, unless duly stipulated as such under the court of law or a government programme.
5. The expenditure should not provide any pecuniary benefit to the recipients; rather, it should be motivated. This is necessary as it has the approval of the legitimate authority and is required to cater to public services.

Public funds should be utilised with the utmost transparency, fairness and zero arbitrariness. The process should follow the norms of efficiency, economy, effectiveness and accountability in the system.

Economy, Efficiency and Effectiveness

The government uses public money to provide public services in order to achieve equitable growth and social justice. It tries to pre-empt the accumulation of wealth in a few hands by imposing taxes, duties, fees, etc., and then distributing the benefits to the public at large. The latter is the most important stage of the whole process; however, the most crucial stage is the execution of such plans on the field, when the output is extracted from the given inputs. These inputs are called allocations, and they comprise human resources, assets, natural resources and public money. The outputs comprise services catered, infrastructure built, and sometimes profit, in terms of surplus.

Economy: The government plans a budget, in accordance to which all expenditure takes place. This budget takes the form of a large corpus of funds that tentatively forecasts the expenditures to be incurred from the public purse. The economy pertains to the reasonable spending of public money in order to procure the best human resources and the finest tangible and intangible assets, ensuring transparency in the whole process. The first component in this definition relates to reasonableness, and the second to transparency. Reasonableness pertains to justified spending under the best available minimum prices, while transparency is explained as following due process and norms in drawing and disbursing the money allotted in the budget. The economy utilises 100 per cent of the budget allotted to that particular head to achieve the objectives of the programme. Initiatives like GEM (Government e-Marketplace) and e-tendering are commendable steps in the public sector.

Efficiency: In mathematical terms, efficiency in government programmes is explained as the ratio of the output achieved and input placed. Thus, efficiency is about realising the value of money in ensuring the best utilisation of all types of inputs. It is not easy to measure inputs and outputs quantitatively. Mere financial allocation is not the sole factor in input; the other factors are:

1. Technical efficiency in terms of the technology used in the process.
2. Scale efficiency pertaining to the scale of activity.
3. Environmental costs while using the natural resources and their after effects.
4. Psychological costs involved in the failure to develop.

Efficiency can be achieved using state-of-the-art technology in the field of administration. At present, the use of information technology (IT) has brought about a revolution, but in India, a long distance is yet to be traversed to harness the maximum potential of IT. Although the use of electronic fund management system (EFMS) for fund transfer, digital signature certificate, and verification through JAM number are the methods being used, lower political willingness to bring all administrative affairs under e-office is a matter of concern. The implementation of e-office in its entirety could reduce the operation time in filing, approval, clearance and fund utilisation to a great extent. Besides, the output measurement is also becoming more accurate, using technology such as geo-tagging, Point of Sale (POS) and biometric verification.

With the help of technology, the overall gestation period of programme implementation can be reduced. Scale efficiency is explained in terms of the growth of output relative to the rate of the growth of resources.

Effectiveness: This describes impact in terms of benefits, with respect to the expenditure of public funds over a period of time. For instance, a metro train service is provided, with the intended occupancy rate set to increase by 50 per cent. If this growth remains at 50 per cent, it will be considered to be 100 per cent effective. However, other factors should also be taken into consideration while assessing the effectiveness:

1. Equal distribution of benefits among all groups in a society.
2. Benefits received by the actual intended beneficiaries.
3. Level of citizen's satisfaction.
4. Achievement of economic development objectives.

The first three can be analysed from citizen report cards, such as social auditing, and the performance audit of the Comptroller and Auditor General (CAG). This can also be gauged from households surveys. The fourth can be measured from the economic survey report of micro-enterprises and industrial sectors. For instance, various studies mention the effectiveness of MGNREGS during the world economic crisis, suggesting that India withstood the impact on its labour markets by virtue of pumping money into rural areas under MGNREGS, which promoted demand and consumption in the domestic market. The regular demand for cement, iron-steel, and labour sustained the Indian domestic economy during the world economic slump.

PROBITY IN GOVERNANCE AND CHALLENGES OF CORRUPTION

Probity is understood as utmost honesty, decency and the strict pursuit of ethical life. With respect to governance, probity aims to bring about a corruption-free attitude in government functioning. Public servants are the trustees of citizen's interests, and therefore probity in governance is inevitable for an efficient and effective system of governance. In India, unfortunately, there is an alarmingly high integrity deficit among public servants.

Corruption is the misappropriation of public resources or authority for personal benefit. Opportunities for corruption in public life increase if there are loopholes in the system, and in the absence of a robust vigilance mechanism. However, despite sufficient provisions for vigilance, corruption in India is rampant, and bureaucrats and politicians shamelessly ask for bribes. This is due to the complete absence of a value system and the lure of wealth, no matter what the means adopted. India's rating in the Corruption Perception Index of Transparency International is very low.

There are a number of extant laws to tackle cases of corruption, but the rate of corruption remains high. The provisions of such laws focus on registering cases of corruption rather than on presenting preventive solutions. Most corruption cases are registered against the lower-level bureaucrats. Officers at the higher echelons and ministers always manage to escape these laws. Western countries like Italy, the UK, and even the USA and Japan also face the menace of corruption. But its impact is more devastating in South Asian countries, where the flow of corruption is top-down as well as bottom-up. At the higher levels, corruption takes place in policymaking, development strategy and the distribution of natural resources to the private sector. Such corruption percolates downwards to the bureaucrats at the ground level. On the other hand, the bottom-up flow takes place with the connivance of politicians and bureaucrats. Public money is extracted by wrongful means at various levels, and it flows up to the top level. For instance, corruption in transfers and postings, contributions for political activities, exploitation of contractors engaged in large development projects, etc., are some areas where corruption is rampant.

Money acquired through corrupt means in South Asia, unlike in other regions, is not invested in the nation's economy; instead, it is smuggled to other nations that serve as safe havens and used to finance private projects. Corruption in India is considered essential practice, so much so that those who choose to not participate face adverse consequences. Corrupt bureaucrats and politicians are rewarded with promotions and good postings because they have the power to purchase authority, and this power is further increased with every new posting. The rate of prosecution and seizing of properties of corrupt bureaucrats and politicians is abysmally low. In contrast, lower-level corruption is prosecuted to a greater extent, to demonstrate commitment to checking corruption. In India and South Asia, most victims of corruption are poor people, while in other parts of the world the victims are largely well-off. The impact of corruption is especially high in India, where people have very low per capita income.

There are two dimensions of corruption: exploitative and collusive. Exploitative corruption takes place where public servants extract money from helpless citizens. In collusive corruption, citizens corrupt the government machinery by offering bribes in lieu of financial benefits with the help of the government. Collusive corruption relies heavily on black money.

India often fails to attract major international investments or world-level production opportunities. The main reason behind this is the heavy top-down corruption; even if clearance from the state is forthcoming, local bureaucrats and politicians can stop operations unless provided with the proper inducement. Any power shuffle in the government gives rise to fresh demands (Fourth Report, Second ARC).

Corruption is the most worrying subject in the field of public administration. This is hardly a new problem; in ancient times, corruption was carefully studied by philosophers like Plato (*The Republic*), Aristotle (*Politics*), Machiavelli (*The Prince* and *Discourses on Livy*) in the West, and by Kautilya in India during the Mauryan period. They focused on the conduct of the governing class, and the risk of their deviating from the common good towards self-interest. The ruling class was subject too higher standards of virtue than the common citizens, because the former will have been prone to corruption of different types. At that time, corruption was principally associated with the political machinery, but in modern times, it has emerged as more complex in nature, and is related to all sectors.

According to the most popular definition, 'corruption is the abuse of power by a public official for private gain'. Corruption is the by-product of the corrosion of ethical values in government, and is the greatest evil hindering the economic and social development of any nation. This downfall in moral standards is due to the skewed belief of public officials that government resources are to be utilised as per their whims and fancies. In 2003, the UN adopted a resolution known as the United Nations Convention Against Corruption, which aims:

1. To promote and strengthen measures to prevent and combat corruption more efficiently;
2. To promote, facilitate and support international cooperation and technical assistance in the prevention of and fight against corruption, including asset recovery.

3. To promote integrity, accountability and proper management of public affairs and public property.

The level of corruption in India can be seen in the Corruption Perception Index reported by Transparency International every year. According to the reports of the Central Vigilance Commission (CVC), it received 3,133 cases of corruption and tendered its advice in 3,162 cases in 2018. The commission tendered first-stage advice in 1,889 cases during 2018. The CBI reported 163 cases after investigation and 1,726 cases were reported by the concerned Central Vigilance Officers or CVOs after their investigation. The commission tendered first-stage advice for criminal proceedings in 42 cases related to CBI investigations and seven cases related to CVO investigations. In other cases, major and minor penalties were advised, including closure in 163 cases investigated by the CBI and 1,726 cases investigated by the CVOs.

In accordance with the Commission's advice in 2018, competent authorities in various organisations sanctioned prosecution against 108 public servants, and imposed major penalties against 1,100 others. The major source of information with respect to misconduct is complaints received through written letters and through those sent online or through the toll-free number provided. Unfortunately, many of the complaints received are frivolous and non-specific, with procedural lapses, and therefore out of the purview of commissions.

A number of complaints are also anonymous and intended to harass individuals. Such anonymous complaints are not entertained by the commission. In 2018, a total of 33,645 complaints were received, out of which 2,922 were anonymous or pseudonymous.

The India Corruption Survey 2019, conducted by Local Circles and Transparency International India, received the responses of 190,000 citizens from 248 districts. It stated that 51 per cent citizens admitted to paying bribes in the past 12 months, although bribery in India had reduced by 10 per cent over the past one year. Twenty-four per cent citizens admitted to giving bribes several times and 27 per cent admitted to paying bribes once or twice in the past year. Cash remains the major mode of paying bribes. Bribes are taken in offices, despite the functional CCTV systems in place. Although there are stringent rules related to cases of bribery, they are often one-sided. The police and investigation agencies are not allowed to initiate investigations against a public servant without the official permission of the competent authority.

MEASURES FOR CURBING CORRUPTION AND ENSURING PROBITY IN GOVERNANCE

A slew of measures have been taken periodically by the Indian government, but these have not been implemented in either letter or spirit. We will discuss some of the important ones, and some measures which need to be taken to ensure probity in governance:

1. Benami Transactions (Prohibition) Act, 1988
2. Misfeasance in public office
3. Confiscation of illegally accumulated assets
4. Public Interest Disclosure Act
5. Freedom of Information Act
6. Lokpal
7. Central Vigilance Commission
8. Civil Services Board
9. Ethics in Government Act
10. Overhauling of Criminal Justice System
11. Prevention of Corruption Act, 1988

Benami Transactions (Prohibition) Act, 1988

The expression 'benami transaction' is defined as 'any transaction in which property is transferred to one person for a consideration paid or provided by another person'. This definition does not segregate *bona fide* from *mala fide* transactions. All properties held as *benami* shall be subject to confiscation by the authority conferred with such power legitimately.

A separate and comprehensive law related to public servants should be appended to this Act, with provisions that stipulate the manner in which the family members and close relatives of a public servant can hold properties. If any such person is suspected of being a *benamidar*, then the burden of proof should lie on that property holder. Besides, the transfer of property to a serving or retired public servant must be through registered instruments with proper scrutiny as per the terms of the Act. Such amendments are required to be appended to the Transfer of Property Act 1882 and the Registration Act 1908.

The Prevention of Corruption Act 1988 and the Indian Penal Code should have more provisions to deal with cases of benami transactions in connection with public servants. Whenever a public servant is found guilty under the scrutiny related to benamidari, her/his assets thus acquired should be confiscated under the Act framed thereunder.

Misfeasance of Authority in Public Offices

Misfeasance in public office is rampant in India. Political executives (ministers) as well as bureaucrats indulge in such activities, taking advantage of their discretionary power. The Supreme Court of India has held that in the matter of the grant of largesse, such authorities should act in a transparent and objective manner, and whosoever causes damage to public interest by misfeasance should be held liable for damages. The UK High Court has interpreted such a situation in the following way:

> The tort of misfeasance in public office is related to abuse of authority and to compensate the damage caused to public interest. The tort could be established in two alternative ways:
> 1. When a public officer intentionally causes harm by performing an act that causes injury due to omission of duty to plaintiff, and
> 2. When he performs an act knowing that he has no authority to perform it and which he knows would harm the plaintiff.

The Supreme Court of India has followed many such decisions of the English Court and concluded, 'We are to view that in legal position, exemplary damage can be awarded in a case where the action of a public servant is oppressive, arbitrary or unconstitutional.' The related decisions of the Supreme Court clearly dictate the position of the law: that howsoever high a person may be, the law is above him.

Public Interest Disclosure Act

In India, the Whistle Blower Protection Act, 2011 is a public interest disclosure Act in which a person may lay information pertaining to any misconduct or malpractice in public office in front of an appropriate public authority. Such an informer should be given the necessary protection against retribution. It is equally essential to ensure that whistle-blowing is not abused by ill-intentioned employees for personal gain. As it happens in public offices, the co-workers lodge false complaints against their competitors, in order to improve their chances of promotion to the limited higher posts. This is done through vindictiveness, or for purposes of retaliation, or to claim rewards in terms of promotions or postings.

Freedom of Information Act

The right to access and disseminate information is a part of the freedom of speech and expression guaranteed by Article 19(a)(1) of the Indian Constitution, subject to reasonable restrictions. Freedom of speech is essential to the growth of an individual. It is important to attain and enhance knowledge. Freedom of speech is a necessary aspect of a democratic system. In a democracy, sovereignty lies with the people. People are the masters and the government is the servant. The Right to Information allows the people to exercise their right and regulate the functions of the government. The press and the media disseminate information; however, their ownership remains in the hands of businessman, and they also remain highly dependent on the government for their survival. On the one hand, they monitor the performance of the government, and on the other, they depend on the government for financial and institutional assistance. Understanding the need for the freedom of speech and expression, some countries have enacted Freedom of Information Acts to facilitate the freedom to receive and impart information. The aim of such Acts is to bring about fair and transparent practices in public offices.

Right to Information (RTI) has brought about a huge change in terms of providing access to government documents. Although RTI is a great instrument to establish transparency in government functioning, some community advocates have turned into RTI activists, hoping to gain undue advantages from public servants by threatening to disclose information pertaining to their offices.

Proactive Vigilance on Corruption

As per the recommendations of the Santhanam Committee, the Government of India established the Central Vigilance Commission (CVC) in 1964. The jurisdiction of the CVC was to be over all public servants of the Central government, PSUs and nationalised banks. The Supreme Court directed the Government of India to provide statutory status to the CVC for the supervision of the CBI as well as the Enforcement Directorate (ED) in the case of *Vineet Narain vs. Union of India 1997*. Now the CVC has been given wider powers, including supervising the CBI and ED. However, while it has vast powers in cases related to corruption, it is only advisory in nature. The recommendations of the Chief Vigilance Officer to the Head of the Department are not binding.

Vigilance and CBI prepare two lists related to corruption cases to identify officers who should not be assigned to sensitive postings. These are the Agreed List and List of Doubtful Integrity. The former is a list of gazetted officers against whom there have been complaints, doubts and suspicion regarding their honesty and integrity. This list is prepared in consultation with the department.

Another list, called 'the list of public servants of gazetted status of doubtful integrity', includes the names of those officers who, after enquiry or during the course of enquiry, have been found to be lacking in integrity. The following actions can be taken against the listed officers:

1. Withholding the certificate of integrity.
2. Transfer from a sensitive post.
3. Non-promotion to a service, grade or post to which s/he is eligible for promotion.
4. Compulsory retirement in the public interest.
5. Refusal to extend service or re-employment, neither in the government nor in the PSU.
6. Non-sponsoring of names for foreign assignments/deputation.
7. Refusal of permission for commercial re-employment after retirement.

Civil Services Board

Frequent shuffling or transfer of public servants is detrimental to good governance. Public servants cannot ensure efficiency or effectiveness without an assurance of fixed tenure. The Supreme Court decided a Public Interest Litigation (PIL), and gave a path-breaking judgment on 31 October 2013, in which it directed the Centre to ensure fixed tenure for bureaucrats. The Supreme Court had asked the Centre to set up boards for deciding transfers, postings and disciplinary action for civil servants within a period of three months until Parliament came up with a proper law for the creation of the Civil Services Board. Various states have still not created this Board, while some which have are not working in accordance with the law. There is no assurance of tenure to bureaucrats. Transfers are done on the whims of politicians, and this practice is corroding the institution of civil service.

Lokpal

The Lokpal is a measure to ensure probity in governance. The Administrative Reforms

Commission (ARC) recommended *inter alia* the setting up of Lokpal in 1966. Following this recommendation, a Bill was introduced in the fourth Lok Sabha, but has not been passed so far in spite of various efforts. This Bill, meant to establish an anti-corruption body, was put forward as many as eight times. In its present form, it goes under the name of the Lokpal and Lokayuktas Act, 2013, after being passed in both Houses of Parliament.

The Act allows the setting up of an anti-corruption ombudsman called the Lokpal at the Centre and Lokayukta at the state level. Lokpal covers all categories of public servants, including the prime minister, but excluding the Armed Forces. The Act also incorporates provisions pertaining to the attachment and confiscation of properties gained disproportionately through corruption, even while the prosecution is underway.

The Lokpal has the power of superintendence and direction over any investigating agency, including the CBI, for cases referred to them. It has the power to summon any public servant if there is a *prima facie* case against such an individual, even before a probe is launched by an investigating agency. There is a provision to institute special courts to conduct trials on cases referred by the Lokpal. The Lokpal can levy fines up to Rs 2 lakh for false, frivolous or vexatious complaints. An investigation must be completed within six months. However, the Lokpal or Lokayukta may allow an extension of a further six months at a time, after being given in writing the reasons why such an extension is needed.

Lokpal and Lokayukta Act, 2013

The predecessor of the Lokpal is the institution of ombudsman in Scandinavian countries (Sweden, Denmark and Norway). Dr L. M. Singhvi coined the terms 'Lokpal' and 'Lokayukta' in 1963. The first and second ARCs both recommended the constitution of the Lokpal Act in India to check the menace of corruption. A countrywide protest led by India Against Corruption (IAC), a civil society movement headed by activist Anna Hazare in 2011–12, played a crucial role in the constitution of the Lokpal in India.

Under the provisions of this Act,

1. The Prime Minister, or a Minister in the Union Government, or a member of Parliament, or all categories of public servants as well as Group A, B, C and D officers are covered under the ambit of the Lokpal's jurisdiction.
2. Lokpal has the power to seize the assets, receipt and benefits of any official which are acquired by corrupt means.
3. Lokpal is conferred with the power to recommend the transfer or suspension of civil servants connected with changes of corruption.
4. It has the power of superintendence over and can give directions to the CBI, and also contains several provisions aimed at making the CBI stronger.
5. The inquiry wing of the Lokpal has been authorised with the power of a civil court in certain cases.
6. Lokpal has the authority to grant sanction for prosecution of public servants in place of the government or other competent authority.

Functions of the Lokpal

1. Lokpal keeps a watch over all public officials and can take suitable action against them in case of failure to act in accordance with the law.
2. It can accept any complaints made by a person or can act *suo moto* (on its own motion).
3. It can summon or question any public official if there is a *prima facie* case against the person, even before an inquiry is started by an investigating agency (CVC or CBI).

4. It can provide adequate protection to those who raised their voices against corruption.

The Lokayukta performs similar functions at the state level. All states have their own Lokayukta Acts. The structure of the Lokayukta differs to some extent; it includes ministers and all public servants under its ambit in the state. It has the power to raid the houses and offices of corrupt officials.

Prevention of Corruption Act, 1988

The Prevention of Corruption Act, 1988 defines public duty and public servant as follows:

'Public duty' means a duty in the discharge of which the State, the public or the community at large has an interest;

'Public servant' means—(i) any person in the service or pay of the Government or remunerated by the Government by fees or commission for the performance of any public duty; (ii) any person in the service or pay of a local authority; (iii) any person in the service or pay of a corporation established by or under a Central government.

Offences and Penalties Defined under the Act

1. Offence relating to a public servant being bribed:

    Any public servant who, (a) obtains or accepts or attempts to obtain from any person, an undue advantage, with the intention to perform or cause performance of public duty improperly or dishonestly or to forbear or cause forbearance to perform such duty either by himself or by another public servant; or (b) obtains or accepts or attempts to obtain, an undue advantage from any person as a reward for the improper or dishonest performance of a public duty or for forbearing to perform such duty either by himself or another public servant; or (c) performs or induces another public servant to perform improperly or dishonestly a public duty or to forbear performance of such duty in anticipation of or in consequence of accepting an undue advantage from any person, shall be punishable with imprisonment for a term which shall not be less than three years but which may extend to seven years and shall also be liable to fine.

    Explanation 1: For the purpose of this section, the obtaining, accepting, or the attempting to obtain an undue advantage shall itself constitute an offence even if the performance of a public duty by a public servant, is not or has not been improper.

    Illustration: A public servant, 'S' asks a person, 'P' to give him an amount of five thousand rupees to process his routine ration card application on time. 'S' is guilty of an offence under this section.

    Explanation 2: For the purpose of this section,

    (i) the expressions 'obtains' or 'accepts' or 'attempts to obtain' shall cover cases where a person being a public servant, obtains or 'accepts' or attempts to obtain, any undue advantage for himself or for another person, by abusing his position as a public servant or by using his personal influence over another public servant; or by any other corrupt or illegal means.

    (ii) it shall be immaterial whether such person being a public servant obtains or accepts, or attempts to obtain the undue advantage directly or through a third party.

    Taking undue advantage to influence a public servant by corrupt or illegal means or by exercise of personal influence—whoever accepts or obtains or attempts to obtain from another person for himself or for any other person any undue advantage as a motive or reward to induce a public servant, by corrupt or illegal means or by exercise of his personal influence to perform or to cause performance of a public duty improperly or dishonestly or to forbear or to cause to forbear such public duty by such public servant or by another public servant, shall be punishable with imprisonment for a term which shall not be less than three years but which may extend to seven years and shall also be liable to fine.

2. Offence relating to bribing of a public servant:

   Any person who gives or promises to give an undue advantage to another person or persons, with intention—(i) to induce a public servant to perform improperly a public duty; or (ii) to reward such public servant for the improper performance of public duty, shall be punishable with imprisonment for a term which may extend to seven years or with fine or with both: Provided that the provisions of this section shall not apply where a person is compelled to give such undue advantage: Provided further that the person so compelled shall report the matter to the law enforcement authority or investigating agency within a period of seven days from the date of giving such undue advantage: Provided also that when the offence under this section has been committed by commercial organisation, such commercial organisation shall be punishable with fine.

   Illustration: A person 'P' gives a public servant 'S' an amount of ten thousand rupees to ensure that he is granted a license, over all the other bidders. 'P' is guilty of an offence under this sub-section.

   Explanation: It shall be immaterial whether the person to whom an undue advantage is given or promised to be given is the same person as the person who is to perform, or has performed, the public duty concerned, and, it shall also be immaterial whether such undue advantage is given or promised to be given by the person directly or through a third party.

3. Offence relating to bribing a public servant by a commercial organisation:

   Where an offence under this Act has been committed by a commercial organisation, such organisation shall be punishable with fine, if any person associated with such commercial organisation gives or promises to give any undue advantage to a public servant intending—(i) to obtain or retain business for such commercial organisation; or (ii) to obtain or retain an advantage in the conduct of business for such commercial organisation: Provided that it shall be a defence for the commercial organisation to prove that it had in place adequate procedures in compliance of such guidelines as may be prescribed to prevent persons associated with it from undertaking such conduct.

   Explanation: For the purposes of this section, a person is said to give or promise to give any undue advantage to a public servant, if he is alleged to have committed the offence under section 8, whether or not such person has been prosecuted for such offence.

4. Criminal misconduct by a public servant.

   A public servant is said to commit the offence of criminal misconduct—(i) if he dishonestly or fraudulently misappropriates or otherwise converts for his own use any property entrusted to him or any property under his control as a public servant or allows any other person so to do; or (ii) if he intentionally enriches himself illicitly during the period of his office.

Attachment and Forfeiture of Property

The provisions of the Criminal Law Amendment Ordinance, 1944 shall, as far as may be, apply to the attachment, administration of attached property and execution of order of attachment or confiscation of money or property procured by means of an offence under this Act (Prevention of Corruption Act, 1988 and Prevention of Corruption [Amendment] Act, 2018).

Prevention of Corruption (Amendment) Act, 2018

This amendment revises certain provisions of the original Act as follows:

1. Any public servant who
   (i) obtains or accepts or attempts to obtain from any person, an undue advantage, with the intention to perform or cause performance of public duty improperly or dishonestly or to forbear or cause forbearance to perform such duty either by himself or by another public servant; or
   (ii) obtains or accepts or attempts to obtain, an undue advantage from any person as a reward for the improper or dishonest performance of a public duty or for forbearing to perform such duty either by himself or another public servant; or
   (iii) performs or induces another public servant to perform improperly or dishonestly a public duty or to forbear performance of such duty in anticipation of or in consequence of accepting an undue advantage from any person

   shall be punishable with imprisonment for a term which shall not be less than three years but which may extend to seven years and shall also be liable to fine.

   Explanation: For the purpose of this section, (i) the expressions 'obtains' or 'accepts' or 'attempts to obtain' shall cover cases where a person being a public servant, obtains or 'accepts' or attempts to obtain, any undue advantage for himself or for another person, by abusing his position as a public servant or by using his personal influence over another public servant; or by any other corrupt or illegal means; (ii) it shall be immaterial whether such person being a public servant obtains or accepts, or attempts to obtain the undue advantage directly or through a third party.

2. Whoever accepts or obtains or attempts to obtain from another person for himself or for any other person any undue advantage as a motive or reward to induce a public servant, by corrupt or illegal means or by exercise of his personal influence to perform or to cause performance of a public duty improperly or dishonestly or to forbear or to cause to forbear such public duty by such public servant or by another public servant, shall be punishable with imprisonment for a term which shall not be less than three years but which may extend to seven years and shall also be liable to fine.

3. Any person who gives or promises to give an undue advantage to another person or persons, with intention—
   (i) to induce a public servant to perform improperly a public duty; or
   (ii) to reward such public servant for the improper performance of public duty

   shall be punishable with imprisonment for a term which may extend to seven years or with fine or with both: Provided that the provisions of this section shall not apply where a person is compelled to give such undue advantage: Provided further that the person so compelled shall report the matter to the law enforcement authority or investigating agency within a period of seven days from the date of giving such undue advantage: Provided also that when the offence under this section has been committed by commercial organisation, such commercial organisation shall be punishable with fine.

FOURTH REPORT OF THE SECOND ADMINISTRATIVE REFORMS COMMISSION: ETHICS IN GOVERNANCE

The Preface of the fourth report of the second ARC starts with the famous quote of Mahatma Gandhi; 'As human beings, our greatness lies not so much in being able to remake the world—that is the myth of the atomic age—as in being able to remake ourselves.' The government's role is to bring about prosperity and equity in society. Corruption is not just immoral, but is also an obstacle in the path of the economic growth of a nation aspiring to match the global pace of development. An efficient government, which includes non-expropriation, enforcement of contracts and few bureaucratic hurdles and malpractices, can give a thrust to the economic growth of a nation. The quality of governance is gauged by six vital indicators: voice and accountability; a stable political environment free of violence; effectiveness of the government machinery; mindful and reasonable regulations; rule of law; and an absence of graft. The last two indicators are directly related to ethical governance. Rule of law relates to the treatment of crimes, which broadly comprises of breach of contract, acquiring of disproportionate assets, tax evasion or tax theft, and interfering with free judicial functioning. An absence of graft presupposes a corruption-free government with no scope for bribes, an end of the licensing raj and an honest judiciary.

It is often said that public servants enjoy immunity from penalties due to the constitutional guarantee. The constitutional safeguards given under Article 311 should be reexamined, and a swift and result-oriented administrative jurisprudence is the need of the hour. Provisions to obtain the sanction of a competent authority before starting a prosecution against a public servant also creates hurdles in the way of faster jurisprudence.

> Law should be so succinct that it can be carried in the pocket of the coat and it should be so simple that it can be understood by a peasant.
> —Napoleon Bonaparte

It is difficult to establish a case of corruption against a public servant in a court of law. The menace of corruption has to be handled systemically. Shrinking the regulatory role of the state in favour of greater regulation and privatisation will not serve any purpose. Corruption, which is considered a low-risk, high-return endeavour, needs to be addressed. To do so, examples have to be set by convicting corrupt public servants expeditiously. Society has to be strengthened to become more vigilant about and intolerant of corruption. The Right to Information has aided this to a great extent. Stress should be laid on e-governance and systemic reforms.

> In 2004, Britain's top law enforcement officer and a key member of Tony Blair's Cabinet, David Blunkett, resigned after it came to light that his department had fast-tracked a visa for his former lover's nanny. Blunkett admitted that his actions had led to preferential treatment for a residence visa for a Filipina nanny employed by his former lover, US magazine publisher Kimberly Quinn.
>
> In 1951, the Lok Sabha discovered that Congress MP H. G. Mudgal had taken Rs 1,000 each on two occasions from the Bullion Merchants Association to ask questions suggested by it. Mudgal resigned from what was then only a provisional Lok Sabha to pre-empt an expulsion motion moved against him by Prime Minister Jawaharlal Nehru.

Ethics are standards that society sets for itself and which guide conduct, preferences and actions. The essence of ethical conduct lies in assimilating such standards and acting in accordance with them, making laws to ensure their enforcement and corrective action in case of violation, and quick adjudication. Corruption results from a failure of ethics in society. The word 'corrupt' is derived from the Latin word '*corrumpere*', meaning 'to mar, bribe or destroy'. Corruption is sadly widespread, and anti-corruption measures have not proven very successful. Such measures have even been used as tools to harass political opponents and resistant public servants. Corruption has been accepted by society; in fact, a large section of society even considers it inevitable and everlasting.

> The objective of the government is making it easy for people to do good and hard to do evil.
> —William Ewart Gladstone

There are two approaches to dealing with corruption and the abuse of public office. The first focuses on mission, vision and values (the high road approach) and the second focuses on punishment for deviant public servants (the low road approach). The first approach believes that human beings are fundamentally inclined to pursuing good, while the second believes that human beings are driven by greed to fulfil their self-interest, to the extent that they can even use public money for their own welfare. In reality, both approaches are important. Values are required to provide guidance to society, and these are found in abundance. Everyone in a society understands right from wrong. Without institutional underpinning, values will collapse. Institutions give shape to values and are critical in dealing with public servants (elected and appointed) endowed with enormous authority and discretion. Public offices that control a vast amount of funds offer both temptation and opportunities for private gain at public cost. Therefore, the institutionalisation of ethical enforcement is important to promote exemplary moral conduct among public servants.

CAUSES OF CORRUPTION

Three major factors are responsible for corruption in Indian society. First, a vision of an unchallenged authority and the wielding of power in an arbitrary manner is a colonial legacy. Indian society reveres power, and hence it is easy for public-office holders to misuse their authority. Second, Indian society is heterogeneity in terms of its power-holding. Most citizens still work in the unorganised sector or are unemployed, and hence a government employee emerges as all-powerful. The third is a conscious choice, which emerged in the initial decades after Independence. India chose a set of policies that Inadvertently placed citizens at the mercy of the state in the name of welfare. In the name of regulation, public servants held enormous power as the government has monopoly in every sector. This created a culture that viewed public servants as masters and the citizens as mendicants.

It is generally understood that monopoly and discretion lead to corruption, while competition and transparency diminish it. Another factor that enables increased corruption is over-centralisation. Between the citizen and the final authority stands a large number of functionaries, with poor accountability and the temptation to misuse their authority. We can see that measures like the RTI, effective Citizen's Charters, public services guarantee acts, public consultation in decision-making, and social auditing have curbed corruption to a great extent.

The political system prevailing in a society is the crucial determinant of its integrity. If political system has a provision for rewarding ethical competence, then the society can be sustainably happy; however, social conditions contrary to this attracts corruption and unwarranted behaviour, aimed at the fulfillment of self-interest by abusing authority and corrupt practices.

In India, certain anti-corruption initiatives, like the Right to Information Act, disclosure of assets and criminal antecedents by contestants who file nominations for elections, and annual disclosure of assets by public servants have proved to be strong measures in the fight against corruption. E-governance in public service delivery has succeeded in mitigating incidences of corruption, and whistleblower legislation protects informants against retribution. It is essential to incorporate ethics in business as well, under the title 'ethics in business'. Eventually, a citizen has to imbibe ethics in their behaviour, as this is what will decide all ethics in government.

All forms of corruption should be discouraged. A policy of zero tolerance for corruption is the need of the hour. However, some forms of corruption need to be handled vigorously and demand closer scrutiny. As corruption is a global phenomenon, the UN General Assembly adopted The United Nations Convention against Corruption in October 2003, which works as an international instrument against corruption. The ADB-OECD Anti-Corruption Action Plan is a broad understanding for inter-regional cooperation to abolish corruption, and India is also a signatory to this. The World Bank has also declared that corrupt governments which do not have a tradition of financial propriety will no longer receive funds.

The following aspects determine ethics in governance:

1. Vigilance and Corruption
   - Strengthening proactive vigilance to abolish corruption and providing safeguards to honest public servants are rational methods to restrict executive discretion.
   - Setting aside the systemic reluctance to punish corrupt public servants.
   - Identifying office procedures and rules that promote corruption, and setting up an effective framework by suggesting measures to weaken factors promoting corruption.
2. Improving the relationship between political executives and permanent executives.
3. Evolving an effective code of conduct for all organs of government.

ETHICAL FRAMEWORK

Before discussing an ethical framework for democratic governance, we need to establish ethical values in politics. It will be impractical to think about an ethical framework for a political system in an unethical environment. Finally, the responsibility lies with politicians, and India has a legacy of political values set by the leaders during the freedom struggle. It is our misfortune that those values were eroded soon after independence and the transfer of power. Excesses displayed during elections, in terms of campaign funding, booth capturing, criminalisation of politics, floor-crossing after elections to seize power, and the abuse of public office have destroyed the value system of Indian politics. The Election Commission and Supreme Court have actively tried to reduce such practices.

> **Election and Other Related Laws (Amendment) Act, 2003**
>
> 1. Full tax exemption to individual and corporate on all contribution to political parties.
> 2. Expenditure by third parties and political parties are brought under ceiling limits, and only travel expenditure of leader of parties is exempted.
> 3. Disclosure of party finances and contribution over Rs 20,000.
> 4. Equitable sharing of time by the recognised political parties on all electronic media (public and private).

The second ARC recommended the partial funding of elections by the state in order to discourage illegitimate and excessive expenditure during elections. The Commission recommended that the President/Governor should decide the issue of disqualification of members on grounds of defection on the advice of the Election

Commission. It also recommended that Section 8 of the Representation of People Act, 1951 should be amended, to ensure that persons facing criminal charges of a grave nature may be disqualified.

In the appointment of the Chief Election Commissioner and Election Commissioners, a collegiums headed by the Prime Minister and comprising the Lok Sabha Speaker, the Leader of the Opposition in the Lok Sabha, Law Minister and Deputy Chairman of the Rajya Sabha should recommend the names for consideration to the President. A special Election Tribunal should be formed at the regional level for speedy disposal of election petitions.

Reasons for Unethical Conduct in Politics

The **involvement of criminals in the electoral process** is one of the evils of the Indian political system. The root cause of increasing crime and violence in society are the large economic disparity, corruption in the public delivery system, protection of criminals by politicians, interference in the investigation of crimes and low prosecution rate, a lengthy judicial process which leads to a delay in punishment, mass withdrawal of cases and indiscriminate granting of parole.

The **enormous expenditure in elections** is another cause of corruption. Although there are formal limits to expenditure in elections, in reality this limit is not followed and political parties indulge in illegal and illegitimate expenditure. When these candidates come to power in the government, they take recourse to corruption to recover this expenditure.

However, there have been recent improvements.

1. Improvement in the accuracy of the Electoral Roll. The Election Commission has tried to make voter registration and revision of Electoral Rolls easier. Voters can easily obtain printed Electoral Rolls and CDs, which are made available for sale. The Electoral Rolls are computerised and photo-identity cards are provided for all voters.
2. Disclosure of the antecedents of candidates. The Supreme Court has directed that while filing a nomination, a candidate has to disclose any conviction by a court or pending criminal case. Similarly, a candidate has to declare her/his assets and liabilities, which would be further checked at the next election.
3. Disqualification of persons convicted of criminal offence. The Supreme Court ruled in 2005 that Section 8(4) of the Representation of People Act was unconstitutional as it violated equality before law. Now, all candidates who are convicted for any criminal offence are on the same footing, regardless of whether they are incumbent legislators. However, if such a candidate is enjoying the term of a legislator and has appealed and sought a stay of their sentence, they will be exempted from disqualification.
4. Enforcement of code of conduct. The Election Commission has provided for a code of conduct under Article 324 of the Constitution. This comprises provisions related to the conduct of candidates, political parties and civil servants during the election process. It provides directions related to the timing of campaigns, insistence on daily expenditure statements, appointment of observers, ordering re-polling in specific polling booths, etc.
5. Free and fearless polling.
6. Reduction in size of the Council of ministers.

The First Administrative Reforms Commission recommended restricting the size of the Council of Ministers to 10 per cent. The Ninety-first Constitutional Amendment Act, 2003 restricts this size to 15 per cent of the strength of the Lower House in Parliament/State legislatures.

The amendment is a step towards moderating the number of ministers.

Ethics in Public Life

Ethics is based on responsibility and accountability. A relation akin to trusteeship exists between public office-holders and citizens. Public functionaries are trustees of the citizens and are endowed with powers to work in the best interest of the people. An ideal framework of ethical behaviour should include:

1. Ethical codes
2. Disclosure of conflict of interest between public interest and self-interest of public functionaries
3. An enforcement mechanism to implement these ethical codes
4. Rules and regulations for qualifying and disqualifying a public office-holder.

RECOMMENDATIONS RELATED TO ETHICAL FRAMEWORK FOR MINISTERS

1. There should be a separate code of ethics to guide ministers to uphold the highest standards of the Constitution and of ethical conduct.
2. A separate unit to monitor the observance of the code of ethics and of conduct should be set up in the offices of the PM and CMs. This unit should also accept public complaints related to all violations of such codes.
3. The PM or CM should be made liable to act according to such observations.
4. A comprehensive annual report, including instances of violation, should be prepared by the unit. This report should be submitted to the legislature and placed in the public domain.
5. The code of ethics should comprise broad principles governing the minister–civil servant relationship.

ETHICAL FRAMEWORK FOR LEGISLATURES

Legislature is the most important pillar of the democratic structure as it carries the expression of the will of the citizens, and the Executive is accountable to it. This relationship compels the creation of ethical standards. Chapter XXIV of the Rules of Procedure and Conduct of Business in the Council of States makes provisions for establishing a Committee on Ethics in the Rajya Sabha. This committee was first formed on 4 March 1997 by the Chairman of the Rajya Sabha, and monitors the ethical conduct of the members.

Code of Conduct for Members of the Rajya Sabha

1. Members must not act in a way that may cause dispute to the Parliament and decrease their credibility.
2. Members must exploit their position as Members of Parliament to enhance the public interest.
3. Members should resolve all conflict between public interest and self-interest by placing public interests above personal interest.
4. Members should never expect or take financial benefit for a vote given or not given by them on the floor of the House with respect to the functions of the House.
5. Members should not accept any gift that may affect their impartial functioning.
6. Members holding public office should utilise public resources for the wellbeing of the people.
7. Members must not reveal confidential and sensitive information obtained while performing various function in their official capacity.
8. Members should strive to maintain social and religious harmony.
9. Members should maintain high standards of ethics, dignity and values in public life.

> **United Nations Convention against Corruption**
> **(Article 8 of the Resolution 58/4 of 31 October 2003)**
>
> Article 8: Codes of conduct for public officials
> 1. In order to fight corruption, each State Party shall promote, inter alia, integrity, honesty and responsibility among its public officials, in accordance with the fundamental principles of its legal system.
> 2. In particular, each State Party shall endeavour to apply, within its own institutional and legal systems, codes or standards of conduct for the correct, honourable and proper performance of public functions.
> 3. For the purposes of implementing the provisions of this article, each State Party shall, where appropriate and in accordance with the fundamental principles of its legal system, take note of the relevant initiatives of regional, interregional and multilateral organizations, such as the International Code of Conduct for Public Officials contained in the annex to General Assembly resolution 51/59 of 12 December 1996.
> 4. Each State Party shall also consider, in accordance with the fundamental principles of its domestic law, establishing measures and systems to facilitate the reporting by public officials of acts of corruption to appropriate authorities, when such acts come to their notice in the performance of their functions.
> 5. Each State Party shall endeavour, where appropriate and in accordance with the fundamental principles of its domestic law, to establish measures and systems requiring public officials to make declarations to appropriate authorities regarding, inter alia, their outside activities, employment, investments, assets and substantial gifts or benefits from which a conflict of interest may result with respect to their functions as public officials.
> 6. Each State Party shall consider taking, in accordance with the fundamental principles of its domestic law, disciplinary or other measures against public officials who violate the codes or standards established in accordance with this article.

The Committee on Ethics of the Lok Sabha

The Lok Sabha also has a Committee on Ethics to monitor the ethical conduct of Members of the House. There are also various norms given in the Rules of Procedure and Conduct of Business in the Lok Sabha, and other related directions and recommendations of various Parliamentary Committees and Speakers from time to time.

The recommendations of the Committee on Ethics of the Lok Sabha are largely similar to those of the Rajya Sabha:

1. Members must exploit their position as Members of Parliament to enhance the public interest.
2. Members should resolve all conflict between public interest and their self-interest by placing public interests above self-interest.
3. Members should never expect or take any financial benefit for a vote given or not given by them on the floor of the House with respect to functions of the House.
4. Members should not accept any gift which may affect their impartial functioning.
5. Members must not reveal confidential and sensitive information obtained while performing various functions in their official capacity.
6. Members should strive to maintain social and religious harmony.
7. Members should maintain high standards of ethics, dignity and values in public life.

Disclosure of Interest

To avoid any conflict of interest, there is a provision for the disclosure of Members' interest in both Houses. A 'Register of Interests' is maintained, which records the disclosure of all such private interests. The Committee on Ethics of Lok Sabha (13th Lok Sabha) made it mandatory for each Member to disclose her/his income from all sources, assets and liabilities. The Committee on Ethics of Rajya Sabha recommended that the remunerative directorship and regular income through various sources should be registered.

The Fourth Report of the Second ARC recommends:

An Office of 'Ethics Commissioner' may be constituted by each House of the Parliament. This Office, functioning under the Speaker/Chairman, would assist the Committee on Ethics in the discharge of its functions, and advise Members, when required, and maintain necessary records.

In respect of States, the Commission recommends the following:

1. All State legislatures may adopt a Code of Ethics and a Code of Conduct for their Members.
2. Ethics Committees may be constituted with well defined procedures for sanctions in case of transgressions, to ensure the ethical conduct of legislators.
3. 'Registers of Members' Interests' may be maintained with the declaration of interests by Members of the State legislatures.
4. Annual Reports providing details including transgressions may be placed on the Table of the respective Houses.
5. An Office of 'Ethics Commissioner' may be constituted by each House of the State legislatures. This Office would function under the Speaker/Chairman, on the same basis as suggested for Parliament.

The Fourth Report also made recommendations with respect to the office of profit:

1. The Law should be amended to define office of profit based on the following principles:
   (i) All offices in purely advisory bodies where the experience, insights and expertise of a legislator would be inputs in governmental policy, shall not be treated as offices of profit, irrespective of the remuneration and perks associated with such an office.
   (ii) All offices involving executive decision making and control of public funds, including positions on the governing boards of public undertakings and statutory and non-statutory authorities directly deciding policy or managing institutions or authorising or approving expenditure shall be treated as offices of profit, and no legislator shall hold such offices.
   (iii) If a serving Minister, by virtue of office, is a member or head of certain organisations like the Planning Commission, where close coordination and integration between the Council of Ministers and the organisation or authority or committee is vital for the day-to-day functioning of government, it shall not be treated as office of profit.

(The use of discretionary funds at the disposal of legislators, the power to determine specific projects and schemes, or select the beneficiaries or authorise expenditure shall constitute discharge of executive functions and will invite disqualification under Articles 102 and 191, irrespective of whether or not a new office is notified and held.)

2. Schemes such as MPLADS and MLALADS should be abolished.
3. Members of Parliament and Members of State Legislatures should be declared as 'Public Authorities' under the Right to

Information Act, except when they are discharging legislative functions.

CODE OF ETHICS FOR CIVIL SERVANTS

The values motivate a public servant to recognise her/his duty as the welfare of the society. Public service values are not just to be assimilated after entering the civil services. These values and attitudes evolve across time, and across generations. Ethics cannot be imposed; it is rather to be inculcated by the individual over time. Rules related to conduct are given in the Central Civil Services (Conduct) Rules 1964, and analogous rules are applicable in the case of All India Services and for various state governments. Specific acts are regularly notified under the Fundamental Rules and Civil Services Regulations; for instance, rules against practices of habitual lending and indiscriminate borrowing was brought in 1869, the banning of gifts in 1876, against commercial investments in 1885, etc., were prescribed to civil servants. Any breach of these rules entailed disciplinary action, such as removal from service. Provisions against illegal gratification or bribery, under Section 409 of the IPC, are still in existence. The Prevention of Corruption Act has now provided a new set of offences. A draft Public Service Bill prescribes a number of expectations from civil servants, which are given as 'values'. The ARC recommended that 'public service values' be applicable to all government organisations, with any violation attracting punishment. Conflict of interest should be exhaustively mentioned in both the code of ethics and the code of conduct, and serving public servants should not be nominated to the Boards of PSUs.

ETHICAL FRAMEWORK FOR THE JUDICIARY

The Supreme Court of India, in its full court meeting held on 7 May 1997, recommended a set of values known as the 'Restatement of Values of Judicial Life'. This is a charter providing a code of conduct for judges. The important points of this code are as follows:

1. Justice must not merely be done but it must also be seen to be done. The behaviour and conduct of members of the higher judiciary must reaffirm the people's faith in the impartiality of the judiciary. Accordingly, any act of a Judge of the Supreme Court or a High Court, whether in official or personal capacity, which erodes the credibility of this perception has to be avoided.
2. A Judge should not contest the election to any office of a club, society or other association; further s/he shall not hold such elective office except in a society or association connected with the law.
3. Close association with individual members of the Bar, particularly those who practise in the same court, shall be eschewed.
4. A Judge should not permit any member of her/his immediate family, such as spouse, son, daughter, son-in-law or daughter-in-law or any other close relative, if a member of the Bar, to appear before her/him or even be associated in any manner with a cause to be dealt with by him.
5. No member of her/his family, who is a member of the Bar, shall be permitted to use the residence in which the Judge actually resides or other facilities for professional work.
6. A Judge should practise a degree of aloofness consistent with the dignity of his office.
7. A Judge shall not hear and decide a matter in which a member of her/his family, a close relation or a friend is concerned.
8. A Judge shall not enter into public debate or express her/his views in public on political matters or on matters that are pending or are likely to arise for judicial determination.
9. A Judge is expected to let her/his judgments speak for themselves. S/he shall not give interview to the media.
10. A Judge shall not accept gifts or hospitality except from her/his family, close relations and friends.

11. A Judge shall not hear and decide a matter in which a company in which s/he holds shares is concerned unless s/he has disclosed her/his interest and no objection to her/his hearing and deciding the matter is raised.
12. A Judge shall not speculate in shares, stocks or the like.
13. A Judge should not engage directly or indirectly in trade or business, either by herself/himself or in association with any other person. (Publication of a legal treatise or any activity in the nature of a hobby shall not be construed as trade or business).
14. A Judge should not ask for, accept contributions or otherwise actively associate herself/himself with the raising of any fund for any purpose.
15. A Judge should not seek any financial benefit in the form of a perquisite or privilege attached to her/his office unless it is clearly available. Any doubt in this behalf must be got resolved and clarified through the Chief Justice.
16. Every Judge must at all times be conscious that s/he is under the public gaze and there should be no act or omission by her/him which is unbecoming of the high office s/he occupies and the public esteem in which that office is held.

LEGAL FRAMEWORK FOR FIGHTING CORRUPTION

In the pre-Independence period, the main tool with which to fight corruption in public life was the Indian Penal Code (sections 161–65 in the chapter 'Offence by Public Servants'). The Prevention of Corruption Act, 1947 offered some new provisions. This act defined a new offence, 'criminal misconduct in discharge of official duty', the punishment for which was imprisonment for a minimum of one year to a maximum of seven years. A new provision stated that no court shall take cognisance of any offence punishable under Sections 161, 164 and 165 of the IPC without the permission of an authority competent to remove the charged public servant. This was stipulated to prevent the harassment of honest officers. The Prevention of Corruption Act, 1988 consolidates the provisions of the 1947 Act and the Criminal Law Amendment Act, 1950, along with some provisions of the IPC to combat corruption effectively. The salient features of the Act are as follows:

1. This Act defines 'public servant' in a broader sense.
2. It incorporates the concept of 'public duty'.
3. The offences related to corruption have been deleted from the IPC and incorporated within the Act.
4. Provision of trial of such cases by special judges.
5. The case has to be decided soon, with hearings held on a day-to-day basis.
6. Penalties are detailed for various offences.

The Prevention of Corruption Act, 1988 lists offences and penalties related to bribery. The offences include acceptance of illegal gratification, obtaining valuable gifts, criminal misconduct involving misappropriation, possessing disproportionate assets, obtaining financial advantage for oneself or another person in a manner that does not serve the public interest, etc.

The Second ARC recommended that under the Prevention of Corruption Act, the following should be considered offences:

1. Gross perversion of the Constitution and democratic system, which may cause the wilful violation of the oath of office.
2. Misuse of authority to favour or harm someone.
3. Presenting hurdles in the delivering of justice.
4. Wasteful expenditure of public funds.

The offence of bribery may be of two types. The first is *coercive bribery*, where the bribe giver is considered a victim, as s/he is coerced to pay bribes in exchange for a public service. This causes delays, harassment, lost opportunities, loss of wages and mental trauma. The second type is is known as *collusive bribery* where the bribe giver and the bribe taker work together to rob the public money.

As per the recommendations of the second ARC, collusive bribery was incorporated as an offence in the Prevention of Corruption Act. The ARC further recommended that the punishment for collusive bribery should be double that of other cases of bribery.

Constitutional Provisions Regarding Civil Servants in India

Article 309: Recruitment and conditions of service of persons serving the Union or a State

Subject to the provisions of this Constitution, Acts of the appropriate Legislature may regulate the recruitment, and conditions of service of persons appointed, to public services and posts in connection with the affairs of the Union or of any State: Provided that it shall be competent for the President or such person as he may direct in the case of services and posts in connection with the affairs of the Union, and for the Governor of a State or such person as he may direct in the case of services and posts in connection with the affairs of the State, to make rules regulating the recruitment, and the conditions of service of persons appointed, to such services and posts until provision in that behalf is made by or under an Act of the appropriate Legislature under this article, and any rules so made shall have effect subject to the provisions of any such Act.

Article 310 (1): Tenure of office of persons serving the Union or a State

Except as expressly provided by this Constitution, every person who is a member of a defence service or of a civil service of the Union or of an all India service or holds any post connected with defence or any civil post under the Union, holds office during the pleasure of the President, and every person who is a member of a civil service of a State or holds any civil post under a State holds office during the pleasure of the Governor of the State.

Article 311: Dismissal, removal or reduction in rank of persons employed in civil capacities under the Union or a State

1. No person who is a member of a civil service of the Union or an all India service or a civil service of a State or holds a civil post under the Union or a State shall be dismissed or removed by a authority subordinate to that by which he was appointed.
2. No such person as aforesaid shall be dismissed or removed or reduced in rank except after an inquiry in which he has been informed of the charges against him and given a reasonable opportunity of being heard in respect of those charges; Provided that where it is proposed after such inquiry, to impose upon him any such penalty, such penalty may be imposed on the basis of the evidence adduced during such inquiry and it shall not be necessary to give such person any opportunity of making representation on the penalty proposed: Provided further that this clause shall not apply
    (a) where a person is dismissed or removed or reduced in rank on the ground of conduct which has led to his conviction on a criminal charge; or
    (b) where the authority empowered to dismiss or remove a person or to reduce him in rank is satisfied that for some reason, to be recorded by that authority in writing, it is not reasonably practicable to hold such inquiry; or
    (c) where the President or the Governor, as the case may be, is satisfied that in the interest of the security of the State, it is not expedient to hold such inquiry.
3. If, in respect of any such person as aforesaid, a question arises whether it is reasonably practicable to hold such inquiry as is referred to in clause (2), the decision thereon of the authority empowered to dismiss or remove such person or to reduce him in rank shall be final.

The Commission recommended that the Corrupt Public Servants (Forfeiture of Property) Bill, as suggested by the Law Commission, should be enacted without further delay. Steps should be taken for the immediate implementation of the Benami Transactions (Prohibition) Act, 1988. The Commission further recommended that a new law on 'serious economic offences' be enacted. A serious economic offence may be defined as an offence which involves a sum exceeding Rs 100 crore, or which is of widespread public concern, or whose investigation requires highly specialised expertise of the financial market and working of financial institutions or involves large international dimensions, or which seems complex to the Union Government, regulators, banks or any financial institutions.

A Serious Fraud Office (SFO), attached to the Cabinet Secretariat, should be established to investigate and prosecute such offences. Special courts should be constituted to try such cases. The SFO should have experts from diverse sectors, particularly from the financial sector, taxation, company laws and information technology.

The second ARC endorsed the suggestions of the 'National Commission to Review the Working of the Constitution' and recommended that Article 105(2) of the Constitution be amended. Corrupt actions of Members of Parliament should not be protected. There should be similar amendments to Article 194(2) in connection to the state legislatures.

Civil servants in India enjoy protection guaranteed by certain provisions mentioned in Part XIV, Article 311 of the Constitution. The Commission deliberated on arguments in favour of retaining Article 311 as well as those in favour of repealing it. With regard to the former, the Commission stated that the Article offers the 'doctrine of pleasure' in relation to certain safeguards vis-à-vis civil servants. A safeguard in the form of an opportunity to be heard has been given under the fundamental principle of natural justice. If Article 311 is repealed, cases related to service matters will increase in the courts.

With regard to repealing Article 311: on several occasions, the apex court has struck down the decisions of the disciplinary authority or the government, citing the provisions of Article 311. If Article 311 is removed, procedure may not be followed while punishing the accused civil servants. In various decisions, the courts have nailed the disciplinary authorities for procedural lapses based on technical details of cases where procedure had replaced the substance of the cases. The Commission observed that no Constitution of any other country granted its civil servants such immunity. The doctrine of pleasure adopted by the Constitution of India stemmed from the Government of India Act, 1919. There are various steps available to government employees in the event of judicial intervention. Sardar Vallabhbhai Patel had argued that senior civil servants should have a free environment in which to render impartial and frank advice to political executives. However, the compulsion of equal treatment of all public servants, along with different judicial decisions, have made such protection applicable to all government employees, including the employees of PSUs, corporations and parastatal organisations. The rights of a civil servant under the Constitution should not be above the public interest or the contractual right of the state. A public servant is an agent of the state, and it is her/his duty to serve the state.

The Commission finally recommended that Articles 310 and 311 of the Constitution be repealed. Article 309 was to be amended by the addition of necessary provisions to protect the *bona fide* actions of public servants, taken in the public interest. Similar provisions should be included in Article 309 to protect public servants from the arbitrary actions of the government.

Institutional Framework

The Administrative Vigilance Division of the Department of Personnel and Training is the nodal agency for dealing with Vigilance and Anti-Corruption. Its objective is to oversee and offer directions to the government's programme to inculcate discipline and remove corruption from the public services. The other agencies are:

1. The Central Vigilance Commission (CVC)
2. Vigilance units in the Ministries/Departments of the Government of India, Central PSUs and other autonomous organisations
3. The Central Bureau of Investigation (CBI)

The Second ARC recommends:

1. A national ombudsman, 'Rashtriya Lokayukta', should be set up by a constitutional amendment.
2. The Rashtriya Lokayukta should have jurisdiction over all Ministers of the Union (except the Prime Minister), all state Chief Ministers, and MPs. It would have the power to investigate any public servant(s) as well, if the need arises.
3. The Rashtriya Lokayukta should undertake a national campaign to enhance the standards of ethics in governance.
4. The Rashtriya Lokayukta should have a serving judge or a retired judge of the Supreme Court as the Chairperson, an eminent jurist as Member, and the Central Vigilance Commissioner as the ex-officio Member.

The second ARC also recommends the constitution of an ombudsman for a group of districts to investigate cases against the functionaries of local bodies. The State Panchayat Raj Acts and Urban Local Bodies Act should be amended in view of the same.

Social Infrastructure

Citizens' participation can be effectively leveraged to ensure good governance. The voices of citizens may prove an effective measure to expose and prevent the corrupt practices of public functionaries. This idea moots the participation of civil society and the media, and training citizens about the evils of corruption. This adds a new dimension to the accountability of public functionaries to the people.

Civil society groups can educate people and raise their level of awareness in combating corruption. Measures taken in this regard are as follows:

1. Inviting civil societies to monitor government schemes
2. Establishing and ensuring good standards of public services
3. Establishing a robust public complaint mechanism
4. Evaluating public trust in anti-corruption measures (anti-corruption institutions, judiciary, etc.)
5. Enforcing access to information
6. Educating people about corruption and upholding moral behaviour
7. Social auditing
8. Spreading awareness campaigns through mass communication
9. Holding training programmes and seminars to discuss problems
10. Incorporating corruption as a topic in the school curriculum
11. Setting up websites on corruption for greater awareness and association of the public.

Systemic Reforms

Corruption may be reduced by an optimal combination of punitive and preventive measures. In India, the government provides important public services in a monopolistic setting. This monopoly creates the scope for taking undue advantages and indulging in corruption. Corruption can be curbed by creating competition in all possible public services.

Monopoly + Discretion − Accountability = Corruption

The Commission recommends that each Ministry/Department identify the area where the existing monopoly can be interfered with competition. Some centrally sponsored schemes could be reshaped by adding provisions for competition in service delivery. Such provisions for competition should be part of all new national policies that have a greater public interface.

Departmental norms in the form of manuals and codes should be revised and updated periodically. All procedures should be simplified. The principle of 'positive silence' should generally be used selectively, and permissions/licenses should be issued in a time-bound manner.

The Commission encourages the mechanism of 'integrity pacts'. A task force may be constituted, with representatives from Ministers of Law and Personnel, to identify the transactions requiring such pacts and the related protocols to establish such pacts.

The government machinery runs on a hierarchical structure. Supervision provides an effective check on the discretion of public servants. Each officer in a supervisory role should carefully oversee all activities in the organisation/office. All major instances of loss to the public exchequer must be inquired into, and the responsibility of the erring officer should be fixed in a time-bound manner.

There should be a column in the Annual Performance Appraisal Report (APAR), indicating the measures a civil servant has taken to curb corruption in the office, and among her/his subordinates. The reporting officer should then give her/his comments on this. Supervisory officers who give 'clean certificates' to subordinate corrupt officers in their APAR should be called to account, in the event that the subordinate is charged with an offence under the Prevention of Corruption Act. Besides, their reports should also reflect their negligence, and the fact that they have failed to comment upon the lack of integrity in the charged subordinates.

All Ministries and Departments should openly adopt the principle of 'first in, first out' and 'single window' for the provision of services to citizens. The Commission recommends that all government organisations carry out a risk profile of jobs in a systematic and institutionalised manner. Risk profiling of officers who have completed 10 years of service should be done, based on their APAR, reports from the vigilance organisation and peer reviews by a 'committee of eminent persons'.

If an audit team detects or suspects major irregularities, the government should take note of it. Proactive vigilance measures should be taken by the head of the office. In this regard, the following tools have been evolved:

1. A 'List of Officers of Doubtful Integrity' is maintained by the organisations/departments that have the names of those against whom disciplinary action is either pending, or who are have been penalised on a vigilance related matter.
2. An 'Agreed List' of suspected officers is prepared by the Chief Vigilance Officer of the organisation and the CBI. These officers are kept under watch.
3. A list of undesirable contact persons (middlemen, touts, etc.) who deal with sensitive organisations should be prepared by the CBI.
4. It is mandatory to furnish the annual property return as on 31 December on 1 January.
5. Vigilance clearance is obtained from the CVC for appointments at the board level in PSUs and PSBs. Additionally, the Government of India has established procedures for vigilance clearance before appointing any officer.

PROTECTING THE HONEST CIVIL SERVANTS

Vigilance activity ought to increase the efficiency and effectiveness of the organisation. Risk-taking should be incorporated in government functioning, and pecuniary or non-pecuniary losses should not attract vigilance enquiry. One criterion to test whether the action was a *bona fide* mistake or an *mala fide* one is to ask: Would a prudent person working under similar circumstances and the same rules and regulations have taken the same decision in the organisational interest? The CVC has recognised the possibility of genuine commercial decisions going wrong, without any ill-intention being attached to such decisions. The Commission recommends that any complaint related to corruption against a public servant must be examined in depth at all initial stages, before initiating any inquiry. An assessment should ascertain whether the allegation is specific, credible and verifiable. In matters related to allegations of corruption, open inquiries should not be initiated merely on the basis of a complaint. Verification of the allegation should be done secretively, and the findings of the verification/inquiries should be evaluated in a competent and just manner. Anti-corruption agencies should strengthen their capacity, and all investigating officers should ensure that only those public servants against whom strong evidence is found are prosecuted.

SEVENTH REPORT OF THE SECOND ADMINISTRATIVE REFORMS COMMISSION

Capacity Building for Conflict Resolution

Conflict is an integral, and unavoidable, part of life in society. People take decisions in their daily interactions with others, and conflict forms part of the internal process of all assessments of pros and cons while making any decision. Development results from this continuous process of conflict resolution. The maturity of a society can be gauged by its ability to manage conflict. A transparent and unbiased mechanism for conflict resolution reduces discontent and disaffection in society, and a fair and independent judiciary acts as an arbiter of all conflicts. However, a society should also evolve a traditional method of conflict management to live a conflict-free life. Conflicts related to family and community should be resolved at the community level, rather than being taken to the courts. India has a very rich and diverse heritage, which contributes to a vibrant culture and nation. This heritage should be preserved from conflict through the process of democratic dialogue.

Democracy has the strength to resolve conflicts and bolster the process of nation-building. Democracy can provide enough opportunities to fulfil the aspirations of all. However, this is possible only through mutual trust, mutual respect and communication, and it is through these that genuine grievances can be redressed and doubts dissipated. Conflicts cannot be managed by a coercive and legal framework or by relying on the government machinery; rather, it will be resolved through democratic instruments. While framing the Constitution of India, in itself a powerful document for conflict resolution, Dr B. R. Ambedkar warned that India should not become complacent with a 'mere political democracy'. India had overcome colonial rule, but it continued to suffer from the evils of inequality and hierarchy. Thus, conflicts in the society of free India would be unavoidable.

After independence, Indian leaders worried about how to deal with tribals, particularly of the Northeast. The Sixth Schedule of the Indian Constitution has provided for the autonomy of many areas. As Pandit Jawaharlal Nehru said, 'Allow the tribals to grow according to their own genius.... In ages long past, Gautam Buddha said that the only real victory was one in which all wins equally and none defeats.'

Conflict occurs when two or more individuals or groups or societies consider their views incompatible. While conflict is usually viewed negatively, they are often desirable for greater change. The famous quote of sixteenth-century poet John Donne, 'No man is an island', states that individuals need to belong to a number of groups in order to fulfil their self-interests. The search for identity is a strong psychological thrust that has propelled human civilisation. Identity often centres around a myth or a powerful community imagined as necessary for political mobilisation. The sense of identity can substantially strengthen interpersonal relations in the community and the nation. The concept of 'social capital' explains why a shared identity with others in a group can produce greater results. Belonging to a social community proves to be a valuable capital. On the other hand, identity can also lead to conflict. We see many such conflicts occur due to illusions of a unique and undesired identity. We live in a world of hatred and violence because of the conflicts we generate.

Conflict does not only cause loss of life, it also destroys public order and affects the public services and economic health of the nation. Once destroyed, physical infrastructure can be rebuilt, but a breakdown in social cohesion and social institutions cannot be repaired easily.

Stages of Conflict: A Lifecycle Approach

A conflict is a dynamic phenomenon and evolves in stages. It takes the form of a cyclical event that involves objectives, approaches, a certain level of intensity and final outcomes. Every phase in the lifecycle of a conflict contains these stages, in varying magnitudes. This makes it necessary to understand the dynamics of conflict so as to formulate conflict prevention and management strategies.

The lifecycle of a conflict may be explained as follows:

1. Individual and Social Tensions: These evolve when an individual or a group feels that they have not received their rightful dues. Socio-economic inequalities of the past may also give birth to social tensions. The major factor behind this phase of conflict is poor quality of governance.
2. Latent Conflict: Individual and social tensions lead to feelings of injustice and give birth to discontent. In this stage, aggrieved individuals turn to the authorities for redress. This is the most critical time in which to prevent conflict, but this fact is often overlooked by the administration.
3. Escalation of Tensions: If the administration does not attend to these grievances, the discontent is aggravated. Inadequate attention to latent conflict may delay the conflict momentarily, but the aggrieved parties may later express their discontent through aggressive instruments such as demonstration, processions, bandhs, strikes, etc.
4. Eruption: If escalations of tension are not handled carefully, a little spark can lead to violence, and to the polarisation of the aggrieved people. The administration usually swings into action in this stage and tries to control the violence by means of coercive action.
5. Stalemate: This situation is similar to latent conflict. If the root cause of conflict is not addressed, mere suppression of violence offers only temporary results. The conflict may continue to recur periodically.

Operational Arrangements for Conflict Management

The Second Administrative Reforms Commission recommends:

1. The institutional capacity of the police should be augmented to contribute to conflict resolution in a proactive and effective manner.
2. Police manuals must be amended by adding suitable provisions for greater scope of involvement of police officials.
3. Executive Magistrates have a greater understanding of the ground situation, by virtue of extensive public interface while working as Revenue Officers. Other field-level officers, particularly in rural areas,

enjoy the respect of the society. These officials should be involved as interlocutors mediating in local conflicts. A suitable institutional framework should be evolved by state governments in this regard.

4. The subordinate judiciary should be strengthened through the allocation of upgraded infrastructure, and greater priority should be given to federal fiscal transfers.
5. Lok Adalats must be strengthened through the allocation of adequate resources.
6. The Ministry of Law may initiate a dialogue with the higher judiciary to find out ways and means of bringing 'greater finality' to the decisions of the quasi-judicial authorities.
7. Encouraging social capital formation.
8. Involvement of local self-governments (panchayats and urban local bodies) in conflict resolution.

Institutional Arrangements for Conflict Management

1. The Inter-State Council should demonstrate greater involvement in conflict resolution under Article 263(a) of the Constitution.
2. The Inter-State Council may be constituted by issuing a suitable Presidential order in the consideration of a dispute.
3. The National Commissions for Scheduled Castes and Scheduled Tribes may look into matters of an individual nature and provide guidance.
4. The role of the National Integration Council may be diversified.
5. District-level Integration Councils (District Peace Committees) should have effective linkages with State Councils. These councils should comprise eminent personalities who enjoy the goodwill and trust of all sections of society.

REFERENCES

Mitta, Manoj. (2005). 'How an MP was expelled for similar scandal'. *The Times of India*, 14 December. Available at https://timesofindia.indiatimes.com/india/how-an-mp-was-expelled-for-similar-scandal/articleshow/1331144.cms (accessed May 2024).

NBC News. (2004). 'British minister and Blair ally Blunkett resigns', 16 December. Available at https://www.nbcnews.com/id/wbna6718251 (accessed May 2024).

Second Administrative Reforms Commission. (2007). 'Ethics in Governance', Fourth Report. Government of India. Available at https://darpg.gov.in/sites/default/files/ethics4.pdf (accessed May 2024).

———. (2008). 'Social Capital—A Shared Destiny', Ninth Report. Available at https://darpg.gov.in/sites/default/files/Social_Capital9.pdf (accessed May 2024).

Supreme Court of India. (1997). 'Restatement of Values of Judicial Life'. Available at https://main.sci.gov.in/pdf/Notice/02112020_090821.pdf (accessed May 2024).

United Nations. (2004). *United Nations Convention Against Corruption*. New York: United Nations. Available at https://www.unodc.org/documents/brussels/UN_Convention_Against_Corruption.pdf (accessed May 2024).

United Nations Development Program (UNDP). (1997). 'Governance for Sustainable Human Development: A UNDP Policy Document'. New York: UNDP. Available at https://digitallibrary.un.org/record/492551?ln=en&v=pdf (accessed May 2024).

QUESTIONS

1. What is the meaning of probity in governance? How does probity play a major role in bringing about good governance in the nation?
2. What are the basic features of good governance?
3. Define the concept of rule of law. Explain its basic components with suitable examples.
4. Determine the key challenges in the modern day governance. Explain with suitable examples.
5. Distinguish between 'code of ethics' and 'code of conduct' with suitable examples. (UPSC 2018)
6. Explain the concepts of economy, efficiency and effectiveness in public service.

20

WORK CULTURE

> **KEY CONCEPT**
> Power Distance, Uncertainty Avoidance, Individualism, Masculinity/Femininity

Work culture is described as the perception of one's work, performance, *modus operandi*, and expectations from a job and the work environment. However, the reasons behind the behaviour demonstrated by both employees and employers are often overlooked. An interesting subject of study can be the clear difference between Japanese workers and Indian workers, in terms of their commitment, dedication and honesty. The Japanese love their work, irrespective of its importance, while Indians, on the other hand, are sometimes considered a little lackadaisical, to the extent that IST (Indian Standard Time) is often translated as 'Indian Stretchable Time'. Work culture is directly related to the culture of a particular place. English scholar Sir Edward B. Tylor (1832–1917) defines culture as 'a complex whole which comprises of cognition, belief, art, morality, custom, law and all other habits and abilities attained by the member of society.' According to Florence Kluckhohm and Fred Strodtbeck, 'Culture includes defined ways of thinking, feeling and reacting, acquired and transmitted mainly by symbols, and constituting their embodiment in artefacts. The essential core of culture includes conventional notions and particularly their pertinent values.'

Culture is inculcated naturally during childhood, through the process of being rewarded or punished for one's behaviour. A behaviour that invites rewards is learnt and repeated, and this becomes a part of a culture. Conversely, a behaviour that leads to punishment is abstained from and delinked from culture. This mechanism applies to every social organisation, such as the State, a community, a workplace, a home and relationships.

In this respect, Swiss-American psychologist Edgar Schein (1928–2023) defines culture as a characteristic of an independently defined social unit, whose members share a considerable amount of common experiences through which they learn to overcome problems. Culture designs people, and vice versa; in other words, people and culture are interlinked, and cultural formations differ from place to place due to the different cultural properties of specific places. Even within a country, we can at times find different cultures, with a distinct overarching culture being considered the common national culture. For example, the culture of Kannada-speaking areas is different from that of the Kumaon region; similarly, the culture of Rajasthan differs from that of Maharashtra.

However, here we are concerned with work culture, which depends on the policies of employers and the culture of employees. This is driven also by work-related values. Dutch social psychologist Geert Hofstede (1928–2020) carried out popular studies on the dimensions of a national culture. The four dimensions he identified distinguished between cultures based on their work-related values. These are:

1. Power Distance
2. Uncertainty Avoidance
3. Individualism versus Collectivism
4. Masculinity versus Femininity

POWER DISTANCE

'Power distance' is defined as the relationship between superiors and subordinates. This explains the relationship with and respect for authority in a hierarchical structure. The Power Distance Index describes the degree of equality or inequality in terms of status in the hierarchy. In a high power distance work culture, there exists a wide gap between employees working at different levels in the hierarchy. Table 20.1 provides a comparison between the work cultures with a high PDI and those with a low PDI.

UNCERTAINTY AVOIDANCE

This pertains to the level of forbearance for uncertainty and risk. This dimension assesses the preference for abiding by strict laws, rules and regulations over high-risk behaviour. Countries with a high uncertainty avoidance steer clear of conflicts and any deviation from set conventions, while countries with low uncertainty avoidance are ready to accept change and different points of views. We can say that a high PDI accompanies fewer innovations and change, while a low PDI displays a greater tendency to change jobs, start new companies, etc. For example, the Japanese are known for sticking to the same job, or having at most two jobs in their entire lives. Indians display a medium PDI. A comparison between the two has been given in Table 20.2.

INDIVIDUALISM

This pertains to a culture's focus on the rights of an individual vis-à-vis those of a group. It emphasises the degree to which individual efforts and achievements are prioritised over collective efforts or teamwork and the overall achievements.

Table 20.1: Implications of power distance on work culture

HIGH PDI	LOW PDI
1. Those in authority do not treat their subordinates with respect. There are open demonstrations of one's rank in the organisation. 2. Highly centralised decision-making. 3. Lower echelons are expected to take the blame for failure.	1. Superiors treat their subordinates with respect. 2. Decentralisation in decision-making. 3. There is a sharing of responsibility, and often the higher echelons accept the overall responsibility for failure.

Table 20.2: Implications of uncertainty avoidance on work culture

HIGH UA	LOW UA
1. Innovative ideas are unwelcome. 2. Promotions are done on the basis of seniority. 3. Salary is based on seniority and expertise. 4. Decision-making takes place on paper and in files.	1. Innovative ideas are encouraged. 2. Promotions are done on the basis of performance and education level. 3. Salary is based on performance. 4. There are very few rules that affect decision-making.

According to Hofstede, individualism indicates a social set-up wherein personal gain becomes more important than group achievement. In collectivism, the welfare of all the members of a team is placed above the self-interest of individual members. An individual work culture prevails in the USA, and does so to a moderate level in India. A collective culture is higher in China, Korea and Japan.

MASCULINITY/FEMININITY

This index emphasises the degree to which traditionally 'masculine' work is assigned to a male employee on a preferential basis, such as jobs related to control, power, assertiveness, achievement and material success. On the other hand, femininity is related to the comparative importance placed on human resources (HR) and a high quality of life. Countries with a higher masculine inclination have well-defined gender roles and work-related values, with greater emphasis on achievement and competition. A higher feminine inclination focuses on the holistic welfare of members rather than on performance.

Table 20.3 shows a comparison of work cultures based on aforementioned indices.

Table 20.3: Work-related values for countries

COUNTRY	POWER DISTANCE	UNCERTAINTY AVOIDANCE	INDIVIDUALISM	MASCULINITY
Argentina	49	86	46	56
Australia	36	51	90	61
Brazil	69	76	38	49
Great Britain	35	35	89	66
Indonesia	78	48	14	46
India	77	40	48	56
Israel	13	81	54	47
USA	40	46	91	62

Source: Hofstede (1980).

REFERENCES

Hofstede, Geert. (1980). *Culture's Consequences*. Beverly Hills, CA: Sage.

Kluckhohn, R. Florence, and Fred L. Strodtbeck. (1961). *Culture: A Critical Review of Concepts and Definitions*. Cambridge, MA: Harvard University Press.

Welsc, Robert Louis, and Luis Antonio Vivanco. (2014). *Cultural Anthropology: Asking Questions about Humanity*. New York: Oxford University Press.

QUESTION

1. Discipline generally implies following the order and subordination. However, this may be counter-productive for the organisation. Discuss. (UPSC 2017)

21

QUALITY OF SERVICE DELIVERY

> **KEY CONCEPTS**
> Introduction; Framework for Quality Service Delivery;
> Six Sigma; Lean Methodology

INTRODUCTION

We have discussed the concept of public service and the responsibility of the State to provide such services to their citizens. With the expansion of the private sector and diversification of market demands, the number of public services has reduced considerably. But though direct involvement in the provision of public services has reduced, the regulatory role of the State still persists, in order to check any breach of public interest and exploitation of the market by private players. The State has delegated a large portion of service delivery to the private sector, after putting in certain mechanisms to address any violation of human rights, liberty and freedom of choice. It is also the State's responsibility to check market monopoly and the threat of cartelisation by private players, which can disrupt the balance of demand and supply.

The State has to run a few public-sector production and delivery units pertaining to certain goods and services (to be referred to henceforth as services) to ensure the minimum welfare of citizens. For instance, besides providing for private catering that offer diverse food products at different prices, the Ministry of Railways also offers inexpensive food, termed 'Janta Khana' to passengers with the help of private vendors. It is essential to deliver public services effectively, efficiently, and economically. The wide range of social deprivations needs to be addressed to bring about justice and equity in the society. Public service delivery should also include an analysis of the type of services to be taken up and their mode of delivery in order to meet its objectives.

As discussed earlier, in India, public services have been badly affected by a bureaucratic attitude and red-tapism. Despite the heavy public expenditure, we have failed to produce the desired results. The principal factor behind this failure is the arrogance displayed by public servants towards citizens, who are considered mere slaves. With the attempt to reinvent governance, this master-slave relation was reversed, and citizens were allowed to take centre-stage. This led to a major shift in the attitude of public servants with respect to the service delivery process, in both the Central and state governments.

Indian society is stratified on the basis of economic status and access to services. Sometimes, even well-off people are denied access to services due to an infrastructure shortage or inadequate spread of information. The situation is worse for poor people, who possess neither sufficient purchasing power nor adequate information with respect to services. The State needs to address such problems. Sometimes, the failure of service delivery can be blamed squarely on the inadequate efforts of public servants. For example, in rural areas, teachers often neglect their teaching duties, thereby compelling their students to take recourse to private tuitions. Such dereliction of duty is rampant in the education and health sectors, a problem that remains unaddressed.

We also see how public services meant exclusively for the poor are misappropriated, with powerful people, who are otherwise ineligible, reaping the benefits of such services. The BPL (Below Poverty Line) list, for instance, was heavily misused by powerful people, with rampant corruption in public offices during the preparation of the BPL list, and in the decisions taken with regard to inclusion and exclusion and the eligibility criteria. The government has recently taken corrective measures to check such fraudulent practices. The new eligibility criteria are based on socio-economic caste census (SECC) data, which takes into consideration the deprivation level of a family, and this has addressed corruption in public service delivery to some extent, despite the errors present in even the SECC data.

FRAMEWORK FOR QUALITY SERVICE DELIVERY

The task of service delivery is assigned to the bureaucracy. Some branches have worked well and successfully implemented various schemes. The quality of work also depends upon the seriousness of state governments in realising good governance on the ground. Service delivery can be improved in the following ways:

1. Putting in place provisions to ensure that the voices and choices of the poor are respected, and encourage their participation in the process of designing schemes and service delivery.
2. Introducing provisions of reward and punishment for public servants in terms of quality service delivery.
3. Provisions for annual social and performance audits.

An efficient public service delivery depends upon the following:

1. Public servants should be accessible to citizens. They should make repeated trips to the field, meet with stakeholders, and conduct public meetings to learn the extant loopholes and improvements needed to ensure an efficient public service delivery.
2. Spread of information through citizens' charters, widespread publicity, public announcements (*munadi*) through loudspeakers, and placing the list of beneficiaries in the public domain to ensure greater transparency.
3. The assurance of greater accountability through various measures such as in-department reviews, complaint handling, grievance redressal, etc.
4. A review of public service delivery through the active participation of citizens groups, local volunteers, management trainees, and research fellows to ensure social auditing.
5. A smart and effective grievance redressal mechanism based on e-governance. For example, the Chief Minister's Helpline in Madhya Pradesh has proved to be a milestone in this regard, with other states now implementing similar projects.
6. Making the public service delivery process simple and free from excessive documentation. It should be based on community verification.
7. A strong vigilance mechanism and quick disposal of corruption cases in fast-track courts especially organised for this purpose.
8. The delivery of public services through IT-enabled applications like e-fms

(Electronic Fund Management System), use of JAM (Jan Dhan bank account, AADHAAR, Mobile number), and the use of the GPS system in geo-tagging assets for progress evaluation and preventing fraud.

Two important models for the implementation of an effective public service delivery system are given below.

ETVX Model

This model was propounded by IBM. Here, 'E' stands for Entry, 'T' for 'Task', 'V' for 'Verification and Validation' and 'X' for 'Exit'.

Entry (E) is defined as the input required for producing the desired results (Exit), in terms of both quality and quantity. It includes the identification of state agencies and provision of resources for implementing the programme. This criterion is decided by political executives with the help of the relevant ministry or directorate.

Task (T) is related to the identification of actions that take place in the process of service delivery. This may include designing policy, providing funds and deciding on manpower.

Verification and Validation (V) is related to the identification of checkpoints during the implementation of the programme. This is used to figure out the weak links and vulnerability of a scheme, which could lead to failure. It validates the satisfactory performance of a task. All identified shortcomings are rectified on a priority basis through necessary amendments.

Exit (X) is defined as the outcome, in terms of quantity and quality. In the government, exit is gauged in terms of infrastructure and asset creation, as well as its impact on the society.

The task can be divided into smaller, more convenient modules, which are further subjected to the process of the MTVX model separately to aid greater control and performance.

SEVOTTAM Model

SEVOTTAM comprises the words '*Seva*' and '*Uttam*', which means 'excellence in service'. This refers to the quality management system (QMS) framed by the Department of Administrative Reforms and Public Grievances, Government of India. It is regulated by the Indian Standard IS 15700:2005, which was specifically designed to certify excellent service delivery works in the government.

It consists of three modules that help to identify the weaknesses of service delivery programmes.

1. Citizen's Charter
2. Public Grievance Redressal Mechanism
3. Service Delivery Capability

We have already discussed citizen's charters in detail in Chapter 19. The public grievance redressal mechanism aims to effectively resolve all public grievances within the prescribed timeframe. Complaints registered under this module provide a useful database to understand the lacunae in the scheme in terms of its design and implementation. Taking such feedback into consideration, necessary amendments are made to reduce the number of complaints. The handling of public grievances involves the registration, redressal and prevention of complaints. Service delivery capability involves an organisation's potential to deliver results, and how these results are reflected. An organisation's capability can be improved by increasing inputs such as human resources, financial provisions and the use of modern technology.

To ensure a successful implementation of quality public service delivery through the SEVOTTAM model, an effective institutional set-up is necessary. The success of any government programme depends upon the level of commitment at the higher levels. Political and bureaucratic will to bring about excellence is imperative. Critical factors to ensure success include the involvement of stakeholders, from policymaking to policy implementation and its auditing (see Figure 21.1.). The other critical factor is change management.

A change in attitude in bureaucrats and the political executive is required under the new dynamics of New Public Management, which puts the idea of 'public first'. Several new initiatives have to be taken in this regard, which can lead to progressive measures; however, the rigid nature of the bureaucracy might lead one to expect some resistance. Vital measures in this area are a focus on transparency, fixing greater accountability, and openness in the working of the government.

SIX SIGMA

Six Sigma is a statistical methodology which enables the enhancement of an organisation's goods and service delivery. It is based on the concept of improving performance and diminishing the process and output variation, which helps in achieving greater product quality, building a brand image, and hence allowing greater customer satisfaction.

The term 'Six Sigma' was coined to indicate a process that is under control with respect to process limits: $\pm 3\sigma$ (three standard deviation in the normal distribution) from the central line (mean value) in the control chart, and within the tolerance limits $\pm 6\sigma$ from the central line.

Six Sigma is based purely on the statistical method used in normally distributed samples. The symbol σ (sigma) represents standard deviation from the mean of the samples. It is known as Six Sigma because it takes into consideration a tolerance limit up to six standard deviation. It means that chances of error is kept at a minimum of 3.4 in numbers out of one million samples. It attempts to ensure the quality of goods and services to the extent that in one million random instances of a particular goods or service delivery, an organisation fails to deliver the stipulated quality in just 3.4 (approximately 4) instances.

In Six Sigma, all activities are viewed as processes that can be represented, measured, analysed, improvised and controlled by learning the reasons responsible for showing any deviation beyond the tolerance limit. Six Sigma was introduced by Motorola in 1986, and is now implemented to identify and eliminate defects, errors and variation in the process. In general, Six Sigma is practised in manufacturing industries in the production process, and has gained popularity in the service sector too. There are very rare instances of achieving a Six Sigma quality standard in government organisations. Six Sigma comprises five steps: define, measure, analyse, improve and control (DMAIC):

1. **Define:** A team constituted for Six Sigma adopts a process in accordance with the objectives of the organisation. The associated problems are then identified and defined explicitly.
2. **Measure:** The team gauges the initial performance of the process, establishing a standard and delineating the reasons affecting the performance of the process. These reasons are taken as independent variables which give effect to the process, and hence control the performance.

Figure 21.1: Critical factors involved in quality service delivery

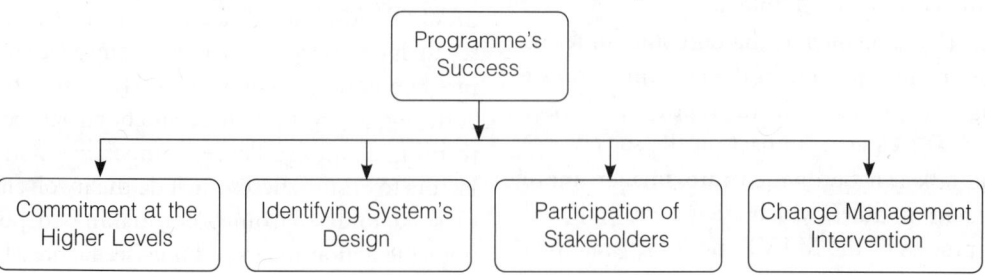

3. **Analyse:** After measuring these steps, the Six Sigma team decides the inputs to be monitored. In this stage, the effect of each input is assessed in isolation, allowing them to discover the reasons for the deviation.
4. **Improve:** Improvements are suggested to treat the variation in performance by incorporating control mechanisms after undertaking the required changes in the system. These variations may be caused by external factors such as human error, environmental factors (natural environment, or the social, political and economic environment), or internal factors such as system error, process error, etc.
5. **Control:** Finally, the team incorporates controls to the process to overcome all instances of deviation beyond the tolerance level.

LEAN METHODOLOGY

Lean methodology is an approach that is popular in manufacturing industries. It has now become an integral part of the management style in all sectors of management, and is based on the principle of eliminating waste and inefficiency so as to make the business profitable. It is a systematic approach towards continuous process improvement. The lean methodology was invented by Toyota to optimise resources and maximise value to its customers. It is now applied in various sectors, like service industries, healthcare and software.

Under lean methodology, eight common wastes are defined as: defects, overproduction, waiting, unutilised human resources, logistic/movement of goods and services, inventory, motion (redundant and unproductive movement of people) and over-processing (additional features that do not create value for the customers). Lean methodology emphasises waste production and workflow efficiencies in the process.

Lean Six Sigma

Governments began showing an interest in quality service delivery with the advent of the New Public Management (NPM). The objectives of governments can be fulfilled by clubbing Six Sigma and Lean Methodology in the service delivery process. Lean Six Sigma comprises the common characteristics of both processes. Customer satisfaction, continuous improvement, finding the causes behind any deviation in the desired results, and intensive worker involvement are some of the characteristics they share.

Lean Six Sigma has been implemented in various projects in the USA in the areas of defence, tax collection, internal security, road maintenance, etc. In India, Six Sigma is yet to become a part of public service delivery. There is huge scope of Lean Six Sigma in sectors like healthcare, agriculture, rural development, logistics and city planning. For instance, in the healthcare sector, major parameters like average patient waiting time in queue for OPD, average recovery time for different ailments, cleanliness of the hospital, and cost of treatment can be focused on to keep the healthcare service delivery process under control. Besides, immunisation and childcare services can also be efficiently delivered using Lean Six Sigma. Incorporation of Lean Six Sigma in e-governance can improve results and diminish costs by controlling waste and leakages.

REFERENCES

CAPAM. (2011). 'Service Delivery, Governance and the Citizen'. *Commonwealth Association for Public Administration & Management* 17(2).

Government of India. (2010). *Guidelines for Designing and Implementing SEVOTTAM Complaints: Citizen's/Client's Charter & Grievance Redress Mechanism*. New Delhi: Performance Management Division, Cabinet Secretariat, and Department of Administrative Reforms and Public Grievances. Available at https://darpg.gov.in/sites/default/files/Sevottam_RFD_Guidelines_August_2010.pdf (accessed March 2024).

Shah, Anwar. (2005). *Public Services Delivery.* Washington, D.C.: The World Bank.

QUESTIONS

1. Explain the role of common citizens in ensuring public service delivery. Do you think that in India, people are aware of their responsibility in this regard? Support your view with the help of examples.
2. Explain the various models which provide guidelines for ideal public service delivery and its monitoring.
3. What are the factors involved in public service delivery? Explain with the help of some examples.
4. Do you think that a bureaucratic attitude hinders the quality of service delivery? Suggest some measures to overcome this problem.

CASE STUDIES

SOLVED CASE STUDIES (UPSC CIVIL SERVICES MAINS EXAMINATION 2013–19)

Case Studies (2013)

Carefully study the cases presented and then answer the questions that follow:

1. A Public Information Officer has received an application under RTI Act. Having gathered the information, the PIO discovers that the information pertains to some of the decisions taken by him, which were found to be not altogether right. There were other employees who were party to these decisions. Disclosure of the information is likely to lead to disciplinary action with possibility of punishment against him as well as some of his colleagues. Non-disclosure or part disclosure or camouflaged disclosure of information will result into lesser punishment or no punishment.

   The PIO is otherwise an honest and conscientious person, but this particular decision on which the RTI application has been filed, turned out to be wrong. He comes to you for advice.

   The following are some suggested options. Please evaluate the merits and demerits of each of the options:

   (i) The PIO could refer the matter to his superior officer and seek his advice and act strictly in accordance with the advice, even though he is not completely in agreement with the advice of the superior.

   (ii) The PIO could proceed on leave and leave the matter to be dealt [with] by his successor in office or request for transfer of the application to another PIO.

   (iii) The PIO could weigh the consequences of disclosing the information truthfully, including the effect on his career, and reply in a manner that would not place him or his career in jeopardy, but at the same time a little compromise can be made on the contents of the information.

   (iv) The PIO could consult his colleagues who were associated in the decision, and then he could take action as per their advice.

   Also please indicate (without necessarily restricting to the above options) what you would like to advise, giving proper reasons. (250 words) 20

---

* The questions provided in this section have been taken from published UPSC examination papers of specific years, and so have been reproduced in their original form, without being edited for language or grammar.

Solution

(i) Merits: He would overcome the burden of taking a decision, whether it works in his own favour or against. He would also refrain from creating any conflict of interest.

Demerit: It is against the rule, as it is the duty of the PIO to provide information about his office. He could not refer the matter to his superior. Besides, it would not reflect the public service value of having the courage of one's convictions.

(ii) Merit: He can again overcome the burden of taking a decision, whether the decision works in his own favour or against. He can avoid a conflict of interest as well.

Demerit: Another PIO's career would suffer because s/he would have to take over the additional charge of the earlier PIO.

(iii) Merit: The PIO can save both her/his career as well as that of their subordinates who are equally at stake.

Demerit: This action goes against the integrity of a public servant. It is also a violation of the RTI Act, 2005. The provisions of the Act may lead to further trouble.

(iv) Merit: A consensual decision may emerge from the consultation with all stakeholders. This can avoid unpleasant consequences arising from the disclosure of the information.

Demerit: This action not an ideal modus operandi, and goes against the spirit of public service values such as integrity, objectivity, transparency and decision-making abilities. This will also suppress the voice of conscience that will always encourage an official to face the consequences of their actions.

My advice will keep in mind the fact that the PIO in question is an honest and conscientious person. The virtue theory of ethics says that the decisions taken by a virtuous person can never be wrong, as the decisions will always be characterised by honesty and will listen to the voice of conscience.

I shall therefore advise the PIO to disclose the information present in the documents without tampering with any of it. This is also her/his duty (*Dharma*). The PIO should exhibit exemplary conduct in front of the public, superior officers, as well as colleagues and subordinates. This will definitely safeguard her/his image as an officer of integrity and a protector of the values of public service. The officer will face any disciplinary inquiry with the same calm and reasoning with which the original decision had been taken. Here, the virtue of 'logos' given by the Stoics would definitely work to defend her/his position.

2. You are working as an Executive Engineer in the construction cell of a Municipal Corporation and are presently in-charge of the construction of a flyover. There are two Junior Engineers under you who have the responsibility of day-to-day inspection of the site and are reporting to you, while you are finally reporting to the Chief Engineer who heads the cell. While the construction is heading towards the completion, the Junior Engineers have been regularly reporting that all construction is taking place as per design specifications. However, in one of your surprise inspections, you have noticed some serious deviations and lacunae which, in your opinion, are likely to affect the safety of the flyover. Rectification of these lacunae at this stage would require a substantial amount of demolition and rework which will cause a tangible loss to the contractor and will also delay completion.

Case Studies

There is a lot of public pressure on the Corporation to get this construction completed because of heavy traffic congestion in the area. When you brought this matter to the notice of the Chief Engineer, he advised you that in his opinion it is not a very serious lapse and may be ignored. He advised for further expediting the project for completion in time. However, you are convinced that this was a serious matter which might affect public safety and should not be left unaddressed.

What will you do in such a situation? Some of the options are given below. Evaluate the merits and demerits of each of these options and finally suggest what course of action you would like to take, giving reasons. (250 words)   20

(i) Follow the advice of the Chief Engineer and go ahead.

(ii) Make an exhaustive report of the situation, bringing out all facts and analysis along with your own viewpoints stated clearly and seek for written orders from the Chief Engineer.

(iii) Call for explanation from the Junior Engineers and issue orders to the contractor for necessary correction within targeted time.

(iv) Highlight the issue so that it reaches superiors above the Chief Engineer.

(v) Considering the rigid attitude of the Chief Engineer, seek transfer from the project or report sick.

Solution

(i) Merits: Early resumption of regular traffic services will take place once the work is completed. It will also avoid any conflict with the Chief Engineer and the contractor.

Demerits: A lot of lives will be jeopardised while travelling over that flyover. This act would also go against my integrity and will highlight the lack of the courage of my convictions.

(ii) Merits: I will follow the exact procedure while exposing the poor quality the work, as this is one of my official duties. I will save my career by avoiding any involvement in this malpractice.

Demerits: Delay in the construction of the flyover, and potential conflict with both the contractor and the Chief Engineer.

(iii) Merits: This will rectify the mistakes in the work. I will assign all responsibility to the Junior Engineers on paper, thereby absolving myself of any legal action.

Demerits: Delay in the construction of the flyover, and potential conflict with both the contractor and the Chief Engineer.

(iv) Merits: Greater attention can be brought to the issue. This will also streamline further courses of action and will definitely usher in corrective measures to avoid adverse consequences.

Demerits: This will invite conflict, which may linger on even after the project is completed.

(v) Merits: I can rid myself of the situation by avoiding any conflict.

Demerits: I can be held accountable for any mishap in the future because the poor construction will have been done during my tenure.

I propose taking methodical, step-by-step actions. First, I will take up option (iii). If I feel that the necessary action is not being taken by the Junior Engineers and the contractor, I will immediately move to option (ii). I will proceed in this way so as to give them a chance to rectify the lacuna, failing which I will start proceedings against the Junior Engineers and the contractor, and inform the Chief Engineer accordingly. If the Chief

Engineer does not take this matter seriously, I will highlight it before higher authorities like the Municipal Commissioner and Mayor, bypassing our immediate superiors who tend to comply with the Civil Services Conduct Rules.

3. Sivakasi in Tamil Nadu is known for its manufacturing clusters on firecrackers and matches. The local economy of this is largely dependent on firecrackers industry. It has led to tangible economic development and improved standard of living in the area.

So far as child labour norms for hazardous industries like firecrackers industry are concerned, International Labour Organization (ILO) has set the minimum age as 18 years. In India however this age is 14 years.

The units in industrial clusters of firecrackers can be classified into registered and non-registered entities. One typical unit is household-based work. Though the law is clear on the use of child labour employment norms in registered/non-registered units, it does not include household-based works. Household-based work means children working under the supervision of their parents/relatives. To evade child labour norms, several units project themselves as household-based works but employ children from outside. Needless to say that employing children saves the costs for these units leading to higher profits to the owners.

On your visit to one of the units at Sivakasi the owner takes you around the unit which has about 10-15 children below 14 years of age. The owner tells you that in his household-based unit, the children are all his relatives. You notice that several children smirk, when the owner tells you this. On deeper enquiry, you figure out that neither the owner nor the children are able to satisfactorily establish their relationship with each other.

(a) Bring out and discuss the ethical issues involved in the above case.

(b) What would be your reaction after your above visit? (300 words)   25

Solution

(a) The ethical issues involved in this case should be analysed through the criteria of different ethical concepts. If we view this problem from the lens of deontological theory, the following points arise:

1. Violation of the law of the land is grossly unethical in the eyes of jurisprudence.
2. Violation of international norms pertaining to child labour goes against the spirit of international ethicism.

A scrutiny under the standards of the teleological theory of ethics tells us that such an activity will not end well. The children are paid very little and are deprived of an opportunity to educate themselves. Any mishandling in the production of firecrackers will place their lives in jeopardy. Thus, this is not supported by consequentialism either.

This activity is also not virtuous because it follows a greed for profit and involves great danger and cruelty. Virtue ethics denounces economic activities such as those taking place in Sivakasi district.

This goes against meta-ethical theories like emotivism and prescriptivism because there is no ethicality in the engagement of children in such activity.

(b) I will take this matter seriously and try to unravel the key points. I will speak to the owner of the factory and try to convince him. I will also speak to the association of owners to take some immediate move in this regard and stop engaging children in such dangerous activites. I will take strict steps against the factory owners—unless they are seen to take substantial steps to rectify the situation. I will also mobilise an awakening in the parents of child labourers with the help of local politicians, social workers and community advocates, warning them about the negative consequences.

4. You are heading a leading technical institute of the country. The institute is planning to convene an interview panel shortly under your chairmanship for selection of the post of professors. A few days before the interview, you get a call from the Personal Secretary (PS) of a senior government functionary seeking your intervention in favour of the selection of a close relative of the functionary for this post. The PS also informs you that he is aware of the long pending and urgent proposal of your institute for grant of funds for modernization, which are awaiting the functionary's approval. He assures you that he would get these proposals cleared.

   (a) What are the options available to you?
   (b) Evaluate each of these options and choose the option which you would adopt, giving reasons. (250 words)   20

Solution

   (a) I am left with the following options:
      1. The first is to act according to the wishes of the senior government functionary.
      2. The second is to politely refuse to compromise my own integrity.
      3. The third is to tell him, 'Let me see how can I help in this case.'
      4. The fourth is to refuse the request and complain about the illegal behaviour of the senior government functionary to the competent authority.
   (b) If I opt for option 1, then it would be easier for me to get my proposal cleared by the senior government functionary. I will also shun all uninvited hassles. However, I will have to compromise my own integrity and value system. The wrong person will be appointed to the post of Professor, and might just destroy the value system of the organisation. An incompetent person can also damage the career of students.

   Option 2 will be the most correct from the perspective of personal and professional ethics. But my decision will jeopardise the future of my institution to a certain extent. I know that that particular functionary will not hold his position for eternity, so while my proposal will be delayed, I can have it cleared later without compromising with my integrity and values.

   Option 3 is the most preferred by people, as it avoids both immediate chaos and any compromise with my professional integrity. But this is also not acceptable as I have to lie, which will have its own inherent negative consequences. Finally, I will be unable to maintain my overall integrity and value system, and also cost the institute my proposal.

   Option 4 is the most appropriate as per the deontological approach to ethical problem-solving, but we have to see whether teleologically, this has any utility. Such incidents are very common, and cannot always be engaged with. At the same time, it is necessary to send a message to the government machinery and society that any misuse of authority will be unacceptable. Thus, I will lead with this option.

5. As a senior officer in the Finance Ministry, you have access to some confidential and crucial information about policy decisions that the Government is about to announce. These decisions are likely to have far-reaching impact on the housing and construction industry. If the builders have access to this information beforehand, they can make huge profits. One

of the builders has done a lot of quality work for the Government and is known to be close to your immediate superior, who asks you to disclose this information to the said builder.

(a) What are the options available to you?
(b) Evaluate each of these options and choose the option which you would adopt, giving reasons. (250 words)   20

Solution

(a) I have the following options before me:
1. I can disclose the information to the builder.
2. I can refuse to disclose the information.

(b) If I go with option 1, then I will avoid conflict with my superior and will have his support as my career progresses. However, this action will compromise my integrity. It will also breach the other foundational values of public service, like impartiality and objectivity. This is a corruption of sorts because it involves unfair practices in the government, which will provide undue financial gain to a particular private player. This also goes against the code of conduct stipulated for a public servant.

If I go with option 2, then I will work in accordance with the values of public service. This will also avoid any breach of conduct and uninvited disciplinary action in case my unethical conduct related to the passing of insider information is disclosed. However, there may be certain repercussions; for instance, my refusal can annoy my superior. But public servants should be prepared to accept all challenges and understand that working honestly in the government system is never easy. Despite pressures and threats, deviation from the norm is never acceptable. If my senior insists that I disclose the information, I will write to my secretary to bring my senior's conduct to notice, and request for a transfer to another office to avoid any potential conflict of interest. Thus, I will opt for this option.

6. You are the Executive Director of an upcoming InfoTech Company which is making a name for itself in the market. Mr. A, who is a star performer, is heading the marketing team. In a short period of one year, he has helped in doubling the revenues as well as creating a high brand equity for the Company so much so that you are thinking of promoting him. However you have been receiving information from many corners about his attitude towards the female colleagues; particularly his habit of making loose comments on women. In addition, he regularly sends indecent SMS's to all the team members including his female colleagues.

One day, late in the evening, Mrs. X, who is one of Mr. A's team members, comes to you visibly disturbed. She complains against the continued misconduct of Mr. A, who has been making undesirable advances towards her and has even tried to touch her inappropriately in his cabin. She tenders her resignation and leaves your office.

(a) What are the options available to you?
(b) Evaluate each of these options and choose the option you would adopt giving reasons. (250 words)   20

Solution

(a) The options available to me are:
1. Ignore the complaint because Mr A is the star performer of the company.
2. Fire Mr A immediately, taking cognisance of his conduct vis-à-vis Mrs X.
3. Initiate an enquiry as per the Sexual Harassment of Women at the Workplace (Prevention, Prohibition and Redressal)

Act 2013, with the help of the internal complaints committee of the company formed for this purpose.

(b) The only merit of option 1 is related to the future growth of the company. On the other hand, this option will jeopardise the entire work culture of the company, and if such cases are not dealt with due diligence, they can invite legal consequences. It is also a fact that in the private sector, there is a high turnover rate of employees, who seek better pay packages. The mere desire to retain Mr A does not appear to be a sound ground vis-à-vis ethics as well as the law.

Option 2 will go against the principle of natural justice as well as the reputation of the company as a fair employer. However, such strict action will set a precedent for other employees of the company.

The proper way to address such issues is option 3. This option will follow the deontological approach that abides with all laws, as well as the teleological approach of pursuing ends that will ultimately prove to be helpful in the growth of the organisation. If the internal complaint committee clears Mr A, I will retain his services, otherwise I will fire him from the company.

Case Studies (2014)

Carefully study the cases presented and then answer the questions that follow.

1. Now-a-days, there is an increasing thrust on economic development all around the globe. At the same time, there is also an increasing concern about environmental degradation caused by development. Many a time, we face a direct conflict between developmental activity and environmental quality. It is neither feasible to stop or curtail the developmental process, nor it is advisable to keep degrading the environment, as it threatens our very survival. Discuss some feasible strategies which could be adopted to eliminate this conflict and which could lead to sustainable development. (250 words)   20

Solution

Environment protection has been a matter of debate in the present time. Some scholars say that nature should not be interfered with because all the things that are natural and undisturbed are good for us all. As per the **teleological tradition** in environmentalism, natural ecosystems are well-ordered and systematic, with every natural thing having its own place and role. In contrast to this teleological idea, some other scholars suggest that all natural phenomena are neither beneficial nor well-planned; rather, they have evolved accidentally.

According to the utilitarian tradition, the consequences of our interference should decide the environmental ethics. **Utilitarianism** is based on the maximisation of pleasure and the minimisation of pain. If interference in the environment leads to maximum happiness in the lives of human beings, then it is permissible.

The next important tradition is **deontology** or duty theory, which focuses on duty without any consideration of the final consequences. It describes environmental protection as a duty; hence, the environment should be preserved, irrespective of its utility to human life.

These conflicts can be mitigated by adopting the following strategies:

1. We should encourage more conclusive research on the environment and development relationship. On the basis of the findings, we should restrict those activities that are harming the environment and will eventually cause pain in human life as well. In this way, we can follow both teleology and deontology in a plausible manner.
2. We should inculcate environmental virtues in all citizens so that the overall biotic pressure can be mitigated.

3. The middle path given by Budhha, or the golden mean principle given by Aristotle are always better options to reconcile the opposing ideas related to environmental ethics.

2. Suppose one of your close friends, who is also aspiring for civil services, comes to you for discussing some of the issues related to ethical conduct in public service. He raises the following points:

   (i) In the present times, when unethical environment is quite prevalent, individual attempts to stick to ethical principles may cause a lot of problems in one's career. It may also cause hardship to the family members as well as risk to one's life. Why should we not be pragmatic and follow the path of least resistance, and be happy with doing whatever good we can?

   (ii) When so many people are adopting wrong means and are grossly harming the system, what difference would it make if only a small minority tries to be ethical? They are going to be rather ineffective and are bound to get frustrated.

   (iii) If we become fussy about ethical considerations, will it not hamper the economic progress of our country? After all, in the present age of high competition, we cannot afford to be left behind in the race of development.

   (iv) It is understandable that we should not get involved in grossly unethical practices, but giving and accepting small gratifications and doing small favours increase everybody's motivation. It also makes the system more efficient. What is wrong in adopting such practices?

Critically analyze the above viewpoints. On the basis of this analysis, what will be your advice to your friend? (250 words)   20

Solution

Pragmatism is beneficial for a hassle-free and happy life. But such happiness is not the objective of human life. Aristotle defined 'Eudaimonia' as 'doing and living well.' The highest happiness is a greater good that leads to a perfect balance in human values such as wisdom, courage, appetite (desire), temperance, fortitude, etc. People opt for the civil services to enjoy the happiness that come from struggling against the odds and gaining respect in lieu of doing good deeds for social welfare. The path of least resistance does not belong to either the middle path or the golden mean.

The second viewpoint is not acceptable because only a chosen few are proven to be leaders, and the civil service is primarily meant for them. While it is true that a minuscule amount of good among a sea of bad will be ineffective, that good can be identified easily. Deontology and Kant's categorical imperative compels us to act according to the norms and duties assigned. Virtue ethics, too, rejects the second viewpoint.

The third viewpoint is grossly incorrect. Virtue ethics explicitly tells us that virtuous deeds beget happiness while bad deeds lead to eventual pain. Several examples support this perspective. The utilitarian tradition also suggests that if the happiness of a few has to be sacrificed to maximise the overall happiness of all, then such a sacrifice is inevitable.

The fourth viewpoint holds good in accordance with utilitarian theory, but is a violation of deontology and virtue theory. One cannot base a decision on ethics on one's own standards. Rules of conduct have been designed to avoid future dilemmas. The values of public service are the hallmark of such services, and there can be no compromise with these.

I will advise my friend to not think along these lines and instead follow constitutional morality in both letter and spirit. Pleasure and pain are two moral motivations. I will explain that s/he will soon realise the happiness that comes from working in an ethical manner, and will ask her/him to read the texts related to ethics and follow the civil services values. I will also offer a warning about the consequences of misconduct, in terms of disciplinary action initiated by the government, in the event that s/he is caught out.

3. You are a no-nonsense, honest officer. You have been transferred to a remote district to head a department that is notorious for its inefficiency and callousness. You find that the main cause of the poor state of affairs is the indiscipline of a section of employees. They do not work themselves and also disrupt the working of others. You first warned the troublemakers to mend their ways or else face disciplinary action. When the warning had little effect, you issued a show cause notice to the ringleaders. As a retaliatory measure, these troublemakers instigated a woman employee amongst them to file a complaint of sexual harassment against you with the Women's Commission. The Commission promptly seeks your explanation. The matter is also publicized in the media to embarrass you further. Some of the options to handle this situation could be as follows:

   (i) Give your explanation to the Commission and go soft on the disciplinary action.
   (ii) Ignore the Commission and proceed firmly with the disciplinary action.
   (iii) Brief your higher-ups seek directions from them and act accordingly.

Suggest any other possible option(s). Evaluate all of them and suggest the best course of action, giving your reasons for it. (250 words)   20

Solution

In option (i), it is mandatory to provide an explanation to the commission because otherwise, a one-sided decision can be taken against me. This will serve no purpose. On the other hand, softening my stance vis-à-vis the notorious employees would encourage them to continue their indiscipline and inefficiency. There might be some relief, in that they might choose to withdraw the fake charges and conspiracy against me. But this will dilute the real purpose and tarnish my reputation, leading me to be known as a spineless officer. Eventually, this will not follow the teleological tradition.

Proceeding with option (ii) will create trouble for me. It will jeopardise my career on the one hand, and project an image of me as a defiant and unruly officer on the other. This goes against the principle of deontology too.

Option (iii) should be followed; the higher authorities should be made aware of the actual situation, but here, too, their advice might not work because the burden of proof in cases of sexual harassment at the workplace will be placed on me. While paying heed to the advice of my seniors, I should proceed after listening to the voice of my conscience.

Finally, I will explain the situation to the higher authorities and take the help of a good lawyer while preparing to present my case to the commission. I will not change my way of working. I will identify the culprits and seek punishment for their indisciplined attitude. I will also speak to the woman employee and use my powers of articulation ('logos', as explained by the Stoics) to persuade her to see reason. I will explain the consequence of lodging false complaints against superior officers. I have faith in the system of jurisprudence, and I know that the truth always emerges victorious. Such instances are common in the life of a civil servant, but this does not mean that one should compromise with one's values system.

4. Suppose you are the CEO of a company that manufactures specialized electronic equipment used by a government department. You have submitted your bid for the supply of this equipment to the department. Both the quality and cost of your offer are better than those of the competitors. Yet the concerned officer is demanding a hefty bribe for approving the

tender. Getting the order is important both for you and for your company. Not getting the order would mean closing a production line. It may also affect your own career. However, as a value-conscious person, you do not want to give bribe.

Valid arguments can be advanced both for giving the bribe and getting the order, and for refusing to pay the bribe and risking the loss of the order. What those arguments could be? Could there be any better way to get out of this dilemma? If so, outline the main elements of this third way, pointing out its merits. (250 words) 20

Solution

First, this is not a case of an ethical dilemma because a dilemma arises due to a conflict between two or more ethical viewpoints. Here, an honest conduct and refusing to pursue a corrupt path are moral obligations.

The benefits to paying a bribe could be the future growth of both my company and my career. If I bribe the concerned officer, then I have to compromise on the quality of my product to match the profit. There is also the risk of this transaction being exposed, and my company being blacklisted by the government. I could even face legal consequences with the corrupt officers in lieu of my corrupt practice.

Refusing to pay the bribe will save me from an act of moral turpitude. Such a practice is also against the law, and not paying a bribe will enable me to follow deontology. Utilitarian theory permits any conduct that leads to a greater outcome, no matter what the means, but in the long run this will degrade the work culture of the company. The argument that the entire production line is dependent upon one particular order is also unconvincing. If my products are unparalleled, then I will find other customers easily.

I will try to win the contract by fair means. If they demand a bribe, I will take recourse to anti-corruption measures (vigilance or the CBI). I will not allow another company to finalise the order by unfair means. If my company's administration refuses to support me, I will resign on moral grounds. My conscience will not allow me to save my career by following corrupt means. I will also expose the *modus operandi* of the bribe-seekers in the media, openly declare the reason behind my resignation. This will increase my prestige as an honest person, which will in turn help my future career.

5. Rameshwar successfully cleared the prestigious civil services examination and was excited about the opportunity that he would get through the civil services to serve the country. However, soon after joining the services, he realized that things are not as rosy as he had imagined. He found a number of malpractices prevailing in the department assigned to him. For example, funds under various schemes and grants were being misappropriated. The official facilities were frequently being used for personal needs by the officers and staff. After some time, he noticed that the process of recruiting the staff was also not up to the mark. Prospective candidates were required to write an examination in which a lot of cheating was going on. Some candidates were provided external help in the examination. Rameshwar brought these incidents to the notice of his seniors. However, he was advised to keep his eyes, ears and mouth shut, and ignore all these things which were taking place with the connivance of the higher-ups. Rameshwar felt highly disillusioned and uncomfortable. He comes to you seeking your advice.

Indicate various options that you think are available in this situation. How would you help him to evaluate these options and choose the most appropriate path to be adopted? (250 words) 20

Solution

The various options available in this situation are as follows:

1. Rameshwar should keep quiet and do his part in overlooking such lapses.
2. He should raise his voice and bring about any changes he can under his authority.

The first option might be better for him if he does not want to get himself into trouble. He can live peacefully, but without the satisfaction of public service. This also goes against public service values such as integrity, transparency, courage of one's conviction and perseverance. It will also not comply with his conscience, resulting in restlessness.

The second option will follow the dictates if his conscience. He can try to change the system, but it will take time and perseverance, as had been rightly pointed out by Mahatma Gandhi. He can choose to be a whistleblower and take recourse to vigilance and other enforcement agencies, but this would not solve the entire problem. Finally, he has to rectify the system on his own. In his department, if things do not run properly, it would be considered his failure. So seeing this situation as an opportunity, he should attempt to realise his duty as a true civil servant.

6. In our country, the migration of rural people to towns and cities is increasing drastically. This is causing serious problems both in the rural as well as in the urban areas. In fact, things are becoming really unmanageable. Can you analyze this problem in detail and indicate not only the socio-economic but also the emotional and attitudinal factors responsible for this problem? Also, distinctly bring out why

(a) Educated rural youths are trying to shift to urban areas;
(b) Landless poor people are migrating to urban slums;
(c) Even some farmers are selling off their land and trying to settle in urban areas taking up petty jobs.

What feasible steps can you suggest which will be effective in controlling this serious problem of our country? (250 words)   20

Solution

(a) The educated rural youth want to shift to urban localities because of the following socio-economic factors:

1. Greater opportunities for jobs in cities.
2. Social backwardness, in terms of rampant casteism, other social evils and oppression by powerful people.
3. Unwillingness to do menial work near their homes for fear of losing prestige in society.

The emotional and attitudinal factors are:

1. Attraction for a modern lifestyle and the high-profile jobs available in cities.
2. Behavioural incompatibility with the rural environment, as they have grown accustomed to city life during their student years.
3. Good medical and educational facilities.
4. Predictive cognition of no sign of advancement in the place of origin in near future.

(b) The landless poor are migrating to urban slums due to the following socio-economic factors:

1. Scarcity of jobs in rural areas and greater opportunities for work in city regions.
2. Low labour wages in rural areas.
3. Failure of government schemes to provide employment under MNREGS.

The emotional and attitudinal factors are:

1. No attachment to their native places because of their landlessness and poverty.
2. Greater opportunities for jobs in urban areas.
3. Higher labour price in cities.

(c) Some farmers are selling their land and shifting to urban areas for petty jobs due to the following socio-economic factors:

1. Agricultural losses and the reduced fertility of land, which makes agriculture less profitable.
2. Prospects of a good education for their children in urban areas, along with better health facilities for parents.
3. The deteriorating social environment of rural areas, in terms of social unrest, deprivation, etc.

The emotional and attitudinal factors facilitating such a move are:

1. No attachment to the land because of the losses faced in agriculture.
2. Attraction for a modern lifestyle and the privacy offered in urban regions.
3. Awareness of the importance of education for the next generation.

Suggestions to ameliorate these situations are:

(i) Introduction of intensive interventions such as modernisation of agriculture and water conservation measures to recharge the water table.
(ii) Creating agriculture infrastructure such as food-processing industries for value addition to farm produce, so that farmers can be paid good prices in lieu of their produce.
(iii) Reinventing the MGNREGS to provide guaranteed employment with asset creation in rural areas.
(iv) Providing good educational facilities in rural areas with the help of technology that will bridge the rural–urban divide.

Case Studies (2015)

1. A private company is known for its efficiency, transparency and employee welfare. The company though owned by a private individual has a cooperative character where employees feel a sense of ownership. The company employs nearly 700 personnel and they have voluntarily decided not to form a union.

One day suddenly in the morning, about 40 men belonging to a political party gate-crashed into the factory demanding jobs in the factory. They threatened the management and employees, and also used foul language. The employees feel demoralized. It was clear that those people who gate-crashed wanted to be on the payroll of the company as well as continue as the volunteers/members of the party.

The company maintains high standards in integrity and does not extend favours to civil administration that also includes law enforcement agency. Such incidents occur in public sector also.

(a) Assume you are the CEO of the company. What would you do to diffuse the volatile situation on the date of gate-crashing with the violent mob sitting inside the company premises?
(b) What could be the long-term solution to the issue discussed in the case?
(c) Every solution/action that you suggest will have a positive and a negative impact on you (as CEO), the employees and the performance of the employees. Analyze the consequences of each of your suggested actions. (250 words) 20

Solution

(a) First, I will try to assuage the mob. I will ask them to choose one among them as a leader whom I will speak to in my office, while the rest wait outside. I will try to persuade their leader that we will accommodate as many people as we can, but to do this, we need to speak with the higher authorities as well. This will take some time, no matter how much we try and expedite this, and he should understand this and cooperate.

(b) The long-term solution to the issue can be summarised as follows:

I will discuss this with the higher management at the board level, and ask them to talk to the concerned minister and related political executives regarding the safety of the employees and the security of the company premises. I will personally talk to the District Collector and Superintendent of Police so they can take the necessary actions, and will increase the private security on the premises. The company has to stop all recruitments through the back door because this might set an unfortunate precedent.

(c) The consequences of this action may be as follows:

1. The mob may become more violent and vandalise the company assets.
2. However, we will now be prepared to tackle any untoward situation with the help of the government and private resources of the company.
3. The employees of the company may be fearful, and this might compromise their work efficiency.

2. You are the Sarpanch of a Panchayat. There is a primary school run by the government in your area. Midday meals are provided to the children attending the school. The Headmaster has now appointed a new cook in the school to prepare the meals. However, when it is found that the cook is from Dalit community, almost half of the children belonging to higher castes are not allowed to take meals by their parents. Consequently the attendance in the school falls sharply. This could result in the possibility of discontinuation or midday meal scheme, thereafter of teaching staff and subsequent closing down the school.

(a) Discuss some feasible strategies to overcome the conflict and to create right ambience.

(b) What should be the responsibilities of different social segments and agencies to create positive social ambience for accepting such changes? (250 words)   20

Solution

(a) Such conflict is quite frequent in rural areas where the caste factor often obstructs government programmes. I will immediately talk to the Headmaster of the school and ask him to convene a meeting of parents and teachers, where I will try and persuade the parents to send their children to school. If my efforts do not yield results, I will inform the Block Development Officer and Sub-Divisional Magistrate and seek their help. I will also seek the help of NGOs, social workers, as well as all prestigious neutral personalities of the locality to visit the village and persuade the parents. If the local MLA or MP are popular personalities, I will urge them to visit the village and urge the parents to send their children to school.

(b) The different social segments and agencies that can be involved are:

Local NGOs, social workers, successful village personalities who are respectful and popular among the villagers, religious teachers (dharma guru), etc.

These people should visit the village and talk to every villager about the social evil of casteism, the importance of brotherhood, humanism and education in the life of children. They should explain the futility of caste considerations, citing the example of the Ramayana (for example, the incident of Lord Rama savouring the plums served by Sabari, a low-caste devotee).

Agencies could involve the Sarpanch, ward members, the education department, BDO (Panchayat Raj department), Sub-Divisional Magistrate/Collector (civil administration), Police, MLA, MP, etc., who should wield their authority and offer rewards and punishment as moral motivators.

3. One of the scientists working in the R & D laboratory of a major pharmaceutical company discovers that one of the company's bestselling veterinary drugs has the potential to cure a currently incurable liver disease that in prevalent in tribal areas. However, developing a variant of the drug suitable for human beings entailed a lot of research and development having a huge expenditure to the extent of Rs. 50 crores.

It was unlikely that the company would recover the costs as the disease was rampant only in poverty-stricken area having very little market otherwise. If you were the CEO, then:

(a) Identify the various actions that you could take;
(b) Evaluate the pros and cons of each or your actions. (250 words)   20

Solution

(a) I am faced with an ethical dilemma: I have to follow professional ethics that compels me to take decisions in the company's benefit. On the other hand, morality compels me to act to produce the drug that can cure the malady of the poverty-stricken tribal people. I can take the following courses of action in this situation:

1. I will try to persuade the Board of the company to develop this drug, using the funds meant for corporate social responsibility.
2. I can try to associate with a social organisation to fund R&D in this regard, with the due approval of the company's Board.
3. I can send a proposal to the Department of Science and Technology, Government of India, under the Collaborative R&D Projects for a grant-in-aid for the research and development of the proposed drug.

(b) The pros and cons of the above actions will be as follows:

1. One of the pros related to the first course of action is that the patent of the drug will remain with the company. If, in the future, the disease spreads on a large scale, the company can make huge profits from the drug production. Also, the prestige and brand value of the company will be enhanced in the drug market. On the negative side, the entire process will take time, during which period the condition of the ill population will worsen further.
2. The pros related to the second course of action will be that research and development will begin at a fast pace, and the drug will soon be available to the ill people. However, the social organisation can intervene unnecessarily in the procedure and the company's credit score may not be adequate, which will be unacceptable to the company's board.
3. This is the best option as it will enhance the reputation of the company in the eyes of the government as well as the drug market. The ill people can all be covered because the government has entered the picture. But there can be procedural delays in the approval of the project due to a bureaucratic attitude.

4. There is a disaster-prone State having frequent landslides, forest fires, cloudbursts, flash floods and earthquakes, etc. Some of these are seasonal and often unpredictable. The magnitude of the disaster is always unanticipated. During one of the seasons, a cloudburst caused devastating floods and landslides leading to high causalities.

Case Studies

There was major damage to infrastructure like roads, bridges and power generating units. This led to more than 100000 pilgrims, tourists and other locals trapped across different routes and locations. The people trapped in your area of responsibility included senior citizens, patients in hospitals, women and children, hikers, tourists, ruling party's regional president along with his family, additional chief secretary of the neighbouring State and prisoners in jail.

As civil services officer of the State, what would be the order in which you would rescue these people and why? Give justifications. (200 words) 20

Solution

I will follow the order given below to rescue the trapped people:

The most vulnerable individuals will be rescued first. In a disaster, vulnerability is decided on the basis of one's capacity to handle the situation, in terms of physical stamina, maturity and knowledge. I will then give priority to the asset values of the nation, and finally to the local people. Children, patients in hospitals, and women will be similarly vulnerable, but as per the utilitarian tradition, women and children (with the family of the regional party president) should be given first priority in rescue. Children are our future and the most innocent individuals; on the other hand, patients in hospitals may belong to different physical categories, with some weaker and unable to survive for longer durations. This is why I will rescue the patients in the hospital after the category of women and children.

Further, I would prioritise the rescue of senior citizens because they are the third most vulnerable group trapped in the disaster. I will then rescue the additional chief secretary of the neighbouring state because of his importance in the government hierarchy, and his value as an asset to the nation. Next in the order of preference will be the ruling party's regional president, tourists, hikers (on the basis of their proximity to the rescue team), and finally, the prisoners in jail.

5. You are heading a district administration in a particular department. Your senior officer calls you from the State Headquarters and tells you that a plot in Rampur village is to have a building constructed on it for a school. A visit is scheduled during which he will visit the site along with the chief engineer and the senior architect. He wants you to check out all the papers relating to it and to ensure that the visit is properly arranged. You examine the file which relates to the period before you joined the department. The land was acquired from the local Panchayat at a nominal cost and the papers show that clearance certificates are available from the two of the three authorities who have to certify the site's suitability. There is no certification by the architect available on file. You decide to visit Rampur to ensure that all is in order as stated on file. When you visit Rampur, you find that the plot under reference is part of Thakurgarh Fort and that the walls, ramparts, etc. are running across it. The fort is well away from the main village, therefore a school here will be a serious inconvenience for the children. However the area near the village has potential to expand into a larger residential area. The development charges on the existing plot, at the fort, will be very high and the question of heritage site has not been addressed. Moreover, the Sarpanch, at the time of acquisition of the land, was a relative of your Predecessor. The whole transaction appears to have been done with some vested interest.

(a) List the likely vested interests of the concerned parties.
(b) Some of the options for action available to you are listed below. Discuss the merits and demerits or each of the options:
  (i) You can await the visit of the superior officer and let him take a decision.

(ii) You can seek his advice in writing or on phone.

(iii) You can consult your predecessor/colleagues, etc. and then decide what to do.

(iv) You can find out if any alternate plot can be got in exchange and then send a comprehensive written report.

Can you suggest any other option with proper justification? (250 words)   25

Solution

(a) The vested interests may be as follows:
1. The appropriate lands near the main village might have been encroached upon, and the Sarpanch of the village might have intended to avoid a clash with the encroachers.
2. Construction of the school building would take place away from the eyes of the villagers, which could provide an opportunity for carrying out inferior quality work without any interruption from the villagers.
3. The building could even be used for illegal activities after school hours due to its distance from the main village.

(b) Merits and demerits of the above options would be as follows:

(i) The first option would avoid all hassles and conflicts. However, the project would linger on, and this might lead to disciplinary inquiries against me. My lethargy could also be mistaken for low administrative capability, which will give me a bad reputation.

(ii) Following the second option would make me seem indecisive when dealing with administrative matters of an urgent nature, and make me seem to be a weak administrator. This is a typical bureaucratic attitude that lies behind the slow progress of the nation. The merit of this option is that it would delay any conflict. This could be helpful while taking decisions, but only to some extent.

(iii) The third option again highlights a weak administrative aptitude. My predecessor had behaved irresponsibly due to his own vested interests, so he would obviously misguide me. The merit of this option is the possibility of my getting some valuable inputs from him, but that too is not very likely.

(iv) The fourth option would give an opportunity to rectify the past wrong and expedite the matter. This would also enhance my administrative reputation in the government. However, this course of action will clash with the stakeholders, whose vested interests would not be served if the site of the school building is changed.

I will form a team comprising a junior engineer and an assistant engineer from the concerned jurisdiction. I will then ask the concerned Tehsildar to send across the revenue officer under whose jurisdiction that village falls. I will explore all possible sites near the main village and select the one most suitable, after consulting with the *panch*es (ward members of Panchayat) and the villagers. If that site is under encroachment, I will mention it in my report, and send the report to the District Collector as well as to Headquarters.

(A common suggestion given often is convening a Gram Sabha for this purpose; however, that is not possible at short notice. A Gram Sabha can only be convened by a notification issued by the District Collector, which is usually not done for deciding a particular case.)

6. You are recently posted as district development officer or a district. Shortly thereafter you found that there is considerable tension in the rural areas of your district on the issue or sending girls to schools.

The elders of the village feel that many problems have come up because girls are being educated and they are stepping out of the safe environment of the household. They are or the view that the girls should be quickly married off with minimum education. The girls are also competing for jobs after education, which have traditionally remained in boys' exclusive domain, adding to unemployment amongst male population.

The younger generation feels that in the present era, girls should have equal opportunities for education and employment, and other means of livelihood. The entire locality is divided between the elders and the younger lot and further sub-divided between sexes in both generations. You come to know that in Panchayat or in other local bodies or even in busy crossroads, the issue is being acrimoniously debated.

One day you are informed that an unpleasant incident has taken place. Some girls were molested, when they were en route to schools. The incident led to clashes between several groups and a law and order problem has arisen. The elders after heated discussion have taken a joint decision not to allow girls to go to school and to socially boycott all such families, which do not follow their dictate.

(a) What steps would you take to ensure girls' safety without disrupting their education?
(b) How would you manage and mould patriarchic attitude of the village elders to ensure harmony in the inter-generational relations? (250 words) 25

Solution

(a) I would talk to the Block Development Officer, Sub-Divisional Magistrate (SDM) and the concerned police officer, as well as to the District Collector and Superintendent of Police to instruct the SDM and relevant police officer, respectively, to arrest the culprits and provide the necessary security to the girls (if possible, women police constables should be deployed for security). I will instruct the BDO to direct the Sarpanch and other officers of the Gram Panchayat to set up a patrol when the girls commute to school. The Panchayat can also take the help of village volunteers in this regard (that is, community policing). I will also arrange for self-defence classes for the girls to make them confident and fearless.

(b) I will use the tools of attitude change, persuasion and emotional intelligence to manage and transform the patriarchal attitude of the village elders. I will organise a 'choupal' (meeting) with villagers and listen to the apprehensions and beliefs of the elders. I will also enlist the help of the new generation to persuade the elders, and explain the importance of education for girls. I will tell them success stories of girls as well as the failure of boys to care for their parents in their old age. I will assure them of the girls' security en route to school.

Case Studies (2016)

1. A fresh engineering graduate gets a job in a prestigious chemical industry. She likes the work. The salary is also good. However, after a few months she accidentally discovers that a highly toxic waste is being secretly discharged into a river nearby. This is causing health problems to the villagers downstream who depend on the river for their water needs. She is perturbed and mentions her concern to her colleagues who have been with the company for longer periods.

They advise her to keep quite as anyone who mentions the topic is summarily dismissed. She cannot risk losing her job as she is the sole bread-winner for her family and has to support her ailing parents and siblings. At first, she thinks that if her seniors are keeping quiet, why she should stick out her neck. But her conscience pricks her to do something to save the river and the people who depend upon it. At heart she feels that the advice of silence given by her friends is not correct though she cannot give reasons for it. She thinks you are a wise person and seeks your advice.

(a) What arguments can you advance to show her that keeping quiet is not morally right?

(b) What course of action would you advise her to adopt and why? (250 words)   20

Solution

(a) I can guide her under the following moral grounds to raise her voice for the sake of the innocent and completely unaware villagers:

1. The teleological tradition of utilitarianism forces us to act in a way that maximises the happiness of the majority. If my happiness needs to be sacrificed for the sake of humanity at large, than that alone should convince me to rebel against the company.

2. The deontological tradition bolsters constitutional morality, which stipulates the fundamental duties of a citizen vis-à-vis the state. She should immediately convey the reality to the district administration.

3. Virtue ethics also compels an individual to act virtuously. Wisdom, courage and justice are the important virtues one must embrace in such situations.

4. 'An unexamined life is not worth living'. This Socratic argument enforces to analyse the aim of our life, and encourages us to be ready to face anything for the sake of the greater good. Gandhi also considered 'commerce without morality' one of the greatest sins.

5. One should not ignore the voice of conscience because it is the most accurate guide in any kind of dilemma.

(b) I would advise her to immediately write to her superior about the imminent dangers posed by the toxic discharge. She should also intimate the district administration about the situation in writing. If the latter seems to be taking prompt action, then she could help them with her knowledge to detoxify the waste. However, if the district administration remains idle, then she should rush to every Sarpanch of the concerned village panchayats and to local public representatives to immediately prohibit the villagers from using the river water, while at the same time applying pressure on the district administration for remedial measures.

2. Land needed for mining, dams and other large-scale projects is acquired mostly from Adivasis, hill dwellers and rural communities. The displaced persons are paid monetary compensation as per the legal provisions. However, the payment is often tardy. In any case, it cannot sustain the displaced families for long. These people do not possess marketable skills to engage in some other occupation.

They end up as Low paid migrant labourers. Moreover, their traditional ways of community living are destroyed. Thus, the benefits of development go to industries, industrialists and urban communities whereas the costs are passed on to these poor helpless people. This unjust distribution of costs and benefits is unethical.

Suppose you have been entrusted with the task of drafting a better compensation-cum-rehabilitation policy for such displaced persons, how would you approach the problem and would be the main elements of your suggested Policy? (250 words) 20

Solution

I would make a policy that can assure the rehabilitation of Adivasis with minimal social cost and the possibility of better living conditions. I will include the following provisions in the rehabilitation plan:

1. An option for land in exchange for land rather than full monetary compensation, so that they can decide their own course of action.
2. Look for land of similar or better quality in terms of fertility and access to existing market centres, thus providing for economic as well as employment options, so that they can continue their previous activities.
3. Provisions for the development of basic infrastructure, like primary school, community-building, access roads and internal roads for the newly settled habitat, with the help of MGNREGS, performance grants, and other schemes.
4. Include compulsory development activities in the acquirement plan, enabling industries to spend their CSR fund on development activities in the newly settled habitat.

The principal ideas behind the rehabilitation policy should be justice, empathy, emotional intelligence, attitude change, persuasion, compassion towards weaker sections, and dedication to public service. The idea of justice pertains to clearing all the dues raised by virtue of land acquisition from the Adivasis. They should be offered exactly what has been snatched from them. The idea of commutative and distributive justice should be included in the rehabilitation plan as well. One should understand the agony of the Adivasis being forced to leave their homeland. To apply empathy and emotional intelligence, large-scale personal communication and interviews should be recorded to include the expectations of the Adivasis. This should be supplemented by rigorous counselling because we have seen that rehabilitated people often do not shift to new regions; rather, they begin living beside the acquired land, thereby increasing their vulnerability.

3. Suppose you are an officer in-charge of implementing a social service scheme to provide support to old and destitute women. An old and illiterate woman comes to you to avail the benefits of the scheme. However, she has no documents to show that she fulfils the eligibility criteria. But after meeting her and listening to her you feel that she certainly needs support. Your enquiries also show that she is really destitute and living in a pitiable condition.

   You are in a dilemma as to what to do. Putting her under the scheme without necessary documents would clearly be violation of rules. But denying her the support would be cruel and inhuman.

   (a) Can you think of a rational way to resolve this dilemma?
   (b) Give your reasons for it. (250 words) 20

Solution

(a) Here, we have ethics under the deontological tradition on the one hand, and morality under a humanistic point of view on the other. Both have served to create an ethical dilemma. I will try to resolve this dilemma by carving a middle path that will ensure a compliance with the norms as well as cater to the needs of the destitute woman.

   I will constitute a team of empathetic and learned subordinates to assist the woman to prepare the necessary documents that will bring her under the purview of the scheme, provided that she meets the eligibility criteria. I will obtain a certificate from the local body (municipality in the case of an urban area, and Gram Panchayat in the case of rural areas) regarding her status, such as BPL, caste, income, land owned by her, etc., to help her meet her eligibility criteria. After ensuring that she is eligible for beneficiary status, I will include her under the scheme immediately.

(b) My reasoning behind these efforts are as follows:

1. My job is to serve all beneficiaries who fulfil the criteria for the scheme. This woman fulfils the criteria, but lacks documents. Therefore, providing her with assistance becomes both an actual duty and a prima facie duty.
2. Compassion towards the weaker sections is one of the fundamental values of civil services.
3. The notion of inclusiveness in good governance demands such efforts.
4. The modus operandi thus laid out strikes a balance between the deontological and teleological traditions, and hence proves that the action is ethical.
5. The Gandhian philosophy of 'taking decisions keeping in mind the last man in the queue' and the notion of 'antyodaya' given by Pt. Deen Dayal Upadhyay also bolster my decision.

4. You are a young, aspiring and sincere employee in a Government office working as an assistant to the director of your department. Since you have joined recently, you need to learn and progress. Luckily your superior is very kind and ready to train you for your job. He is a very intelligent and well informed person having knowledge of various departments. In short, you respect your boss and are looking forward to learn a lot from him.

Since you have a good tuning with the boss, he started depending on you. One day due to ill health he invited you at his place for finishing some urgent work.

You reached his house and before you could ring the bell you heard shouting noises. You waited for a while. After entering the house the boss greeted you and explained the work. But you were constantly disturbed by the crying of a woman. At last, you inquired with the boss but his answer did not satisfy you.

Next day, you were compelled to inquire further in the office and found out that his behaviour is very bad at home with his wife. He also beats up his wife. His wife is not well educated and is a simple woman in comparison to her husband. You see that though your boss is a nice person in the office, he is engaged in domestic violence at home. In such a situation, you are left with the following options.

Analyze each option with its consequences.

(a) Just ignore thinking about it because it is their personal matter.
(b) Report the case to the appropriate authority.
(c) Your own innovative approach towards the situation. (250 words)   20

Solution

(a) The advantage of ignoring the behaviour of my boss at home is being able to continue with his support at the workplace. I am not responsible for his personal conduct with his family. Proving any merit to these allegations is the job of the higher authorities. However, ignoring such behaviour does not allow me to be a good citizen. I come across as egocentric and suppress the voice of my conscience. It also goes against the teleological tradition, as some day, some mishap might occur and my boss might find himself facing legal consequences, thereby robbing me of my opportunity to learn from him.

(b) The advantage of reporting the case to the appropriate authority is that it will help me overcome my guilt and moral turpitude. It will also be legally and teleologically appropriate. However, fostering a bad relationship with my boss can jeopardise my career.

(c) I will not jump to a conclusion on the basis of one instance; rather, I shall discuss this further with my colleagues and try to glean the truth. If I find that my boss is completely in the wrong, then I will wait for an opportune moment to discuss the matter further with him. I will warn him of the consequences of his behaviour, and possible legal action against him, in case his wife or someone else lodges a complaint. As I am not his neighbour and do not know much about his personal life, I will inform his wife's family about the situation discreetly and anonymously. I cannot lodge a police complaint because I am not an eyewitness to the domestic violence, nor is this my actual duty.

5. ABC Ltd. is a large transnational company having diversified business activities with a huge shareholder base. The company is continuously expanding and generating employment. The company, in its expansion and diversification programme, decides to establish a new plant at Vikaspuri, an area which is underdeveloped. The new plant is designed to use energy efficient technology that will help the company to save production cost by 20%.

The company's decision goes well with the Government policy of attracting investment to develop such underdeveloped regions. The Government has also announced tax holiday for five years for the companies that invest in underdeveloped areas. However, the new plant may bring chaos for the inhabitants of Vikaspuri region, which is otherwise tranquil. The new plant may result in increased cost of living, aliens migrating to the region, disturbing the social and economic order.

The company, sensing the possible protest and tried to educate the people of Vikaspuri region and public in general that how its Corporate Social Responsibility (CSR) policy would help to overcome the likely difficulties of the residents of Vikaspuri region. In spite of this the protests begin and some or the residents decided to approach the judiciary as their plea before the Government did not yield any result.

(a) Identify the issues involved in the case.
(b) What can be suggested to satisfy the company's goal and to address the resident's concerns? (300 words)   25

Solution

(a) The issues involved in the case are: residents' apprehensions regarding the possible cultural downfall of the region; the entry of social evils into the community; an increasing desire among youngsters to follow new and expensive lifestyles, aping the employees of the company.

These issues may be addressed through recourse to attitude change, persuasion, emotional intelligence, and following the ethics of corporate governance. The attitude of Vikaspuri residents can be changed through different methods; for example, meaningful communication with the help of agreeable employees, a promise of employment generation, and intensive CSR activities in Vikaspuri, which will increase the overall prosperity of the region. The company also has to empathise with the emotions of the residents. The meticulous use of emotional intelligence on the part of the company's officer can resolve this issue. The apprehension of local residents pertaining to economic and cultural degradation can be addressed with the help of regular communication, convincing the residents and unemployed youngsters of their intention to generate new jobs and build social, educational and health infrastructure for them, and how such endeavours would give a new direction to the lives of the residents.

(b) The company should make a plan for employment generation that will explicitly project the average income of the employees, as well as a plan of activities under CSR funds. This plan should be presented before the Vikaspuri residents after convening a meeting. The company should promise to create a committee of local residents that will be invited every quarter to present their concerns to the management.

6. Saraswati was a successful IT professional in USA. Moved by the patriotic sense of doing something for the country she returned to India. Together with other like-minded friends, she formed an NGO to build a school for a poor rural community.

The objective of the school was to provide the best quality modern education at nominal cost. She soon discovered that she has to seek permission from a number of Government agencies. The rules and procedures were quite confusing and cumbersome. What frustrated her most were the delays, callous attitude of officials and constant demand for bribes. Her experience and the experience of many others like her has deterred people from taking up social service projects. A measure of Government control over voluntary social work is necessary. But it should not be exercised in a coercive or corrupt manner.

What measures can you suggest to ensure that due control is exercised but well meaning, honest NGO efforts are not thwarted? (300 words)   25

Solution

I can offer the following suggestions to ensure control over the NGOs and social work institutions without jeopardising their objectives:

1. The initial formalities should be reduced. These procedures should be made available online, with minimum human intervention in the formation and registration of NGOs. If an NGO intends to start work without government assistance, the relevant rules should be relaxed and the NGO should remain independent of rigorous regulatory mechanisms.

2. There should be a mechanism to screen these institutions on the basis of their work and the impact they have on society. That should be the sole basis for government funding, or any crowd-funding or monetary assistance these institutions seek from the public in lieu of services provided by them.

3. There should be a social audit of the work done by these NGOs. The social audit reports should be intensively studied and taken into consideration while either rating or blacklisting them.

4. Provision should be made for an online recordkeeping system where all the ongoing and previous projects undertaken by each registered NGO should be included, This information should be disclosed in the public domain, and the public should have direct access to a complaint register as well.

Case Studies (2017)

1. You are an honest and responsible civil servant. You often observe the following:

   (a) There is a general perception that adhering to ethical conduct one may face difficulties to oneself and cause problems for the family, whereas unfair practices may help to reach the career goals.

   (b) When the number of people adopting unfair means is large, a small minority having a penchant towards ethical means makes no difference.

   (c) Sticking to ethical means is detrimental to the larger developmental goals.

(d) While one may not involve oneself in large unethical practices, but giving and accepting small gifts makes the system more efficient.

Examine the above statements with their merits and demerits. (250 words)   20

Solution

(a) The merits of statement (a) can be as follows:
   1. One can avoid clashes with seniors, politicians and public figures.
   2. Problems pertaining to frequent transfers, intra-office resentment, and bad postings can be overcome.
   3. An 'yes man' is always the first choice of politicians and higher authorities.
   4. Key postings and promising assignments, which may prove to be milestones in career growth, are usually given to favourite officers.

   The demerits are as follows:
   1. Such a modus operandi may lead to unpleasant situations.
   2. This goes against public service values.
   3. This also goes against deontological, teleological, and virtue ethics.

(b) The merits of statement (b) are as follows:
   1. An ethical person who later follows the norm and starts using unfair means will no longer be part of a minority.
   2. People in a minority make very little difference, and hence the utility of their efforts remains nil. By following the conduct of the majority of officers, they will at least gain prosperity and happiness in their personal lives.

   The demerits are:
   1. Changes are always brought about by a leader who is different from the mob, unique, and identified for his deeds. One defies one's own conscience when becoming like others.
   2. This will corrupt the virtue and intuitions of a virtuous civil servant.

(c) The merits of statement (c) are:
   1. Ethical compliance usually retards the pace of programme implementation.
   2. A reliance on ethical persuasion may result in cynicism and scepticism. This leads to a deficit of trust, which slows down decision-making and proved detrimental to larger objectives.

   The demerits are:
   1. Larger goals cannot be built on a foundation made of a fragile integrity, overwhelming self-interest, and a compromise with ethics and public service values.
   2. Pursuing self-interest would divert public money from the objectives for which it is meant, which will not conform to deontology or teleology.

(d) The merits of statement (d) are:
   1. This will enhance the efficiency of public servants.
   2. If the credit of achieving a larger goal does not have to be shared, one can easily accept personal gains in monetary terms.
   3. This would not cause huge losses because planning is usually done with an augmented budget, and efficiency can help to save costs even while determining the stipulated quality in public delivery.

   The demerits are:
   1. Integrity needs to remains beyond any doubt. A compromised integrity is no integrity at all.
   2. Involvement in corrupt practices, no matter how small, deteriorates the reputation of public office.

3. Even accepting small gifts leads to an obligation to reciprocate, giving rise to a conflict of interest.

2. You are aspiring to become an IAS officer and you have cleared various stages and now you have been selected for the personal interview. On the day of the interview, on the way to the venue you saw an accident where a mother and child who happen to be your relatives were badly injured. They needed immediate help.

What would you have done in such a situation? Justify your action. (250 words)   20

Solution

This is a moral dilemma. On the one hand, the lives of two persons are at stake, and on the other, my career and dreams are at stake. Different moral principles will lead to different answers in this situation. This is also a test of my emotional intelligence. I will try to arrive at the most convincing answer by drawing guidance in the following manner:

1. Plato defines justice as the virtuous condition of the soul, in which the rational part of the soul rules over the whole. Social functions have been divided among the different classes in a society. In this case, the government has put in place emergency services that cannot be matched by any personal assistance I can offer to the victims of an accident. My function as a Good Samaritan is to immediately call the emergency service; anything other than this is beyond my expertise and ability. My role involves informing everyone concerned about the situation. This view is also supported by the utilitarian tradition.
2. I must learn to distinguish between *prima facie* and actual duty. Weighing my duties related to providing assistance to the victims on the one hand and rushing to the interview on the other leads me to realise that the latter is more important. My actual duty is to realise my dream of being selected for the Indian Administrative Service (IAS) as a lot of efforts and the expectations of many people are tied up with this. This view also conforms to the utilitarian tradition.

I will immediately stop and call the emergency services (an ambulance) and the police. I will then inform the closest relatives of the victims. Since I am no medical expert, I cannot provide any assistance to them. If time permits, I will pursue the emergency service and try to get them on the scene as soon as possible. Then, I will proceed to my interview.

3. You are the head of the Human Resources department of an organisation. One day one of the workers died on duty. His family was demanding compensation. However, the company denied compensation because it was revealed in investigation that he was drunk at the time of the accident. The workers of the company went to strike demanding compensation for the family of the deceased. The Chairman of the management board has asked for your recommendation.

What recommendation would you provide the management?

Discuss the merits and demerits of each of the recommendations. (250 words)   20

Solution

I would provide the following recommendations:

1. Strictly deny the provision of any compensation if it is proved that the death was caused due to the worker being intoxicated on duty.
2. Provide compassionate employment to an eligible member of the deceased's family.

The merit of the first recommendation is the strong message conveyed to all employees. In future, no employee will dare to indulge in such indiscipline. Such an act also goes against professional ethics and the laws of the company. Thus, this recommendation conforms to the deontological tradition. The demerit is that the strike may last longer, which may cause financial loss to the company.

The merit of the second recommendation relates to the human value of compassion and empathy towards weaker sections. This sends a message that while the company does not compromise with its norms, it is, at the same time, serious about employee welfare. However, while this action will ensure the future of the concerned employee's family, there is a risk that other employees might misuse this policy in the future.

4. You are the manager of a spare parts company A and you have to negotiate a deal with the manager of a large manufacturing company B. The deal is highly competitive and sealing the deal is critical for your company. The deal is being worked out over a dinner. After dinner the manager of manufacturing company B offered to drop you to the hotel in his car. On the way to hotel he happens to hit a motorcycle injuring the motorcyclist badly. You know the manager was driving fast and thus lost control. The law enforcement officer comes to investigate the issue and you are the sole eyewitness to it. Knowing the strict laws pertaining to road accidents you are aware that your honest account of the incident would lead to the prosecution of the manager and as a consequence the deal is likely to be jeopardized, which is of immense importance to your company.

What are the dilemmas you face? What will be your response to the situation? (250 words) 20

Solution

Here, the dilemma is: Should I save the culprit, or should I follow the law of the land? In a real sense, this is not a moral dilemma at all; rather, this dilemma relates to a conflict of interest. On the one hand, my personal interest is clashing with my organisational interest, and on the other hand, the crime against the state committed by the manager of company B should be punished, on the basis of my statement to the law agencies.

I will tell the truth and cooperate with the law enforcement officer. The reasons behind my stand are as follows:

1. According to deontological ethics, one should abide by and cooperate with the law.
2. The utility lies in the fact that the truth will lead to the manager of company B being punished under torts or some other traffic rules, but it will ensure that in the future, he rectifies his conduct and avoids any accident that may endanger his life and that of others. In this way, my decision to tell the truth will determine the greater good in the future.
3. 'An unexamined life is not worth living'. This statement by Socrates reminds me of the value of self-assessment and its implications.
4. I should understand that the case is no longer confined to a private relationship. It has now become public, and I should act according to the ethics governing public relationships.

5. A building permitted for three floors, while being extended illegally to 6 floors by a builder, collapses. As a consequence, a number of innocent labourers including women and children died. These labourers are migrants of different places. The government immediately announced cash relief to the aggrieved families and arrested the builder.

Give reasons for such incidents taking place across the country. Suggest measures to prevent their occurrence. (250 words) 20

Solution

The reasons behind such incidents are:

1. Vertical development reduces the building costs and increases the builders' profits.
2. Permission for fewer floors requires fewer specifications. This low specification drastically reduces the construction cost, because high-rise construction includes norms and provisions of structural safety, more space for parking, greater width of the plot, hard surface approach road, etc.
3. In urban areas, the connivance of revenue officers, municipal authorities, and engineers lead to a plan being approved, often overlooking safety norms. The actual construction on the field follows lower standards than those approved.

Measures to prevent the occurrence of such incidents:

1. Determining public service values and emotional intelligence in regulating construction works because most disasters take place due to the weakness of the structures.
2. Provisions for strong vigilance in construction activities, and severe consequences for any negligence and corruption in building permission and regulation.
3. RERA has emerged as a milestone in this regard, but we should ensure that it remains immune to corruption.
4. Frequent and timely surveys should be conducted by neutral engineers and social audit teams.
5. Intensive IEC activities over television and radio to educate people about the plan and standards required for a building they plan to purchase. They should also be asked to inspect the construction quality by visiting the site from time to time.

6. You are a Public Information Officer (PIO) in a government department. You are aware that the RTI Act 2005 envisages transparency and accountability in administration. The act has functioned as a check on the supposedly arbitrarily administrative behaviour and actions. However, as a PIO you have observed that there are citizens who filed RTI applications not for themselves but on behalf of such stakeholders who purportedly want to have access to information to further their own interests. At the same time there are these RTI activists who routinely file RTI applications and attempt to extort money from the decision makers. This type of RTI activism has affected the functioning of the administration adversely and also possibly jeopardizes the genuineness of the applications which are essentially aimed at getting justice.

What measures would you suggest to separate genuine and non-genuine applications? Give merits and demerits of your suggestions. (250 words) 20

Solution

I would suggest the following measures to filter genuine RTI applications from those that are not so genuine:

1. The handling of RTI applications should be done online, with procedures that will immediately identify frequent information seekers and blacklist them.
2. I cannot prevent anyone from seeking information if the application comes through the proper channel in accordance with the norms. However, I can establish a system to identify whether that information is being sought in an individual's personal interest, and whether it will serve a larger public interest. This can be done through proper training of the staff.
3. I will try to put this information out in the public domain, as the act permits me to do. Further, I will not entertain application

pertaining to information already present in the public domain.
4. I would organise workshops and seminars on the RTI Act to educate the staff about RTI provisions. This will enable them to screen RTI applications effectively, particularly regarding any exemption from disclosure under Section 8 of the RTI Act.

Merits of these suggestions:

These measures would drastically reduce the staff workload. Fraudulent applicants would be discouraged, and the prestige of the public office will be enhanced. Individuals in a fiduciary relationship with the public office would largely trust the government to protect their interests and privacy.

Demerits of the suggestions:

There may be certain problems relating to the implementation of the RTI Act, in letter and spirit. Implementing the RTI on an online platform may cause troubles to villagers and citizens who are technically uneducated or unable to access the internet. It can also be misused by fraudulent yet technically sound people. Suggestion 2 may involve a lot of scrutiny and cause delays in providing information to genuine applicants if an adequate number of staff is not deputed.

Case Studies (2018)

1. Rakesh is a responsible district level officer who enjoys the trust of his higher officials. Knowing his honesty, the government entrusted him with the responsibility of identifying the beneficiaries under a health care scheme meant for senior citizens.

The criteria to be a beneficiary are the following:

(a) 60 years of age or above.
(b) Belonging to a reserved community.
(c) Family income of less than 1 Lakh rupees per annum.
(d) Post-treatment prognosis is likely to be high to make a positive difference to the quality of life of the beneficiary.

One day, an old couple visited Rakesh's office with their application. They have been the residents of a village in his district since their birth. The old man is diagnosed with a rare condition that causes obstruction in the large intestine. As a consequence, he has severe abdominal pain frequently that prevents him from doing any physical labour. The couple has no children to support them. The expert surgeon whom they contacted is willing to do the surgery without charging any fee. However, the couple will have to bear the cost of incidental charges, such as medicines, hospitalization, etc., to the tune of rupees one lakh. The couple fulfils all the criteria except criterion 'b'. However, any financial aid would certainly make a significant difference in their quality of life.

How should Rakesh respond to the situation? (250 words) 20

Solution

While this seems to be a genuine case, the beneficiary does not fulfil the very important criteria 'b', by which the scheme is aimed solely at the reserved community. Violation of this criterion is legally and rationally unacceptable, legally because the scheme is meant for a particular section of society and duly approved by the legal authority, and rationally because there may be many other similar cases of genuine illness which do not meet the criteria. It is not Rakesh's actual duty to look into such cases. On humanitarian grounds, every rational person should contribute to societal welfare, but public servants should especially ensure that they work within the norms of the ideal code of conduct.

Rakesh can help that elderly man by taking a quotation from the hospital management related to expenditure on incidental charges. He can then talk to some NGOs that work for such causes.

While doing so, Rakesh must ensure there is no *quid pro quo* attached to this arrangement, by which the NGO can seek undue official assistance in the future. He should also avoid all conflict of interest. Rakesh should also endeavour to bring all needy people on a common platform so that they can be helped by honest and humanitarian organisations.

2. As a senior officer in the Ministry, you have access to important policy decisions and upcoming big announcements such as road constructions projects before they are notified in the public domain. The Ministry is about to announce a mega road project for which the drawings are already in place. Sufficient care was taken by the planners to make use of the government land with the minimum land acquisition from private parties. Compensation rate for private parties was also finalized as per government rules. Care was also taken to minimize deforestation. Once the project is announced, it is expected that there will be a huge spurt in real estate prices in and around that area.

Meanwhile, the Minister concerned insists that you realign the road in such a way that it comes closer to his 20 acres farmhouse. He also suggests that he would facilitate the purchase of a big plot of land in your wife's name at the prevailing rate which is very nominal, in and around the proposed mega road project. He also tries to convince you by saying that there is no harm in it as he is buying the land legally. He even promises to supplement your savings in case you do not have sufficient funds to buy the land. However, by the act of realignment, a lot of agricultural lands have to be acquired, thereby causing a considerable financial burden on the government, and also the displacement of the farmers. As if this is not enough, it will involve cutting down of a large number of trees denuding the area of its green cover.

Faced with this situation, what will you do? Critically examine various conflicts of interest and explain what your responsibilities are as a public servant. (250 words)

Solution

In this situation, I will take the following course of action:

1. I will clearly lay out before the Minister arguments relating to the loss of public money, the level of environmental damage, and problems attending such a realignment of the road and the consequent rehabilitation. I will use my virtue of speech (logos) to persuade the Minister to leave this project in the public interest.
2. If the Minister does not agree and continues to put pressure on me, I will talk to my seniors and seek their help. If they refuse to help, I will go on leave and seek a transfer to another ministry. I will then try to expose that Minister, using the provisions of the Whistleblower Protection Act.

There can be two conflicts of interest:

1. My personal interest versus the public interest
2. The Minister's personal interest versus the public interest

In the case of the first, there will be both an actual and a potential conflict of interest, since I will be planning the project and so will know the real value of the information I possess. I should work in the public interest, but I should try to escape any situation of conflict by either leaving the ministry and disclosing the conflict of interest, or by not succumbing to the Minister's pressure. I should complete the plan in the public and environmental interest and submit it to the Ministry.

The Minister should disclose his personal interest as it is his private land that will benefit from the realignment of the road. There is such a provision in the rules of conduct for the ministers and legislatures. Not following this may invite both legal consequences and future investigation.

My responsibility as a public servant is to advise the Minister about the consequences of such behaviour, and the trouble it might cause both of us. It is also my responsibility to take care of the public interest.

3. It is a State where prohibition is in force. You are recently appointed as the Superintendent of Police of a district notorious for illicit distillation of liquor. The illicit liquor leads to many death, reported and unreported, and causes a major problem for the district authorities. The approach till now had been to view it as a law and order problem and tackle it accordingly. Raids, arrest, police cases, and criminal trials—all these had only limited impact. The problem remains as serious as ever.

Your inspections show that the parts of the district where the distillation flourishes are economically, industrially and educationally backward. Agriculture is badly affected by poor irrigation facilities. Frequent clashes among communities gave boost to illicit distillation. No major initiatives had taken place in the past either from the government's side or from social organizations to improve the lot of the people.

Which new approach will you adopt to bring the problem under control? (250 words)

Solution

Reward and punishment are two forms of moral motivation, as rightly pointed out by St. Thomas Aquinas. Punishment, however, has its limits, and when it starts losing its impact, one should move towards rewards. In this situation, raids, arrests, police cases and criminal trials had no effect because the root of the problem lies elsewhere. I will start by finding out the real problem after talking to people across the district, without revealing my identity to them. Armed with this feedback, I will talk to the District Magistrate and the Collector, and propose a meeting with MLAs, MPs, and other public representatives of local self-governments like Panchayats and Municipalities. I will also invite NGOs and social activists to comprehensively discuss the issue. Social transformation cannot take place only through police action; it will require the participation of the various departments controlled by the District Magistrate/Collector.

We will try to institutionalise all sales of liquor and engage local people as per the excise policy of the state. We will also organise rehabilitation camps for habitual drinkers. Advanced agriculture practices, promoted under various schemes of the government, will be offered to the farmers. We will aim to design a comprehensive package, which involves land improvement, irrigation facilities, agricultural inputs supply, and land dispute resolution, incorporating all the schemes of rural development and agriculture.

I will use the approaches of attitude change, persuasion, social influence, rewards, transparency, impartiality and emotional intelligence to address the issue, and inculcate these in the police officers who work at the grassroots level.

4. A big corporate house is engaged in manufacturing industrial chemicals on a large scale. It proposes to set upon the additional unit. Many states rejected its proposal due to the detrimental effect on the environment. But one state government acceded to the request and permitted the unit close to a city, brushing aside all opposition.

The unit was set up 10 years ago and was in full swing till recently. The pollution caused by the industrial effluents was affecting the land, water and crops in the area. It was also causing serious health problems to human beings and animals. This gave rise to a series of agitation thousands of people took part, creating a law and order problem necessitating stern police action. Following the public outcry, the State government ordered the closure of the factory.

The closure of the factory resulted in the unemployment of not only those workers who were engaged in the factory but also those who were working in the ancillary units. It also very badly affected those industries which depended on the chemicals manufactured by it.

As a senior officer entrusted with the responsibility of handling this issues, how are you going to address it? (250 words)

Solution

My job is to address the issues that stemmed from the shutting down of the factory, which primarily pertain to unemployment and the resulting poverty. Most of the workers belong to urban areas, while some are from villages. I will ask for a list of the factory workers who continue to remain unemployed, and meet them in groups at their nearest Gram Panchayat or Municipality offices.

I will talk to them empathetically and try to assess their suitability for work. I will also inform them about all the schemes being conducted under the aegis of the government. After assessing their educational background and skill sets, I shall speak to other industries and private units and seek employment for them. I will also organise vocational training according to the demands of the market, so that some of them can be absorbed easily. I will explain the MGNREGS to the uneducated workers and encourage them to seek work under this scheme and in other farming activities. I will also explore self-employment programmes by means of SHGs (Self-Help Groups) and micro-financing under the NRLM (National Rural Livelihood Mission).

5. Dr X is a leading medical practitioner in a city. He has set up a charitable trust through which he plans to establish a super-speciality hospital in the city to cater to the medical needs of all sections of the society. Incidentally, that part of the State had been neglected over the years. The proposed hospital would be a boon for the region.

You are heading the tax investigation agency of that region. During an inspection of the doctor's clinic, your officers have found out some major irregularities. A few of them are substantial which had resulted in considerable withholding of tax that should be paid by him now. The doctor is cooperative. He undertakes to pay the tax immediately.

However, there are certain other deficiencies in his tax compliance which are purely technical in nature. If these technical defaults are pursued by the agency, a considerable time and energy of the doctor will be diverted to issues which are not so serious, urgent or even helpful to the tax collection process. Further, in all probability, it will hamper the prospects of the hospital coming up.

There are two options before you:

1. Taking a broader view, ensure substantial tax compliance and ignore defaults that are merely technicalin nature.
2. Pursue the matter strictly and proceed on all fronts, whether substantial or merely technical.

As the head of the tax agency, which course of action will you opt and why? (250 words) 20

Solution

This case study relates to the conflict of means and ends. The nature of the work of a charitable trust is not a matter of consideration for an enforcement agency. As the head of a tax enforcement agency, my duty is to follow the law. If certain relaxations with respect to technical compliance can be brought under the legal ambit, I will help to that extent, but the trust has to comply with the law in all respects.

The deontological ethics emphasises means. In the government, officers are unable to decide their *modus operandi* on a case by case basis. The charitable trust was found to be withholding a substantial amount of tax, and this raises doubts over his conduct. I would not be inclined to relax the tax norms on the basis of the trust's philanthropic works.

It is true that reinventing the government depends on cooperation from public servants, but an enforcement agency has very little scope to do so, especially in matters of non-compliance. I will help him to understand the law and the procedures by which to comply with the technical aspects. I will expect him to fulfil all the necessary formalities and pay the required amount of tax assessed.

6. Edward Snowden, a computer expert and former CIA administrator, released confidential Government documents to the press about the existence of Government surveillance programmes. According to many legal experts and the US Government, his action violated the Espionage act of 1971, which identified the leak of State secret as an act of treason. Yet, despite the fact that he broke the law, Snowden argued that he had a moral obligation to act. He gave a justification for his 'whistle blowing' by stating that he had a duty 'to inform the public as to that which is done in their name and that which is done against them.'

According to Snowden, the Government's violation of privacy had to be exposed regardless of legality since more substantive issues of social action and public morality were involved here. Many agreed with Snowden. Few argued that he broke the law and compromised national security, for which he should be held accountable.

Do you agree that Snowden's actions were ethically justified even if legally prohibited? Why or why not? Make an argument by weighing the competing values in this case (250 words)

Solution

Ethics is very subjective. But a minute study of the philosophy of ethics will give us a clear idea of right and wrong. Every person in society has been assigned their duty, and going outside that stipulated duty disturbs the mechanism of justice. Plato had pointed out that justice is the citizen's sense of their own duty. The four cardinal virtues mentioned are wisdom, courage, justice and temperance, of which justice is the most difficult to ascertain because it demands the assistance and contribution of society as a whole. The government is not run by a single individual in a democratic country. The decisions of the government are considered the decisions of the collective. Snowden held a responsible public office, and he had to follow the relevant deontology in letter and spirit. He should not have leaked the classified information because that amounted to a breach of public trust. Whistle-blowing is different concept, related to gross injustice, acts against the public interest, and misappropriation of public funds.

Snowden's conscience might have compelled him to raise his voice, but his conscience should not supersede the popular will of the government. There are other ways to register one's dissatisfaction with government functioning which do not violate the law (in this case, the Espionage Act). Snowden's act may have been morally correct, but it was not ethically appropriate. He examined his life and took a decision that was wrong ethically. The philosopher Socrates had defied the government, but he did not disrespect it. Even when offered the chance to escape from prison, he did not do so.

Case Studies (2019)

1. You are heading the rescue operations in an area affected by severe natural calamity. Thousands of people are rendered homeless and deprived of food, drinking water and other basic amenities. Rescue work has been disrupted by heavy rainfall and damage to supply routes. The local people are seething with anger against the delayed limited rescue operations. When your team reaches the affected area, the people there heckle and even assault some of the team members. One of your team members is even

severely injured. Faced with this crisis, some team members plead with you to call off the operations fearing threats to their life.

In such trying circumstances, what will be your response? Examine the qualities of a public servant which will be required to manage the situation. (250 words)   20

Solution

In such a situation, my response would be as follows:

(i) I will motivate my team members to proceed with the operation against all odds, because dedication to service is the hallmark of public service. I am convinced that once my team members display their commitment to rescue work, the public opinion will turn in their favour.

(ii) I will talk to the local public representatives and respected people of the affected areas. I will take their help to maintain a positive environment for the government employees involved in the rescue operation, and in turn, assure them of all possible assistance and prompt rescue services.

The qualities indispensible to managing such a situation are:

1. Integrity
2. Impartiality
3. Perseverance
4. Dedication to public service
5. Empathy
6. Compassion towards weaker sections.

Integrity: A public servant must carry out her/his duties and obligations responsibly. S/he should act professionally and retain the faith of superiors, legislatures, ministers and the public at large. S/he should utilise public funds and resources carefully, and conduct all fiduciary obligations sensitively. The media should only be engaged with after due authorisation from the government or a minister.

Impartiality: This means to not discriminate on the basis of religion, caste, creed, region, or membership of a particular group while taking any decision, instructing subordinates and team members, or following the advice of superiors.

Empathy: This is a powerful tool with which to provide information regarding the impact of one's professional duty as well as personal behaviour. Knowing others' expectations, and how one's actions can impact others will help a person to adjust her/his behaviour while discharging their professional duties.

Perseverance: This is about ensuring an efficient service delivery system of public goods in the public interest. Public servants must understand the obstacles that can come in the way of service delivery, due to stringent rules and regulations, the low spirit of the government machinery, and the continuous struggle for the betterment of society.

Dedication to public service: A public servant is considered a trustee of the public goods and services entrusted to them. Dedication to public service is an indispensable core value of a public servant. A public servant has to dedicate quality time, complete attention, and all possible effort to work incessantly for the welfare of the people.

Compassion towards weaker sections: The sections of society affected during natural calamities find themselves in deplorable living conditions. Their houses are inferior and their finances are low. The weaker sections deserve special administrative care, and should be treated sympathetically.

2. Honesty and uprightness are the hallmarks of a civil servant. Civil servants possessing these qualities are considered as the backbone of any strong organization. In line of duty, they take various decisions, at times some become bonafide mistakes. As long as such decisions are not taken intentionally and do not benefit personally, the officer cannot be said to be guilty. Though such decisions may, at times,

lead to unforeseen adverse consequences in the long-term.

In the recent past, a few instances have surfaced wherein civil servants have been implicated for bonafide mistakes. They have often been prosecuted and even imprisoned. These instances have greatly rattled the moral fibre of the civil servants.

How does this trend affect the functioning of the civil services? What measures can be taken to ensure that honest civil servants are not implicated for bonafide mistakes on their part? Justify your answer. (250 words)   20

Solution

Civil servants are the chosen few who are selected through a rigorous process of competition. There is no scope for error in decision-making and conduct taken in the public interest. Civil servants are privileged for the nature of their job. If *bona fide* mistakes do occur, they should be overlooked; however, a mistake that causes severe damage to the state exchequer, or repeated misconduct, cannot be forgiven. The present system, based on good governance and a corruption-free administration, poses a threat to the functioning of civil servants. There have been cases where honest civil servants have been implicated for genuine mistakes on their part. This usually happens when discretionary power is utilised under emotional duress, albeit with *bona fide* intentions. The prevailing system of vigilance is based on strict adherence to rules and regulations. A civil servant must not bypass any rule and should be aware of the negative consequences of their decisions.

Measures which can be taken to ensure that honest civil servants are not implicated in mistakes are as follows:

1. They should be helped to understand, by means of official as well as informal communication, the negative consequences of decisions that do not follow established procedure.
2. Periodic seminars should be conducted by the vigilance department and the CBI to educate young civil servants about grey areas where their decisions can create trouble.
3. There should be a system of allocating mentors to young civil servants. These mentors should be selected from among seasoned officers, who can provide guidance.

Finally, every civil servant has to protect her/himself and avoid taking any decision that deviates from rules and regulations.

3. An apparel manufacturing company having large number of women employees was losing sales due to various factors. The company hired a reputed marketing executive, who increased the volume of sales within a short span of time. However, some unconfirmed reports came up regarding his indulgence in sexual harassment at the workplace.

After sometime, a woman employee lodged a formal complaint to the management against the marketing executive about sexually harassing her. Faced with the company's indifference in not taking cognizance of her grievance, she lodged an FIR with the Police.

Realizing the sensitivity and gravity of the situation, the company called the woman employee to negotiate. In that she was offered a hefty sum of money to withdraw the complaint and the FIR and also give in writing that the marketing executive is not involved in the case.

Identify the ethical issues involved in this case. What options are available to the woman employee? (250 words)   20

Solution

The ethical issues involved in this case are:

1. Deontological issue: Violation of the guidelines of the Sexual Harassment of

Women at the Workplace (Prevention, Prohibition and Redressal) Act, 2013.
2. Teleological issue: The current volume of sales will not be sustained in the future because of the behaviour of the marketing executive.
3. Virtue ethics: A non-virtuous man cannot be trusted. He can jeopardise the future of the company.

The woman employee is left with the following options:

1. She can accept the company's offer and rescind her complaint and the FIR. This is unethical and would make it seem as if the complainant had fabricated a story in an attempt to extort money. It would damage her career prospects as well as her social reputation. Besides, this will violate the law of the land, and might set an unfair precedent.
2. She could refuse to tolerate any disrespect and immediately lodge a complaint about the company's behaviour, thereby compelling her to turn hostile. The employer, on their part, should protect her rights and dignity rather than lowering it further, and thereby protect the sanctity of the law of the land.
3. She should stay silent and seek other opportunities elsewhere. While this will take care of this particular problem, she might face similar incidents in other companies. Keeping quiet will go against the values of courage and perseverance.

The second option is the most correct as per the ethical point of view.

4. In a modern democratic polity, there is the concept of political executive and permanent executive. Elected people's representatives form the political executive and bureaucracy forms the permanent executive. Ministers frame policy decisions and bureaucrats execute these.

In the initial decades after independence, relationship between the permanent executive and the political executive were characterized by mutual understanding, respect and co-operation, without encroaching upon others domain.

However, in the subsequent decades, the situation has changed. There are instances of the political executive insisting upon the permanent executive to follow its agenda. Respect for and appreciation of upright bureaucrats has declined. There is an increasing tendency among the political executive to get involved in routine administrative matters such as transfers, postings, etc. Under this scenario, there is definite trend towards 'politicization of bureaucracy'. The rising materialism and acquisitiveness in social life has also adversely impacted upon the ethical values of both the permanent executive and the political executive.

What are the consequences of this 'politicization of bureaucracy'? Discuss. (250 words)   20

Solution

The bureaucracy and political institutions complement each other and provide checks and balances on their functioning. This crucial function is now being diluted. We cannot place the blame solely on the political masters because bureaucrats are equally complicit. The consequences of this 'politicisation of the bureaucracy' can be explained as follows:

1. Honest bureaucrats are disliked by politicians. The latter prefer flexible bureaucrats who can be easily persuaded. This practice discourages honest bureaucrats.
2. Politicisation of the bureaucracy leads to rampant corruption in public offices.
3. The public money and other resources are misused and diverted to benefit politicians and bureaucrats.

4. It also gives rise to crony capitalism, which is more dangerous because the capitalists engulf enormous amounts of public resources.
5. Politicisation of the bureaucracy also harms democratic values and a fair election process.
6. The ruling political party misuses public funds in their political promotions.
7. The bureaucrats are tagged with political parties, a trend which goes against the values of impartiality and non-partisanship.

5. In one of the districts of a frontier state, narcotics menace has been rampant. This has resulted in money laundering, mushrooming of poppy farming, arms smuggling and near stalling of education. The system is on the verge of collapse. The situation has been further worsened by unconfirmed reports that local politicians as well as some senior police officers are providing surreptitious patronage to the drug mafia.

At that point of time a woman police officer, known for her skills in handling such situations is appointed as Superintendent of Police to bring the situation to normalcy.

If you are the same police officer, identify the various dimensions of the crisis. Based on your understanding, suggest measures to deal with this crisis. (250 words)   20

Solution

The various dimensions of this crisis are:
1. Illegal activities lead to problems of law and order, chaos, social evils and criminalisation.
2. Weak internal administration and poor law and order are detrimental to national security. Frontier states are crucial because they share international boundaries with neighbouring countries. This may give rise to problems of infiltration, cross-border terrorism and insurgency.
3. The youth will be spoiled and perverted by growing up in a polluted social environment.

Measures to deal with the crisis are:
1. I have been posted to bring about normalcy, which means that the government is willing to eradicate the menace. I will exploit this opportunity and initiate a probe to expose the names of corrupt police officers and local politicians.
2. I will select a team of honest young officers, and train them in the required expertise.
3. I will enlist the help of the District Magistrate and involve local representatives willing to bring about a change in the society. I will involve local self-governments and NGOs who can educate the youth and prepare them to be both informers and educators.
4. I will try to persuade poppy cultivators to stop their illegal cultivation.
5. Finally, I will treat the accused with an iron fist, and make sure they are brought to justice with the support of strong evidence.

6. In recent times, there has been an increasing concern in India to develop effective civil service ethics, codes of conduct, transparency measures, ethics and integrity systems and anti-corruption agencies. In view of this, there is a need being felt to focus on three specific areas, which are directly relevant to the problems of internalizing integrity and ethics in the civil services. These are as follows:
1. Anticipating specific threats to ethical standards and integrity in the civil services,
2. Strengthening the ethical competence of civil servants and
3. Developing administrative processes and practices which promote ethical values and integrity in civil services.

Suggest institutional measures to address the above three issues. (250 words)   20

Solution

To maintain the public service ethos and good governance, various measures have been taken. But they are either very rigid or not implemented in both letter and spirit. The following suggestions can be incorporated to address these issues:

1. An ethics committee should be set up in every department and ministry, headed by a senior bureaucrat with a good service record and vast experience in dealing with issues related to corruption. They should research the scope of corruption and possible potential threats to the ethical standards and integrity of the officers of the concerned department and ministry. The ethics committee should have access to the classified information collected by enforcement agencies like the CBI and vigilance departments, which maintain various lists like the agreed list, list of doubtful integrity, etc., related to officers, and a list of touts in every department.
2. To strengthen the ethical competence of civil servants, workshops or seminars on ethics should be organised. The ethics committee can be endowed with this task.
3. Administration based on information technology should be introduced in the public offices. The concept of e-office and online procurement should be implemented in every public office to ensure greater transparency. Transfers and postings of civil servants should be done through e-office by a committee, rather than by a single person. The notion of security of tenure of a public office-holder should be followed in letter and spirit, and should any officer be transferred before the maturity period of her/his tenure, a proper reason must be recorded and should be passed by the majority members of the committee.

These proceedings should be tagged with the dossier of the individual officer in perpetuity.

UNSOLVED CASE STUDIES (UPSC CIVIL SERVICES MAINS EXAMINATION 2020–23)

Case Studies (2020)

1. Rajesh Kumar is a senior public servant with a reputation of honesty and forthrightness, currently posted in the Finance Ministry as Head of the Budget Division. His department is presently busy organizing the budgetary support to the states, four of which are due to go to the polls within the financial year.

This year's annual budget had allotted Rs. 8300 crores for the National Housing Scheme (NHS), a centrally sponsored social housing scheme for the weaker sections of society. Rs 775 crores have been drawn for the NHS till June.

The Ministry of Commerce had long been pursuing a case for setting up a Special Economic Zone (SEZ) in a southern state to boost exports. After two years of detailed discussions between the centre and state, the Union Cabinet approved the project in August. The process was initiated to acquire the necessary land.

Eighteen months ago, a leading Public Sector Unit (PSU) had projected the need for setting up a large natural gas processing plant in a northern state for the regional gas grid. The required land is already in possession of the PSU. The gas grid is an essential component of the national energy security strategy. After three rounds of global bidding, the project was allotted to an MNC, M/s XYZ Hydrocarbons. The first tranche of payment to the MNC is scheduled to be made in December.

Finance Ministry was asked for a timely allocation of an additional Rs. 6000 crores for these two developmental projects. It was decided to recommend re-appropriation of this entire amount from the NHS allocation. The file was forwarded to the Budget Department for their comments and further processing. On studying the case file, Rajesh Kumar realized that this re-appropriation may cause inordinate delay in the execution of NHS, a project much publicized in the rallies of senior politicians. Correspondingly, non-availability of finances would cause financial loss in the SEZ and national embarrassment due to delayed payment in an international project.

Rajesh Kumar discussed the matter with his seniors. He was conveyed that this politically sensitive situation needs to be processed immediately. Rajesh Kumar realized that diversion of funds from the NHS could raise difficult questions for the government in the Parliament.

Discuss the following with reference to this case:

(a) Ethical issues involved in re-appropriation of funds from a welfare project to the developmental projects.
(b) Given the need for proper utilization of public funds, discuss the options available to Rajesh Kumar. Is resigning a worthy option?

2. The Chairman of Bharat Missiles Ltd (BML) was watching a program on TV wherein the Prime Minister was addressing the nation on the necessity of developing a self-reliant India. He subconsciously nodded in agreement and smiled to himself as he mentally reviewed BML's journey in the past two decades. BML had admirably progressed from producing first generation anti-tank guided missiles (ATGMs) to designing and producing state of the art ATGM weapon systems that would be the envy of any army. He sighed in reconciliation with his assumptions that the government would probably not alter the status quo of a ban on exports of military weaponry.

To his surprise, the very next day he got a telephone call from the Director General, Ministry of Defence, asking him to discuss the modalities of increasing BML production of ATGMs as there is a possibility of exporting the same to a friendly foreign country. The Director General wanted the Chairman to discuss the details with his staff at Delhi next week.

Two days later, at a press conference, the Defence Minister stated that he aims to double the current weapons export levels within five years. This would give an impetus of financing the development and manufacture of indigenous weapons in the country. He also stated that all indigenous arms manufacturing nations have a very good record in international arms trade.

(a) As Chairman of BML, what are your views on the following points?
(b) As an arms exporter of a responsible nation like India, what are the ethical issues involved in arms trade?

List five ethical factors that would influence the decision to sell arms to foreign governments.

3. Rampura, a remote district inhabited by a tribal population, is marked by extreme backwardness and abject poverty. Agriculture is the mainstay of the local population, though it is primarily subsistence due to the very small landholdings. There is insignificant industrial or mining activity. Even the targeted welfare programs have inadequately benefited the tribal population. In this restrictive scenario, the youth has begun to migrate to other states to supplement the family income. Plight of minor girls is that their parents are persuaded by labour contractors to send them to work in the Bt Cotton farms of a nearby state. The soft fingers of the minor girls are well suited for plucking the cotton. The inadequate living and working conditions in these farms have caused serious health issues for the minor girls. NGOs in the districts of domicile and the cotton farms appear to be compromised and

have not effectively espoused the twin issues of child labour and development of the area.

You are appointed as the District Collector of Rampura. Identify the ethical issues involved. Which specific steps will you initiate to ameliorate the conditions of minor girls of your district and to improve the overall economic scenario in the district?

4. You are a municipal commissioner of a large city, having the reputation of a very honest and upright officer. A huge multipurpose mall is under construction in your city in which a large number of daily wage earners are employed. One night, during monsoons, a big chunk of the roof collapsed causing instant death of four labourers including two minors. Many more were seriously injured requiring immediate medical attention. The mishap resulted in a big hue and cry, forcing the government to institute an enquiry.

Your preliminary enquiry has revealed a series of anomalies. The material used for the construction was of poor quality. Despite the approved building plans permitting only one basement, an additional basement has been constructed. This was overlooked during the periodic inspections by the building inspector of the municipal corporation. In your enquiry, you noticed that the construction of the mall was given the green signal despite encroaching on areas earmarked for a green belt and a slip road in the Zonal Master Plan of the city. The permission to construct the mall was accorded by the previous Municipal Commissioner who is not only your senior and well known to you professionally, but also a good friend.

Prima facie, the case appears to be of a widespread nexus between officials of the Municipal Corporation and the builders. Your colleagues are putting pressure on you to go slow in the enquiry. The builder, who is rich and influential, happens to be a close relative of a powerful minister in the state cabinet. The builder is persuading you to hush up the matter, promising you a fortune to do so. He also hinted that if this matter is not resolved at the earliest in his favour; there is somebody in his office who is waiting to file a case against you under the POSH Act.

Discuss the ethical issues involved in the case. What are the options available to you in this situation? Explain your selected course of action.

5. Parmal is a small but underdeveloped district. It has rocky terrain that is not suitable for agriculture, though some subsistence agriculture is being done on small plots of land. The area receives adequate rainfall and has an irrigation canal flowing through it. Amria, its administrative centre, is a medium sized town. It houses a large district hospital, an Industrial Training Institute and some privately owned skill training centres. It has all the facilities of a district headquarters. A trunk railway line passes approximately 50 kilometres from Amria. Its poor connectivity is a major reason for the absence of any major industry therein. The state government offers a 10 years tax holiday as an incentive to new industry. In 2010 Anil, an industrialist, decided to take benefits to set up Amria Plastic Works (APW) in Noora village, about 20 km from Amria. While the factory was being built, Anil hired the required key labour and got them trained at the skill training centres at Amria. This act of his made the key personnel very loyal to APW. APW started production in 2011 with the labour drawn fully from Noora village. The villagers were very happy to get employment near their homes and were motivated by the key personnel to meet the production targets with high quality. APW started making large profits, a sizable portion of which was used to improve the quality of life in Noora. By 2016, Noora could boast of a greener village and a renovated village temple. Anil liaised with the local MLA to increase the frequency of the bus

services to Amria. The government also opened a primary health care centre and primary school at Noora in buildings constructed by APW. APW used its CSR funds to set up women's self-help groups, subsidize primary education to the village children and procure an ambulance for use by its employees and the needy. In 2019, there was a minor fire in APW. It was quickly extinguished as fire safety protocols were in place in the factory. Investigations revealed that the factory had been using electricity in excess of its authorized capacity. This was soon rectified. The next year, due to a nationwide lockdown, the requirement of production fell for four months. Anil decided that all employees would be paid regularly. He employed them to plant trees and improve the village habitat. APW had developed a reputation of high-quality production and a motivated workforce.

Critically analyse the story of APW and state the ethical issues involved. Do you consider APW as a role model for development of backward areas? Give reasons.

6. Migrant workers have always remained at the socio-economic margins of our society, silently serving as the instrumental labour force of urban economics. The pandemic has brought them into national focus.

On announcement of a countrywide lockdown, a very large number of migrant workers decided to move back from their places of employment to their native villages. The non-availability of transport created its own problems. Added to this was the fear of starvation and inconvenience to their families. This caused the migrant workers to demand wages and transport facilities for returning to their villages. Their mental agony was accentuated by multiple factors such as a sudden loss of livelihood, possibility of lack of food and inability to assist in harvesting their rabi crop due to not being able to reach home in time. Reports of inadequate response of some districts in providing the essential boarding and lodging arrangements along the way multiplied their fears.

You have learnt many lessons from this situation when you were tasked to oversee the functioning of the District Disaster Relief Force in your district. In your opinion what ethical issues arose in the current migrant crisis? What do you understand by an ethical care giving state? What assistance can the civil society render to mitigate the sufferings of migrants in similar situations?

Case Studies (2021)

1. Sunil is a young civil servant and has a reputation for his competence, integrity, dedication and relentless pursuit of difficult and onerous jobs. Considering his profile, he was picked up by his bosses to handle a very challenging and sensitive assignment. He was posted in a tribal dominated district notorious for illegal sand mining. Excavating sand from river belt and transporting through trucks and selling them in black market was rampant. This illegal sand mining mafia was operating with the support of local functionaries and tribal musclemen who in turn were bribing selected poor tribals and had kept the tribals under fear and intimidation.

Sunil being a sharp and energetic officer immediately grasped the ground realities and the modus operandi followed by the mafia through their devious and dubious mechanism. On making inquiries, he gathered that some of their own office employees are in hand and glove with them and have developed close unholy nexus. Sunil initiated stringent action against them and started conducting raids on their illegal operations of movement of trucks filled with sand. The mafia got rattled as not many officers in the past had taken such strong steps against the mafia. Some of the office employees who were allegedly close to mafia informed them that the officer is determined to clean up the mafia's illegal sand mining operations in that district and may cause them irreparable damage.

The mafia turned hostile and launched counter-offensive. The tribal musclemen and mafia started threatening him with dire consequences. His family (wife and old mother) were stalked and were under virtual surveillance and thus causing mental torture, agony and stress to all of them. The matter assumed serious proportions when a muscleman came to his office and threatened him to stop raids, etc., otherwise, his fate will not be different than some of his predecessors (ten years back one officer was killed by the mafia).

(a) Identify the different options available to Sunil in attending to this situation.
(b) Critically evaluate each of the options listed by you.
(c) Which of the above, do you think, would be the most appropriate for Sunil to adopt and why?

2. You are Vice Principal of a degree college in one of the middle-class towns. Principal has recently retired and management is looking for his replacement. There are also feelers that the management may promote you as principal. In the meantime, during annual examination the flying squad which came from the university caught two students red-handed involved in unfair means. A senior lecturer of the college was personally helping these students in this act. This senior lecturer also happens to be close to the management. One of the students was son of a local politician who was responsible in getting the college affiliated to the present reputed university. The second student was son of a local businessman who has donated maximum funds for running of the college. You immediately informed the management regarding this unfortunate incident. The management told you to resolve the issue with flying squad at any cost. They further said that such incident will not only tarnish the image of the college but also the politician and businessman are very important personalities for the functioning of the college. You were also given hint that your further promotion to Principal depends on your capability in resolving this issue with flying squad. In the meantime, you were intimated by your administrative officer that certain members of the student union are protesting outside the college gate against the senior lecturer and the students involved in this incident and demanding strict action against defaulters.

(a) Discuss the ethical issues involved in the case.
(b) Critically examine the options available with you as Vice Principal. What option will you adopt and why?

3. An elevated corridor is being constructed to reduce traffic congestion in the capital of a particular State. You have been selected as project manager of this prestigious project on your professional competence and experience. The deadline is to complete the project in next two years by 30 June, 2021, since this project is to be inaugurated by the Chief Minister before the elections are announced in the second week of July 2021. While carrying out the surprise inspection by inspecting team, a minor crack was noticed in one of the piers of the elevated corridor possibly due to poor material used. You immediately informed the chief engineer and stopped further work. It was assessed by you that minimum three piers of the elevated corridor have to be demolished and reconstructed. But this process will delay the project minimum by four to six months. But the chief engineer overruled the observation of inspecting team on the ground that it was a minor crack which will not in any way impact the strength and durability of the bridge. He ordered you to overlook the observation of inspecting team and continue working with

same speed and tempo. He informed you that the minister does not want any delay as he wants the Chief Minister to inaugurate the elevated corridor before the elections are declared. Also informed you that the contractor is far relative of the minister and he wants him to finish the project. He also gave you hint that your further promotion as additional chief engineer is under consideration with the ministry. However, you strongly felt that the minor crack in the pier of the elevated corridor will adversely affect the health and life of the bridge and therefore it will be very dangerous not to repair the elevated corridor.

(a) Under the given conditions, what are the options available to you as a project manager?

(b) What are the ethical dilemmas being faced by the project manager?

(c) What are the professional challenges likely to be faced by the project manager and his response to overcome such challenges?

(d) What can be the consequences of overlooking the observation raised by the inspecting team?

4. The coronavirus disease (COVID-19) pandemic has quickly spread to various countries. As on May 8th, 2020, in India 56342 positive cases of corona had been reported. India with a population of more than 1.35 billion had difficulty in controlling the transmission of coronavirus among its population. Multiple strategies became necessary to handle this outbreak. The Ministry of Health and Family Welfare of India raised awareness about this outbreak and to take all necessary actions to control the spread of COVID-19. Indian Government implemented a 55-day lockdown throughout the country to reduce the transmission of the virus. Schools and colleges had shifted to alternative mode of teaching-learning-evaluation and certification. Online mode became popular during these days.

India was not prepared for a sudden onslaught of such a crisis due to limited infrastructure in terms of human resource, money and other facilities needed for taking care of this situation. This disease did not spare anybody irrespective of caste, creed, religion on the one hand and 'have and have not' on the other. Deficiencies in hospital beds, oxygen cylinders, ambulances, hospital staff and crematorium were the most crucial aspects. You are a hospital administrator in a public hospital at the time when coronavirus had attacked large number of people and patients were pouring into hospital day in and day out.

(a) What are your criteria and justification for putting your clinical and non-clinical staff to attend to the patients knowing fully well that it is highly infectious disease and resources and infrastructure are limited?

(b) If yours is a private hospital, whether your justification and decision would remain same as that of a public hospital?

5. A reputed food product company based in India developed a food product for the international market and started exporting the same after getting necessary approvals. The company announced this achievement and also indicated that soon the product will be made available for the domestic consumers with almost same quality and health benefits. Accordingly, the company got its product approved by the domestic competent authority and launched the product in Indian market. The company could increase its market share over a period of time and earn substantial profit both domestically and internationally. However, the random sample test conducted by inspecting team found the product being sold domestically in variance with the approval obtained from the competent authority. On further investigation, it was also discovered that the food company was not only selling products

which were not meeting the health standard of the country but also selling the rejected export products in the domestic market. This episode adversely affected the reputation and profitability of the food company.

(a) What action do you visualise should be taken by the competent authority against the food company for violating the laid down domestic food standard and selling rejected export products in domestic market?

(b) What course of action is available with the food company to resolve the crisis and bring back its lost reputation?

(c) Examine the ethical dilemma involved in the case.

6. Pawan is working as an officer in the State Government for the last ten years. As a part of routine transfer, he was posted to another department. He joined in a new office along with five other colleagues. The head of the office was a senior officer conversant with the functioning of the office. As a part of general inquiry, Pawan gathered that his senior officer carries the reputation of being difficult and insensitive person having his own disturbed family life. Initially, all seemed to go well. However, after some time Pawan felt that the senior officer was belittling him and at times unreasonable. Whatever suggestions given or views expressed by Pawan in the meetings were summarily rejected and the senior officer would express displeasure in the presence of others. It became a pattern of boss' style of functioning to show him in bad light highlighting his shortcomings and humiliating publicly. It became apparent that though there were no serious work-related problems/shortcomings, the senior officer was always on one pretext or the other and would scold and shout at him. The continuous harassment and public criticism of Pawan resulted in loss of confidence, self-esteem and equanimity. Pawan realised that his relation with his senior officer was becoming more toxic and due to this, he felt perpetually tensed, anxious and stressed. His mind was occupied with negativity and caused him mental torture, anguish and agony. Eventually, it badly affected his personal and family life. He was no longer joyous, happy and contented even at home. Rather without any reason he would lose his temper with his wife and other family members. The family environment was no longer pleasant and congenial. His wife who was always supportive to him also became a victim of his negativity and hostile behaviour. Due to harassment and humiliation suffered by him in the office, comfort and happiness virtually vanished from his life. Thus, it damaged his physical and mental health.

(a) What are the options available with Pawan to cope with the situation?

(b) What approach Pawan should adopt for bringing peace, tranquility and congenial environment in the office and home?

(c) As an outsider, what are your suggestions for both boss and subordinate to overcome this situation and for improving the work performance, mental and emotional hygiene?

(d) In the above scenario, what type of training would you suggest for officers at various levels in the government offices?

Case Studies (2022)

1. Prabhat was working as Vice President (Marketing) at Sterling Electric Ltd., a reputed multinational company. But presently the company was passing through difficult times as the sales were continuously showing downward trend in the last two quarters. His division, which hitherto had been a major revenue contributor to the company's financial health, was now desperately trying to procure some big government order for them. But their best

efforts did not yield any positive success or breakthrough. His was a professional company and his local bosses were under pressure from their London-based HO to show some positive results. In the last performance review meeting taken by the Executive Director (India Head), he was reprimanded for his poor performance. He assured them that his division is working on a special contract from the Ministry of Defence for a secret installation near Gwalior and tender is being submitted shortly. He was under extreme pressure and he was deeply perturbed. What aggravated the situation further was a warning from the top that if the deal is not clinched in favour of the company, his division might have to be closed and he may have to quit his lucrative job. There was another dimension which was causing him deep mental torture and agony. This pertained to his personal precarious financial health. He was a single earner in the family with two school-college going children and his old ailing mother. The heavy expenditure on education and medical was causing a big strain to his monthly pay packet. Regular EMI for housing loan taken from bank was unavoidable and any default would render him liable for severe legal action. In the above backdrop, he was hoping for some miracle to happen. There was sudden turn of events. His secretary informed that a gentleman—Subhash Verma—wanted to see him as he was interested in the position of Manager which was to be filled in by him in the company. He further brought to his notice that his CV has been received through the office of the Minister of Defence. During interview of the candidate Subhash Verma, he found him technically sound, resourceful and experienced marketeer. He seemed to be well-conversant with tendering procedures and having knack of follow-up and liaising in this regard. Prabhat felt that he was better choice than the rest of the candidates who were recently interviewed by him in the last few days. Subhash Verma also indicated that he was in possession of the copies of the bid documents that the Unique Electronics Ltd. would be submitting the next day to the Defence Ministry for their tender. He offered to hand over those documents subject to his employment in the company on suitable terms and conditions. He made it clear that in the process, the Sterling Electric Ltd. could outbid their rival company and get the bid and hefty Defence Ministry order. He indicated that it will be win-win situation for both him and the company. Prabhat was absolutely stunned. It was a mixed feeling of shock and thrill. He was uncomfortable and perspiring. If accepted, all his problems would vanish instantly and he may be rewarded for securing the much awaited tender and thereby boosting company's sales and financial health. He was in a fix as to the future course of action. He was wonder-struck at the guts of Subhash Verma in having surreptitiously removing his own company papers and offering to the rival company for a job. Being an experienced person, he was examining the pros and cons of the proposal/situation and he asked him to come the next day.

(a) Discuss the ethical issues involved in the case.
(b) Critically examine the options available to Prabhat in the above situation.
(c) Which of the above would be the most appropriate for Prabhat and why?

2. Ramesh is State Civil Services Officer who got the opportunity of getting posted to the capital of a border State after rendering 20 years of service. Ramesh's mother has recently been detected [with] cancer and has been admitted in the leading cancer hospital of the city. His two adolescent children have also got admission in one of the best public schools of the town. After settling down in his appointment as Director in the Home Department of the State, Ramesh got confidential report through

intelligence sources that illegal migrants are infiltrating in the State from the neighbouring country. He decided to personally carry out surprise check of the border posts along with his Home Department team. To his surprise, he caught red-handed two families of 12 members infiltrated with the connivance of the security personnel at the border posts. On further inquiry and investigation, it was found that after the migrants from neighbouring country infiltrate, their documentation like Aadhaar Card, Ration Card and Voter Card are also forged and they are made to settle down in a particular area of the State. Ramesh prepared the detailed and comprehensive report and submitted to the Additional Secretary of the State. However, he has summoned by the Additional Home Secretary after a week and was instructed to withdraw the report. The Additional Home Secretary informed Ramesh that the report submitted by him has not been appreciated by the higher authorities. He further cautioned him that if he fails to withdraw the confidential report, he will not only be posted out from the prestigious appointment from the State capital but his further promotion which is due in near future will also get in jeopardy.

(a) What are the Department options available to Ramesh as the Director of the Home Department of the bordering State?
(b) What option should Ramesh adopt and why?
(c) Critically evaluate each of the options.
(d) What are the ethical dilemmas being faced by Ramesh?
(e) What policy measures would you suggest to combat the menace of infiltration of illegal migrants from the neighbouring country?

3. The Supreme Court has banned mining in the Aravalli Hills to stop degradation of the forest cover and to maintain ecological balance. However, the stone mining was still prevalent in the border district of the affected State with connivance of certain corrupt forest officials and politicians. Young and dynamic SP who was recently posted in the affected district promised to himself to stop this menace. In one of his surprise checks with his team, he found loaded truck with stone trying to escape the mining area. He tried to stop the truck but the truck driver overrun the police officer, killing him on the spot and thereafter managed to flee. Police filed FIR but no breakthrough was achieved in the case for almost three months. Ashok who was the Investigative Journalist working with leading TV channel, suo moto started investigating the case. Within one month, Ashok got breakthrough by interacting with local people, stone mining mafia and government officials. He prepared his investigative story and presented to the CMD of the TV channel. He exposed in his investigative report the complete nexus of stone mafia working with blessing of corrupt police and civil officials and politicians. The politician who was involved in the mafia was no one else but local MLA who was considered to be very close to the Chief Minister. After going through the investigative report, the CMD advised Ashok to drop the idea of making the story public through electronic media. He informed that the local MLA was not only the relative of the owner of the TV channel but also had unofficially 20 per cent share in the channel. The CMD further informed Ashok that his further promotion and hike in pay will be taken care of in addition the soft loan of 10 lakhs which he has taken from the TV channel for his son's chronic disease will be suitably adjusted if he hands over the investigative report to him.

(a) What are the options available with Ashok to cope up with the situation?
(b) Critically evaluate/examine each of the options identified by Ashok.

(c) What are the ethical dilemmas being faced by Ashok?
   (d) Which of the options, do you think, would be the most appropriate for Ashok to adopt and why?
   (e) In the above scenario, what type of training would you suggest for police officers posted to such districts where stone mining illegal activities are rampant?

4. You have done MBA from a reputed institution three years back but could not get campus placement due to COVID-19 generated recession. However, after a lot of persuasion and series of competitive tests including written and interview, you managed to get a job in a leading shoe company. You have aged parents who are dependent and staying with you. You also recently got married after getting this decent job. You were allotted the Inspection Section which is responsible for clearing the final product. In first one year, you learnt your job well and was appreciated for your performance by the management. The company is doing good business for last five years in domestic market and this year it is decided even to export to Europe and Gulf countries. However, one large consignment to Europe was rejected by their Inspecting Team due to certain poor quality and was sent back. The top management ordered that ibid consignment to be cleared for the domestic market. As a part of Inspecting Team, you observed the glaring poor quality and brought to the knowledge of the Team Commander. However, the top management advised all the members of the team to overlook these defects as the management cannot bear such a huge loss. Rest of the team members except you promptly signed and cleared the consignment for domestic market, overlooking glaring defects. You again brought to the knowledge of the Team Commander that such consignment, if cleared even for domestic market, will tarnish the image and reputation of the company and will be counter-productive in the long run. However, you were further advised by the top management that if you do not clear the consignment, the company will not hesitate to terminate your services citing certain innocuous reasons.

   (a) Under the given conditions, what are the options available to you as a member of the Inspecting Team?
   (b) Critically evaluate each of the options listed by you.
   (c) What option would you adopt and why?
   (d) What are the ethical dilemmas being faced by you?
   (e) What can be the consequences of overlooking the observations raised by the inspecting Team?

5. Rakesh was working as Joint Commissioner in Transport Department of a city. As a part of his job profile, among others, he was entrusted with the task of overseeing the control and functioning of City Transport Department. A case of strike by the drivers' union of City Transport Department over the issue of compensation to a driver who died on duty while driving the bus came up before him for decision in the matter.

He gathered that the driver (deceased) was plying Bus No. 528 which passed through busy and congested roads of the city. It so happened that near an intersection on the way, there was an accident involving the bus and a car driver by a middle-aged man. It was found that there was altercation between the driver and the car driver. Heated arguments between them led to fight and the driver gave him a blow. Lot of passerbys had gathered and tried to intervene but without success. Eventually, both of them were badly injured and profusely bleeding and were taken to the nearby hospital. The driver succumbed to the injuries and could not be saved. The middle-aged driver's condition was also critical but after a day, he recovered and was discharged. Police had immediately come at the spot of accident and FIR was registered. Police investigation revealed that the quarrel in question was started by the bus driver and he had resorted to physical violence. There was exchange of blows between them. The City Transport Department management is considering of not giving any extra compensation to the driver's (deceased) family. The family is very aggrieved, depressed and agitated against the discriminatory and non-sympathetic approach of the City Transport Department management. The bus driver (deceased) was 52 years of age, was survived by his wife and two school-college going daughters. He was the sole earner of the family. The City Transport Department workers' union took up this case and when found no favourable response from the management, decided to go on strike. The union's demand was two-fold. First was full extra compensation as given to other drivers who died on duty and secondly employment to one family member. The strike has continued for 10 days and the deadlock remains.

(a) What are the options available to Rakesh to meet the above situation?
(b) Critically examine each of the options identified by Rakesh.
(c) What are the ethical dilemmas being faced by Rakesh?
(d) What course of action would Rakesh adopt to diffuse the above situation?

6. You are appointed as an officer heading the section in Environment Pollution Control Board to ensure compliance and its follow-up. In that region, there were large number of small and medium industries which had been granted clearance you learnt that these industries provide employment to many migrant workers. Most of the industrial units have got environmental clearance certificate in their possession. The environmental clearance seeks to curb industries and projects that supposedly hamper environment and living species in the region. But in practice most of these units remain to be polluting units in several ways like air, water and soil pollution. As such, local people encountered persistent health problems. It was confirmed that majority of the industries were violating environmental compliance. You issued notice to all the industrial units to apply for fresh environmental clearance certificate from the competent authority. However, your action met with hostile response from a section of the industrial units, other vested interest persons and a section of the local politicians. The workers also became very hostile to you as they felt that your action would lead to the closure these of industrial units, and the resultant unemployment will lead to insecurity and uncertainty in their livelihood. Many owners of the industries approached you with the plea that you should not initiate harsh action as it would compel them their units, and cause huge financial loss, shortage of their products in the market. These would obviously add to the sufferings of the labourers and the consumer alike. The labour union also sent you representation requesting against the closure of the units. You simultaneously started receiving threats from unknown corners. You however received supports from some of your colleagues, who advised you to act freely to ensure environmental compliance. Local NGOs also came to your support and they demanded the closure of the polluting units immediately.

(a) What are the options available to you under the given situation?
(b) Critically examine the options listed by you.
(c) What type of mechanism would you suggest to ensure environmental compliance?

(d) What are the ethical dilemmas you faced in exercising your option?

Case Studies (2023)

1. You are working as an executive in a nationalised bank for several years. One day one of your close colleagues tells you that her father is suffering from heart disease and needs surgery immediately to survive. She also tells you that she has no insurance and the operation will cost about 10 lakh. You are also aware of the fact that her husband is no more and that she is from a lower middle class family. You are empathetic about her situation. However, apart from expressing your sympathy, you do not have the resources to fund her. A few weeks later, you ask her about the well-being of her father and she informs you about his successful surgery and that he is recovering. She then confides in you that the bank manager was kind enough to facilitate the release of Rs 10 lakh from a dormant account of someone to pay for the operation with a promise that it should be confidential and be repaid at the earliest. She has already started paying it back and will continue to do until it is all returned.

   (a) What are the ethical issues involved?
   (b) Evaluate the behaviour of the bank manager from an ethical point of view.
   (c) How would you react to the situation?

2. A landslide occurred in the middle of the night on 20th July, 2023 in a remote mountain hamlet, approximately 60 kilometres from Uttarkashi. The landslide was caused by torrential rains and has resulted in large-scale destruction of property and life. You, as District Magistrate of that area, have rushed to the spot with a team of doctors, NGOs, media and police along with numerous support staff to oversee the rescue operations. A man came running to you with a request for urgent medical help for his pregnant wife who is in labour and is losing blood. You directed your medical team to examine his wife. They return and convey to you that this woman needs blood transfusion immediately. Upon enquiry, you come to know that a few blood collection bags and blood group test kits are available in the ambulance accompanying your team. Few people of your team have already volunteered to donate blood. Being a physician who has graduated from AIIMS, you know that blood for transfusion needs to be procured only through a recognized blood bank. Your team members are divided on this issue; some favour transfusion, while some others oppose it. The doctors in the team are ready to facilitate the delivery provided they are not penalized for transfusion. Now you are in a dilemma. Your professional training emphasizes on prioritising service to humanity and saving lives of individuals.

   (a) What are the ethical issues involved in this case?
   (b) Evaluate the options available to you, being District Magistrate of the area.

3. At 9 pm on Saturday evening, Rashika, a Joint Secretary, was still engrossed in her work in her office. Her husband, Vikram, is an executive in an MNC and frequently out of town in connection with his work. Their two children aged 5 and 3 are looked after by their domestic helper. At 9.30 pm her superior, Mr. Suresh calls her and asks her to prepare a detailed note on an important matter to be discussed in a meeting in the Ministry. She realises that she will have to work on Sunday to finish the additional task given by her superior. She reflects on how she had looked forward to this posting and had worked long hours for months to achieve it. She had kept the welfare of people uppermost in discharging her duties. She feels that she has not done enough justice to her family and she has not fulfilled her duties in discharging essential social obligations. Even as recently as last month she had to leave her

sick child in the nanny's care as she had to work in the office. Now she feels that she must draw a line, beyond which her personal life should take precedence over her professional responsibilities. She thinks that there should be reasonable limits to the work ethics such as punctuality, hard work, dedication to duty and selfless service.

(a) Discuss the ethical issues involved in this case.

(b) Briefly describe at least four laws that have been enacted by the Government with respect to providing a healthy, safe and equitable working environment for women.

(c) Imagine you are in a similar situation. What suggestions would you make to mitigate such working conditions?

4. Vinod is an honest and sincere IAS officer. Recently, he has taken over as Managing Director of the State Road Transport Corporation, his sixth transfer in the past three years. His peers acknowledge his vast knowledge, affability and uprightness. The Chairman of the State Road Transport Corporation is a powerful politician and is very close to the Chief Minister. Vinod comes to know about many alleged irregularities of the Corporation and the highhandedness of the Chairman in financial matters. A Board Member of the Corporation belonging to the Opposition Party meets Vinod and hands over a few documents along with a video recording in which the Chairman appears to be demanding bribes for placing a huge order for the supply of QMR tyres. Vinod recollects the Chairman expediting clearing of pending bills of QMR tyres. Vinod confronts the Board Member as to why he is shying away from exposing the Chairman with the so-called solid proof he has with him. The member informs him that the Chairman refuses to yield to his threats. He adds that Vinod may earn recognition and public support if he himself exposes the Chairman. Further, he tells Vinod that once his party comes to power, Vinod's professional growth would be assured. Vinod is aware that he may be penalized if he exposes the Chairman and may further be transferred to a distant place. He knows that the Opposition Party stands a better chance of coming to power in the forthcoming elections. However, he also realizes that the Board Member is trying to use him for his own political gains.

(a) As a conscientious civil servant, evaluate the options available to Vinod.

(b) In the light of the above case, comment upon the ethical issues that may arise due to the politicization of bureaucracy.

5. You have just been appointed as Additional Director General of the Central Public Works Department. The Chief Architect of your division, who is to retire in six months, is passionately working on a very important project, the successful completion of which would earn him a lasting reputation for the rest of his life. A new lady architect, Seema, trained at Manchester School of Architecture, UK joined as Senior Architect in your division. During the briefing about the project, Seema made some suggestions which would not only add value to the project, but would also reduce completion time. This has made the Chief Architect insecure and he is constantly worried that all the credit will go to her. Subsequently, he adopted a passive and aggressive behavior towards her and has become disrespectful to her. Seema felt it embarrassing as the Chief Architect left no chance of humiliating her. He would very often correct her in front of other colleagues and raise his voice while speaking to her. This continuous harassment has resulted in her losing confidence and self-esteem. She felt perpetually tense, anxious and stressed. She appeared to be in awe of him since he has had a long tenure in the office and has vast experience

in the area of her work. You are aware of her outstanding academic credentials and career record in her previous organizations. However, you fear that this harassment may result in compromising her much needed contribution in this important project and may adversely impact her emotional well-being. You have also come to know from her peers that she is contemplating tendering her resignation.

(a) What are the ethical issues involved in the above case?

(b) What are the options available to you in order to complete the project as well as to retain Seema in the organization?

(c) What would be your response to Seema's predicament? What measures would you institute to prevent such occurrences from happening in your organization?

6. You hold a responsible position in a ministry in the government. One day in the morning you received a call from the school of your 11-year-old son that you are required to come and meet the Principal. You proceed to the school and find your son in the Principal's office. The Principal informs you that your son had been found wandering aimlessly in the grounds during the time classes were in progress. The class teacher further informs you that your son has lately become a loner and did not respond to questions in the class, he had also been unable to perform well in the football trials held recently. You bring your son back from the school and in the evening, you along with your wife try to find out the reasons for your son's changed behaviour. After repeated cajoling, your son shares that some children had been making fun of him in the class as well as in the WhatsApp group of the students by calling him stunted, duh and a frog. He tells you the names of a few children who are the main culprits but pleads with you to let the matter rest. After a few days, during a sporting event, where you and your wife have gone to watch your son play, one of your colleague's son shows you a video in which students have caricatured your son. Further, he also points out to the perpetrators who were sitting in the stands. You purposefully walk past them with your son and go home. Next day, you find on social media, a video denigrating you, your son and even your wife, stating that you engaged in physical bullying of children on the sports field. The video became viral on social media. Your friends and colleagues began calling you to find out the details. One of your juniors advised you to make a counter video giving the background and explaining that nothing had happened on the field. You, in turn posted a video which you have captured during the sporting event, identifying the likely perpetrators who were responsible for your son's predicament. You have also narrated what has actually happened in the field and made attempts to bring out the adverse effects of the misuse of social media.

(a) Based on the above case study, discuss the ethical issues involved in the use of social media.

(b) Discuss the pros and cons of using social media by you to put across the facts to counter the fake propaganda against your family.

SAMPLE CASE STUDIES WITH SOLUTIONS

1. A village is facing the menace of theft continuously. A vigilant group of villagers decides to provide security to its village when police failed to check the menace. One night, some sadhus going for pilgrimage passed by the village. They were stopped by the vigilant group of villagers which also included some minors. They suspected the sadhus to be thieves masquerading as saints, and they lynched them with sticks without informing the concerned police station. Such incidents have been rampant in recent days. The local people have started taking law into their own hands which

exhibits the failure of administrative machinery and burgeoning unethical practices in the society.

You are Superintendent of Police of the district. You immediately rush to the crime scene and find a severe crisis of law and order which is responsible for this incident. You also find apathy in your subordinates to address the menace that resulted in the lynching of innocent sadhus.

(a) What are the ethical concerns involved in this case?
(b) How should you deal with such incidents? Suggest some preventive actions that should be taken to stop the emergence of such incidents.
(c) What is the role of educational institutions and parents to prevent the involvement of their children in such criminal activities?

Solution

(a) The following ethical issues are present in this case:
- Violation of contract between citizens and the State that is against the ideal of contractarianism of normative ethics. A citizen should follow the law of the land. If State machinery has failed to execute its duty, there are other ways to compel it to carry out its duty rather than taking law into one's own hands.
- This act also comes under the ambit of violation of the deontological principle. The police should do its duty and citizens should remain under the purview of law.
- All citizens should possess the virtue of temperance, justice, pity and compassion. The lack of empathy and emotional intelligence in the society and State machinery is the cause behind the frequent occurrence of such incidents.

(b) I will immediately organise an investigation committee under skilled and honest police officers, and personally look into the case. I will talk to the District Magistrate and local leaders and ask them to explain to the citizens why such incidents should not happen again. I would mobilise the police to control theft and other crimes taking place in the society frequently.

The preventive measures would be rigorous counselling of the police to inculcate in them the sense of duty and emotional intelligence. I will organise visits and meetings with common people in the villages to explain to them why they should not take law in their own hands.

(c) The educational institution should take responsibility to cater civic sense and moral attitude to the students besides imparting formal education. Good citizenry is formed through good education. Character is built in school and colleges, and it is the duty of a teacher to impart values and virtue to students. Parents too should contribute and make an effort to form good citizens in homes. The role of parents, especially that of the mother, is important and they can keep watch on their children's activities.

2. A deadly epidemic took place in a state, which resulted in hundreds of deaths and thousands of patients due to the quick spread of the virus through air and person-to-person contact. You are Chief Secretary of the state. The disease can spread beyond the state if it is not confined immediately.

The demand on health services is increasing rapidly. Private hospitals have started ruthlessly extracting money from the patients. On the other hand, the public health services are unable to cater to the high demands, and the facilities too are not up to the mark.

(a) Suggest some measures to confine the disease and to ensure that common people can access the necessary health facilities.

(b) How would you deal with the ethical crisis among the medical practitioners?

Solution

(a) I would immediately seal the borders of my state. I would immediately plan to create infrastructure and set up systems to screen people crossing the borders in the coming days. I would control the private health service providers with an iron fist. I will try to increase and improve the health facilities in public hospitals. The prices of healthcare services would be fixed, and I would bring about provisions of heavy penalty if someone is caught charging patients disproportionately. I will immediately start a dedicated grievance cell where people can seek health services related to the symptoms of the prevailing disease, and they can also register their complaints related to malfunctioning of the health units.

(b) The integrity approach of ethics would work in such cases. There should be the provision of classes on medical ethics, and frequent seminars on the subject of integrity to be organised in the medical colleges. Every medical practitioner would have to compulsorily pass the certificate course on ethics especially designed for them before they can receive their registration, and also before extending the registration in case of already registered medical practitioners.

3. You are the Municipal Commissioner of a city. Every day you see families residing on the footpaths. You ignore this and keep on doing your routine functions. One night, a car ran over three people including a child of five years. This incident became a burning issue and your ignorance is seen as a sign of your administrative incapacity.

(a) What are the ethical issues involved with your administrative aptitude?

(b) What are the factors behind such administrative apathy in the civil servants of our country?

(c) How would you react in this situation in response to your voice of conscience?

Solution

(a) The ethical issues involved with my administrative aptitude are lack of compassion towards weaker sections, and lack of empathy, prudence and wisdom. Certainly, I lack virtue because virtue cannot be defined as mere possession of good characteristics—rather it should be a habit. When administrative aptitude becomes habit, there is very little chance to be careless in sensitive issues like this.

(b) The factors responsible for such administrative apathy among the present day's civil servants are feeble connection with the poor and downtrodden marginal population. The civil servants are not properly sensitised with regards to the issues of the weaker sections of society. Mere bookish knowledge cannot match the first-hand experiences gained in the field. Regular visits to meet the people, caring attitude towards their grievances and the desire to serve them can only come with being empathetic and emotionally intelligent. In the present era of the internet and digital media, people-to-people contact has reduced. Even e-governance has some shortcomings; for instance, the grievance redressal mechanism on e-platforms are not sufficient to accurately convey the real condition of the aggrieved.

(c) I would listen the voice of conscience, and try to understand the issues of the poor and the marginalised. I would admit that the incident occurred due to the lethargy of administrative machinery. I would direct the officers to take all such issues into cognisance and make a plan to address them. I can provide the benefits of government schemes to the people on the streets. I would also provide inputs to the Development and Welfare Board for the Denotified, Nomadic and Semi-Nomadic Communities for planning schemes which can address the real problem of the disenfranchised people.

4. In the district of Rajnagar, five uppercaste men gang-raped a Dalit girl while she was working in her farm. She was severely injured and succumbed to death. This incident took shape of a caste conflict. The accused are well connected people, and a strong politician of the ruling party belonging to the same high caste is striving to protect the culprits. The local administration and police were instructed to suppress the issue to save the rapists.

You are the District Magistrate of Rajnagar. The ruling political authority tries to compel you to assuage the parents of the rape victim and handle the caste conflict by any means. You are an honest officer, and you know if you don't follow the instructions of your political boss, you have to pay a heavy cost in terms of your career.

(a) What are the ethical issues involved in such events that happen on a regular basis in every nook and corner of the country?

(b) How would you handle this situation while keeping your career secure?

Solution

(a) The ethical issues related to this incident are lack of virtue—particularly temperance in society, shift of human values, and uncontrolled animal desires of men. Compassion towards weaker sections and women must be inculcated in everyone through educational institutions. As described by Plato, the four cardinal virtues—courage, moderation, wisdom and justice—must be possessed by the people for the successful functioning of society. To overcome such an unruly 'state of nature' as explained in social contract theory, the sovereign authority should deal with issues like this with an iron fist.

(b) I would immediately get all the alleged men arrested and put them before the court of law. I would not help the culprits in any way. If political authority compels me to make the case weaker, I would persuade them with the help of my skill of 'logos' (power of speech) and explain that such blind support in this case may become a cause of degradation of his party's image, and even may cause severe political loss. I would try to explain to the political authority that we all are public servants, and we must ensure justice in society.

In this way, I would try to handle the situation. If the political authority does not agree with me, I would act as per my voice of conscience, and according to my duty. In other words I will follow deontological ethics. No political authority has power to spoil the career of a civil servant, I possess this courage of conviction. I would leave behind the ambition of key postings if I cannot bring about any positive change in the society.

5. Ramesh is an honest servant working in your house. You and your family trust him. Over a period of time, you have realised that things around the house are getting lost, and you often find that money is missing from your wallet. You suspect that one of the other servants is involved in this pilferage. One day, you suddenly spot Ramesh stealing money from your wallet. You don't reveal to him that now you have come to know everything. You know

that Ramesh is very poor and the sole earner in his family. If you fire him immediately, his family would certainly end up on the verge of starvation.

(a) What are the various issues involved in this case?
(b) How would you take a decision in this situation of ethical dilemma?

Solution

(a) The various issues in this case are ethical dilemma, compassion towards weaker sections, and virtues of wisdom and justice. In this case of ethical dilemma I have two possible options: I can fire him or give him another chance, explaining to him why he must not repeat his wrongdoings. Both these options are ethical from different perspectives and different ways of reasoning. But one should opt for the ethical path that has the minimum impact in terms of producing bad in the society. An employer should be a philosopher while taking decisions with regards to his/her employees. S/he should be prudent and also merciful keeping in mind all the potential risks involved in the decision. The major drawback of consequentialism is nobody knows the exact consequence of any action. Justice is explained by Aristotle as the golden mean between two extreme vices. A radical decision should be shunned, and one must always try to find a middle path, as sermonised by Lord Buddha.

(b) I would talk to Ramesh at an appropriate time, and ask him calmly why he did this. I would try to analyse the circumstances in which he had committed the sins. Human beings have the natural tendency to deviate from the right path, and it is value education that makes one adjustable in society. If I realise that there was a strong reason for the theft done by him, although I know that no reason can justify a bad deed, I would explain to him that any kind of stealing is a moral as well as a legal crime. And if he repeats and steals again, he would be treated as a criminal, and must face very harsh consequences. I would help him as much as is possible for me if he has any genuine problems because of which he was stealing.

6. You are the Block Development Officer of a Block. You are highly motivated to serve the poor villagers. One day, during your village visit, you see an old and poor lady outside the Panchayat Office in a very deplorable situation. After some initial enquiry, you come to know that she is very poor, and her children have left her in the village and escaped to a big city, having sold off all their property. She is now struggling for food, shelter and clothes.

You want to improve her condition. What may be the ethical dilemma in front of you? Also suggest some measures which you can take in such a situation to take care of similar cases which have been rampant in villages in recent times.

Solution

The potential ethical dilemma in this situation may mean the following choices:

- I can get the case registered under the Maintenance and Welfare of Parents and Senior Citizens Act, 2007.
- I can instruct the Panchayat-level government functionaries to make arrangements for the old lady. However, there is no fund allocated by the government to address such issues.
- I can personally bear the responsibility to provide care to that old lady.

All the above points have ethical validity, but every ethical action has some limitations in practicality. This is not my personal duty to bear the expenditure of her survival. If I help her, then I must help all those people who are facing the same situation in my block, otherwise my behaviour would come under the definition of bias and impartiality. I can go for legal action against the children of that lady, but it will take time to deliver justice. But I can make arrangements with the help of different governmental schemes in the meanwhile: I would instruct local self-help groups that provides mid-day meals to schools to provide food to the old lady in the daytime. I would request the Panchayat community to provide her with a meal at night on a rotational basis, setting in place a modus operandi. I would also request the Panchayat community to donate some clothes to her.

If this model is successful, I would apply this model across the Block. I would also try to find some NGOs to join in on this sacred task. I would prepare a list of similar victims, and try to get cases registered against all their children. I would also start nukkad-natak (small street plays) in the villages to eradicate this evil of abandoning elderly parents.

7. You are the District Collector in a district where bi-elections are going to be held in two legislative constituencies. These two seats are important to the ruling party for the sustenance of the government in the state. You are pressurised by the ruling party's high command to support its candidates in the bi-election to gain both the seats. You are also given assurance of good postings in the future in lieu of this favour.

   Although you are an honest and committed civil servant, you also know that your contribution to society is possible only when you can holding key posts in the administration.

   (a) What are the ethical issues involved in this case?
   (b) Suggest some measures to overcome such situations while protecting your career and your contribution to the society.

Solution
(a) The ethical issues involved in this case are related to ethics in public administration. A public servant should follow impartiality and non-partisanship. He should remain aloof from politics. In India, public servants are career bureaucrats, so they should support the politicians in framing and implementing the schemes rather than being involved in political games. Free and fair election is the spirit of the constitution. If I do not follow the constitutional provisions, this would show lack of integrity. Woodrow Wilson famously said that politics and bureaucracy are two opposite extremes, and a bureaucrat must not be involved in political affairs. It is also against the notion of Weberian bureaucracy.

(b) I would not follow the order of the ruling party's high command. I would politely explain to him that such a manoeuvre would be a breach of constitutionality, and I am committed to obey the law of the land. I would also assure him that elections can be won on the ground of development done by the government. In spite of that if he tries to compel me, I would write to the Election Commission about the present circumstances, and request them to transfer me to another post to curb the possibility of a conflict of interest.

8. A granite mining company is operating near a small village where employment opportunities are rare. The company has generated a good amount of employment for the villagers. Over a period of time, the mining company has earned great reputation in the village as well as in the state for taking care of the local economy, and it has proved itself to be a responsible corporate citizen.

   A lot of new cancer cases have been arising after the inception of the company's activities in the region. The district administration while processing the applications of health benefit schemes run by the state government has realised that the cases have increased due to mining activities. However, the company follows all the pollution- and environment-related norms strictly.

(a) What are the ethical issues involved in this case?

(b) How should the company respond to prove itself to be an ethical corporate citizen?

Solution

(a) The case involves corporate ethics. It is related to the notion of corporate citizenry and corporate social responsibility. A private organisation exploits the public resources, and although they pay for this, all human and physical resources belong to public. In lieu of the utilisation of these resources, a private firm must take into consideration all the potential consequences that may take place during the process of production. If something wrong happens then that firm must take the onus on moral ground, and it should immediately strive to alleviate the pain of the community which has suffered the consequences.

(b) The company should immediately constitute a committee of neutral experts in concerned fields—health experts, social researchers and scientists—to enquire about the issue. It should openly accept the findings and recommendations of the committee. The company should immediately start relief measures and grievance redressal. It should start funding the treatment of victims by using its CSR funds. It should also incorporate modern technology to curb the spread of the disease by checking the cause of the disease.

9. You are newly appointed as the District Magistrate of a district. A powerful ruling party MLA runs illegal mining activities in your area. An opposition party's MLA is also involved in similar activities. The ruling party MLA compels you to take stringent action against the MLA of the opposition party to stop his illegal activities so as to establish monopoly in mining activities. You are an honest civil servant, and after enquiring about the illegal mining activities, you come to know that the state exchequer has suffered a heavy loss of revenue from mining due to such malpractices.

You start taking strong action against all mining mafias including the MLA of the ruling party. The ruling party's MLA complains to the Chief Minister about your unsupportive attitude. The Chief Minister calls you and instructs you to support the MLA of his party.

(a) What are the ethical issues involved in the case?

(b) How would you proceed with respect to your voice of conscience?

Solution

(a) The ethical issues in this case involve values of public service like integrity, impartiality, non-partisanship, transparency and courage of conviction. A public servant should act according to the rule of law. The notion of equality before law should be followed to obey deontological ethics.

(b) I would listen to the voice of conscience and treat every offender equally. I would control the illegal mining activities with an iron fist. I would explain to the Chief Minister that illegal mining activities are causing a huge loss to the public exchequer. I would also explain to him that a wrong message is being conveyed to the common public that the ruling party is not serious about controlling illegal activities in the region.

10. You are a newly appointed Group-A officer in a department. Your senior officer is very cordial and supportive to you, and he is willing to train you in all respects. One day, a female employee comes to you, and complains that your senior officer has been physically exploiting her for six months. She solicits your help and support to get out of this grim situation.

You have a good opportunity to learn while working under a supportive and talented senior officer. But your voice of conscience compels you to help the female employee.

(a) How would you help her in overcoming this situation?
(b) How would you proceed to follow the law of the land while protecting your self-interest?

Solution

(a) I would guide and inform her about legal resorts like lodging a complaint with the internal complaint committee. I would suggest her to take a clear decision about the way forward after shedding all dilemmas. She should not bear this pain anymore, and she should fight for justice.

(b) Being a responsible officer of the organisation, it is my duty to take cognisance and try to stop the harassment of the lady employee. Although this is not my actual duty, it is a *prima facie* duty. The principle of division of functions given by Plato also suggests that one should do his/her own work. He says that justice can be defined as doing your own thing. Government has devised a separate internal complaint committee to take up such issues. My duty would cease once I counsel the lady officer about the way she can get justice in her case. I would talk to my senior officer about the whole episode, and request him to stop the exploitation. I would also emphasise that I want to work under him to learn, but I would not accept subordination or work under an unethical senior.

BIBLIOGRAPHY

CHAPTER 1

Annas, Julia. (1995). *The Morality of Happiness*. New York: Oxford University Press.

Anscombe, G. E. M. (1958). 'Modern Moral Philosophy'. Philosophy 33(124): 1–19.

Crabtree, Vexen. (2014). 'Do We Need Religion To Have Good Morals?' 3 October. Available at http://www.vexen.co.uk/religion/ethics.html (accessed February 2018).

Dewey, John. (2014). *Ethics*. Landor Press.

Haidt, Jonathan. (2006). *The Happiness Hypothesis: Finding Modern Truth in Ancient Wisdom*. Basic Books.

Myers, David. (2001). 'Godliness and Goodliness'. *Sightings* (online public religion newsletter from the Martin Marty Center at the University of Chicago).

Ryan, Mckay, and Harvey Whitehouse. (2014). 'Religion and Morality'. *Psychological Bulletin* 141(2): 447–473.

Singer, Peter. 'Neil Cooper's Concepts of Morality'. *Mind* 80(319): 421–423.

CHAPTER 2

Adams, R. M. (1976). 'Motive Utilitarianism'. *Journal of Philosophy* 73(14): 467–481.

———. (2001). 'Scalon's Contractualism: Critical Notice of T. M. Scanlon's *What We Owe to Each Other*'. *Philosophical Review* 110(4): 563–586.

———. (2006). *A Theory of Virtue*. New York: Oxford University Press.

Alexander, L. (1985). 'Pursuing the Good—Indirectly'. *Ethics*, 95(2): 315–332.

Allison, Henry. (2011). *Kant's Groundwork for the Metaphysics of Morals*. Oxford University Press.

Bloomfield, Paul. (2014). *The Virtue of Happiness: A Theory of Good Life*. New York: Oxford University Press.

Brandt, Richard. (1959). *Ethical Theory*. New Jersey: Prentice Hall.

Gilligan, C. (1982). *In A Different Voice: Psychological Theory and Women's Development*. Cambridge, MA: Harvard University Press.

Hare, R. M. (1952). *The Language of Morals*. Oxford: Oxford University Press.

Jackson, Frank. (1998). *From Metaphysics to Ethics: A Defence of Conceptual Analysis*. New York: Oxford University Press.

Rawls, John. (1971). *A Theory of Justice*. Cambridge, MA: Harvard University Press.

CHAPTER 4

Graves, Clare W. (2002). *Levels of Human Existence*. ECLET Publishing.

Rokeach, Milton. (1973). *The Nature of Human Values*. Free Press.

CHAPTER 5

Carson, C. ed. (1998). *The Autobiography of Martin Luther King Jr*. New York, NY: Warner Books.

Chopra, P. N. ed. (1998). *The Collected Works of Sardar Vallabhbhai Patel*. Vol. 9. New Delhi: Konark Publishers Pvt. Ltd.

Das, Sisir Kumar. (1994). *The English Writings of Rabindranath Tagore*. Volume II and Volume III. New Delhi: Sahitya Akademi.

Gandhi, Mahatma. (2009 [1929]). *The Story of My Experiments with Truth*. New Delhi: Fingerprint Publishing.

Nehru, Jawaharlal. (2008 [1946]). *The Discovery of India*. Penguin UK.

Parameswaran, P. ed. (1978). *Gandhi, Lohia, and Deendayal*. Deendayal Research Institute.

Radhakrishnan, S. (1952). *History of Philosophy: Eastern and Western.* Volume II. London: George Allen and Unwin.

Rajagopalachari, C. (1993). *Kural: The Great Book of Tiru-Valluvar.* Bharatiya Vidya Bhavan.

Schroeder, John Frederick. (2015). *Maxims of Washington: Political, Social, Moral and Religious.* Andesite Press.

T. Babyak, Andrew. (n.d.). *The Moral Leadership of Martin Luther King, Jr.* Chowan University. Available at https://anyflip.com/ncuf/zqoh/basic/ (accessed June 2024).

Trigunayat, Govind. (1957). *Kabir Ki Vichardhara.* Kanpur: Sahitya Niketan.

Upadhyaya, Deendayal. (1965). *Integral Humanism.* New Delhi: Bhartiya Jan Sangh.

Vivekananda, Swami. (1892). *The Complete Works of Swami Vivekananda.* Volumes II, III, IV. Kolkata: Advaita Ashrama.

West, T. C. (2008). 'Gendered Legacies of Martin Luther King Jr.'s Leadership'. *Theology Today* 65(1).

CHAPTER 6

Ajzen, I. (2001). 'Nature and Operation of Attitudes'. *Annual Review of Psychology* 52: 27–58.

———. (2012). 'Attitudes and Persuasion'. In *The Oxford Handbook of Personality and Social Psychology,* eds. K. Deaux and M. Snyder, 367–393. Oxford University Press.

Ajzen, I., and M. Fishbein. (1980). *Understanding Attitudes and Predicting Social Behaviour.* New Jersey: Prentice-Hall.

———. (2005). 'The Influence of Attitudes on Behaviour'. In *The Handbook of Attitudes,* eds. D. Albarracin, B. T. Johnson and M. P. Zanna, 173–221. New York: Lawrence Erlbaum Associates.

Albarracín, D. (2002). 'Cognition in Persuasion: An Analysis of Information Processing in Response to Persuasive Communications'. In *Advances in Experimental Social Psychology,* Vol. 34, ed. M. P. Zanna, 61–130. Academic Press.

Anderson, N. H. (1974). 'Cognitive Algebra: Integration Theory Applied to Social Attribution'. *Advances in Experimental Social Psychology* 7: 1–101.

Bassili, J. N., and R. D. Brown (2005). 'Implicit and Explicit Attitudes: Research, Challenges, and Theory'. In *The Handbook of Attitudes,* eds. D. Albarracin, B. T. Johnson and M. P. Zanna, 543–574. New York: Lawrence Erlbaum Associates.

Connell, R. W. (1967). 'The Origin of Political Attitude: An Introduction'. *Politics* 2(2): 141–156.

D. Albarracín, B. T. Johnson, and M. P. Zanna. (2005). *The Handbook of Attitudes.* New York: Lawrence Erlbaum Associates.

Fazio, R. H. (1995). 'Attitude as Object-Evaluation Associations: Determinants, Consequences, and Correlations of Attitude Accessibility'. In *Attitude Strength: Antecedents and Consequences,* eds. R. E. Petty and J. A. Krosnick, 247–282. New York: Lawrence Erlbaum Associates, Inc.

Festinger, L. (1957). *A Theory of Cognitive Dissonance.* Stanford: Stanford University Press.

Fishbein, M., and I. Ajzen. (1975). *Belief, Attitude, Intention and Behaviour: An Introduction to Theory and Research.* Reading, MA: Addison-Wesley.

CHAPTER 8

Blickle, G. (1996). 'Personality traits, learning strategies, and performance'. *European Journal of Personality* 10(5): 337–352.

Cherniss, Cary and Daniel Goleman. (2001). *The Emotionally Intelligent Workplace.* John Wiley & Sons Inc.

Goleman, Daniel, Richard Boyatzis, and Annie Mckee. (2004). *Primal Leadership: Learning to Lead with Emotional Intelligence.* Harvard: Harvard Business School Press.

Goleman, Daniel. (2008). *Working with Emotional Intelligence.* New York, NY: Bantam Doubleday Dell Publishing Group.

CHAPTER 10

Algra, K., J. Barnes, J. Mansfeld and M. Schofeld. eds. (1999). *The Cambridge History of Hellenistic Philosophy.* New York: Cambridge University Press.

Aquinas, Thomas. (1920–22). *The 'Summa Theologica' of St. Thomas Aquinas.* Trans. Fathers of the English Dominican Province. London: Burns Oates and Washbourne.

Aurobindo, Sri. (1919). *The Life Divine.* Pondicherry: Sri Aurobindo Ashram Publication Department.

———. (1971). *The Supramental Manifestation.* Pondicherry: Sri Aurobindo Ashram Publication Department.

Barnabas, A., and P. S. Clifford. (2012). 'Mahatma Gandhi: An Indian Model of Servant Leadership'. *International Journal of Leadership Studies* 7(2).

Barnes, J. ed. (1984). *The Complete Works of Aristotle.* 2 vols. Princeton University Press.

Bilimoria, Purushottama, Joseph Prabhu and Renuka Sharma. (2007). *Indian Ethics: Classical Traditions and Contemporary Challenges,* Vol. 1. New Delhi: Routledge.

Brook, R. (2007). 'Deontology, Paradox and Moral Evil'. *Social Theory and Practice* 33(3).

Cooper, John M. (1997). *Plato: Complete Works.* UK: Hackett Publishing.

Crawford, S. Cromwell. (1984). *Raja Rammohun Roy: His Era and Ethics.* New Delhi: Arnold-Heinemann.

Dundar, Hakan, Erdi Erdogan and Erdem Hareket. (2016). 'A Role Model in Light of Values: Mahatma Gandhi'. *Educational Research and Reviews* 11(20): 1889–1895.

Gagarin, M. and P. Woodruff. (2008). 'The Sophists'. In *The Oxford Handbook of Presocratic Philosophy,* eds. Patricia Curd and Daniel Graham. Oxford University Press.

Gupta, V. K. (1987). *Kautilyan Jurisprudence.* B. D. Gupta Publishers.

Harman, G. (1977). *The Nature of Morality.* New York: Oxford University Press.

Hobbes, Thomas. (1968). *Leviathan.* Baltimore: Penguin Books.

Kangle, R. P. (1960). *The Kautilya Arthashashtra. Part 2.* Bombay: University of Bombay.

Kant, Immanuel. (1886). *The Metaphysics of Ethics,* trans. J. W. Semple, ed. Rev. Henry Calderwood. Edinburgh: T. & T. Clark.

Kaushik, Ashok. ed. (2007). *Srimad Bhagavad Gita,* English trans. Janak Datta, 7th ed. New Delhi: Star Publications.

Kumar, R. (n.d.). 'Gandhi on Value Education'. Available at https://www.gandhiashramsevagram.org/gandhi-articles/gandhi-on-value-education.php#:~:text=Therefore%20we%20can%20say%20that,education%20we%20finally%20attain%20salvation (accessed June 2024).

Long, A. A., and David Sedley. (2012). *The Hellenistic Philosophers, Vol. 2.* Cambridge: Cambridge University Press.

Moreton, Catherine. (n.d.). 'Ten qualities that made Abraham Lincoln a Great Leader'.

O' Donnell, James J. (2012). *Augustine Confessions.* Oxford: Oxford University Press.

Radhakrishnan, S. (2009). *An Idealist View of Life.* New Delhi: Harper Collins.

Vivekananda, Swami. (1892). *The Complete Works of Swami Vivekananda, Vol. 2,3 and 4.* Kolkata: Advaita Ashrama.

Yogi, Ramesh T. (2000). *Ethics of Chanakya.* Delhi: Sahni Publishers.

CHAPTER 11

Cooper, T. L. ed. (2006). *The Responsible Administrator: An Approach to Ethics for the Administrative Role.* San Francisco: Jossey-Bass.

Mantysalo, Venla. (2016). *Ethical Minimum or Ethical Maximum?* Vaasan Yliopisto, University of Vaasa, Helsinki. Available at https://www.uwasa.fi/materiaali/pdf/isbn_978-952-476-657-9.pdf (accessed February 2024).

Rohr, John A. (1989). *Ethics for Bureaucrats.* New York: Routledge.

Sheeran, Patrick J. (1993). *Ethics in Public Administration: A Philosophical Approach.* Praeger Publishers Inc.

Wakefield, Susan. (1976). 'Ethics and the Public Service': A Case for Individual Responsibility'. *Public Administration Review* 36(6).

CHAPTER 12

Devlin, Patrick Baron. (1965). *The Enforcement of Morals.* Oxford University Press.

Fuller, Lon. (1964). *The Morality of Law.* New Haven: Yale University Press.

Lloyd, Dennis. (1959). *Introduction of Jurisprudence.* London: Sweet & Maxwell.

Mitchell, Basil. (1970). *Law, Morality and Religion in a Secular Society.* Oxford University Press.

Scheller Jr, Arthur. (1953). 'Law and Morality'. *Marquette Law Review* 36(3).

CHAPTER 13

Bar Cendon, Antonio. (1999). 'Accountability and Public Administration: Concepts, Dimensions, Developments.' In *Openness and Transparency in Governance: Challenges and Opportunities,* ed. Michael Kellly. Maastricht, The Netherlands: EIPA.

Bovens, M. (1999). 'The Quest for Responsibility: Accountability and Citizenship in Complex

Organisations'. *Administrative Science Quarterly* 44(4): 846.

Brereton, M., and M. Temple. 2002. 'The New Public Service Ethos: An Ethical Environment for Governance'. *Public Administration* 77(3): 455–474.

Jabbra, J. G., and O. P. Dwivedi. (1988). *Public Service Accountability: A Competitive Perspective.* Kumarian Press.

CHAPTER 14

Administrative Training Institute, Mysore. (2013). *Training Module on Ethics in Governance.* Available at http://darpg.gov.in/sites/default/files/Ethics_in_Governance_2nd_ARC.pdf (accessed June 2024).

Organisation for Economic Co-operation and Development (OECD). (2013). *Ethics Training for Public Officials. A Study Prepared by the OECD Anti-Corruption Network for Eastern Europe and Central Asia (ACN), and SIGMA, a joint EU-OECD initiative, principally financed by the EU, in co-operation with the OECD Public Sector Integrity Network.* Available at http://www.oecd.org/corruption/acn/resources/EthicsTrainingforPublicOfficialsBrochureEN.pdf (accessed June 2024).

CHAPTER 15

Cathcart, Thomas. (2013). *The Trolley Problem or Would You Throw the Fat Guy off the Bridge?: A Philosophical Conundrum.* New York: Workman Publishing.

Gowans, Christopher W. (1987). *Moral Dilemmas.* Oxford: Oxford University Press.

CHAPTER 16

Amstutz, Mark R. (2013). *International Ethics: Concepts, Theories, and Cases in Global Politics.* Rowman & Littlefield Publishers.

Cassidy, John. (2002). 'Helping Hands: How Foreign Aid Could Benefit Everybody'. *The New Yorker.* 18 March.

Hoffmann, Stanley. (1981). *Duties beyond Borders: On the Limits and Possibilities of Ethical International Politics.* Syracuse University Press.

Singer, Peter. (2004). *One World: The Ethics of Globalization.* Yale University Press.

Walzer, Michael. (1977). *Just and Unjust Wars.* New York: Basic Books.

CHAPTER 18

Bailey, S. (1964). 'Ethics and the Public Service'. *Public Administration Review* 24(4): 234–243.

Bozeman, B. (2007). *Public Values and Public Interest: Counterbalancing Economic Individualism.* Georgetown University Press.

Duguit, Leon. (1923). 'The Concept of Public Service'. *Yale Law Journal* 32(5).

Government of India. (2007). *Ethics in Governance.* Fourth Report, Second Administrative Reforms Commission. Available at https://darpg.gov.in/sites/default/files/ethics4.pdf (accessed June 2024).

OECD. (2005). *Managing Conflict of Interest in the Public Sector.* OECD Publishing.

CHAPTER 20

CAPAM. (2011). 'Service Delivery, Governance and the Citizen'. *Commonwealth Association for Public Administration & Management* 17(2).

Department of Administrative Reforms and Public Grievances, Ministry of Personnel, Public Grievances and Pensions. (2010). *Guidelines for Designing and Implementing SEVOTTAM Compliant Citizen's/Client's Charters and Public Grievance Redress Mechanisms.* Available at https://darpg.gov.in/sites/default/files/Sevottam_RFD_Guidelines_August_2010.pdf (accessed June 2024).

———. (2011). *Guidelines for Implementing SEVOTTAM.* Available at https://himachal.nic.in/WriteReadData/l892s/15_l892s/1411537043.pdf (accessed June 2024).

Shah, Anwar. (2005). 'Public Services Delivery'. Washington D.C.: The World Bank.